POST-MODERNISM

THE NEW CLASSICISM IN ART AND ARCHITECTURE

POST-MODERNISM

THE NEW CLASSICISM IN ART AND ARCHITECTURE

CHARLES JENCKS

RIZZOLI
NEW YORK

To Maggie

Library of Congress Cataloging-in-Publication Data

Jencks, Charles.
Post Modernism.

Bibliography: p.
Includes index.
1. Arts, Modern--20th century. 2. Postmodernism.
I. Title.
NX456.5.P66J46 1987   700'.9'04   87-9481
ISBN 0-8478-0835-1

Published in the United States of America in 1987 by
RIZZOLI INTERNATIONAL PUBLICATIONS INC
597 Fifth Avenue, New York, NY 10017

First published in Great Britain in 1987 by
ACADEMY EDITIONS
an imprint of the Academy Group Ltd, 7 Holland Street, London W8 4NA

Printed and bound in Hong Kong

Contents

Preface

Most people have heard of Post-Modernism and don't have a very clear idea of what it means. They can be forgiven this confusion because Post-Modernists don't always know and, even when they think they do, often find themselves disagreeing. Like the Modernists before them they are sometimes divided over essential issues: whether their activities and programme represent a fundamental break with the recent past and a negation of Modernism, or alternatively, a reweaving of this tradition with strands of western humanism. This book argues the second position, supporting it with the evidence of recent art and architecture, particularly that work which can be termed classical.

Since the end of the 1970s the majority of Post-Modern artists and architects have taken a diverse tradition and consolidated it with what I call Free-Style Classicism – a rich, broad language of form, going back to Greece and Italy, but also to Egypt and so-called 'anti-classical' movements such as Mannerism. In effect they have returned to the archetypes and constants which underlie Canonic Classicism, those that are familiar to everyone who has looked at a Poussin or strolled through a Palladian house. The result is an eclectic mixture which freely combines elements of Modernism with the wider classical tradition. To call it 'free' however is not to say that it is without direction, order or precepts, and in the last chapter I've attempted to define the new, emergent rules of the genre.

It is obvious, but worth stating, that there are other valid traditions at work today which have little to do with this recent synthesis. Late-Modernism in art and architecture, for instance, continues to develop avant-garde tendencies of Modernism, such as the new abstraction and high-tech building. Vernacular, regional and revivalist traditions are also flourishing. Let us hope that they all continue to compete, for if one thing is clear from the nineteenth century, it is that nothing is so successful at finishing off a movement than unchallenged commercial success. For this reason and others, I favour a pluralism of approach, although it will become obvious where my own values and prejudices lie – with the emerging Post-Modern Classicism. Form and content are ultimately related and, in the final analysis, if you care about the rebirth of a classical style, you are also involved with seeing western culture as a reversible continuum where the past makes its claims on the present just as the present must revalue the past. A commitment to both classicism and Modernism is required to effect a credible synthesis. Obviously it's inadequate to simply dress up a building with a few classical mouldings or paint an Arcadian shepherd lolling about in a California cow field. Free-Style Classicism is undoubtedly a fashion, but I am concerned more with its broader implications.

Case blocking and title page:
Michael Graves and Lennart Anderson, *Bacchanal*, 'Artist-Architect Collaboration', New York, 1981
Endpapers:
Robert Stern, *Family Room Rug* design, 1986
Frontispiece:
O.M. Ungers, *Skyscraper*, Frankfurt-Am-Main, 1983-5 (Photograph Dieter Leistner)
Opposite:
Lincoln Perry, *Morning Embankment*, 1985, detail, oil on canvas, 50 x 62in (Courtesy Tatistcheff and Co. Inc., NYC)

I started writing this book seven years ago and the editorial problem can be imagined: as I described the movement it kept growing, changing and becoming more interesting. The result has been, in the interim, four little booklets – *Post-Modern Classicism*, 1980, *Free-Style Classicism*, 1982, *Abstract Representation*, 1983, and *What is Post-Modernism?*, 1986 – for which purchasers of those tracts and this book may justifiably curse me. I apologise for this promiscuous fecundity and would like to repay these kind supporters with a thousand thank you notes, but I must say that if there is one thing worse than buying several incomplete and partially digested versions of a similar idea, it is having to rethink and rewrite them. That is a Sisyphean labour, the endless push of the familiar ball up the same old hill, both of which get bigger and more familiar. As the Chinese say 'May you be cursed to live in interesting times', and doubly cursed to continuously write about them while they are becoming more interesting.

There's another sin for which I feel reluctant to apologise, that will, no doubt, be pointed out by some specialists and art critics. I'm an architectural writer who has mistakenly wandered into the special preserve of what may be one of the fastest growing commercial markets, apart from micro-chips and Rubik cubes, that is the art-world-market. It's a wide, complex and changing world, as various as its architectural counterpart, and I wouldn't claim to have mastered the entire terrain. Quite a few Post-Modern artists are not discussed here, such as Julian Schnabel, either because they are not concerned with the recent classical synthesis, or because I don't find their work very convincing. Others, such as Frank Stella and Richard Diebenkorn, are not discussed either, because, inspite of claims to the contrary, they are Late-rather than Post-Modernist. No doubt I have missed some important figures and have also viewed art from a non-specialist perspective. However after reflecting on the current orthodoxy that sanctions books devoted solely to either art or architecture, I'm less inclined to apologise than to indict others in both fields for perpetuating a closed shop which ought to be declared uncultured by the Intellectual Monopolies Commission. If the reader is annoyed at my combining two 'specialisms' (suitably horrible word) than he or she can at least be thankful that I have stopped short at two and not, except for a momentary and I believe necessary lapse in the first chapter, discussed Post-Modern literature or philosophy. Someone else, with much wider horizons, will have to draw a picture of all these movements together, a picture that is hard to see today because the fields are so discontinuous and over-specialised. What I have tried to do in the text and with evolutionary charts is show the variety of Post-Modernism in its third, classical phase and make clear the relative worth of the main protagonists.

*   *   *

A book of this kind incurs large personal and intellectual debts, especially because it has taken so long to work out. Many of the latter are acknowledged implicitly or explicitly in the footnotes rather than here in the preface since,

Venturi, Rauch and Scott Brown, *The Sainsbury Wing*, proposed extension to the National Gallery (Photograph courtesy the National Gallery)

like all bad debtors, I have long forgotten the original source. Others stand out in my memory and I'm happy to repay them here, however insufficiently, with acknowledgement. Linda Nochlin and Gabriela de Ferrari read the chapters on art and gave me some very useful suggestions for inclusion. Robert Schoelkopf, whose gallery in New York exhibits several of the artists discussed, has been helpful with advice and in allowing me to reproduce work, as indeed have all the gallery owners who are acknowledged at the end of the book. My eye for, and ideas on, the new classical architecture have been immeasurably improved by discussions I have had over the years with Leon Krier, Michael Graves, Robert Stern, Demetri Porphyrios, Arata Isozaki, Conrad Jameson and Mathias Ungers. They don't always agree with my views, nor does John Summerson who has also given his time, advice and criticism most liberally; but I have been the beneficiary of their opinions for which I'm indeed grateful.

Getting the text, photos, captions, notes, rewrites and grammar into a reasonably proportionate shape in a book like this is a labour of care and design. For the former I'm indebted to Freda Emery who typed several sections and to Nick Jones who proof-read and corrected them; for the latter I'm beholden to Frank Russell and to Sue Walliker who did the layout. Andreas Papadakis, my publisher, has had the faith to see all this through to completion. But the greatest dept of all I owe, once again, to Maggie Keswick for her patience while I wrote and for her suggestions about what I wrote – a debt which the dedication of this book recognises if not adequately repays.

Charles Jencks

CHAPTER I
The Values of
Post-Modernism

After more than twenty years the Post-Modern Movement has achieved a revolution in western culture without breaking anything more than a few eggheads. It has successfully challenged the reign of Modern art and architecture, it has put Positivism and other twentieth-century philosophies in their rightfully narrow place, brought back enjoyable modes in literature without becoming populist and slowed, if not halted altogether, the wanton destruction of cities. In at least one city, San Francisco, it has instituted positive laws for growth. This revolution has cut across film, music, dance, religion, politics, fashion and nearly every activity of contemporary life and, like all revolutions, including planetary ones, it entails a return to the past as much as a movement forward. In painting the human figure has returned with proportions compared to classical architecture, while in architecture there's been a return to painting and sculpture with the human figure compared to the column (1,2). These simultaneous returns are, however, tradition with a difference and that difference is the intervention of the modern world and the tenuous place of humanism within it. The figure of man and woman that emerges is sometimes frail, occasionally mutilated and often paradoxical – an acknowledgement that our place within the universe, or even a technological civilisation, is no longer as central as it was in the Renaissance. But the human presence is back, even if it's on the edge.

Contrary to common belief Post-Modernism is neither anti-Modernist nor reactionary. It accepts the discoveries of the twentieth century – those of Freud, Einstein and Henry Ford – and the fact that two world wars and mass culture are now integral parts of our world picture, but doesn't make from this an entire ideology. In short, as its name implies, it acknowledges the debt to Modernism but transcends this movement by synthesising it with other concerns. Anyone who has come under the sway of Post-Modernism owes allegiance to two quite different pasts – the immediate and the more distant one. But, like any trend and all movements of the last two hundred years, it has also produced its fair share of pretentious nonsense and bad art. Thus, the reader will be forgiven a little scepticism and encouraged to see at least some of the work shown in this book as partially flawed. Now in the 1980s, when Post-Modernism has become respectable and academic and its products are starting to turn up on every coffee table, we can anticipate its kitsch and pomposity – those twin spectres which did so much to bring down Modernism in the 1960s. But the real accomplishments of Post-Modernism remain and it is the purpose of this book to summarise some of them,

1.1 John Nava, *D.A.K. Arms Raised/Capital*, 1984, acrylic, oil, collage on canvas, 5x4ft (Collection of Gail and Barry Berkus / Courtesy Koplin Gallery, NYC)

1.2 Robert Krier, *Human Figure and Apartments*, Ritterstrasse, Berlin-Kreuzberg, 1977-81 (Photograph A. Papadakis)

11

especially those of its third 'classical' phase, the period starting in the late 1970s.

Like any cultural movement its defining characteristics have changed shape and meaning since its inception in the late 1950s. Its subtle changes in name, such as post-Modern, postmodern and Post-Modern Movement, have to be distinguished from events which took place quite independently, such as Pop Art, the counter culture, feminism and pluralism. Both its concept and historical activity changed simultaneously until the mid 1970s when they merged and we could speak of a Post-Modern *Movement*, at least in architecture.

In other areas confusion persisted for a while, burgeoning around a series of related hybrids: 'Postminimalism' (Pincus-Witten), 'Post-Performance' (Dennis Oppenheim), 'Post-Civilisation' (Kenneth Boulding) and 'Post-Logical Positivism' (Mary Hesse) to name but a few.[1] These categories had little in common other than the liberating potential of their prefix, the desire to go beyond what were perceived as constricting dogmas. Being 'Post' in this sense might mean a strange even paradoxical thing: becoming more modern than Modern, more avant-garde. This inherent double meaning of the term has led to much confusion which it is best to clear up at the beginning.

The prefix 'post' has several contradictory overtones, one of which implies the incessant struggle against stereotypes, the 'continual revolution' of the avant-garde – and hence, by implication, the fetish of the new. The French philosopher Jean-François Lyotard has focused exclusively on this connotation, reducing the movement to this incessant battle of the generations and concluding with perfect logic and a little perversity that – 'A work can become modern only if it is first postmodern. Postmodernism thus understood is not modernism at its end but in the nascent state, and this state is constant.'[2] In effect Lyotard's paradox amounts to a play on words, the fact that Picasso and Braque were 'Post-Cézanne' just before they became 'Modern' and that all subsequent Modernists overthrow those immediately before them. This is of course true, but so is the opposite generalisation that they carried on the work of their predecessors – that is, both are not very revealing truisms. In fact Lyotard's argument in *The Postmodern Condition* stems from that of Ihab Hassan's advocating ultra-Modernism. Fearing the 'death of the avant-garde' which for the last twenty years has been so widely reported by Irving Howe, Hilton Kramer and other writers (evidently a malingering last act), Lyotard intends to give it a large jab of experimental adrenaline. He needn't bother: 'The *Late*-Modern Condition', as his book should have been called, is alive and economically flourishing in most of the world's galleries, corporate headquarters, and university literature ('Deconstructionist') departments. The Hong Kong and Shanghai Bank is there in all its wealthy splendour to celebrate, if not support, it. Late-Modernism – the exaggerated, purified and incessantly revolutionary form of Modernism –will go on thriving as long as technology changes, the youth need counter-challenges and fashion rules consumer society; i.e. from now on. But Post-

Modernism is something different, based on further connotations of the prefix 'post' which stress that it comes 'after' not before Modernism. As implied it's a reweaving of the recent past and western culture, an attempt to rework its humanist tenets in the light of a world civilisation and autonomous, plural cultures. The way this new tradition has grown slowly and fitfully out of Modernism and away from Late-Modernism shows amusing similarities with previous movements.

The Creative Paranoia of Labels

It has been argued by E.H. Gombrich and other historians that artistic terms often grow from fear and loathing, from the abusive epithets critics invent in order to stop the newest form of heresy.[3] Thus 'Baroque' and 'Rococo' were, before they became descriptive categories, derogatory labels, meant to stop the 'illogical', and excessively decorated forms to which they originally referred ('Baroque' meant a 'misshapen pearl', 'Rococo' meant 'shell like'). 'Impressionism' was thought deficient because it gave only hazy, subjective impressions; 'Romanesque' meant sub-Roman (most 'esque' forms implied degeneracy); 'Gothic' meant 'not yet classic' and also created by the barbarian Goths who sacked Rome, and 'Mannerism' meant overly mannered. Ironically, these negative epithets did not always work as intended. Indeed, reworking the old adage, we might say that 'some paranoid critics create real enemy movements' – fears continuously voiced often establish the very movements they seek to quash.

Of course living movements depend on much more than the hostility they provoke, but these attacks do often provide energy and direction. A quick summary of the term 'Post-Modern' reveals both this creative paranoia and the growing conceptual maturity. Its first cousin *postmodernismo* was referred to in 1934 by Frederico De Onís in his *Antología de la poesía española e hispanoamericana* as a 'minor reaction to modernism already latent within it', a usage that was picked up by Dudley Fitts in his *Anthology of Contemporary Latin-American Poetry*, 1942.[4] Its second cousin 'post-Modern' was then used in Arnold Toynbee's *A Study of History* published in abridged form in 1947 where, in referring to the end of western dominance, Christian culture and individualism, it acquired an element of Spenglerian doom. The modern era, beginning with the Renaissance, seemed to be giving way to internationalism, the rise of the proletariat and non-western cultures. Toynbee's anxiety that western spirituality had declined was tempered, if not contradicted, by his belief that a synthetic religion might arise from the fusion of Muslim, Christian, Buddhist and Hindu faiths. This pluralism has remained a defining aspect of all subsequent Post-Modernisms, but the syncretic faith has, in spite of later attempts, failed to gel. Toynbee's sense of 'post-Modern' thus represents its first apocalyptic usage signifying 'breakdown and disintegration' for us 'the children of a post-Christian world'. It took thirty-seven years for this argument to be inverted by Harvey Cox who recently pointed to the emergence of a 'postmodern theology' – a liberation movement based on the activities of local Christian communities in places like Latin America.[5] But this anticipates a later shift in meaning.

In the late 1950s and early 1960s the notion of a 'postmodern fiction' was invented by Irving Howe and Harold Levin, a term retaining much of the dreaded overtones of Toynbee's usage in its suggestion of a posthumous Modernism, or one in need of a postmortem.[6] The death of High Modernism was implicitly equated with the end of high culture, but again there was a glimmer of hope with the emergence of such distinctly postmodern writers as J.D. Salinger, Norman Mailer and Jack Kerouac. Howe, Levin and later Hilton Kramer (*The Age of the Avantgarde,* 1973) saw in postmodern literature a decline in standards, which reflected the inherent nihilism of the consumer society which it portrayed. Most intellectuals agreed with Clement Greenberg's essay on *Avant Garde and Kitsch* (1938) or Dwight MacDonald's distinctions between highbrow, midcult and masscult. These tracts claimed that there was an unbridgeable and widening division between elitist and mass culture, and that the former although tiny and carried on by a dwindling avant-garde was the only one worth having. The stage was thus set for a double attack on this theory; either its valuations could be inverted and low become a form of high culture, or the stratified layers within any group, or individual, could be seen as a continuum. Both positions and a mixture of them emerged about the same time and together constitute the first positive phase of Post-Modernism.[7]

1960s Postmodernism: Pop Art, Counter Culture and adhocism

Pop Art was started, significantly, by a small group of English intellectuals and artists who consumed American mass culture both unselfconsciously and as an acquired taste. They met as an avant-garde elite, the Independent Group, in the 1950s and lectured on the way the new media – TV, films, advertisements and mass-produced machinery – shaped consciousness. Marshall McLuhan came to some of these meetings, at which anthropology and semiology were discussed, and these disciplines showed the way all culture is a tissue of signs or a form of information exchange. Members of the Group collected mass media ephemera, displayed them in juxtaposition on tackboards and explained the rationale behind these compositions: in this way quite naturally developing an art form of collage. Lawrence Alloway, founder and protector of the concept of Pop Art, describes how it developed from meetings between young working class and urban professionals who made up this London advance guard:

> The Independent Group missed a year and then was reconvened in winter 1954-5 by John McHale and myself on the theme of popular culture. This topic was arrived at as a result of a snowballing conversation in London which involved [the artist] Paolozzi, [the architects] the Smithsons, [the photographer] Henderson, [the critic] Reyner Banham, [the painter] Hamilton, [the theorist] McHale and myself. We discovered that we had in common a vernacular culture

that persisted beyond any special interest skills in art, architecture, design or art criticism that any of us might possess. The area of contact was mass-produced urban culture: movies, advertisement, science fiction, Pop music. We felt none of the dislike of commercial culture standard among most intellectuals, but accepted it as a fact, discussed it in detail, and consumed it enthusiastically . . .[8]

Richard Hamilton and the others produced several Pop collages illustrating this new enthusiasm and they were always, significantly, tied with Modernist modes such as abstraction and complex irony (3). One should emphasise that they were neither populist nor clichéd, as their detractors made out, however much they might use mass cult imagery. Nor admittedly were they very profound syntheses of high and low art, the present and the past. Rather they were *ad hoc* amalgamations of a wide spectrum of tastes – a mixture which the contemporary Modernists found distasteful.

Five years later Pop Art grew independently in America where it was more brash and immediate, but equally mixed in method and intention. Robert Rauschenberg was the most original of these *ad hocists*, aggregating a violent heterogeneity of material into his 'combines'; for instance an angora goat and a car tyre alongside Abstract Expressionist patches and mass media signs formed the work *Monogram*. The mixed audience of young and old, scruffy and establishment, which came to see his work in 1959 and at several retrospectives in the 1960s more or less mirrored the disparities inherent within these combines. Like *Monogram* the audience may not have added up to anything as a whole – certainly not an integrated taste culture – yet this fragmented pluralism has remained both a fundamental fact and aesthetic of Post-Modernism ever since. By 1965 it had already matured into a shared style and was applied with great skill by hundreds of Pop Artists – the number reflecting the democratisation of the new art scene.

James Rosenquist's *F111* is characteristic of this phase (4). Its scale is that of the billboards he had once worked on – ten feet high and eighty-six feet long. Its bright, acid, enticing images were taken directly from the mass media but then montaged. It's meaning? Ambiguous, but with the F111 fighter – by then an *obsolete* airplane in the Vietnam War – it was an obvious protest against the use to which taxes were put, as was the A-bomb exploding in the painting under an umbrella (tax shelter). On one level the point of the work was the impossibility of its whole meaning, underlined by the impossibility of viewing it as a single entity. Even reading it from left to right, as implied, is difficult because the subject, slick image, scale and colour keep oscillating like a TV set which has gone into terminal multiple exposure. Inevitably its provocative ambiguity and media style agitated the Modernist critics. Hilton Kramer, attacked it as 'slick, cheerful, overblown, irredeemably superficial… [it] leaves the spectator feeling as if he ought to be sucking a popsicle'.[9] Here is the paranoiac response which the artist must have expected when he aimed his dayglo canvas at the well exposed Modernist nerve ends.

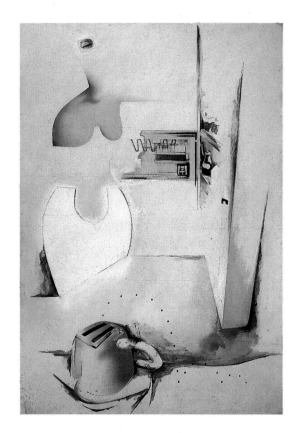

1.3 Richard Hamilton, *$he*, 1958-61 (veiled fragments of advertisement, shoulders, breast, a toaster, vacuum cleaner and refrigerator) oil, cellulose, collage on panel, 48x32in (Photograph John Webb/Courtesy Tate Gallery, London)

It is probable that both Rosenquist and Kramer were involved in some sort of implicit contract here; the former using heightened emotional images such as the too knowing Doris Dayette under a hairdryer: the latter throwing back popsicle barbs. The work became the most controversial of Pop paintings and Rosenquist would be disingenuous if he didn't concede that a prime motive was to inspire dread and panic. But is the *F111* 'irredeemably superficial'? Only by Pop-Modernist standards. As the reader will discover in Chapters III and IV, there is so much 'suggestive narrative' and 'implicit allegory' in Post-Modern art that it amounts to a genre as conventional as historical painting or still-life. The fact that Rosenquist will not make a single political point out of this Vietnam protest, for that is its implicit meaning, accurately reflects his culture's mixed feeling about the war. The painting is more a heroic celebration of this ambiguous feeling than a resolution or reasoned synthesis of arguments as it might have been if painted by Nicolas Poussin or Jacques Louis David.[10] It is not as beautiful and organically related as these historical genre paintings, because it tries to make a virtue of schizophrenia; but it is more plausible for its time than an integrated Neo-classical version would have been.

The dramatisation of social and urban reality underlay postmodernism in its first phase in the 1960s. It could be found in such disparate undercurrents as the work of the Advocacy Planners, the defence of local interest groups, the writings of Robert Venturi on Main Street and Route 66, the anti-war movement, the overstated speculations of McLuhan on the new media, the counter culture and Susan Sontag's *Notes on Camp*; and even to an extent the youth movement and student uprisings in 1962 at Berkeley and May 1968 in Paris. A characteristic *ad hoc* architecture to emerge from this period was Lucien Kroll's buildings for the students in Belgium – full of ornament, humour, metaphor and looking in their vital jumble altogether like a constructed version of May 1968 (5). All these different movements and demonstrations were anti-establishment in their celebration of specific political and social realities. They were undoubtedly one-sided and in some ways as infantile as their critics claimed; but as particular strategies they were more responsive to social realities than the reigning Modernist culture.

Modernism, in its several forms, had become an orthodoxy by the 1960s, at least in America. It was built in the business centre of every growing city, taught in the literature and art departments of major universities and, as a form of art, collected by the major galleries and institutionalised by the Museum of Modern Art. But the very success of Modernism as a style and ideology, its adoption by bureaucratic power structures and its fatal alignment with the program of modernisation, left it morally weak and aesthetically boring. The Modern Movement which was radical, critical and lively in the 1920s had now been coopted by the *Pax Americana* and corporate life. The architecture of this time well illustrates this compromise, with Walter Gropius designing the brutally commercial Pan Am building in New York, Le Corbusier churning out heavy inhuman *Unités d'Habitations*

1.4 James Rosenquist, *F111*, 1965, oil on canvas with aluminium, 10x86ft (Private Collection, New York/Courtesy Whitney Museum of American Art, NYC)

1.5 Lucien Kroll and Atelier, *Dormitory and Medical Faculty Buildings*, University of Louvain, Belgium, 1969-74 (Photograph C. Jencks)

for West Berlin and other sensitive sites, and Mies' followers constructing the equivalent of Madison Avenue in every western city. Early defenders of Modernism, such as Lewis Mumford, were as quick as the the younger postmodernists to point out 'The case against "Modern Architecture"' and by 1960 he had already launched an attack on Mies and 'the apotheosis of the compulsive, bureaucratic spirit'.[11]

If America was the leader of the Free World in the 1960s and if its orthodoxy was a form of Modernism tied to liberal capitalism, then the time was ripe for writers and artists to declare a new culture as an inversion of everything established. This explains Leslie Fiedler's radical use of the prefix 'post' used in an article like an incantation to support all the mini-movements against the centre. The counter cultures, he proclaimed in 1965, were 'post humanist, post-male, post-white, post-heroic . . . post-Jewish'.[12] He didn't however, have a fully articulated concept of postmodernism for, as we have seen, there was at this time no positive and synthetic view of the movement as a whole. This had to await the 1970s when, ironically, most of its tendencies had withered or changed course; notably dead or collapsing were the anti-war and student movements, Pop Art and the McLuhanite celebration of TV. In part the postmodernism of the 1960s was an unselfconscious Pop culture inspired by rock and folk music and made up of various groups – such as Hippies, Yippies and *groupuscules* – representing specific ideologies of protest. Tom Wolfe, developing a neo-hysterical style by combining Pop Art and stream-of-consciousness, used Las Vegas and its sign artists to criticize the elite sterilities of Modernist formalism. Like others, he set a Pop and populist culture against the late Bauhaus and the followers of Mondrian and Shoenberg. Andy Warhol, for 'fifteen minutes', produced a series of radical images of mass-production, summarising the death-wish of commercial culture. His electric chairs, silkscreens of *suicide* and portraits of Jackie and Marilyn Monroe had a tough, poetic dignity which was to become dissipated in the 1970s when Warhol himself became such a social machine. Much of this aggressive Pop culture, like Warhol's, was aimed simply at the commercial success of Modernism and aimed to supplant it with a blatant form of exploitive cynicism. However, it would be as wrong to dismiss this Pop culture as mere opportunism as it would to say that the Modern Movement was fought to make Madison Avenue safe from communism; but in both cases commercial success eroded the life and direction of these movements.

1970s Post-Modernism: Pluralistic Politics and Eclectic Style

It wasn't until 1971 and Ihab Hassan's essay 'POSTmodernISM: A Paracritical Bibliography' that the movement was *actually* christened and a pedigree provided although even then the term, like its inconsistent capitalisation, wasn't clearly defined. Nevertheless, from this and Hassan's later writings a clear enough picture emerged of a *literary* movement which focused mainly on the *Late*-Modernism of William Burroughs, Jean Genet and Samuel Beckett, the music of John Cage and the 1960s futurisms of McLuhan and

Buckminster Fuller. 'Post-Modernism', he wrote, 'is essentially subversive in form and anarchic in its cultural spirit. It dramatises its lack of faith in art even as it produces new works of art intended to hasten both cultural and artistic dissolution.'[13] The emphasis was thus on ultra-avantgardism, and some literary critics, philosophers and not a few artists accepted it uncritically as the historical truth. In his 1978 definitions Hassan lists the kind of modes POSTmodernISM involves: 'Pataphysics/Dadaism, Antiform (disjunctive, open), Play, Chance, Anarchy, Exhaustion/Silence, Process/Performance/ Happening, Participation, Decreation/Deconstruction . . . Antinarrative, the Holy Ghost, Desire, Polymorphous/Androgynous, Schizophrenia . . . etc.'[14] Ironically, except for the notion of participation, this list represents the antithesis of what was going on in the Post-Modern Movement in architecture at the time. Even as an analysis of literature these definitions were inaccurate and were in fact inverted in the 1980s by writers such as John Barth and Umberto Eco. But for a period, such Late-Modern concerns dominated discussion within literary circles, conspicuous among which was William Spanos' journal devoted to postmodern literature, *boundary 2*, which featured the oral poetry of Olson, Creely, David Antin and Jerome Rothenberg.

Hassan was soon to generalise the concept to include other eras and, significantly, claimed James Joyce's *Finnegan's Wake* as a key example of postmodernism since it had a plethora of anarchic and disjunctive qualities: no plot, no character, no chronological sequence, no subject, no imitation, no symbolism and no meaning. It required a Readers Guide and, as Barth wryly observed, a staff of tenured professors to act as a 'necessary priestly industry of explicators'. This excessive difficulty, Barth adds, is no reason to dismiss High Modernist literature which is what *Finnegan's Wake* really is. Joyce, Pound and others had many historical reasons for adopting such modes and meeting the challenge of twentieth-century discoveries in physics, psychology, anthropology and technology. Because of its very high standards of artistry High Modernist literature repays the close analysis it demands.

But John Barth does take exception to Hassan's definition of postmodernism. In a most cogent essay on the subject, 'The Literature of Replenishment, Postmodernist Fiction', 1980, he writes: 'In my view, if it has no other and larger possibilities than those noted by, for example, Professors Alter, Graff and Hassan, then postmodernist writing is indeed a kind of pallid, last-ditch decadence, of no more than minor symptomatic interest'.[15] Barth outlines a very different programme for postmodernism – similar to the architectural one – that accepts the Modern Movement as a necessary stage of the first half of our century, but as something which now has to become more democratic and accessible, and retain its appeal on rereading.

> A worthy program for postmodernist fiction, I believe, is the synthesis or transcension of these antitheses, which may be summed up as premodernist and modernist modes of writing. My ideal postmodernist author neither merely repudiates nor merely imitates either his

twentieth-century modernist parents or his nineteenth-century pre-modernist grandparents. He has the first half of our century under his belt, but not on his back...he nevertheless aspires to a fiction more democratic in its appeal than such late-Modernist marvels (by my definition and in my judgement) as Beckett's *Stories and Texts for Nothing* or Nabokov's *Pale Fire*. He may not hope to reach and move the devotees of James Michener and Irving Wallace – not to mention the lobotomised mass-media illiterates. But he *should* hope to reach and delight, at least part of the time, beyond the circle of what Mann used to call the Early Christians: professional devotees of high art.[16]

As examples of successful syntheses Barth recommends Italo Calvino's *Cosmicomics* (1965) and, even more, Gabriel Garćia Márquez's *One Hundred Years of Solitude* (1967) '. . . as impressive a novel as has been written so far in the second half of our century an one of the splendid specimens of that splendid genre from any century'. It's interesting to contrast Barth's list of postmodernists with Hassan's – writers such as William Gass, Donald Barthelme, Thomas Pynchon, Kurt Vonnegut Jr., the Englishman John Fowles, the expatriate Argentine Julio Cortázar – and see that he distinguishes them from 'late-Modernists' such as John Hawkes, 'comparative preModernists' such as Saul Bellow and Norman Mailer, and 'consistently traditionalist' writers such as John Cheever and John Updike. Here we find the important conceptual distinctions between major traditions with each one correctly labelled – 'traditional', 'post', 'late' and 'pre-modern'. These mutually illuminate and define each other, and are distinctions which I had proposed quite independently for architecture. Their importance cannot be overstated because they allow the autonomy and legitimacy of different approaches. This pluralism, necessarily founded on conceptual clarity and the ability to make such distinctions, is the defining aspect of postmodernism in the 1970s. Before we examine it in the other arts, we should note two aspects that Umberto Eco adds to Barth's discussion of postmodernist literature: the new use of history and irony.

Eco, in his *Postscript to the Name of the Rose* (1983), gives a witty characterisation of the way the avant-garde proceeds forward by a series of self-cancelling steps until it reaches the all white canvas, the glass and steel curtain wall, the literature of silence and, in music, 'the passage from atonality to noise to absolute silence (in this sense, the early Cage is modern)'. Eco continues with this fine parody:

> But the moment comes when the avant-garde (the modern) can go no further, because it has produced a metalanguage that speaks of its impossible texts (conceptual art). The postmodern reply to the modern consists of recognising that the past, since it cannot really be destroyed, because its destruction leads to silence, must be revisited: but with irony, not innocently.[17]

And here, if I may emphasise the point because it is the most amusing illustration of why postmodernists must use irony when dealing with the past,

Eco comes to a classic formulation.

> I think of the postmodern attitude as that of a man who loves a very cultivated woman and knows he cannot say to her 'I love you madly', because he knows that she knows (and that she knows that he knows) that these words have already been written by Barbara Cartland. Still, there is a solution. He can say 'As Barbara Cartland would put it, I love you madly'. At this point, having avoided false innocence, having said clearly that it is no longer possible to speak innocently, he will nevertheless have said what he wanted to say to the woman: that he loves her in an age of lost innocence. If the woman goes along with this, she will have received a declaration of love all the same. Neither of the two speakers will feel innocent, both will have accepted the challenge of the past, of the already said, which cannot be eliminated; both will consciously and with pleasure play the game of irony . . . But both will have succeeded, once again, in speaking of love.[18]

Irony and all this knowing that everyone else knows that we know that innocence is lost can get rather tiring, but self-consciousness is a natural consequence of living in a post-Freudian age – one that has created several well-paid professions from linguistic and sexual analysis. There's no going back in time, as Barth would say, no way of eradicating Nietzsche, Einstein, Levi-Strauss and our view of the expanding universe. But thankfully we *can* move beyond these discoveries and are not limited to any particular world view which may derive from them.

This open pluralism, both political and cultural, was one of the great accomplishments of the 1970s, at least in America where it replaced the Modernist notion of an elite avant-garde set against mass culture. The women's movement typifies certain key changes in this respect. Starting in the early 1960s with the writings of Betty Friedan and soon turning into an active political forum, by the early 1970s it had become a large middle-class movement which could point to several legislative victories among its successes – including abortion and employment rights – and a generally changed attitude in society. Feminism, with its unremitting critique of hidden assumptions, aimed its attack on elitism *per se*. Thus one of its main antagonists was Modernism and the previously hidden male dominance of its programme.

The women's movement arrived relatively late on the art scene in the early 1970s, when it challenged the major New York museums to put on mixed shows, set up several galleries devoted solely to female artists (A.I.R. in 1972, Sotto 20 and Women's Interart Gallery in 1975) and staged polemical exhibitions and demonstrations to propagate their aims.[19] Much of the art produced had an implicit didactic basis like eighteenth-century historical painting, and an explicit sexual bias.

Judy Chicago's *The Dinner Party*, 1979, was an inventively lugubrious demonstration of the number of ways a feminine triangle and other sexual parts could be used symbolically. They are turned into place settings at a mythical meal attended by thirty-nine historical painters and the living artist Georgia O'Keefe (who resented this use of her name and imagery). More subtle and amusing, though no less polemical, was Dotty Attie's erotic narratives such as *A Dream of Love*, 1973, which consists of a hundred-and-forty-four small drawings arranged in a grid, an idea which derives from the Pop artists' use of the tackboard. In this work Attie appropriates images from Gainsborough and Ingres, from cigarette ads and pornography, to build up a checkerboard of sexual fantasy that reads partly like a novel, partly like a classical painting. Each one of the images tends to become the word of a sentence, repeated with variations of scale and meaning (6). A headless nude, a stabbed man, a boot crushing a face, signs of sexual fetishism and repulsion follow each other from left to right, up and down or anyway we want to read them. Their totality does not, however, add up to any discernible single message beyond the representation of erotic fantasy and repression. What makes this work typical of feminist and Post-Modern art in the 1970s is its pluralism of technique and reference.

Sylvia Sleigh, wife of Pop Art theorist Lawrence Alloway, also characteristically mixes images of high and low art in her sensual portraits. These sometimes take the classical pose of the voluptuous odalisque, displayed horizontally on a sofa for our visual delectation, and transforms it into the figure of a hairy man as in *Imperial Nude*, 1975. This change of sex has a double punch. Not only does it make us aware of the voyeuristic assumptions behind the odalisque tradition, but also, and this is accentuated, the feminine eroticism of the male body.

Such mixing of categories and genres became the style of 1970s Post-Modernism in all the arts. In this era of eclecticism the past was consulted (and plundered), lovingly revived (and ridiculed). Often it was hard to tell whether the artist or architect was making a serious attempt at combining traditions, critically contrasting them, or was simply confused. Modernism and popular culture were combined in the synthetic music of Terry Riley and Phil Glass, the buildings of Charles Moore and Hans Hollein and in the New German Cinema, especially in the films of Rainer Werner Fassbinder. Jeremy Dixon's low cost housing in London is characteristic of the architecture that is eclectic because it must appeal to plural taste-cultures. At St. Mark's road, for instance he mixed an Edwardian typology with vernacular and Modernist elements (7). It even includes anthropomorphism – each house suggests a face – and classical symmetries.

The common element in such eclecticism was its assault on the notion of a stable category such as high art, good taste, classicism or Modernism. As Craig Owens has argued: 'otherness' and eclecticism were two strategies used against elitism by both the women's movement and Post-Modern culture generally.[20] Thus Pop Art theory of the 1950s which had shown culture to be a continuum had, by the 1970s, created an eclecticism which represented this continuum. But there were also specific trends in Post-Modern art towards allegory and narrative, still-life and landscape, ornament and pattern

1.6 Dotty Attie, *A Dream of Love*, 1973, pencil on paper, 3x12ft (Courtesy the artist)

1.7 Jeremy Dixon, *St. Mark's Road Housing*, London, 1976-80 (Photograph Martin Charles)

painting. There was even a return to complex didactic and moralistic art.

Pluralism thus existed both as a tactic within particular works and as a very real variety within the art world as a whole. It is worth summarising some of this variety to highlight the main currents. Within the realist tradition there were the main shifts from Pop Art to Photo-Realism and the various neo-realisms. Richard Estes, basically a Photo-Realist, cuts across several of these categories. He often focuses on the new urban landscape with its signs and ephemera, just as a Pop artist would, but then invests these signs with an almost classical *gravitas*. Selecting details from a series of randomly shot photos of city streets, he will create a powerfully ambiguous montage. Thus the *Boston Bank Building* simultaneously emphasises both the permanence of architecture and the immateriality of light (8). Columns and metal mullions are layered frontally while the interior lighting and reflections recede on the diagonal; the ambiguity between foreground, background and reflection mirrors the ambiguity of the subject matter – present and reflected past. These double readings give his form of realism a timelessness not immediately appreciable; at first we may confuse the images with the deadpan neutrality of the camera shot, deriving as they do so clearly from the conventions of photography.

Ron Kitaj, an entirely different type of realist and one of the most significant Post-Modern painters, takes a more obviously interpretative attitude towards subject matter. Indeed in this respect he is more traditional than Estes, and he has declared his humanist intentions not only in his work, but as curator of an important exhibition in 1976 entitled *The Human Clay*. Along with David Hockney, Peter Blake and others he called for a return to traditional concerns: the life class and drawing, with an emphasis on relevant subject matter. Nevertheless his work always retained a Modernist flavour in style and content, resulting in the typical hybrid combination of Post-Modernism. *To Live in Peace (The Singers)*, portraying an Easter dinner in Spain, uses Modernist formal devices such as cropped figures, flat graphic planes of colour and shallow, layered space (9). Figures are bent and distorted and sometimes even reduced to fuzzy silhouettes. But there is a suggested narrative in the title and a peaceful landscape to the left, so we are bound to read it as a characteristic 'enigmatic allegory' – albeit as troublesome to decipher as it is for the singer in this painting to follow her score. T.S. Eliot's poetry, which suggests more than it states, is often an inspiration for this work. Here the suggestion conveyed is one of a contemporary ritual fragmented by discontinuities of character, dress and ambience. It's a haunting scene full of anomalies – the sun shines, an electric light competes with it. Kitaj turns these non-sequitors and juxtapositions into a believable portrayal of the dissociated ritual typical of our time.

The way the realist tradition built up momentum through the 1970s and into the 1980s is evident from the many exhibitions devoted to the movement during this period. There was the Documenta Show in 1972 called *5 Realismus;* the *Hyperrealists Americains* at the Galerie des 4 Movements in

1.8 Richard Estes, *Boston Bank Building*, 1974, gouache, 12x18in (Collection Mr. and Mrs. Barry Hirschfield, Denver/Courtesy Louis K. Meisel Gallery, NYC)

1.9 Ron Kitaj, *To Live in Peace (The Singers)*, 1973-7, oil on canvas, 30x84in (Private Collection, New York/Courtesy Marlborough Fine Art (London) Ltd.)

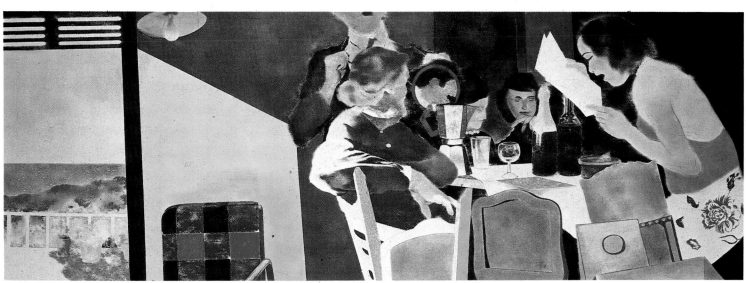

Paris 1972-3; *Trends in Contemporary Realist Painting* at Boston's Museum of Fine Arts, 1975; *Figurative/Realist Art* at the Artists' Choice Museum, New York, 1979; *Contemporary American Realism Since 1960* at the Pennsylvanian Academy of Fine Arts, 1981-2 (organised by Frank H. Goodyear, the most balanced and thoughtful of the American exhibitions);[21] *Eight Figurative Painters* at the Yale Center for British Art, 1981-2; *Real, Really Real, Super Real* at the San Antonio Museum 1981-2; *Les Realismes 1919-39* at the Pompidou Centre, Paris, 1981 (rightfully stressing the variety of interwar realisms during the height of Modernism); and *The Hard Won Image* at the Tate Gallery, London, 1984. From this representative selection, it is apparent that the realist tradition continually gathered strength and diversity from the 1970s onwards and that it is largely, though not exclusively, based in America. A further point should be emphasised: although all Post-Modernists are interested in figuration, not all figurative painters are Post-Modern. Some have never faced the Modernist predicament – the secularisation and fragmentation of culture – and have thus never absorbed this into a greater synthesis.

There have been other tendencies within Post-Modernism in addition to realism, some of which are as much the creation of curators as they are of artists. Hostile critics tend to ascribe the need for new 'directions' or 'waves' to the demands of the market place – the very real commercial necessity for new products and a quick turnover. No doubt the expanded art market has caused overproduction and inflation (it is said that there are ninety thousand artists in New York City) along with the mass production of Schnabels and Clementes, but one must keep this in perspective by remembering how Modernism itself celebrated industrialisation, and how Rubens, aided by assistants, practiced his own cottage industry of self-forgery. When Giorgio Vasari boasted to Michelangelo that he had high-speed-painted the Palazzo Cancelleria in 'one hundred days', the laconic and exact reply was 'It looks like it'. Fast-food painting, like fast-food architecture, has been around for some time and it nearly always has the same watery flavour.

Admittedly some of these trends are thin, but cumulatively they have played a part in shaping Post-Modernism and should be mentioned: there was the 'Pattern Painting' of 1976-7, and the related tendencies of the new ornamentalism; the 'New Image' painting of 1979; 'Bad Painting' and the 'New Wave' of 1981; and – the most conspicuous 'ism' of 1983 – Neo-Expressionism. All these currents and eddies need to be seen as part of the ever-widening river of Post-Modernism and appreciated for their particular quality or dismissed for their lack of it. As in other cases, quality depends on skill, integrity and the imaginative use of a language – aspects which are rarely combined in any one movement.

The Post-Modern Movement in Architecture

While Post-Modernism remained a diffuse series of trends within the arts it quite quickly crystallised into an architectural movement during the mid

1970s. One reason for this, suggested by Andreas Huyssen, is that architecture more than any other art form succumbed to the alienating effects of modernisation.[22] The Modern Movement in architecture promoted industrialisation and correspondingly demoted local communities and the existing urban fabric, as it did virtually everything that stood in the way of the bulldozer. There was a tragic, indeed fatal, connection between Modern architecture and modernisation which was more or less directly opposed by the Modern Movement in the other arts. T.S Eliot's *The Waste Land* portrays the characteristic attitude to these other Modernisms. But this split on the question of industrialisation is understandable. Architects, to protect their livelihood, must adopt an upbeat attitude towards development, towards the new technology and increased efficiency. There is no such thing as a Dadaist or Existentialist architecture because the profession, or an individual within it, could not bear the contradiction of building a better world for a nihilistic world view. Imagine Marcel Duchamp or Jean-Paul Sartre as the heroic subject of Ann Rand's *The Fountainhead*, and you'll appreciate the profound difference in perspective between Modern architecture and all other forms of Modernism.

The tragic association of Modern architecture with modernisation became very obvious in the late 1950s. The first critique of this situation from within the Movement came from the Team Ten architects such as Aldo Van Eyck, which quickly resulted in a type of Revisionist Modernism. This philosophy and practice substituted the notion of place for abstract space, promoting a high-density low-rise building and an abstract form of regionalism, still championed today by Kenneth Frampton under the banner of 'critical regionalism'. Mario Botta and the Ticino architects in Switzerland characterise this departure at its best with thin abstract classical constructions, although whether they are 'regional' can be doubted (10). But the critique was not very radical (it was after all an in-house revolution) and stopped far short of Jane Jacobs' withering attack of 1961, *The Death and Life of Great American Cities*. As I argue in Chapter IX, the rise of Post-Modern architecture and urbanism really dates from this attack which, along with the succession of urban and social critiques it spawned, resulted in the widespread demolition of Modernist housing estates.

Again the other Modernisms did not suffer such violent and clear refutations, did not have their Pruitt-Igoes to watch on TV, lifting off the ground in a slow-motion of dust, dynamite and fractured abstraction. This explosion of 1972, copied countless times throughout the world as a radical way of dealing with such housing estates, soon came to symbolise the mythical death of Modern architecture (11). That was how I used it when starting to lecture on the subject in 1974 and the notion of a sudden demise, coupled with slides of the explosion, had an enormously liberating impact. For the next two years, in lectures around the world, I used this rhetorical formula – Death of Modernism/Rise of Post-Modernism – aware that it was a symbolic fabrication (I even invented a false date) and yet pleasingly

1.11 *Pruitt-Igoe Blowing Up*, St. Louis, USA, 1972 (Courtesy Minoru Yamasaki)

surprised to find that nearly everyone (especially the press) accepted it as truth. If I pointed out that many Modern architects were still at work and that my arguments were symbolic, or ironic caricatures, these disclaimers were ignored. The public response was extremly strong in every country I visited, especially communist ones where Modern architecture, being state supported, was the only option for housing. In fact the response to my lectures and articles was so forceful and widespread that it created Post-Modernism as a social and architectural movement. I am not claiming, of course, to have coined the term or invented the trend, but rather to have discovered that the public needed its social purpose. This point should be stressed especially now when so many people discuss the issue as if it were a matter of style, or reviving the past. The Post-Modern Movement was then, and remains today, a wider social protest against modernisation, against the destruction of local culture by the combined forces of rationalisation, bureaucracy, large-scale development and, it is true, the Modern International Style. But style was only one of eleven causes I cited as responsible for its death in *The Language of Post-Modern Architecture*, 1977. The other ten concerned the actual production *system* that architects found themselves saddled with. This system had two major flaws, the scale of its projects and the speed with which they were executed: a billion dollar chunk of the environment could be designed by one man and built within a couple of years.

A consensus amounting to a movement started to gel in 1975 when several architects such as Robert Stern and Michael Graves began working along similar lines to European architects such as Aldo Rossi, Robert Krier and James Stirling. Although they had some significant differences of approach and might question my labelling them Post-Modern at this time, they all sought to transcend Modernism while hearkening back to a wider architectural language. Not long after, Hans Hollein (12) and Arata Isozaki produced their eclectic buildings and Philip Johnson designed the AT&T Corporate Headquarters. The 'new wave' became a flood, in which I well remember getting wet. On 31 March 1978, at precisely 7.46 a.m. several architectural students from Yale University burst into my hotel room and thrust a copy of *The New York Times* in my face. On the front page was a photo of Johnson's new foray into Post-Modernism (13) and, inside, an article by Paul Goldberger proclaiming it to be the 'first monument' of the movement. The students enquired of this monolith (from one perspective it looks funereal) 'Is Post-Modernism Dead?' The logic of their question was compelling. If Modernism failed because it got too big and corporate, then this structure to the world's biggest corporation must be the movement's kiss of death. Success had once again taken its toll, as in the nineteenth century, littered with the corpses of changing styles which could survive every persecution, cope with any situation, except the loving embrace of a commercial society.

I almost agreed with this diagnosis, one which has been made repeatedly; at times with photo-collages of Michael Graves' Portland Building being blown up, at others under the rubric 'Post-Post-Modern' and even more

1.10 Mario Botta, *The State Bank at Fribourg*, 1977-82, banking hall (Courtesy the architect)

1.12 Hans Hollein, *Perchtoldsdorf Townhall Renovation*, Austria, 1975-6 (Photograph J. Surwillo)

1.13 Philip Johnson and John Burgee, *AT&T Headquarters Building*, model, New York, 1978-82 (Photograph courtesy the architects)

frequently with the simple epitaph 'The Death of P-M'.[23] The linguistic life and death of movements, noted by Vasari in the Renaissance and reaching a high pitch in the 1920s, had now become an integral part of cultural politics. Tony Vidler, a Princeton professor of architecture, took aim at my writings (and head) and accompanied by graphics which showed my cranium disintegrating in slow motion freeze frames, like Pruitt-Igoe, took a certain pleasure in the hit job.[24] Perhaps I deserved such summary treatment after announcing the death of Modern architecture – the idea of each young art movement devouring its parent was in the air, to be appropriated by any critic or trend so inclined. But, to return to Post-Modernism's health after the AT&T, the obituaries are evidently premature. The movement had not so much died as a result of this media 'success' (its image promptly appeared on the covers of the London *Times*, *Time* magazine, the *Observer* colour section etc.) as become visibly older. It moved straight into middle age and won the acceptance of the establishment as had its brother, Late-Modernism, and aged parent, Modernism. All three exist partly to deal with very real social forces and partly in response to each other; in other words, they dialectically define each other in relation to other, external forces. As long as one exists, it is likely the other two will carry on, as will aspects of traditional culture. For, as has been stressed, this pluralism represents an important rediscovery and principle of Post-Modernism.

By 1980, there were several events which confirmed the movement's widespread acceptance. Most important was the Venice Biennale section on architecture, organised by Paolo Portoghesi, and a committee on which I sat. Entitled 'The Presence of the Past', it highlighted the element of historicism within Post-Modernism – the most conspicuous trend within the movement. The virtue of the exhibit lay in its celebration of architecture as a representational art and its recognition of the new consensus within the Post-Modern Classical style (14). The public's response to this display was over two thousand visitors per day – a large number for an architectural exhibition. Because of its success it was demounted and reassembled the following year in both Paris and San Francisco. This popular response should be stressed since it vindicated the Post-Modernists' notion that architecture is a public art which must not only be comprehensible, but also colourful and amusing.

The other significant event which occurred at this time was the competition for the Portland Public Service Building, a contest Michael Graves won with an eclectic facade that could have come from the Venice Biennale, if it hadn't been designed beforehand. Partly urbanist with its green arcades, it was also partly Modernist – its black glass wall signifying the public space within (15). The Rationalist Style was acknowledged as well in the little square windows (prompted also by the energy crisis) while its proportions and garlands hinted at Egyptian and Baroque influences. Calling it eclectic is an understatement, but its virtue lay not only in these diverse references (which related to nineteenth-century arcaded building in Portland), but also

1.14 *Strada Novissima,* Venice Biennale, 1980. Facades of Robert Venturi, Leon Krier and J.P. Kleiheus in view (Photograph C. Jencks)

1.15 Michael Graves, *Portland Public Services Building*, Portland, 1980-2 (Photograph Proto Acme Photo)

1.16 Raymond Kaskey, *'Portlandia'*, Portland, 1985 (Photograph Ed Wundrum)

1.17 Skidmore, Owings and Merrill, (Design Partner, Adrian Smith), *Rowes Wharf,* east elevation, N-S section, Boston, Mass., 1987 (Drawing Peter Van Vechten)

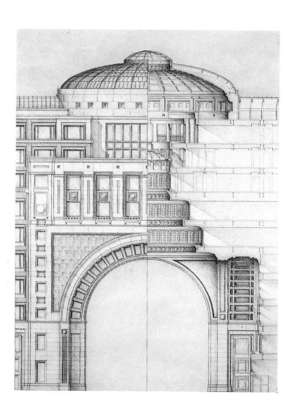

in the way they were pulled together into what Robert Venturi called 'the difficult whole'. Here was a building which, with all its undeniable faults, really was inclusive on a visual and urban level. It related to the adjacent city hall as well as the surrounding Modernist slabs, it incorporated veiled references to the human body and face, and reintegrated sculpture and polychromy as essential parts of its mixed language. The installation of the sculpture 'Portlandia' over the front door was a cause for public celebration by the citizens, as well as a small victory for Post-Modernists supporting the collaboration of artists and architects (16). No doubt, as critics contend, it is diagrammatic and two-dimensional, but this is partly because of its extremely low cost – something like fifty dollars per square foot. And it would have been better if Modernist critics had refrained from imposing several oversimplifications on its roof and sides: in their unremitting attacks on Graves they effectively censored parts of the architecture.[25] On the whole it was far more creative than contending designs, and a lot more humane than the surrounding slabs which were reducing Portland to a cemetery of inarticulate blandness. It also ushered in the Post-Modern Classical style, the third and most mature phase of the movement.

In other spheres Post-Modernism was also coming into focus partly as a result of clearer definitions within the architectural movement. Once such events are labelled and defined they reach a new stage of development. Artists reflect on their goals and the way they are part of a growing tradition; architects become conscious of the values and rules they are using (as we will see in the last chapter); while Post-Modernist writers and philosophers start to define a corpus of key texts and concepts. Characteristic of this gathering tradition were several exhibitions on the new classical art, and a large overview of Post-Modernism at the Hirshorn Museum in Washington DC 1984-5, called rather bluntly *Content.*[26] The argument behind the show, as might be guessed, was that a new concern with content, or 'the will to meaning', unites the pluralistic trends of the recent past, trends which stem from the conceptual art of the early 1970s. This argument was indeed compelling even if, in forwarding it, the organisers failed to distinguish Late- from Post-Modern works and included too much (what doesn't have content?). In the academic sphere there was a sudden outburst of conferences and specialist journals devoted to Post-Modernism with one such jamboree in Japan attended by 10,004 concerned participants.[27] The movement became big business in the architectural world, with large corporate practices such as Skidmore, Owings and Merrill switching styles (17) and Kohn Pedersen Fox streamlining the Gravesian synthesis. I had written *Post-Modern Classicism* in 1980 and by 1985, when the bulk of the present book was written, it had become one of the world's leading approaches with a short history, set of monuments and key protagonists. To clarify this type of classicism one must define its broad outlines and distinguish it from the traditional mode of the language.

Post-Modern Classicism – the Third Stage of Post-Modernism 1979–

What I wrote in the 1980 monograph on the subject of architecture is still largely true today. 'In the past year there has been a convergence of styles within Post-Modernism, a convergence towards a manner which could be called classical. In the past, classical revivals have been associated with the ancient norms of perfection and harmony, a perfect human body and perfect architecture both being equated with an assumed cosmic harmony. The Greeks, the major but not sole originators of classicism, postulated a universal order which could be represented through well-proportioned buildings, sculpture and music. In classical revivals, notably the Italian Renaissance, a rebirth of this perfection, order and harmony is evoked, if not invoked, and later revivals, even in the nineteenth and early twentieth centuries, contained an element of this idealism. Today Post-Modern Classicism is also reviving the classical languages to call up an idealism and a return to a public order, but it is doing so notably without a shared metaphysics or a belief in a single cosmic symbolism . . . Some architects wish to adopt a full language of architecture that will make discourse with the past richer, and will use the full spectrum of rhetorical means – including polychromy, writing, nature and ornament. Others wish an urban comprehensibility; some want to build like the Ancients, in stone and real oak; others wish to jump quickly on the bandwagon.

1.18 Ricardo Bofill and Taller de Arcquitectura, *Les Arcades du Lac*, St. Quentin-en-Yvelines, France, 1974-81 (Photograph C. Jencks)

'But perhaps this variety of motivation is of less importance than the fact that a loosely shared approach has emerged, for some commonality and consensus must develop in order for architects to communicate with an audience and create significant innovations. The maturity of any movement depends on it forging a style which combines both constancy and change, a duality more easily expressed than achieved. What are the examples that make Post-Modern Classicism such a consensus? James Stirling's Museum in Stuttgart, Michael Graves' Fargo-Moorehead project, Ricardo Bofill's Arcades du Lac (a 'Versailles for the people') (18), Philip Johnson's AT&T, Charles Moore's Piazza d'Italia, and most all of the recent work of Robert Stern, Arata Isozaki, Robert Venturi and Hans Hollein. In short, nearly every major Post-Modern architect has adopted parts of a classical vocabulary.'[28]

Even as I was writing these lines other major architects were shifting towards the style – Aldo Rossi, Mario Botta, Robert Krier and Tom Beeby – and were soon followed by their many disciples listed in the chart on page 176. Once the shift had been made and defined it became, like the International Style of fifty years previously, a self-conscious mode to be improved through imitation. In my monograph and the subsequent publication, *Free-Style Classicism*, I sought to heighten this self-awareness by articulating the 'new rules' and values: i.e. urban contextualism, visual anthropomorphism, the semantic use of invented 'Orders', the preoccupation with ruins and fragments, and some new rhetorical figures – erosion, amplification, oxymoron and saturated polychromy.[29] Some of these same rules and figures crop up and are discussed within this present text and are to be found summarised in the concluding section, 'The Emergent Rules'.

However, two major objections could be made to my formulation: namely that this new synthesis was neither classical nor commendable. The first objection was voiced by Nicholas Penny, among others, in the *Times Literary Supplement*.[30] Penny argued that a true classicism must have ideal proportions, monumentality, solemnity and grandeur – aspects which do indeed characterise some of its canonic revivals. However, as I pointed out there *is* monumentality, solemnity and grandeur in the work of Ricardo Bofill, Philip Johnson and Aldo Rossi. Ideal proportions are indeed missing, except for a few schemes by Leon Krier and others, but the reason for this is partly explained by my initial statement that the synthesis is 'without a shared metaphysics or a belief in a single cosmic symbolism'. Whereas Alberti and Palladio believed in the harmony of the spheres and that the world's order can be captured by simple ratios and musical harmonies, Post-Modernists coming after Einstein and the Big Bang Theory of the universe, couldn't believe in such a simple picture. Harmonies inevitably play a part within this new approach but do not make up the whole picture. Thus when a Post-Modern artist or architect uses simple ratios and composed figures he will fracture this beauty in some respects, or place it in tension with counter forms. One will continually find in art and architecture the oxymoron of 'disharmonious harmony', 'dissonant beauty', 'syncopated proportions' – that is, simple ratios which are set up and then consciously fragmented or violated.

In effect we are dealing with *Free-Style Classicism* as distinct from the *Canonic Classicism* of Vitruvius, Palladio and today Quinlan Terry. Canonic Classicism, conventionally defined, means 'Graeco-Roman' and 'of the first rank'. The latter notion stems from its original use by the Roman writer Aulus Gellius who contrasted the *scriptor classicus* with the *scriptor proletarius* – authors of the upper, tax-paying class versus proletarian writers. When classicism became a tradition, and later an architectural language, it retained these intrinsic connotations, always referring to a restricted pedigree, or a set of 'classic authors'. In asserting a wider tradition, Free-Style Classicism expands this definition so it more closely approximates the historical truth: invented by the Egyptians, the style was used in many 'anti-classical' periods such as the Mannerist epoch, and by vulgarians on proletariat building tasks such as the Roman thermae and colosseum. It is this freer, sometimes vulgar, usage which is relevant today when architects like Bofill and Stirling build for the masses using non-canonic materials such as glass and steel. And this commitment to both industrial reality *and* classicism forces us, like all revolutions, to reassess our most basic terms.

If we expand our notion of classicism to include the continuum of western architecture – Egyptian, Graeco-Roman, Romanesque, Gothic, Renaissance, Mannerist, Baroque, Rococo, Neoclassical – we do so because, in spite of great differences in articulation, they share many aspects including a related grammer. Gothic architecture at Chartres, for instance, used simple harmonic ratios, composite capitals, classical mouldings and a transformation of the Roman basilican plan. Some of the Gothic architects, we now know, even used Vitruvius' writings as a departure point. The same is true of the Baroque period which, for a long time, was censored as anti-classical. With hindsight, theories of transformational grammar and Wittgenstein's notion of 'language games', we can appreciate more clearly the similarities between all these styles. Within Free-Style Classicisms there are a series of overlapping concerns, 'family resemblances' which all of them share, inspite of the fact that none of them are identical. To decide whether an architect is a Post-Modern Classicist would amount to noting these family resemblances, to decide whether he belonged to the wider tradition – in effect the course I have followed in selecting examples for this book (19).

But this brings us to the other objection: what if the architecture is not of 'the first rank'? Here we encounter aesthetic judgements which relate to our understanding of overlapping traditions. Sir John Summerson, trained by the traditional classicist Albert Richardson, has strong reservations about the new tradition. Summerson's *The Classical Language of Architecture* is, of course, the standard short work on the subject and although in the 1980s he extended his approval to encompass such previously *outré* periods as Baroque and Rococo, he stops short of the recent synthesis. This is primarily due to his preference for, and notion of, Canonic Classicism. He openly admits to finding the Post-Modern Classicism of Venturi, Moore and Graves distasteful, looks on Ricardo Bofill's work as that of 'the devil' (because it reminds him of fascist schemes) and alternates in his attitude towards James Stirling – initally finding the Clore Gallery 'drivel': later an exemplary instance of *Vitruvius Ludens*.[31] Here we come to the crux of the problem. It's an obvious point, but one worth making, that value judgements are made within a frame of reference and this frame is mostly formed by the past. To an eye and mind trained in Canonic Classicism, the Free-Style variety is going to look odd and ungrammatical, impure and sometimes malevolent.[32] How could it be otherwise, when old canons are broken and supplanted? We should remember Le Corbusier's famous reminder, written three times lest we forget, of 'Eyes Which Do Not See' – the beauty of 'I) Liners II) Airplanes, III) Automobiles'. Now that these beauties have been celebrated too frequently in architecture, they have lost their charm. But the point holds true and can be generalised to 'The Mind's Eye takes Time to See' or 'Tastes Will Only Change Slowly'. One cannot expect, nor is it desirable, that a new language or architecture be appreciated by everyone in the first years of its use. As it becomes more widely used, as experiments and not a few mistakes are made, we learn to recognise the limitations of a particular language, what can be said in it and said well. Architects, critics and public are involved in discovering these qualities and bringing them to consciousness in the form of articulated values and rules. When this process is working well we can speak of limited progress towards a goal: for instance the way Stirling and Wilford's

1.19 Jan Digerud and Jon Lundberg, *Skogbrand Insurance*, Oslo, Norway, 1985-6. An addition to Heinrich Bull's Free-Style Classical building of 1917 (Photograph courtesy the architects)

1.20 James Stirling and Michael Wilford, *Neue Staatsgalerie*, 'domeless dome', Sculpture Gallery, Stuttgart, 1977-84 (Photograph C. Jencks)

Museum in Stuttgart realises the goal of contextualism, pluralism and symbolic ornament in a way superior to previous work in this tradition. Its central rotunda establishes the public realm in a beautiful outdoor room; a fresh version of a classical shape where the sky above creates the illusion of the 'domeless dome'(20). This building, as remarked in Chapter IX, sets new standards and, along with Michael Graves' Humana Building, is one of the high points of Post-Modernism. This doesn't mean that the building is without faults, nor that it will be appreciated by those whose tastes have been formed by Modernism or Canonic Classicism, even though Richard Rogers and Colin Amery, for instance, do happen to admire the museum. The norm in our pluralistic age is a conflict of taste-cultures and a rejection, or disregard, of architecture and art which falls outside our own relatively limited tastes and knowledge. We can deplore this fragmentation of culture, but it has deep historical and social roots that go back to the nineteenth century with the growth of professionalism, the avant-garde, the middle-class and a host of other, more or less discontinuous, taste-cultures.[33]

A major goal of Post-Modernists in the 1960s and 1970s, we have seen, was to cut across this spectrum of tastes by using tactics of eclecticism. Today it tries to pull this variety together within a more public language; a Free-Style Classicism inclusive of both current realities (technology in architecture and everyday content in art) and plural tastes. Canonic Classicism, contrary to Quinlan Terry's protestations, cannot do this any more than can High Modernism. For the language must be sufficiently rich and flexible to deal with the complexities of urban life in an industrial and post-industrial society. This entails a hybrid language which can absorb neologisms while simultaneously drawing on a storehouse of memories. Quality, according to these specifications, involves mixing languages and elements which both the Modernists and Canonic Classicists would suppress. It is therefore a new quality which we must seek out and define.

The role of the critic then, is to construct a new interpretive framework which makes sense of these emergent qualities: to lay out the field, define the key concepts, rhetorical tropes and values, identify the major and minor figures and discriminate between them. Like the architect, the critic builds a new structure which, if effective, changes the historical landscape, the relation between present and past figures and between key terms. I have here attempted to map out this new landscape and facilitate navigation through it by providing two charts, or evolutionary trees, of key artists and architects (see pages 41 and 176). E.H. Gombrich has made the point that artists and art historians take stock of such landmarks from the past to form objective standards against which present efforts can be measured. For a pluralist era which tries to avoid making judgements of relative worth, the idea of a firm landscape is most welcome. Where absolute values have lost credibility, tradition and the historical continuum replace them as the new departure points. This notion, to which I shall return in the last chapter, is especially relevant for today and is recognised as such in my charts.

Canonic and Free-Style Classicism in Art

Canonic Classicism in art can be defined as the depiction of momentous subject matter in a clear, idealized style that relates to the antique manner of Greece, Rome and their many revivals.[34] This broad definition has been adopted in Michael Greenhalgh's book, *The Classical Tradition in Art*, to encompass an intermittent tradition extending from the Roman Empire 'to the time of Ingres'. Its exhaustion in the early nineteenth century, Greenhalgh argues, was prompted by misunderstanding and the lack of imagination of artists working within the genre, and it was finally killed off by the rise in popularity of realism.

This view has something to recommend it, even if it is too dismissive of the 'American Renaissance' of the 1890s. It gives a consistent picture of a spontaneous academic tradition before it was precisely formulated and while it flourished. Raphael's *The School of Athens* and Poussin's *The Judgement of Solomon* represent the canonic viewpoint, where an epic subject is rationally integrated within a philosophical and artistic system. This definition of Canonic Classicism suggests how difficult it would be to practice today when science, philosophy and the different arts each go their separate ways. Canonic Classicism points to a time when knowledge, faith and practice were unified and artists trusted in this unity. Yet such a definition fails to incorporate the wider Free-Style Classicism which always existed on the periphery and sometimes even took centre stage, as in Mannerist and Baroque periods. A single definition of this larger tradition cannot be given in a sentence because it is so wide. Ultra realistic, when loyal to the classical goal of mimesis, it can at other times be extremely suggestive, hazy and full of *chiaroscuro* when practiced by the Mannerist Caravaggio or the Neo-classicist Angelica Kauffmann. If one compiled all the attributes of these classical artists from the Egyptians down to the present day, an interesting conclusion would emerge: there are fifty or sixty definers of the tradition and artists from any particular period crystallise only a small set of them.[35] Robert Rosenblum has shown, for instance, four different strands of Neo-classical art and charted a changing set of preoccupations within that revolutionary period.[36] Our own classicism is just as divided and contradictory.

And yet it still makes sense to speak of Neoclassicism or today Post-Modern Classicism, because the artists so designated draw from a common list of attributes. This is not to say that they each select all the attributes, nor even the same five or six, but rather that they individually choose different subsets from the pool as a whole. Again we return to Wittgenstein's notion of a unity formed through family resemblances, or overlapping sets of preoccupations, coupled with the further idea that these preoccupations may be thematic as well as formal – questions of content as much as of style.

The Free-Style tradition even includes small trends within Modernism. It has long been pointed out that artists as different as Giorgio de Chirico, Balthus and Henry Moore have a sensibility that is partly classical, and that Picasso and the Cubists used a variety of classical motifs in their work. One

1.21 Pablo Picasso, *Seated Bather*, 1930, oil on canvas, 64½x51in (Courtesy Mrs. Simon Guggenheim Fund, Museum of Modern Art, NYC)

1.22 Pablo Picasso, *Minotauromachy*, 1935, etching, 19½x27¼in (Rosenwald Collection/Courtesy National Gallery of Art, Washington DC)

1.23 Odd Nerdrum, *The Water Protectors*, 1985, oil on canvas, 60½x72in (Courtesy the artist)

historian, O.J. Brendel, has even found classical precedents for that most Modern of paintings, Picasso's *Les Demoiselles d'Avignon*.[37] The subject matter may be a brothel (not Olympus), the faces broken into stylised interpenetrating planes based on African masks, but the motifs are analogous to the classical statuary of Jean Goujon *(The Fountain of Innocents)*, 1547-9, the composition has a clear geometrical basis, and a monumental, classical presence pervades the scene. This is the typical Free-Style hybrid, an eclectic mix which, because of its intention and date, 1907, we should properly term 'Modernist Classical'. Picasso continued to play on the combination especially in the 1920s so called Neoclassical period. His *Two Women Running on the Beach*, 1922, may be related to the *Medes Sarcophagus* of the Roman Antonine period as Brendel claims, but their modelling and heroic gestures are clearly derived from Romantic Classicism. Even the tortured *Seated Bather*, 1930, with its fractured body and eroded face, conveys a classical air (21). This is due partly to the Mediterranean background, but also stems from the austere *gravitas* of its balance. Indeed nothing is so classical as this mood of high seriousness and sustained depth – instantly recognisable, yet eluding formal definition. It is this quality that characterises those artists I group under the notion of 'Classical Sensibility'; they share an attitude and method rather than a specific set of forms (see the Evolutionary Tree and Chapter VI).

Picasso's *Minotauromachy* and especially his *Guernica*, of the 1930s, are also within this tradition, partly because of their classical quotes, but more because of their tone. They convey T.S. Eliot's 'historical sense' – the 'feeling that the whole [art] of Europe . . . has a simultaneous existence and composes a simultaneous order'. In spite of the non-canonic composition and violent fragmentation, they convey an epic seriousness through handling eclectic quotes in an awesome and frightening manner. The minotaur, for instance, is part Cretan bull on the rampage, part the European beast of fascist ignorance and part a serene force of nature (22). The Christ figure and other characters regard this monster with attitudes varying from the classically stoic to the sublime and dignified. Yet all of them share a classical generality.

Guernica must be considered with the genre of history painting – the highest of the several types – along with such works as J.L. David's *The Intervention of the Sabine Women*, 1799. Epic treatment of historic or contemporary events was always considered the primary role of the classical painter, who was obliged to depict the great deeds, or mistakes, of great men. Grandeur, dignity and a belief that historical characters shape history are its basic tenets, and this makes the tradition somewhat problematic for today. Nevertheless there are some painters of note – Alfred Leslie, Jack Beal, David Hockney and above all Ron Kitaj – who aspire to dignity in depicting historical events. The work of such artists constitute what I have called the 'Narrative Classical'; a tradition which can be subversive, serious and satirical by turn. It relates closely to another stream, 'Allegorical Classical', but this one is more explicitly traditional, especially in its use of nostalgia.

Most current classicists have turned away from historical narrative and adopted a more ambivalent attitude towards the meaning of present events. They either explore symbolic ambiguity, as did Rene Magritte, or employ realist conventions, as do John De Andrea and Michael Leonard. Such endeavours create two further distinctive trends; 'Metaphysical Classical' stemming from de Chirico, and 'Realist Classical' coming from the hyper-realism of those such as Richard Estes. But obviously the decision to place an artist in one category or another is based on those aspects of his work we wish to emphasise. For instance the Norwegian artist Odd Nerdrum uses the conventions of historical narrative adapted from the Old Masters and more recent Symbolist painters such as Ferdinand Hodler. *The Water Protectors* could be considered a narrative of three gunners about to depart into the northern wilderness to hunt for the animal skins that shield their bodies and heads (23). Or it could be read, as critics have done, as an allegory about future survival in a 'post-apocalyptic' world after a nuclear war, where isolated individuals wander in a desolate landscape without the shelter of either a structure or a religious creed.[38] Survival depends, in this reading, on minimum forms of social existence such as hunting in small groups, and a very primitive technology. Alternatively this work can be considered in the genre of classical realist portraits, or even biblical, didactic art (although it lacks a clear moral). It alludes as much to a Viking past as an Existentialist future, the work of Rembrandt as much as the writings of Derrida. Often the more profound an artist is the more categories his work illustrates, since a good measure of this quality is multivalence itself. If a supreme goal of an artist is to be unclassifiable, then the antithetical duty of the critic is to make distinctions of value and divide up a complex and flowing river into comprehensible streams.

In all the five streams we will discuss, classical motifs are mixed with present day elements and filtered through a sensibility which is responsive to the realities of our time. It is this mixture which makes these artists Post-Modern Classicists rather than revivalists or Canonic Classicists. To be the latter would be difficult today, partly because this tradition was broken in the nineteenth century, and partly because our sensibility has been fragmented and modified by pluralism, Modernism and current science. If by chance we met someone who painted very much like Poussin, we would find him a charming but unlikely figure. It is such a nostalgia for the mythic Golden Age of the Renaissance – when western culture was integrated and appeared to hang together – that we'll encounter in the next chapter, 'The Metaphysical Classicists', but these artists acknowledge a unity which has been lost.

Opposite:
The Five Traditions of Post-Modern Classical Art, 1960-1985

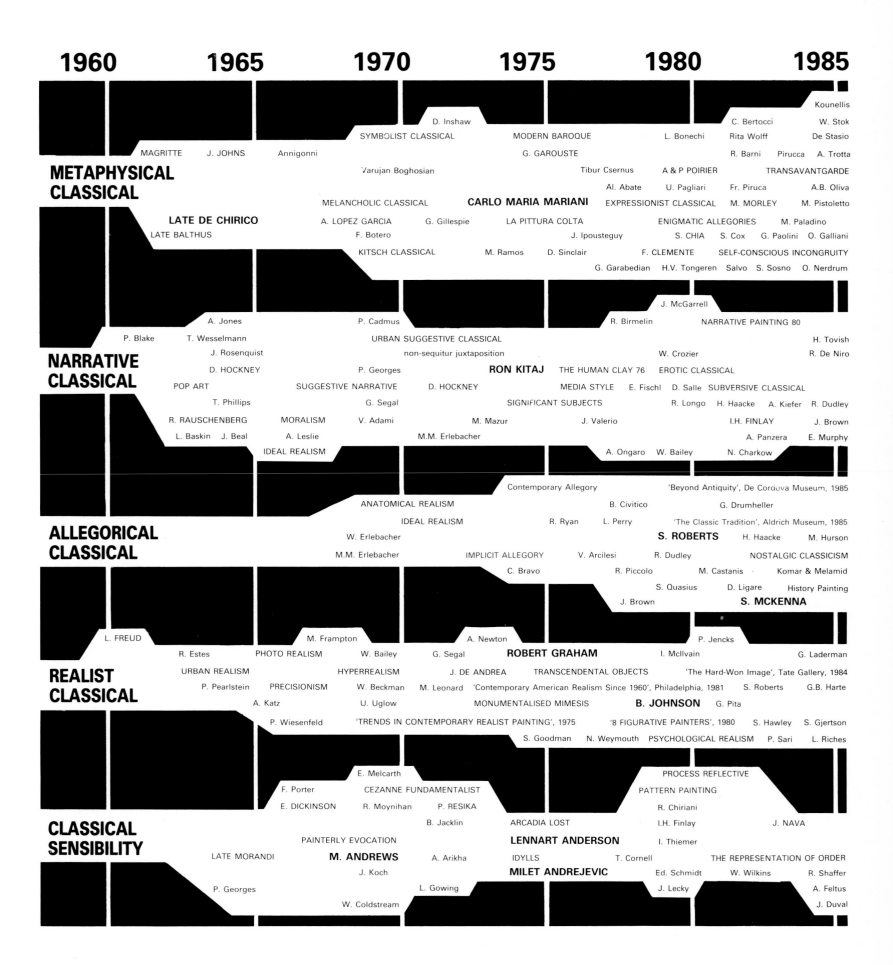

1960 **1965** **1970** **1975** **1980** **1985**

Kounellis

D. Inshaw
SYMBOLIST CLASSICAL   MODERN BAROQUE   L. Bonechi   C. Bertocci   W. Stok
G. GAROUSTE   Rita Wolff   De Stasio
MAGRITTE   J. JOHNS   Annigonni   R. Barni   Pirucca   A. Trotta

Varujan Boghosian   Tibur Csernus   A & P POIRIER   TRANSAVANTGARDE
Al. Abate   U. Pagliari   Fr. Piruca   A.B. Oliva
MELANCHOLIC CLASSICAL   **CARLO MARIA MARIANI**   EXPRESSIONIST CLASSICAL   M. MORLEY   M. Pistoletto

METAPHYSICAL CLASSICAL

LATE DE CHIRICO   A. LOPEZ GARCIA   G. Gillespie   LA PITTURA COLTA   ENIGMATIC ALLEGORIES   M. Paladino
LATE BALTHUS   F. Botero   J. Ipousteguy   S. CHIA   S. Cox   G. Paolini   O. Galliani
KITSCH CLASSICAL   M. Ramos   D. Sinclair   F. CLEMENTE   SELF-CONSCIOUS INCONGRUITY
G. Garabedian   H.V. Tongeren   Salvo   S. Sosno   O. Nerdrum

J. McGarrell
A. Jones   P. Cadmus   R. Birmelin   NARRATIVE PAINTING 80
P. Blake   T. Wesselmann   URBAN SUGGESTIVE CLASSICAL   H. Tovish
J. Rosenquist   non-sequitur juxtaposition   W. Crozier   R. De Niro
D. HOCKNEY   P. Georges   **RON KITAJ**   THE HUMAN CLAY 76   EROTIC CLASSICAL
POP ART   SUGGESTIVE NARRATIVE   D. HOCKNEY   MEDIA STYLE   E. Fischl   D. Salle   SUBVERSIVE CLASSICAL

NARRATIVE CLASSICAL

T. Phillips   G. Segal   SIGNIFICANT SUBJECTS   R. Longo   H. Haacke   A. Kiefer   R. Dudley
R. RAUSCHENBERG   MORALISM   V. Adami   M. Mazur   J. Valerio   I.H. FINLAY   J. Brown
L. Baskin   J. Beal   A. Leslie   M.M. Erlebacher   A. Panzera   E. Murphy
IDEAL REALISM   A. Ongaro   W. Bailey   N. Charkow

Contemporary Allegory   'Beyond Antiquity', De Cordova Museum, 1985
ANATOMICAL REALISM   B. Civitico   G. Drumheller
IDEAL REALISM   R. Ryan   L. Perry   'The Classic Tradition', Aldrich Museum, 1985
W. Erlebacher   **S. ROBERTS**   H. Haacke   M. Hurson

ALLEGORICAL CLASSICAL

M.M. Erlebacher   IMPLICIT ALLEGORY   V. Arcilesi   R. Dudley   NOSTALGIC CLASSICISM
C. Bravo   R. Piccolo   M. Castanis   Komar & Melamid
S. Quasius   D. Ligare   History Painting
J. Brown   **S. MCKENNA**

L. FREUD   M. Frampton   A. Newton   P. Jencks
R. Estes   PHOTO REALISM   W. Bailey   G. Segal   **ROBERT GRAHAM**   I. McIlvain   G. Laderman
URBAN REALISM   HYPERREALISM   J. DE ANDREA   TRANSCENDENTAL OBJECTS   'The Hard-Won Image', Tate Gallery, 1984

REALIST CLASSICAL

P. Pearlstein   PRECISIONISM   W. Beckman   M. Leonard   'Contemporary American Realism Since 1960', Philadelphia, 1981   S. Roberts   G.B. Harte
A. Katz   U. Uglow   MONUMENTALISED MIMESIS   **B. JOHNSON**   G. Pita
P. Wiesenfeld   'TRENDS IN CONTEMPORARY REALIST PAINTING', 1975   '8 FIGURATIVE PAINTERS', 1980   S. Hawley   S. Gjertson
S. Goodman   N. Weymouth   PSYCHOLOGICAL REALISM   P. Sari   L. Riches

E. Melcarth   PROCESS REFLECTIVE
F. Porter   CEZANNE FUNDAMENTALIST   PATTERN PAINTING
E. DICKINSON   R. Moynihan   P. RESIKA   R. Chiriani
B. Jacklin   ARCADIA LOST   I.H. Finlay   J. NAVA

CLASSICAL SENSIBILITY

PAINTERLY EVOCATION   **LENNART ANDERSON**   I. Thiemer
LATE MORANDI   **M. ANDREWS**   A. Arikha   IDYLLS   T. Cornell   THE REPRESENTATION OF ORDER
J. Koch   **MILET ANDREJEVIC**   Ed. Schmidt   W. Wilkins   R. Shaffer
P. Georges   L. Gowing   J. Lecky   A. Feltus
W. Coldstream   J. Duval

CHAPTER II
Metaphysical Classicism

Melancholic Classicism

A strong motive for the return to classicism is the interest in reestablishing the urban realm, epitomised by the traditional Italian city centre. Focusing on its heart, the piazza, which is overlooked by church, town hall and marketplace, this image has come to represent for westerners the essence of the homeland. Today, architects such as Leon Krier and Aldo Rossi evoke its power, while artists such as Rita Wolff paint melancholic visions of the ideal urban square, where public buildings huddle next to communal loggia under the benign gaze of a belvedere (1). The public realm in these visions appears perfectly scaled, picturesque and secure in its monumental clothing. Ricardo Bofill actually builds such *places* in French cities and suburbia, making the image as powerful today as its former manifestations must have been in the Renaissance.

Yet as social fact this reality has changed completely. The city-fathers no longer walk leisurely in the piazza, perhaps no longer even control the city, and live, inevitably, in suburbia. No one has painted this loss more effectively than Giorgio de Chirico. His early metaphysical period from 1911-18 created a language of loss: a flat blue-green sky, clear like the end of a summer's day, and the evening light casting menacing shadows across empty streets. The stilted arcades of lonely piazzas, made lonelier still by stick figures and the classical sculpture of a former civilisation, send up prison-like shadows (2). Everything is awkward and ill-fitting: the perspective points vanish in all directions at oblique angles, pantiled roofs don't curve but rather grimace unhappily with downturned mouths, and a sailboat departs in the distance. Even in a painting called *Joy of Return*, 1915, it seems that everybody has left, so empty are the arcades, so black the shadows. Sometimes de Chirico shutters his windows, implying that the inhabitants have left for the winter; other times he blows out the panes and mullions, implying that the city is a well-preserved ruin, a cemetery city, or one burnt out but then strangely repainted white.

De Chirico studied in Munich, which was rebuilt by Ludwig I as a kind of misplaced Florence. The city's strange sense of loss (conveyed by *déjà vu*) is even more poignant today, after its long, dolorous arcades have been rebuilt and repainted following the Second World War. Studying under the Symbolist painter Arnold Böcklin, de Chirico formulated his theories of enigmatic symbolism. He used mannequins, shadows, drawing instruments, trains in the distance and vernacular, classical architecture to create this symbolic emptiness. The occurrence of a tower, smokestack or train often

2.1 Rita Wolff, *Filadelfia*, 1983, watercolour, 7¾ x 5½ in (Photograph Steven Sloman / Courtesy the artist)

2.2 Giorgio de Chirico, *Piazza d'Italia*, 1933-5, oil on canvas, 23½ x 19½ in (Courtesy Robert Miller Gallery, NYC)

memorialises the loss of his own father, a railroad engineer: 'My father was a man of the nineteenth century; he was an engineer and also a gentleman of olden times, courageous, loyal, hard-working, intelligent and good. He had studied in Florence and Turin, and he was the only one of our large family of gentry that wanted to work.'[1]

After 1918 de Chirico started to paint 'in the manner of' several styles and this is the cut-off date of his respectability, at least for the Museum of Modern Art.[2] And yet although there is a change in his style (he makes the pronouncement '*Pictor Classicus Sum*') there is also continuity. Even in the 'Late de Chirico 1940-76', as an exhibition was called, one can trace the influence of his first metaphysical period.[3] This era saw him repaint his early work, producing some eighteen versions of *The Disquieting Muses* and forty-five of the *Piazza d'Italia*. Dismissed as self-forgeries, their subject was, in a sense, the same one as that of his youth: the feeling of loss. For what he painted was always the absence of the present civilisation and the revival of a dead one. Occasionally in some of his one-hundred-and-six self-portraits, he would paint himself in period costume, for instance as a seventeenth-century gentleman standing by a ruin with a gauntlet in hand to throw down at the twentieth century. The ambivalent gesture was both a serious challenge, in its depiction of a lost tradition, and self-mockery.

His *Capriccio Veneziano alla Manièra di Veronese*, 1951 (3), uses many of the metaphysical elements – the differing vanishing points, the frozen statuary, the columns that blank out space – to tell again an enigmatic story of deprivation. Sick birds spin about in disarray as if something has just happened, or is about to happen: 'Things fall apart/The centre cannot hold.' The birds are harbingers of a classical culture – sickly sweet in its Veronese dress – that is almost camp, but still enticing. What more vivid symbol of Venice do we have today than this: so equally attractive and repulsive?

All the late de Chiricos are about nostalgic loss and many of them are simply nostalgic. But the best make use of a previous style, sometimes even of the painter's own early period, at the level of symbolic allusion: that is, their style functions like the subject matter, the smokestacks and empty streets, to evoke both what is and is no longer. De Chirico was quite knowing about the double meaning of his revivalism, something that the dismissive critics have not yet cared to deal with. Rather they read the paintings straightforwardly as sentimental. But this is a dangerous thing to do, as de Chirico's first self-portrait of 1911 suggests. The classical inscription, '*Et quid amabo nisi quod aenigma est?*' (What shall I love if not the enigma?) could be put beneath every one of his works, both good and bad. Their unifying theme is the notion that all European culture has returned to us and is open for appreciation, but only as a melancholic museum, a place for disinterested speculation and enjoyment: not action. Nothing of *public* consequence ever happens here – de Gaulle or Margaret Thatcher do not stride across open squares – because European culture has gone on a perpetual holiday, leaving its enticing forms and enigmatic equipment behind.

2.3 Giorgio de Chirico, *Capriccio Veneziano alla Manièra di Veronese*, 1951, oil on canvas, 103½ x 146in (Photograph Steven Sloman/Courtesy Robert Miller Gallery, NYC)

2.4 Antonio Lopez Garcia, *Madrid from Vallecas*, 1962-3, oil on canvas, 40 x 51in (Courtesy Marlborough Gallery, NYC)

Other European painters such as Balthus and Magritte have likewise explored in a classical manner this extreme melancholia but with different results: the former conveying a beautiful claustrophobia, the latter an attractive madness. Magritte's *Perspective of Madame Recamier* shows her sitting up on the famous couch but now enclosed by a sit-up coffin.[4] This mordant joke, done in Neoclassical style, is yet another sad comment on our relation to the past: at once accurate in its archaeological detail and truthful in its stiff portrayal of Recamier's present state. Pushing truth and melancholia in a more realist direction, Antonio Lopez Garcia has carried on the de Chirican tradition of urban anomie. Nothing is quite so hopeless (or dignified) as his urban landscapes of Madrid (4). Sometimes painted from the rooftops, or the edge of the city, they show the tranquil desolation of industrial civilisation: very few people wander around this city which sprawls on endlessly. Black shadows and empty streets again tell the story of loss, now with a stoic serenity reminiscent of Piero della Francesca.

Piero's harmonious asceticism has influenced three generations of twentieth-century painters, especially Balthus who has spanned all three.[5] A great compositionalist, who makes the empty areas he depicts as charged with presence as those of Piero, Balthus tends to layer images on the canvas frontally so their silhouettes become clear and complete, almost like architectural elevations. Indeed, the architecture and furniture are often squared up to the picture plane as in a classical composition. Everyday objects are given the sensuality and dignity that the classical tradition since Giotto made into such a norm. The depiction of three-dimensional objects in clear space, their sculptural presence, used to be taught as an adjunct to other skills, but with Balthus the objects have become enigmatic ends in themselves. In *The Moth*, 1959-60 (5), the chequered bedcover and kerosene lamp are as significant as the protagonists, the young girl and the moth she dangles in the light. In *Getting Up*, 1975-8 (6), the girl, the toy bird and the quizzical cat charging out of the mailbox are equal in importance to the pillows and bed. Classical hierarchy and plot are gone to be replaced by a democratic association of enigmatic presences breathing an antique air. There is no allegory, no riddle of the universe to be solved, no idea that art is an intensely public activity, but rather a strange, domestic vision. Using classical means for private ends again conveys a melancholic loss, because these paintings suggest they are about something of great significance, when we know they are ultimately about fleeting moods.

This suggestion may be summarised as 'the presence of the absence', the feeling that culture has departed and the feast is somewhere else. Alienation is too strong a word for it and privacy too weak. Some critics find Balthus claustrophobic and pretentious – 'Pierrot not Piero' as Robert Hughes has put it – but there can be no doubt he is the master of the enigmatic bedroom and dignified emptiness. The backgrounds of so much Post-Modern Classicism have this quality, a kind of noble, timeless void: a Platonic stillness. Gregory Gillespie has achieved this in his haunting interiors, *Lady and Dog*, 1973 (7),

2.5 Balthus, *The Moth*, 1959-60, oil on canvas, 63¾ x 51¼in (Private Collection/Courtesy the artist)

2.6 Balthus, *Getting Up*, 1975-8, oil on canvas, 66½ x 62¾in (Private Collection/Courtesy the artist)

2.7 Gregory Gillespie, *Lady and Dog*, 1973, mixed media, 9 x 13in (Courtesy Forum Gallery, NYC)

and Carlo Maria Mariani has made it the particular virtue of his Neoclassical allegories. These last take place not in real existential space, but in an idealised flat space of timeless mythology. At first glance one might think these were very good pastiches of Jacques-Louis David. Here are the cool, sexy bodies placed in the austere chambers that Mario Praz has characterised as the 'Erotic Frigidaire'.[6] Adonis-like nudes, often accompanied by *putti*, are engaged in some unspecified activity (usually to do with painting) that shows off their polished bodies in all their mammary roundness (8). Idealised athletes in their early twenties are displayed in the conventional poses of heroic statuary.

To Modernists, Mariani seems the most reactionary of the classicists. Termed a 'protofascist' or 'bad' artist by those committed to the 'Shock of the New', he gives their mental habits a 'Shock of the Old'. At first glance his work does indeed resemble dreary academic reconstructions. On a second look, however, his conceptual strategy becomes clearer, as does his invention.

In the mid-1970s Carlo Maria Mariani started to build up a fictional, ideal academy – the 'School of Rome' – presided over by such luminaries as Angelica Kauffmann, Goethe, Mengs and Winkelmann. His paintings, some based on photographs, others incorporating literary supplements, were full of historical quotes used both naively and with point. Mariani revived the notion of a polished, straightforward 'beauty', along with an interest in *tekhné* and grand historical painting. The combination, termed '*la pittura colta*' by Mariani, Italo Mussa and other critics, really was 'cultured painting' in the sense that it took a certain scholarly knowledge to decipher. This has, of course, led it to be damned as elitist by Modernists, and accepted by scholars as an endless opportunity for exegesis. But not all of it is straight mythology, and here lies Mariani's contribution.

He will take the abduction of Ganymedes, the 'most beautiful youth alive', as a subject and rework it as part of a current mythology. In one painting Zeus, disguised as an eagle, descends to the Trojan plain and picks up the beautiful boy's leg with one of his gruesome claws (9). There is a certain melodrama in this scene of male rape as the two gaze at each other with bemused interest. But the postures and juxtapositions of incongruous figures make this not a hackneyed illustration of Greek mythology but a surreal 'remythification' of the homosexual world. In another elaborate allegory *Costellazione del Leone (La Scuola di Roma)* (Constellation of Leo (School of Rome)), 1980-1 (10), the figure of Ganymedes can now be seen holding onto the eagle Zeus as they fly heavenwards towards Olympus. Mariani was no doubt aware that the royal ascent to heaven on eagleback is a widespread religious fancy shared by the Greeks, Babylonians and Celts.[7] In any case, he here extends the myth, casting one of his fictional 'School of Rome' – the performance artist Luigi Ontani, complete with stick and hoop – in the role of Ganymedes. What could be more appropriate in this allegory than Ganymedes as an airborne performer?

The other figures involved are current artists remythologised through

2.8 Carlo Maria Mariani, *Poseidon*, 1984, oil on canvas, 27½ x 19½in (Photograph Hanover Studios, London / Courtesy Edward Totah Gallery, London)

2.9 Carlo Maria Mariani, *Rape of Ganymedes*, 1981, oil on canvas, 23½ x 20½in (Courtesy Artra Studio, Milan)

2.10 Carlo Maria Mariani, *Costellazione del Leone (La Scuola di Roma)*, 1980-1, oil on canvas, 133¼ x 177⁹⁄₁₉in (Courtesy Sperone Westwater Gallery, NYC)

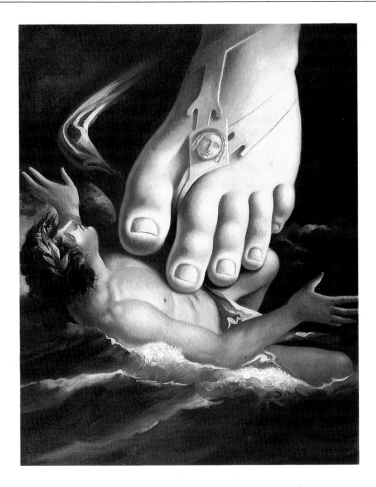

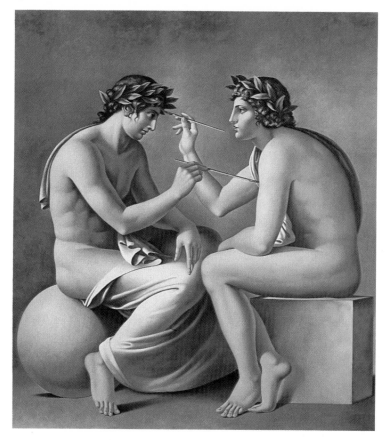

Mengs' and Raphael's versions of *Parnassus*. If Anton Raphael Mengs reworked Raphael's *Parnassus*, the *Apollo Belvedere* and the *Borghese Dancers* in his allegory of the artists in heaven, then Mariani is reworking this imitation. Here versions of mythology and art constitute together an extended text most accessible to our age of paperback scholarship. The painter has conveyed this density with a certain irony: friends, foes, art critics and dealers, a personification of the Tiber and a reclining hermaphrodite surround the blue-robed Mariani. New Yorkers will recognise Cy Twombly on horseback, looking a bit ridiculous with a Roman SPQR in hand; Francesco Clemente gazes past a canvas held by Sandro Chia; Mario Merz is Hercules in an understated bathtub; a well-known New York art dealer waddles to the water as a turtle; critics write and admire their own profiles; Kounellis, a *putto*, grins behind one of his masks; and a German dealer beside Goethe's Altar of Good Fortune wears that poet's famous hat (memorialised in Wilhelm Tischbein's *Goethe in the Roman Campagna*, 1786-7). Today's art scene is in fact rather like Mariani's pretentious collection of assorted types. It has its arcane pathways and esoteric knowledge, its self-admiring fancy-dress balls and critical wrangles. Portraying it as Mengs' *Parnassus* (even with the dancers in the distance) makes us aware how much that venerated master-piece must likewise have been based on an arbitrary conceit lifted from a previous century; similarly with Raphael's *Parnassus* and so on through one mythological text after another.[8] When Post-Modernists have recourse to allegory, they often slip in small incongruous elements to give the painting a contemporary meaning, and, as we shall see with the work of Lennart Anderson and Milet Andrejevic, it is these little touches which make the remythifications ironic as well as 'truthful'.

Post-Modernists can't have their ideals and myths straight, but they will nonetheless have them. Most of Mariani's myths, like the Modernists', concern the painter's craft. *E' Vietato Redeture gli Dei* (It Is Forbidden to Doubt the Gods), 1984 (11), shows the sleeping painter and *putto* as gods who shouldn't be awakened from their slumber; the artist in a classical pose ironically holds his brushes where one might expect something else. *Il Pittore Mancino* (The Left-Handed Painter), 1983 (12), shows the same laurel-wreathed painter holding a surprised *putto* upside down while he puts the finishing touches to his golden wing. The claustrophobic, slightly acid background, with its suggestion of a floor and wall, makes the Neoclassical ball look like an orange. In *La Mano Ubbidisce all'Intellètto* (The Hand Submits to the Intellect), 1983 (13), Goethe's Altar of Good Fortune is again the setting for this strange act of double painting. The allusion is perhaps to the Greek legend of the origin of painting in which Dibutade, knowing her lover is about to depart, traces his shadow on the wall – an idea that has inspired other Post-Modern irony.[9] In Mariani's allegory the meaning is intentionally ambiguous. Both hands are submitting to both intellects: the past paints the present, the present the past. The implication is that art and

2.11 Carlo Maria Mariani, *E' Vietato Redeture gli Dei*, 1984, oil on canvas, 22¾ x 39½in (Photograph Hanover Studios, London / Courtesy Edward Totah Gallery, London)

2.12 Carlo Maria Mariani, *Il Pittore Mancino*, 1982, oil on canvas, 78½ x 69in (Courtesy Sperone Westwater Gallery, NYC)

2.13 Carlo Maria Mariani, *Il Mano Ubbidisce all'Intellètto*, 1983, oil on canvas, 78½ x 69in (Courtesy Sperone Westwater Gallery, NYC)

2.14 Jasper Johns, *Target with Plaster Casts*, 1955, encaustic and collage on canvas with objects, 51 x 44 x 3½in (Courtesy Leo Castelli Gallery, NYC)

culture are created from nothing except themselves, but this interpretation of auto-invention remains *just* an implication, even if it is an apt satire on Modernist hermeticism. In an often quoted statement – 'I am not the picture, I am not the artist, I am the work' – Mariani conveys both the Neoclassical commitment to an impersonal tradition *and* the Modernist commitment to process, although ultimately the utterance is as Delphic as the paintings.

'Precise obscurity' is the oxymoron conveyed by the Metaphysical Classicists, perhaps because this paradox implies a knowledge of what has been lost from the past, but not of what has been regained. Some Pop artists have explored this de Chirican territory as much as Mariani and one is tempted to see some of them, like Jasper Johns, as Free-Style Classicists. In the early 1960s Johns painted 'things the mind already knows', such as beer cans, flags and targets, giving them a monumental stasis. As in Balthus' work the full frontal placement of the image combined with its generality raises it above the banality of realism. The two beer cans in bronze become tough, primitive dolmens; the diminishing American flags telescoped inside each other become a heraldic emblem – as fresh and strong an image as the flag might originally have been. Johns' use of encaustic, the subtle impasto markings of his canvases, shows a commitment to the classical signs of painting, while his freely controlled brushstrokes were noteworthy at a time when other painters were stressing the mechanical and flat image (14). Does the use of symmetrical composition, painterly surface and archetypal (if prosaic) subject matter – these three definers – make a painter classicist? Probably not, if the attitude and intention are not serious and historical. There can be no doubt about Johns' seriousness, but his ironic subject matter, which is limited to small areas of the present tense, puts him at the edge of the classical tradition. Like Magritte, from whom he has benefited, he operates in a paradoxical area, treating the banal as if it were heroic, either with irony or a self-fulfilling naivety. He can make beer cans look majestic, a bull's eye profound; like Morandi he can give objects a dignity and like Balthus he can invest them with sensual presence. Considered within the totality of classicism, however, they are, as Jack Beal likes to characterise Modernism, 'not Art but (P)art'; that is a specialisation on a few parts of the classicist's much wider repertoire.

Expressionist Classicists and Enigmatic Allegory

Many Post-Modern painters are quite happy to work within this limited tradition while making overtures to the larger one. Malcolm Morley is characteristic of these in that he oscillates back and forth between traditions and attitudes. Some of his early work was Superrealist in appearance, while some was Impressionist; some of the motifs were drawn from classicism, others from the world of modern travel. His *School of Athens*, 1972, was a formal investigation of this most classical painting, yet it didn't deal with semantic significance at all. In this sense it epitomised today's paradoxical movement of iconography without meaning, that is, the Expressionist use of symbols. His later work, such as *Farewell to Crete*, 1984 (15), is also Expressionist in its use of classical imagery, but now the associational overtones are related to suggest a meaning.

He has described his method, and it's one that relates to most of the '*trans-avantgarde*', as Achille Bonito Oliva has termed them,[10] or the Expressionist Classicists, as I prefer to call them. In the quote that follows what he says of his painting *The Palms of Vai* relates also to *Farewell to Crete* since he used the former painting as a departure for the latter.

I'm after making pictures that contain a combination of images that have the power to brand, in the way that a branding iron sears. I figured that a combination of unique image arrangements could have a similar effect, the way de Chirico hits . . .

Each of the paintings is a revelation because I don't know until I begin what it implies . . . For example, the image of the bull in *The Palms of Vai*. It's from a small Minoan sculpture that's 6,000 years old and fresh as a biscuit. It's a votive thing that would be filled up with wine for offerings, then the wine would be drunk from the vessel's mouth. Originally, the Minoans had the cult of the bull, which represented fertility. They'd get the blood and sperm and the whole thing and they'd go around pouring it . . . In the painting, there's a headless torso in the centre, underneath the bull.

In the picture I'm working on now, of a Greek horse over a crowded beach, the top is very clear and crisp. It's like a criticism of painting going on now – so-called Expressionist, Neo-Realist this or that. It's a call for a standard. And it's a retreat, in a way, back to that idea of what's infinite . . .[11]

2.15 Malcolm Morley, *Farewell to Crete*, 1984, oil on canvas, 80 x 164in (Saatchi Collection, London/Courtesy Xavier Fourcade Inc., NYC)

The primitivist attitudes expressed here ('a branding iron sears') could well be those of Francis Bacon, and the raw bodies on the beach in *Farewell to Crete* also recall this Modernist painter. The Minoan and Greek images are, however, juxtaposed with this rather horrific suburban beach scene in a way which is indeed reminiscent of the enigmatic combinations of de Chirico. What are we to make of the Trojan (?) horse confronting the fertility vessel? No doubt the brutal cult of Crete and the title with its 'farewell' suggests that it is Theseus' boat sailing off, as well as the painter leaving this subject matter and place.

Is the lugubrious, lipsticked matron a contemporary version of Ariadne? The divisions in the sky suggest that we read this remythification in four parts: Minoan past/Greek past/Minoan present/Mythic past. And the spattered blood, the comic-book images (that resemble late de Chirico) and vital colours suggest this is a contemporary myth. But the painter has stopped short of this intention. Like an Expressionist he proceeds empirically, following the canvas and his feelings as the primary agents: 'I get more of an implication as I go along, like the public prosecutor mounting up evidence bit by bit. I don't paint from faith or belief, only evidence.'[12]

By contrast the Canonic Classicist has both a preexisting plan and some faith or belief in the iconography, which explains why his aim is so sure compared to the Expressionist Classicist who believes in his subject matter only in so far as it's realised aesthetically. There are quite a few painters who might be put in this category: Roberto Barni, Lorenzo Bonechi, Gérard Garouste, Christopher Le Brun, Mimmo Paladino, Stephen Cox, Hermann Albert, Odd Nerdrum, Charles Garabedian, Francesco Clemente, Sandro Chia and at times even Robert Rauschenberg and Anselm Kiefer. Although often discussed as part of other movements, they all, at times, use classical images and myths in an expressive and enigmatic way.

Lorenzo Bonechi, born in Tuscany in 1955, has developed a rather hopeful, wispy version of de Chirico's cityscapes. Centrally planned temples and churches are combined in a convention of an 'ideal city', and set against a Tuscan mountain landscape from which thin, giant figures stare out with an unfathomable gaze. *Città*, 1983 (16), is a painting both inside and outside of the frame, just as the dream imagery has an obvious double existence as both real and fictitious. All his work has the faded, stretched-out and spindly feeling of dreams. Figures are aetiolated into hatchings and squiggles; mountains become haystacks and even buildings start to dissolve into thin wisps (17). The brush treatment seems perfectly suited to the evanescent subject matter.

Christopher Le Brun, a young British artist of the same generation, also paints archetypal dream-like images in a way that is as fleeting as a reverie. Often called *Untitled* (18), his works portray faceless white horses let loose in indeterminate, misty landscapes – a symbol of nature and escape into it. Using a painterly surface that stems ultimately from Turner, Le Brun obviously wants to exploit the ambiguous qualities of impasto, imperfections

2.16 Lorenzo Bonechi, *Città*, 1983, tempera on paper, 78½ x 117½in (Courtesy Fabian Carlsson Gallery, London)

2.17 Lorenzo Bonechi, *Visitazione*, 1985, oil on canvas, polyptych, 64 x 145in (Private Collection/Courtesy Fabian Carlsson Gallery, London and Galleria Carini, Florence)

2.18 Christopher Le Brun, *Untitled*, 1984-5, oil on board, 9½ x 12½in (Private Collection/Courtesy Nigel Greenwood Gallery, London)

on the canvas and ambiguous shadow. The mythology, such as it is, never gets much beyond the Jungian archetype, the basic Expressionist minimum.

Stephen Cox, another British artist (born 1946), also makes links between Turneresque abstraction and classicism by fragmenting his sculptures into suggestive areas of colour and textured travertine. *View from the Loggia (after Turner)*, 1983 (19), is a curious mixture of a smashed Renaissance fragment (such as inspires Peter Sari today)[13] and a perspective view of the courtyard of St. Peter's. It is meant to recall the Englishman's view of Italy – aestheticising like Adrian Stokes whose writings have influenced Cox, and restrained in imagery and temper. Neither Le Brun nor Cox would ever be so vulgar as to carry through a whole iconographic programme so that its parts could be named and completely understood. And Cox in particular tries to capture the whole through an obsessive display of the parts. Thus the view through the lunette is truncated at the top, only part of the building is seen and the geometric shape is broken up by white, linear voids, as if the relief were really stained glass. Ageing is implied by the 'bone-like' travertine and the application of minerals, these last based on techniques elaborated by Vasari.

Extreme refinement is also suggested by the flat relief, a delicacy which one associates with Renaissance aesthetics. Cox has also been influenced by Agostino di Duccio's reliefs at Rimini, and their delicate swirling clouds can be seen in his *Ecstasy: St Agnes*, 1983 (20). What a strange ecstasy this is. A saint who has had her breasts severed in a protracted martyrdom finds a transcendent happiness in death. Her breasts and buttocks are here suggested in the sensuous pockmarked rossi di Verona marble. Folds of drapery or hair slide around this freckled red surface, leaving shapes that recall the feminine sex. At the edges the stone is broken raw to suggest some violent end, and the three fragments can be read on the diagonal to suggest a dual religious and sensual ascension. Everything is suggested with a delicacy which leaves a lot up to the interpreter: is this an aesthetic, Christian or mythic ecstasy? Following Oscar Wilde and British understatement, Cox would probably answer: 'To name something is to kill it'.

A similar ambiguity is apparent in Mimmo Paladino's work, which is more primitive, seemingly inspired by African masks, Picasso and the crude ritualistic sculpture of Sumer. In *Canto Notturno* (Night Song), 1984 (21), we seem to be present at the birth of civilisation, as we witness a powerful king entreating a masked force of nature to save him from a wild dog. But such interpretations may appear gratuitous, as they sometimes do of Sumerian images, which were conceived as concrete symbols. Neverthless, this extreme primitivism, which does not distinguish between the product of art and its meaning, is inevitably a difficult regression to sustain in our culture where everything is quickly labelled and separated. 'Being natural is such a difficult pose to keep up', as Oscar Wilde put it, especially if one has annual shows opening in New York and London. But of course primitivism has been an artistic staple for more than two hundred years and artists quite naturally

2.19 Stephen Cox, *View from the Loggia (After Turner)*, 1983, travertine marble, oxides and black cement, 88¼ x 98in (Private Collection / Courtesy Nigel Greenwood Gallery, London)

2.20 Stephen Cox, *Ecstasy: St Agnes*, 1983, rossi di Verona marble, 117½ x 156¾in (Photograph Eileen Tweedy / Private Collection / Courtesy Nigel Greenwood Gallery, London)

2.21 Mimmo Paladino, *Canto Notturno*, 1984, bronze, 78¾ x 41⅜ x 90½in (Photograph Salvatore Licitra/Courtesy Waddington Galleries, London)

like the open-air life of the noble savage. Paladino keeps his studio by an olive grove in Benevento, southern Italy, close to the place he was born in 1948, as if to draw on the long source of underground cults – Egyptian, Graeco-Roman and Christian – that have superseded one another. He turns them all, as does Christopher Le Brun, into Jungian dream symbols.

Francesco Clemente's dream symbolism is even less general and classical, and more private. His obsessive concerns are the driven state of adolescence and the portrayal of his own desires, often associating food and sex. *Untitled*, 1983 (22), shows a Dionysian rage driving a naked dancer in the foreground, a red-raw self-portrait in the midground and a hell scene of copulating couples in the background. These three areas are lapse-dissolved as in a film or dream. For instance the dancer's *lei* of flowers transmutes into Clemente's hair, while his face turns into the classical symbol of lust – the satyr. It's an acute interpretation of moods and ideas. The flare of nostrils and the single jutting tooth immediately convey the obsessive drive, as does the blank, animal stare. Eddies and slashes of murky red paint accentuate the frenzy. We are here far away from the elevated idealism of Canonic Classicism and only the Dionysian ecstasy and classical allusions give the painting a connection with the wider tradition. Indeed most of Clemente's work, like Julian Schnabel's, is anti-classical in both subject and intent.

Another Italian, often grouped with him, Sandro Chia, also occasionally reuses classical iconography in a private way. *The Idleness of Sisyphus* has been interpreted as an ironic attack on the Modernist notion of progress in the arts, showing that the artist's true role is instead a superior form of fruitless repetition, pushing the ball of painterly creation to the top of a mountain of similarly ruined canvases only to have it roll down again and become part of the heap.[14] Sisyphus is here characterised not as the stoic hero carrying out his labour with resignation, but as a cocky youth with a broad smile. For Chia, like the other Expressionist Classicists, appropriates mythology to his own ends.

Son of the Son, 1981 (23), is another play on Mediterranean mythology with a gargantuan farmer (holding golf clubs with his sack of produce) looking back to the sun while his son pulls at his apron. *Three Boys on a Raft*, 1983 (24), is again about giants and midgets of the Aegean. The protagonists appear engaged in some portentous activity on a sea of humour – 'they were not waving but drowning' – except that one of them is strangely asleep. Very often Chia reinterprets archetypal imagery in an amusing way. *Perpetual E(motion)*, 1978, shows the happy peasant drinking wine and passing water at the same time, reversing the cycle of turning water into wine. Chia's art, a cross between Rabelais and the Futurist Boccioni, exuberantly mocks pretension, while cashing in on 'the return to painting'. The pneumatic strong-men set in a beautiful Elysium of vibrating space celebrate undulating brushstrokes and the voluptuous palette as much as they do any subject matter, and thus his work is another illustration of that dominant category, the Enigmatic Allegory (ultimately about art).

2.22 Francesco Clemente, *Untitled*, 1983, oil on canvas, 78 x 93in (Gerald S. Elliot Collection, Chicago / Courtesy Mary Boone Gallery, NYC)

2.23 Sandro Chia, *Son of the Son*, 1981, oil on canvas, 96 x 107in (Courtesy Leo Castelli Gallery, NYC)

2.24 Sandro Chia, *Three Boys on a Raft*, 1983, oil on canvas, 97 x 111in (Paine Webber Collection / Courtesy Leo Castelli Gallery, NYC)

Gérard Garouste, the fashionable French artist, is the most enigmatic of these allegorists. He appropriates myths of Adhara, Columba and most of all the giant hunter Orion to create narrative scenes that imply more than they mean. Alternatively he will create the same kind of charged riddles from overstuffed interiors and Christian mythology. He mixes myths as he does stylistic quotes from Tintoretto, Titian, Bernini and Magnasco to produce what some critics damn as 'Decorator-Surrealism' and others, like Robert Hughes, dismiss as a muddy porridge. 'All he has done with [the legend of Orion] is produce a set of murky canvases with loud patches of local colour, full of posturing figures who flap and twist about in the pervasive dung-coloured twilight like parodies of the eighteenth-century Italian Mannerist Alessandro Magnasco.'[15]

Such hostility towards this artist and Enigmatic Allegory in general can be partly explained as the result of dashed hopes – the realisation that this sort of painting cannot be the equivalent of a Titian allegory with the power to revive myths for our secular age. Yet if we don't approach Garouste with such a demanding task, but rather see his work as a painter's speculation on ambiguous narrative, it is more acceptable, even interesting. His *Orion le Classique – Orion l'Indien*, 1981 (25), an unlikely mixture of two sources, locates the battle of this great hunter in nocturnal gloom – hence the murky browns and silvery moon highlights. Orion is poised to spear a woolly beast that crouches ready to jump while a long Mannerist tiger (?) and mad bull circle around his dancing body. Ghost-like trees and white grass undulate weirdly in this compressed space. Odd heads sprout from Orion's body – accidents of paint turned into appropriate beasts. The brushstrokes, sometimes incessant approximations of a shape, take up the struggle. Orion's boast that he would exterminate the wild beasts on the island of Chios can be read as the fable of the rising sun, at whose appearance all the wild beasts return to their dens; this would explain the murky light of the battle scene.[16] Another myth connecting Orion's name with Urion tells how his birth resulted from an old man urinating on a bull's hide – an idea which may come from a primitive African rain-producing ritual. Orion is also connected to deadly insects, such as the scorpion, and his constellation (chased by Scorpio) is a sign of both rain and the hottest part of the summer. So many of the fabulous and real objects that Garouste mixes in his allegories do relate to the various texts of Orion and do have the logic of myth with their many encrustations and elaborations. In fact, his style seems well suited to the transformational logic and ambiguity of layered myth.

More directly derivative of de Chirico are the domestic interiors which often show nude and dressed figures engaged in some kind of Proustian plot. In *La Chambre Rouge* (The Red Room), 1982 (26), classical pediments and a red baroque couch set the scene for some mysterious passion: has the distracted woman just murdered her lover, by poison, or with one of the leaden instruments by the bed? Or is he just stretching out a disjointed arm? Again, dream symbolism seems to be the ultimate reference of this

2.25 Gérard Garouste, *Orion the Classic – Orion the Indian*, 1981, oil on canvas, 98½ x 116¼in (Courtesy Leo Castelli Gallery, NYC)

2.26 Gérard Garouste, *The Red Room*, 1982, oil on canvas, 98⅞ x 116in (Courtesy Sperone Westwater Gallery, NYC)

2.27 Gérard Garouste, *The Wrestlers*, 1982, oil on canvas, 100 x 118in (Courtesy Sperone Westwater Gallery, NYC)

2.28 William Stok, *The Dream*, 1984, tempera on paper, 55 x 27½in (Courtesy the artist)

2.30 Anne and Patrick Poirier, *Mimas*, 1983, bronze, wood, charcoal and water, 8 x 16½ x 6¾ft (Courtesy Sonnabend Gallery, NYC)

2.31 Anne and Patrick Poirier, *Mimas*, 1983, bronze, wood, charcoal and water, 8 x 16½ x 6¾ft (Photograph André Morain/Courtesy Galerie Daniel Templon, Paris)

ambiguity, as it does with *Les Lutteurs* (The Wrestlers), 1982 (27). According to one interpretation this painting is a parody of a late antique allegory which contrasts a dying paganism (the surrounding viewers) with an emergent Christianity (the fighting gladiators). Another reading sees it as a parody of a Francis Bacon bed fight with dismembered heads and screaming shirts strewn across a king-size couch while a distracted and voyeuristic public looks on. No doubt the *mis-en-scène* does relate to late de Chiricos where, for instance, you find a young Ulysses rowing across a very thick-pile carpet to return home (to a bourgeois living room). It is Garouste's virtue, as well as his limitation, that his allusive paintings can call up this halo of meanings while resisting any explicit solution.

There are so many painters systematically mining this territory of illusive allusion that we could call it a major convention of the time. It's almost as if an artist knows he will start with a paradox and end with a conundrum without ever passing through the normal channel of comprehensible plots. In this sense it is a continuation of trends started by Symbolists in the late nineteenth century and it is probably as rarefied and hermetic as that work.[17] Its quality and expressive power in some instances is not in question, even if its public meaning is. For instance William Stok, the Anglo-Italian painter, will place heroic, mythical figures in an unfinished limbo of eternal suggestion (28). Dramatic figures are photographed, then drawn, half finished in tempera and cut off in the style of Degas to accentuate their momentary presence, their unresolved meaning. The background will suggest a perfect Renaissance city, or its dream image, but the overall plot and the connection of events is left to skills of free association.

No doubt such vaguely focused work has produced its share of portentous art, but whether it's any more pretentious than during periods of precise focus – Napoleonic history painting for instance – is debatable. What we can say with assurance is that enigmatic allegories have become so conventionalised as to constitute both a subject matter and a view of life. They are self-consciously pursued as an end in themselves and are thus elevated to the level of symbols. It's hardly surprising, in a secular age, that the meaning of myth should be mythology itself, or the mythic function; nor that it should be combined with disguised allegories about art and the myths of Modernism and Post-Modernism.

Anne and Patrick Poirier, two Parisian sculptors, work together on very polished allegories which connect these myths in an implicit way. Some are enigmatic suggestions showing archaeological sites – a ruined temple with remains of stone walls covered in a shallow pool of water – all watched over by a giant eye suggestive of the artist, critic or perceiver (29). Miniaturisation, contrast of scales, bronze painted black and fragmentation displace these creations from the customary realm of sculpture. In *Mimas*, 1983 (30, 31), a huge bronze eye is all that is left of the giant who, with his sight, created Mount Etna, symbolised by the charcoal amphitheatre. A bronze arrow, 'sign of the gods', pierces the reflecting pool, while a trickle of water from the eye is both an ironic fountain and a comment on ruins, death and presumably the current art scene.

The Birth of Pegasus, 1985 (32), is even more melodramatic. A wingless stallion in classical pose is covered in glowing blue pigment and mired up to the knees in post-nuclear rubble. Black charcoal is again used for the walls and an amphitheatre to achieve a sad beauty. The ghost-like horse and charred ruins show how much of the classical past and mythology has been irreversibly lost, yet is still present and reborn as art. The melancholic classicism of de Chirico, where the ordered past is both eternally lost *and* present, is recalled as much as the Surrealists' use of incongruous juxtapositions. The Poirier sculptures provide us with quick parables about layering and fragmentation within mythology and Modernism. Their melancholia is heightened because the allegory is unspecific. Just as we're not always sure if Modernism and Post-Modernism mean anything or have any direction, and this uncertainty introduces a note of panic, so the Poiriers convey an ambiguity about the meaning of the past and their own work.

From these trends some speculative conclusions may be drawn. Just as in the nineteenth century Matthew Arnold could predict that art might become a substitute religion, now we can see it becoming a very real social mythology. Artists are now treating an implicit subject which is the convergence of two myths: mythology itself and the significance and history of art. Given the hyperactivity of the art market, where a Jasper Johns can sell for a million dollars and Julian Schnabel can paint a well-publicised portrait of God, we can assume a further convergence of these myths.[18] It wouldn't be surprising if the forces became more explicit and artists started to work on narratives like Mariani's *Costellazione del Leone (La Scuola di Roma)*, but with more circumstantial plots and higher ideals. If remythification is the hidden agenda of these artists, then their own profession with its heroes and scoundrels, drama and pseudo-profundity, would seem to be an adequate subject for epic treatment. And it might even be right out in the open, where it was first conventionalised and then rendered intelligible. For, as we shall see in the next chapter, there are Post-Modern Classicists who are treating contemporary narrative without falling into reductive illustration.

2.29, Anne and Patrick Poirier, *Untitled*, 1984, bronze and water, 17 x 38 x 38in (Courtesy Sonnabend Gallery, NYC)

2.32 Anne and Patrick Poirier, *The Birth of Pegasus*, 1984, charcoal and plaster, 117½ x 156¾in (Photograph G. Poncet/Collection of Marc and Livia Strauss, Chappaqua, New York)

CHAPTER III
Narrative Classicism

The Aesthetic Moralists and Suggestive Narrative

For the longest time, roughly from 1480 to 1840, historical painting was considered the most elevated type of art within the classical tradition. Often it illustrated a significant event and pointed to a moral. At best it would show the great actions of leading statesmen, or their mythological representatives. Jacques-Louis David's *Oath of the Horatii* and *Death of Socrates* (1), two of the best-known moralising paintings in this genre, show historical figures renouncing private duties for public virtues. Such paintings were meant to be read as uplifting moral sermons about the present, and so they were, especially just after the French Revolution when public virtue subjugated individual desires. The Reign of Terror, it is often said, was a Reign of Virtue engendered by the high-minded idealism of those such as Robespierre, Saint-Just and Jacques-Louis David.

Perhaps all narrative painting has an implicit moral goal, since in any recognisable plot there lurks a potential parable. In the late eighteenth century this implicit meaning became more explicit as artists and writers insisted on the *exemplum virtutis* – the work of art intended to teach a lesson in virtue. Historical events, usually taken from the Graeco-Roman past and filled out with classical dress and architecture, might illustrate the ideal of the chaste mother's worldly sacrifice, the uncommon charity of a Roman general, or, like Socrates taking the hemlock, some unyielding dedication to abstract beliefs.[1] These scenes should, in the ringing phrases proclaimed during the Revolution, '*Faire haïr le vice, adorer la vertu en charmant les yeux*'.[2] This elevated purpose took art above and outside aesthetics – although it was still supposed to 'charm the eye' – and set it against the decadence of Rococo and art for art's sake. The major way it could do this was by illustrating 'the virtuous and heroic actions of great men, the exemplars of humanity who showed generosity, courage, disdain for danger, a passionate zeal for honour and the well-being of the Nation, and above all the defense of its religion'.[3] These lofty sentiments, expressed by La Font de Saint-Yenne in 1754, might appear embarrassing today to anyone apart from the 'moral majority' – and they have yet to inspire great art in this century. Patriotism and organised religion, like the belief in myths and heroes, have succumbed to moral relativity and social pluralism, at least when it comes to art. Serious artists have not tried, except in extremely rare instances, to portray public virtues, and those few who have – the Social Realists, the WPA artists or, today, those involved in protest and mural art – have come dangerously close to creating illustration or propaganda. The social *imagina-*

3.1 Jacques-Louis David, *The Death of Socrates*, oil on canvas, Salon of 1787, detail, 51x77¼in (Catharine Lerillard Wolfe Collection/Courtesy Metropolitan Museum of Art, NYC)

67

tion seems either to be seduced by power or dwarfed by events such as Hiroshima. In either case it is deflected from the classical goal of imagining great men involved in noble actions. There are however some good paintings of ignoble men involved in questionable deeds, and these *do* have a didactic purpose.

Paul Georges, who has been patiently engaged in modern narrative since the 1950s, painted *My Kent State*, 1971-2 (2), as an imaginative comment on a significant event: the brutal killing of Vietnam protestors at Kent State University. He uses here a figure of the 'muse', a strong feminine personification of freedom and the arts, which was to inspire his work for the next decade. The muse tries to flee evil, rendered explicit in the gas-masked paratrooper, while Georges holds her back; Nixon washes his hands of the whole affair over the bloodied corpse of one of the students. This combination of realism, the depiction of an important event that catalysed Americans, and the imaginative representation of artistic inspiration as a central actor in the plot – all three work to lift the painting above illustration. In *Return of the Muse*, 1969-70 (3), Georges shows this same sexual and poetic power coming back to the artist in the midst of New York skyscrapers, and he has continued to transform this presence in a series of classical allusions: *The Mugging of the Muse*, 1974, *Venus and Cupid*, 1984, etc.

Alfred Leslie, a realist who is explicitly committed to the moral purpose of art, again makes use of Christian and classical iconography. In a cycle of paintings devoted to the death of his friend, the poet/critic Frank O'Hara, he has used traditional themes – such as the deposition of Christ – in a modern context (4). Here young girls in bathing dress and jeans help lower the body in a compositional grouping that recalls so many Mannerist depositions from the Cross. The dramatic lighting is reminiscent of Caravaggio and is also a realistic portrayal of the night-time lighting when a beach taxi accidentally hit the poet. The other paintings in the cycle show the variety of people involved – Leslie believes in portraying all conditions of people – some of whom are reminiscent of Paul Georges' muse: that is nude women acting in a quasi-allegorical role. The problem with some of Leslie's realism is that the particularity can overwhelm the idea. When the sharp-focused eyes of his teenagers stare out from the canvas, as if caught by a flash camera, the event suddenly looses its classical *gravitas*. Leslie's intention, however, is to find a straightforward realism that can dignify democratic, ethnically diverse, everyday life.

The same intention can be seen in George Segal's plaster sculptures which often take everyday people and put them in prosaic situations. *The Butcher Shop*, for instance, portrays a Jewish New Yorker's shop. The ethnicity is indicated by the spare lettering, but the rest of the environment is portrayed in fundamental shapes and abstract contrasts, mostly black and white. This abstraction, or generalisation, gives to the frail characters a classical dignity which they sometimes lack in Leslie's work. Often, as in the *Two Bathers*, 1983 (5), figures and background are reduced to a Minimalist white on white,

3.2 Paul Georges, *My Kent State*, 1971-2, oil on canvas, 8½x12ft (Courtesy the artist)

3.3 Paul Georges, *Return of the Muse*, 1969-70, oil on canvas, 10x20ft (Courtesy the artist)

3.4 Alfred Leslie, *The Killing Cycle VI: Loading Pier*, 1975, oil on canvas, 108x72in (Photograph Eeva Inkeri/Courtesy Allan Frumkin Gallery, NYC)

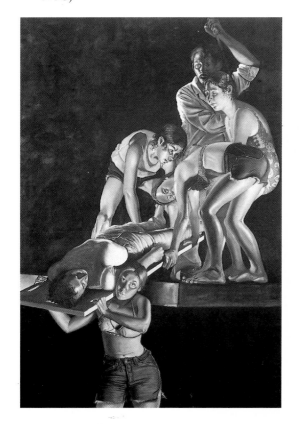

3.5

3.5 George Segal, *Two Bathers*, 1983, plaster and wood, 68½x36x22in (Photograph Allan Finkelman/Courtesy Sidney Janis Gallery, NYC)

3.6 Jack Beal, *Prudence, Avarice, Lust, Justice, Anger*, 1977-8, oil on canvas, 72x78in (Photograph Eeva Inkeri/Courtesy Allan Frumkin Gallery, NYC)

3.7 Jack Beal, *Danae* (second version), 1972, oil on canvas, 68x68in (Courtesy Allan Frumkin Gallery, NYC)

3.8 James Valerio, *Studio Figures*, 1982, oil on canvas, 92x100in (Courtesy Allan Frumkin Gallery, NYC)

3.6

before the Greek polychromers have arrived, and the work is set in an architectural context. Poses and expression are twentieth century, but distanced by generality while the foam of the water is both a particular sexual sign and an abstract set of swirls and drips.

Jack Beal, also committed to merging opposite traditions of narrative and abstraction, is not always entirely successful. His *Prudence, Avarice, Lust, Justice, Anger*, 1977-8 (6), could be a Mannerist allegory of card-players in modern jeans who have imbibed too much Schlitz beer. The subject is plausible both as a timeless parable and a modern illustration of these traditional virtues and vices. The problem is, however, that Beal's characters do not portray the depth or complexity of the classical types, but remain a dramatic, even melodramatic, illustration of the very real American models. Realism has always been one of the classical armoury's double-edged swords, respected as the ultimate goal of verisimilitude but attacked for its endless empiricism. If a painter becomes too involved in the details, colour and chiaroscuro, for instance, he will lose sight of the overall idea, the *concetto* that should guide selection.

Sometimes Jack Beal aims for generality through the illustration of details, and this is particularly true of his *Danae* (second version), 1972 (7). Danae, the mythic heroine who conceived Perseus in a shower of gold as she waited by the window, has been a subject for several Post-Modern Classicists, perhaps because the archetypal figure of a nude in a room full of sunlight is a natural subject for painting.[4] Beal has completed many such portraits since the mid-1960s – *Nude with Suitcase, Nude on a Red Sofa*, etc. – that contrast the intimate view of a woman's body caught in raking light with a strongly textured bed cover and quilt. The build-up of richly coloured details which fold and undulate equate the skin with its surroundings and, since a strong orange glow suffuses everything, the theme of Danae is successfully suggested in terms of painting. Exaggerated and tilted perspective (a device often used by Beal) makes the room and mattress as much a part of the narrative as the musings of the two women and the supposed miraculous act of conception. One imagines that the classical subject and title were found by Beal during the process of painting; that they resulted from his commitment to realism.

James Valerio also adopts this open-ended approach towards subject matter. Some of his narrative paintings such as *The Card Trick*, 1980, are premeditated genre scenes which tell a story, but more often their plot is suggested and discovered slowly. *Studio Figures*, 1982 (8), came from a fascination Valerio had with a photograph he took of a man on a tightrope. This led to a drawing which suggested a Thomas Eakins painting of a modelling class. Further photographs of figures that fascinated Valerio – the head emerging from the body of a swimmer, a crouching nude – were drawn and added to the composition. Slowly the narrative was built up with other figures, artist-friends, posing for the art class and Valerio himself looking tentatively out from behind a canvas. The subject remains caught between

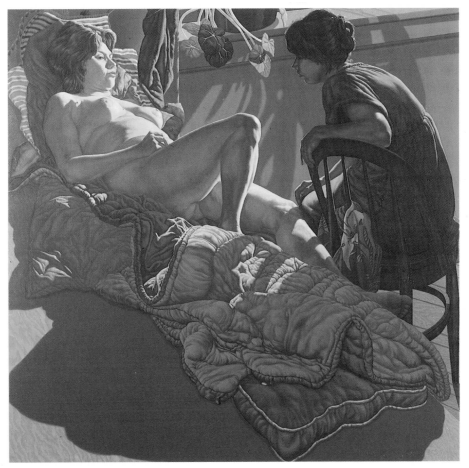

3.7

3.8

the painter's uncertain gaze and the other artists' intense concentration. A black painter wears a Mickey Mouse shirt; the kimono of the model, and the dress and faces of the female painters suggest further diverse viewpoints, both of ethnicity and purpose. The three easels are set at discordant angles and no one is paying attention to the model swimming on the floor.

We are close here to the category of Enigmatic Allegory, but the title *Studio Figures* and the realism of details, a form of Photo Realism, verge on what might instead be called the Suggested Narrative. We can guess that the story is of Valerio's uncertainty in a time of valid pluralism. He has painted a haunting *Self-Portrait*, 1981 (9), which some critics have read as a 'closet anti-nuclear statement' because the alarm clock shows four minutes to midnight (where we are according to the Committee of Concerned Scientists). One can see why this interpretation makes sense and Valerio has admitted its point.[5] There's a black (nuclear?) submarine on a glass table, a cube with a falling aeroplane, a torn photograph, the telephone (about to ring?) and Valerio's look of profound dismay as he reaches up to his staring face – again with uncertain gesture. His impotence as a painter in a nuclear age is suggested by the adjacent easel and his floating presence placed against a black void. The green velvet chair and cashmere sweater suggest how luxurious are our last four minutes.

This is perhaps as close as a painter has come to giving us 'the man of the 1980s': concerned, distracted, anxious, well-off and waiting. Although Valerio denies didactic intentions and explicitly distances himself from painters such as David, his paintings gravitate in this direction because of their lay-out and control. Even such an erotic work as *Reclining Dancer*, 1978 (10), suggests the Neoclassical tradition through the spare background, frontal layering and one-point perspective. What is the narrative here? A jumping cat suggesting the danger of the woman's fickle libido? The afternoon light and her stretching towards it suggest that she is about to act. No doubt Valerio wants to suggest many scenarios and consciously goes about loading his canvases with meaningful details that spin the viewer from plot to plot. Some of the elements are actually called 'decoys' and are meant to pull in the mind's eye as much as the different easels and paintings within paintings.

Michael Mazur in *Incident at Walden Pond*, 1978-9 (11), has produced one of the great narrative paintings of our time. Again, imaginative suggestion is used as a very positive aspect of the context. Has there been a rape or murder? Is the fleeing figure towards whom the runners gesture the criminal, or has he disappeared into the space of the viewer? The violence and heat of the drama are increased by the punctuation of trees and light, the way streaks of colour fall across the contorted faces, the way the calm of the pond is broken by the staccato of tree trunks. Indeed, the extremely wide-angle view and the fact that there are three stages of this painting increase our pursuit of the solution and the heat of the chase. And then there are the extraneous details, so real in everyday tragedies: the panting dog, the

3.9 James Valerio, *Self Portrait*, 1981, oil on canvas, 92¼x76in (Courtesy Allan Frumkin Gallery, NYC)

unconcerned jogger, and the domesticated suburban landscape of Walden Pond. These dramatically gratuitous elements remain in the background to give added weight to the foreground event, to give it that odd psychological twist which Dostoyevsky has shown to so often accompany criminal acts. Finally, the combination of elements from traditional iconography (for instance the pietà scene to the right) adds a resonant mystery to this unnamable crime.

The master of Suggested Narrative on a public level is certainly David Hockney who has managed to evolve a sad, accessible gaiety with which many people can identify. Few artists could attempt such pretty painting without becoming trivial, but Hockney has managed to give this taboo genre a special wistful stamp. Prettiness, like quaintness, has been a term of opprobrium for Modern artists since before the First World War. However for Hockney, and some other painters who were connected with Pop Art, an ornamental prettiness is a natural part of one's mental environment. Many of their narrative paintings take place in beautiful settings, whether Los Angeles, Provence or cleaned-up studio bedrooms (as we'll see in Eric Fischl's work (25)). With Hockney such settings have become so conventionalised that even restaurants have started incorporating the look: it might be called 'Habitat-Hockney' after the formula made famous by Terence Conran, Design Research and other purveyors of pretty, minimalist good taste.

There is a lot of room for Suggestive Narrative in this environment and occasionally it is even literary and classical. In *Homage to Michelangelo* two similar women cross paths while T. S. Eliot's lines are scrawled near Michelangelo cartoons drawn on the wall: 'In the room the women come and go / Talking of Michelangelo'. The drawing is just as evocative and daunting as Eliot's lines, especially since these women are not about to say anything of importance concerning Michelangelo. Of more substance, and more direct classical lineage, are *A Bigger Splash*, 1967, *Mr and Mrs Clark and Percy*, 1970-1, and *Contra-Jour in the French Style*, 1974. All three are frontally layered, well-proportioned paintings which owe much to the classical tradition, especially its use of architecture to frame action and give it a noble permanence. The action may be absent (the splash) or private (Mr Clark's vulnerable nervousness) but the scene and geometrical harmony are reminiscent of Piero and the classical sensibility in general.

Hockney might not claim this pedigree for himself as he was hardly trained in the full academic tradition. His subject matter remains modest and sometimes provincial, but it is a provinciality nourished on the western tradition. As if to show that he is a self-trained amateur in the classical tradition his debts are often explicitly acknowledged with a written label, or title of a book. Thus one can find small quotes in his work alluding to Picasso, Michelangelo or, in one of his most moving series, *My Parents*, 1977 (12), to Piero and Chardin. The humble atmosphere of this portrayal – the spartan A-frame of the furniture, the bent figure of his father attentively and awkwardly

3.10 James Valerio, *Reclining Dancer*, 1978, oil on canvas, 84x100in (Courtesy Allan Frumkin Gallery, NYC)

3.11 Michael Mazur, *Incident at Walden Pond*, 1978-9, oil on canvas, triptych, 48x150in (Courtesy Barbara Mathes Gallery, NYC)

reading, the resigned repose of his mother, the carefully tidy trolleyscape –
are all ironic and timeless images which fall somewhere between the heroism
of David's revolutionary figures and the realism of Courbet. One can see why
Hockney is the heroic subject of Peter Blake's *The Meeting*, 1981-3 (13), and
the sometime mock-heroic subject of Ron Kitaj's brush. He has again
discovered that modesty and prettiness can be as real as austerity and
ugliness. However, if his Suggestive Narratives remain domestic, then their
moral and political purpose also remain underdeveloped.

This is not true of Ron Kitaj's work, which is the most deeply serious of
the Post-Modernists' on a moral and political level. Here, such issues are
dealt with imaginatively and in all their complexity. Kitaj avoids treating
historical events either as illustration or private myth, two of the most
obvious failings of so much narrative painting, and he can insert a personal
and moral figure into a historical situation without becoming banal or
simplistic. For instance his epic *Juan de la Cruz*, 1967, which concerns a
negro helicopter pilot flying in Vietnam, suggests violation, passions and
destruction without making them melodramatic. Thus the pilot is allowed to
convey a classical dignity even though surrounded by acts of outrage
committed on women – an ambiguous and powerful allegory of war.

Much of his later painting also deals with serious issues, both domestic
and political, and such significant figures as Walter Benjamin and the poet
Cavafy. His first ambitious attempt at a synthesis, *If Not, Not*, 1975-6 (14), is
based on *The Wasteland* of T. S. Eliot not only in part of its subject matter,
but also in its fragmentary references. Survivors of war crawl through the
desert towards an oasis, survivors of civilisation (Eliot himself) are engaged
in quizzical acts, some with representatives of an exotic culture. Lamb, crow,
palm tree, turquoise lake and a Tuscan landscape, consciously adapted from
the classical tradition, resonate with common overtones. They point towards
a western and Christian background overlaid by Modernism – the cult of
primitivism and disaster. The classical barn/monument at the top, so
reminiscent of the work of the Italian architect Aldo Rossi and of other Post-
Modern face buildings, is suggestive also of death camps. Indeed, the
burning inferno of the sky, the corpse and broken pier, the black and
truncated trees all suggest life after the Second World War: plural, confused
and tortured on the whole, but containing islands of peace (and a search for
wholeness?). The title, with its double negative, was taken from an ancient
coronation oath: 'We who are as good as you swear to you who are no better
than we, to accept you as our King, provided you observe all our liberties and
laws; but if not, not . . .'[6] This curious oath, combining the opposites of
monarchy and democracy in extreme contrast, underscores the tentative
nature of the artist's commitment to society. If the State or its representatives
break the rules then the artist, and we, can break our allegiance.

This double negative attitude towards leadership is also suggested in
Kitaj's *Rise of Fascism*, 1975-9 (15). Three women, hardly the classical Three
Graces, display attitudes to which the title of the painting points in different

3.12 David Hockney, *My Parents*, 1977, oil on
canvas, 72 x 72in (Photograph John Webb/Cour-
tesy Tate Gallery, London)

3.13 Peter Blake, *The Meeting, or Have a Nice
Day Mr. Hockney*, 1981-3, oil on canvas,
38½ x 48¾in (Courtesy Tate Gallery, London,
and the artist)

ways. The central figure, a fat, false blond reminiscent of the fascist types depicted by Grosz and Beckmann, strides menacingly towards the dark beachline. The bodies and sea immediately recall classical prototypes including Titian's *The Rape of Europa*. But here the violence is ambiguous and coupled with an attractive sensuality. A middle-aged figure, a model or prostitute, looks up in a dazed lethargy, the frame of mind that allows fascism, while the suave, rich vixen, exposing her sex, seems to be part Egyptian sphinx, part whore. At the upper left a phallic bomber, presumably another fascist presence, looms out of the sky threatening the three women. The sensuality of the paint and pastel nicely underscores the shape of the bodies. One's eye is led from area to area, rather like a lapse-dissolve in film, in search of the meaning. And, in so far as this is public, it concerns the archetypes which may lead to fascism: sensual decadence, inattentive passivity, explicit display and power.

This interpretation is inferential rather than public or conventional, as didactic, historical painting would have been in the Renaissance. But the work has both dignity and monumentality: it conveys a grandeur of decadence with a high moral purpose – however much the latter may be obscured by intentional ambiguities. Kitaj characterises the intellectual's moral dilemma in the twentieth century when confronted by oversimple alternatives which demand total commitment. In refusing to simplify, or to back away from depicting the dilemma, he produces the most suggestive of narratives which allows competing readings.

The Autumn of Central Paris (*After Walter Benjamin*), 1972-3 (16), is ambiguous in title and make-up. The Jewish writer Walter Benjamin is shown sitting at a café not long before he committed suicide. Other archetypal figures can be inferred: a fascist type in black leather, the caricature of 'reds under the bed' in the foreground, a gangster and an intellectual. All these figures press into a tight space which also appears to hold the broken windows of Notre Dame (?) and a café awning. The montage technique is used here with flat graphic boldness, loud colours and a subtle, blurred *sfumato* which together create a violent mixture of moods. The eclectic, politically charged café life of Paris 1940 is reflected in the clash of styles. Just what is going on in this Suggestive Narrative is not clear beyond the general confrontation of the intellectual with rising European thuggery. Kitaj presents his view of the world as a struggle between twentieth-century heroes (the writers and philosophers in exile) and villains (the leaders of organised violence). As with Paul Georges, or Ian Hamilton Finlay (as we'll see) the good and bad are clearly cast. Kitaj does not have recourse to classical mythology, but the consistency and depth with which he presents the implicit allegory place him closer to the great tradition of historical painters, to Raphael, Poussin and David, than many of those who use the classical style. Kitaj revives its spirit while bending its language in an Expressionist direction.

3.14 R. B. Kitaj, *If Not, Not*, 1975-6, oil on canvas, 60x60in (Courtesy Scottish National Gallery of Modern Art, Edinburgh)

3.15 R. B. Kitaj, *The Rise of Fascism*, 1975-9, pastel, charcoal and oil on paper, 33½ x 62⁵/₁₆in (Courtesy Tate Gallery, London)

Erotic and Subversive Classicism

If the subject of narrative painting often poses a problem in an agnostic age there is one issue which remains eternally real and attractive: eroticism. The painter's muse is often personified as an appealing woman, as Paul Georges reminds us, and the human body is a perennial metaphor for investigation, as current architects have shown us.[7] When all else fails there is sex and gossip, as the tabloids prove. This would seem to be rather arid territory for classicists to investigate, but they have always kept an eye on it. Not only have erotic situations been portrayed in almost every period of classicism, but in some eras, notably the Pompeiian, sexual appetites in the ordinary burghers' houses are celebrated and lampooned as a matter of course. Classicism and sensuality have been willing partners since the Egyptian ithyphallic Min gave his fertility blessing to the Pharoahs of the Old Kingdom and it is only relatively recently, since the seventeenth century and the French Academy, that they've gone separate ways. Thus their present reunion, especially in an eclectic manner, is bound to cause a double resistance. Some artists even use sexual innuendo and taboo as forms of Subversive Classicism to challenge conventional notions of art and morality.

James McGarrell, a midwestern artist in his fifties, has painted an elaborate narrative of twentieth-century debauchery. *Travestimento*, 1980 (17), has so many allusions and layers of narrative that one can read it as a meticulous detective story about art history and affluent society. Men, half-dressed in black tie and masks, play music and sport with women. The tuxedo finds an echo in the tiny photograph of Max Beckmann stuck on the pillar to the right, *Self Portrait in Tuxedo*, 1927: the artist is here the detached, tough, urban dandy. Above this is another photograph, this one of the Dionysian initiation ceremony in the Villa of Mysteries in Pompeii. The Roman figure who drops her veil in apprehension as she dances (?) or flees (?) from flagellation finds an echo in McGarrell's figure who spreads her flowing red cape over the central action – an orgiastic last supper where women in pearls caress a cat or expose their unhealthy sunburns. The Pompeiian frieze, representing a marriage ceremony or mystic ritual, is the classical counter-part to McGarrell's work with its similar subject matter and similar objects of mirrors and masks. For instance to the far left of *Travestimento* a masked figure holds a mirror revealing the dancer's back and a phallus suspended on a string. In the background are further postcard references to erotic and religious themes, also taken from the wider classical tradition.

The density and disturbing juxtaposition of so much colourful detail remind one of those traffic jams in hell that Hieronymus Bosch loved to paint. Here too the mind and eye can rove into the far distance finding one horizon after another, cars bigger than cypress trees, trains and boats travelling irrationally over each other, the whole pastoral landscape so rich with produce as to drive the inhabitants mad. Red and blue apples float miraculously through the window towards the viewer, the malachite green arcade and floor seem to fall away as the ground outside rushes up. These

3.16 R. B. Kitaj, *The Autumn of Central Paris (After Walter Benjamin)*, 1972-3, oil on canvas, 60x60in (Private Collection, New York / Courtesy Marlborough Fine Art (London) Ltd.)

3.17 James McGarrell, *Travestimento*, 1980, oil on canvas, 96x226in (Courtesy Allan Frumkin Gallery, NYC)

disorientations and the multiple horizons work effectively to heighten what is already a very disturbing and raucous orgy.

This is not exactly an *exemplum virtutis*, an example meant to teach a lesson in virtue, yet one can read into it moral attitudes towards consumption and play; after all the party is hellishly overripe, in its second day perhaps, and the pleasure is beginning to become a torture. We could call this the Suggestive Ethical; a counterpart to the Enigmatic Allegory on the moral plane. Even Erotic Classicists intending to promote a more open sexuality have an ethical strain to their work. William Crozier's bronzes, for instance, show women on bed-like plinths aggressively offering themselves to men in a way which could be interpreted as insisting on feminine sexuality (18). Such frank expression of desire has not been seen often since Roman sculpture, and the few examples usually portray male lust. Crozier's work, somewhat reminiscent of Rodin, is usually explicit in its narrative of sexual desire and intercourse and, as a result, somewhat limited in its range of meaning.

The artist who has been criticised and even attacked by feminists for his portrayal of women's sexuality, Allen Jones, is in fact much more subtle and complex in his narrative. It is true his women still show the stylisation of a fetish – the curvaceous and shiny leg ending in an ultra high heel – but these are now absorbed into a greater narrative which includes men. Jones' series of party paintings and lithographs done in 1984-5 show a development in his work towards a richer handling of paint and subject matter. In *Night Moves*, 1985 (19), one can see the iconographic motifs built up from several different sources including Poussin, Kitaj and Jones' own past work. Here the kneeling waitresses and dancers of previous paintings are blended together into the synchronic space of colourful dreams. Flat graphic forms merge into decorative patterns, outlined caricatures and then modelled, three-dimensional shapes. The notion of the artist as the outsider, the voyeur at the party, is suggested by the draughtsman and the man with the flashlight crawling on the floor. What is the typical Allen Jones party – is it like McGarrell's frenetic and unhappy orgy? On a painterly level it is much more sensual and involving, if less detailed and precise. Dancers are always falling into embraces or bent over in a provocative pose, or tied up in a corset to accentuate their shape; some wear phallic masks, as with McGarrell, and the men seem to be having a pretty miserable time. For the most part they crawl around on the ground with dunces' caps pulled over their eyes (20), or play a banjo, like Father Time, as they gaze longingly at the happy, voluptuous women in their prime. In fact Jones' women are eternally twenty-five and beautiful, a race of robust Amazons taken from the pages of *Vogue* and undressed, never at a loss for dominating men's desires. The enigmatic figure in *Night Moves* of the crucified mermaid in a green rubber suit is one of the few victims of pleasure. More often the moral of a Jones party is that women rule society by manipulating male desire. Although the message emerging is ambiguous and not didactic, it may be that these are then, on the whole, 'examples meant to teach a lesson in virtue', which is one reason why their

3.18 William Crozier, *Marilyn*, 1975-80, bronze 44½x34¾x38⅛in (Courtesy Xavier Fourcade Inc., NYC)

3.19 Allen Jones, *Night Moves*, 1985, oil on canvas, 114x132in (Courtesy Waddington Galleries, London)

3.20 Allen Jones, *Swing*, 1984, oil on canvas, 96x92in (Photograph Prudence Cuming Associates Ltd./Courtesy Waddington Galleries, London)

sensuality has proved so provocative.

There are two younger American artists who use sexuality in a similarly provocative manner: David Salle and Eric Fischl. Salle has cultivated a very urbane way of representing stereotypes, taken from the mass media and the world of art, which has affinities with Jasper Johns' early classicism, such as the *Target with Boxes*. Parts of the human body, usually the erogenous zones, are fragmented and recombined in a diptych as part of an enigmatic collage. *The Cruelty of the Father*, 1983 (21), shows poses taken from 'How to Draw' manuals and mass-circulation magazines like *Penthouse*, overlaid with splotches of abstraction and a nervous map outline; this is then contrasted with the representation of a Joan Crawford head stuck unnaturally on top of the water, as if left there by an absent-minded swimmer. What cruelty is this? What father? To understand any one of Salle's paintings one has to understand their overall meaning since, like the film techniques they use and comment on, they are slices from a larger narrative.

The basic text concerns middle-class life as seen through television, newspapers and glossy monthlies. This is a nonsensical life as Salle portrays it; full of glamour, disjointed sex and violence. These three elements, as reduced to the media image or sometimes a comic strip, are the characters of the story. Disparity is the key, as in *Burning Bush*, 1982 (22), where two pornographic images contrast with a political cartoon and burning bush (?) of abstraction. The implication is that they are all the same at the level of imagery. We make no sense of the First World War caricature fleeing with his loot of clocks; nor of the girl peering at the viewer from between her legs. What does give pause is the way these images jump back and forth in successive readings. No sooner has one finished decoding the outline cartoon than one is off chasing a three-dimensional girl with a headache (and her aspirin relief at the top of the canvas?). This is mildly amusing, as are Salle's wry juxtapositions.

His deadpan approach has been considered by some as a form of subversion, the 'deconstruction' of habitual categories of perception.[8] Since 'meaning is intimated but tantalisingly withheld' and its 'obscurity is its source of strength', 'Salle follows a strategy of infiltration and sabotage, using established conventions against themselves in the hope of exposing cultural repression'.[9] The avant-garde military metaphor has this 'deconstructor' blowing up 'ideological institutions' by using the conventions of classicism against classicism, the Pop image against the assumptions of TV, the pornographic still against *Penthouse*. On a certain level this subversion is probably effective: anyone coming to Salle's work with the assumptions of an authoritarian classicist, or the values of a suburbanite, is bound to feel betrayed. They are enticed into the painting by the use of seductive imagery and then slapped in the face by its obvious nihilism. On the other hand, its ambiguous aesthetic approach can be, and has been, criticised for precisely the opposite reason: for exploiting debased imagery for personal gain.[10] This reading, although contradictory at one level, is also correct inasmuch as

3.21 David Salle, *The Cruelty of the Father*, 1983, oil and acrylic on canvas, 75x100in (Victor Smorgon Collection, Australia / Courtesy Larry Gagosian Gallery, LA)

3.22 David Salle, *Burning Bush*, 1982, oil and acrylic on canvas, 92x118in (Bruno Bischofberger Collection, NYC / Courtesy Mary Boone Gallery, NYC)

Salle's own strategy, in his career, is quite calculated. But he wouldn't be the first artist in history to make a fine living out of subversive, seductive satire.

What Salle's art shows as a whole is an effective dualism that cancels out each side of his equation: high art questions low art, abstraction negates representation, male attacks female, depth is set off against flatness, impulsive scrawl against academic realism, and so on in a series of mutual negations. Ultimately the meaning of middle-class imagery itself is cancelled as the narratives lead us directly to zero, or nihilism – a meaning Salle would probably also reject as being too explicit and singular. But like the Dadaist works of Picabia, which were based on similar techniques of overlaid contradictions, we have the choice of reading both erotic imagery and its cancellation.

By contrast Eric Fischl's eroticism is more seductive, less cancelling, but still disturbing. Again, the subject is middle-class eroticism, but now it is not the media, but the viewers who are put on stage to be shown in all the ages of concupiscence. Again, taken as a whole, the work implies a morality which is ultimately ambiguous, implicating the viewer of the painting as a voyeur, as well as a character caught in the act. The self-conscious irony of this exposed hypocrisy is positively Stendahlian: to be seen enjoying a Fischl, as one should, provokes adolescent guilt. This helps explain why the most moving paintings concern young boys or girls trapped in the snare of adult sexuality. One rather innocent work, *Father and Son Sleeping*, 1980, shows two males on a clean Hockney-like bed in exactly the same curled-up pose, presumably having the same dream. They are identical in every way but age, Fischl implies, engaged in the ultimate stereotypical act of sleeping. A corresponding work is *Mother and Daughter*, 1984 (23), which portrays them as engaged in the typical suburban activity of sunning themselves in a garden while they peruse *Vogue* and gossip. Their concentration on developing a sexual suntan is positively aggressive. Beaches, parks and homes are full of this animal activity every summer, but it took Fischl to bring this social convention to our eyes for psychological inspection. 'The animal in the home' could be the title of the overall narrative, the depiction of the desires which are so ordinary and legitimised that we overlook their subversive fetishism. Every suburbanite strokes his dog, cuddles his children and spends a significant part of his income on improving his body, cosmetically and physically. These everyday actions have a dark, illicit side which Fischl expresses through obsessive concentration on a psychologically revealing detail – a quality he admires in the work of Max Beckmann.

The Old Man's Boat and the Old Man's Dog, 1982 (24), suggests in its title a menacing, Hemingwayesque plot. Knowing in Fischl's universe that dogs are the acceptable subjects of suburban libido and seeing the position and expression of this animal over the 'odalisque', we have the inference of some bestial act. The 'old man' is of course an American euphemism for the father of the family (as well as a reference to *The Old Man and the Sea*) and he's seen here sipping beer in an unconcerned way. In back a storm is brewing and 'off

3.23 Eric Fischl, *Mother and Daughter*, 1984, oil on canvas, 84x204in (Gerald S. Elliot Collection, Chicago/Courtesy Mary Boone Gallery, NYC)

3.24 Eric Fischl, *The Old Man's Boat and the Old Man's Dog*, 1982, oil on canvas, 84x84in (Saatchi Collection, London/Courtesy Mary Boone Gallery, NYC)

canvas' as if 'off stage' something has disturbed the two adolescent males, while the daughter raises her finger as if to say 'Haven't you forgotten the tiller?' Somehow this innocent fishing party has gotten out of hand and the family is threatened with destruction. Or so it seems. The best work of Fischl has this dramatic implication which we've seen Michael Mazur use to such effect. Something unspeakable or bestial has just happened and now a train of action is set off – which cuts through the heart of the family.

In *Bad Boy*, 1981 (25), an adolescent watches his mother (?) stretch and reaches into her purse while illicitly peering at her sex. Clearly she knows what is going on, just as we, the viewer placed behind the boy, know that she knows. Implicating the audience in this kind of compromising situation is similar to what Manet did with *Olympia*: exposing the hypocrisy of the distanced perceiver, the objective aesthete. If we become the 'bad boy' by looking from his position, we also recognise in the Hockney-Hollywood bedroom the stereotypes of this situation. Here is that attention to psychological detail which makes Fischl's comment on the media and its conventional images so compelling. The soap-operatic quality pulls one in to reveal what often happens, but is rarely shown, on the other side of Sitcom Land.

Using this formal language in a subversive way, like Salle, to undermine accepted values allows us to speak of a common 'media style' running through this work. Like Salle's, Fischl's paintings have an archetypal quality that relates as much to TV as to classicism. The titles – *Dog Days, Birthday Boy*, etc. – read like entries in a TV guide, although TV does not show the explicit sexual acts of these works, or deal with their complexity of attitude. But the bodies and poses, even the sky, water and lawns are well known to us through the media. It is to Fischl's credit that he can move through this world of cliché and give it some meaning and mystery. *The Women*, 1982 (26), again shows some indeterminate but disturbing act. Women of different ages warm themselves by a fire, or are lost in ecstatic reveries or contemplation. One walks towards another as if to rouse her from sleep. The night-time light reveals the suburban furniture and ordinary car, and gives this enigmatic scene a frightening reality. This is an average American beach scene, but these night-time Amazons, reminiscent of Gauguin's Polynesian women, are about to engage in some menacing action. Or are they innocent mothers and daughters? And if they are suburban innocents, has the camp fire kindled some forgotten instincts, some ancient feelings that no amount of televised behaviour can suppress? Fischl has described the psychological states he conveys as partly the result of living in an inadequate culture.

> Central [to his work is] the feeling of awkwardness and self-consciousness that one experiences in the face of profound emotional events in one's life. These experiences, such as death, or loss, or sexuality, cannot be supported by a life style that has sought so arduously to deny their meaningfulness, and a culture whose fabric is so worn out that its public rituals and attendant symbols do not make

3.25 Eric Fischl, *Bad Boy*, 1981, oil on canvas, 66x96in (Saatchi Collection, London/Courtesy Mary Boone Gallery, NYC)

3.26 Eric Fischl, *The Women*, 1982, oil on canvas, 66x96in (Jerry & Emily Spiegel Collection, NYC/Courtesy Mary Boone Gallery, NYC)

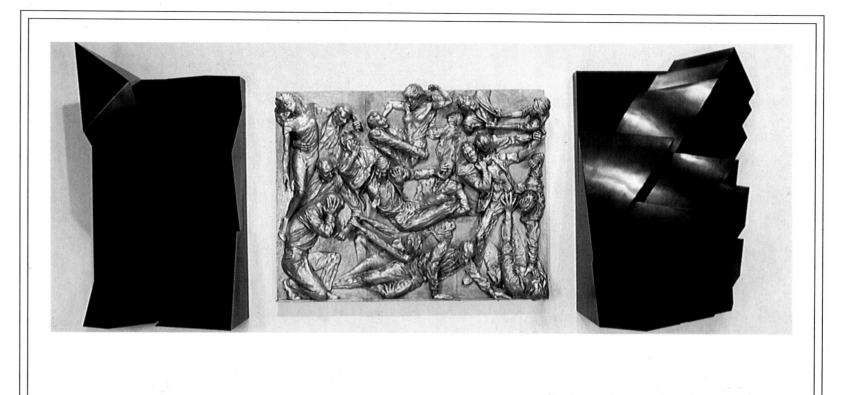

for adequate clothing . . . Each new event is a crisis, and each crisis . . . fills us with much the same anxiety that we feel when, in a dream, we discover ourselves naked in public.[11]

Awkwardness and a feeling of crisis pervade his work and as he gets older (Fischl was born in New York, 1948) his limited suburbanite cosmology might expand so that his very real gifts are applied to a wider subject. As it is now, his compelling view has shown us some truths behind the upper-middle class American dream and the truths appear as astonishing as they are normal.

Robert Longo, a contemporary of Fischl and a fellow New Yorker, is also instrumental in evolving a 'media style' to deal with everyday life, but here it tends to be urban. *Men in Cities*, 1980, shows well-dressed executives jumping, falling or twitching about as if shot or pushed onto a strong current of electricity. *Corporate Wars, Wall of Influence*, 1982 (27), reveals what life is really like when one multinational takes over another. The Brooks Brothers' jackets come off and everyone gouges and pummels each other just as they do in a spaghetti western or a Last Judgement of Jan van Eyck. As with Salle and Fischl, low and high art are mixed. Indeed, *Corporate Wars* is, characteristically, a triptych of mixed media: a cast aluminium relief depicts the battle scene, and two black, alienating Art Deco buildings stand to either side. The impersonal sophistication of this piece catches the cruel professionalism of New York corporate life where blood is spilled, and cleaned up, with consummate style and disinterest. All the legs and flailing arms are as stylised and posed as the faces. Although death is here, it's a suave generalised death of executives without names, reminiscent, as Robert Hughes has pointed out, of a Roman battle sarcophagus.[12] Even the glistening suits resemble classical drapery.

If Longo is right in his depiction of the business world, it is as seedy and cruel as the suburban family life of Fischl. Constant struggle, with no heroes or winners, is the implication of the *White Riot Series*, 1982(28) – a ballet of hammerlocks, half-nelsons and dislocated necks. The abstract beauty of these darkly suited professionals is a wry comment on their selfish activity, as is the implicit equation with a black riot in uptown Harlem. Is the yuppie as vicious and stereotyped as he looks, is life-on-the-way-up at IBM really like this?

The idea of displacing one convention, a TV gangster film, with another, a man in a grey flannel suit, is a rather interesting formula that reminds one of the ironic combinations of Warhol and Rauschenberg in the 1960s. Like them, Longo is interested in performance art, mixed media and producing films, and, again like them, he keeps a cool distance from all his material, refusing to take a stance beyond a tense and ambiguous presentation. On the other hand he sees his role as pointing up the power and violence of American life – an authoritarianism he often considers as worse than that of Nazi Germany. Responding to this he casts himself in the role of policeman or guardian.

3.27 Robert Longo, *Corporate Wars, Wall of Influence*, 1982, mixed media, 9x26x4ft (Courtesy Metro Pictures, NYC)

3.28 Robert Longo, *Untitled (White Riot Series)*, 1982, charcoal, graphite and ink on paper, 95½x116in (Courtesy Metro Pictures, NYC)

3.29 Robert Longo, *Still*, 1984, acrylic and silkscreen on wood; charcoal and graphite on dyed paper; oil and copper leaf on carved oak; granite and metal; oil on hammered lead, 96x288in (Courtesy Larry Gagosian Gallery, LA)

The artist has to . . . be like a policeman. A great deal of my art, particularly the relief *The Sleep*, is about blowing the whistle on society. I made the piece right after Jonestown [massacre] and right before the Phalangist murders. Here they are selling the image of genocide in family sportswear [the image is actually taken from a family leisure-wear ad]. *The Sleep* is the perfect example of the artist serving as the guardian of culture.[13]

Here again we are close to the moralist role of the artist and the *exemplum virtutis* except that it is vice – aggressive sex, brute power, the macho personality – which is being celebrated in order to chastise the viewer. Ultimately, like a dramatist, Longo wants to present the truth of society in a sequence of acts to produce a catharsis, not a parable. It's Aristotelian poetics without the metaphysics.

Still, 1984 (29), mixes all sorts of images and materials in a staccato five-part sequence like a series of movie stills. This ordering is a good example of a widely used technique – 'non-sequitur juxtaposition' – which leaves the working out of connections up to the hard-pressed viewer. In the first frame a fist squashes a tomato-like heart; second, a muscular red-coloured woman engages in some unspeakable act; third, a black fascist (American?) eagle strikes down; fourth, a soulless panel of black granite implies an urban skyscraper; fifth, a stereotyped knight engages in battle. This is another enigmatic allegory about 1. the violence of today's surgery (?); 2. the media; 3. the State; 4. the corporation; and 5. ideas of warfare. The five-part

organisation and near symmetry are fundamentally classical even if it's a Mannerist Classicism of violent juxtaposition and suppressed centre. In the Los Angeles installation, 1984, the whole piece acted as the embracing 'arms' of other mixed media intended to represent the whole body and all its appetites.

Occasionally Longo delivers Warholian boasts: 'I make art that's going to kill you either way, mentally or physically'; 'I'm like the revenge of the media'. And the monumental scale of his work, the sculpted reliefs, the references to Albert Speer show a love of megalomaniac classicism of the terrorist sort. This sado-masochism is, of course, ultimately ambiguous, being a subversive form of art in one context and a heightening of bombast and careerism in another. It's tempting to say of Robert Longo, as of the Post-Modern Classical architect Ricardo Bofill, that the megalomania is quite salutary as long as it isn't catching and the monuments remain singular. Rather like the Pompidou Centre in Paris – one is invigorating, two a disaster.

An artist who bears comparison with Robert Longo, and who would no doubt be surprised to hear it, is the Scottish poet Ian Hamilton Finlay. His works, although not erotic or bombastic, are good examples of the current Subversive Classicism. Like Longo's, his work is very autobiographical and he creates it with other artists and helpers, including his wife Susan Finlay. Instead of being based on performances, its location is the political and media event itself. And the media is so mixed – including photos, pamphlets, sculpture, gardens, art works, model battleships and engraved stones – as to defy any simple marketing strategy New York City might come up with. When the time comes to collect Finlay's classicism, it's going to take a grand gesture from the National Monument's Board, or an Act of Parliament, because it will involve declaring a previously desolate Scottish hillside an important national treasure. What Finlay has been doing, systematically since 1978, is turning this windswept moor into a rural Acropolis while, at the same time, showing how recalcitrant are the official powers of law and culture. Finlay has declared 'war' on these powers and although he is losing the legal battles, he is winning the fight of ideas: 'The battle of Little Sparta' as he has termed this long-term art/political event.

Finlay, called 'Scotland's greatest concrete-poet' in the 1960s, combines writing, conceptual art and sculpture into an effective and amusing whole. In his picturesque garden, for instance, is one small memorial stone, a Neoclassical slab placed under a tree with a double-entendre cut into the surface: 'Bring Back the Birch'. Allusions to Poussin and Claude in his landscape designs get the stone inscriptions 'See POUSSIN Hear Lorrain'. Where one comes across configurations of reeds and trees that resemble an Albrecht Dürer, Finlay hangs on a branch in front of this view a stone with the artist's monogram AD, 1975. (30). This art of labelling and writing captions, out of fashion in an aesthetic age, is as much in the tradition of the Chinese garden as the classical one. The visual arts aren't really 'finished' until the captions are written; or at least they remain necessarily ambiguous without such strong conventions.

Some of the most provocative captions are those Finlay wrote for *The Third Reich Revisited*, 1982; graphic works that he and Ian Appelton realised together. These show, for instance, the elevation of Albert Speer's *Reichskanzlei* in Berlin – the ultimate piece of fascist classicism – with the central lintel inscribed 'Small is Quite Beautiful', and a revealing, witty comment below the image. Another drawing shows the National Monument on Carlton Hill – the unfinished Parthenon of Edinburgh's unfinished Acropolis (Edinburgh used to be known as the 'Athens of the North'). Finlay describes the reason for the chiselled lettering 'EVENTS ARE A DISCOURSE', and tells how his eighteenth-century vigilantes would have managed to inscribe this polemical slogan.

> Working overnight with muffled chisels, Saint-Just Vigilantes letter-carvers have added lettering to the frieze of the unfinished classical monument . . . The classic Roman letter-style harmonised with the architecture to the extent that the aphorism went unnoticed by citizens and city authorities for several weeks. Once it was discovered, there was little the authorities could do but accept the fait accompli; to *restore* an embarrassingly uncompleted, historical monument would have been too much . . .[14]

A wonderfully mad but just and creative idea this. 'Events are a discourse' is Finlay's basic point and he is tireless in creating events. Another,

3.30 Ian Hamilton Finlay, *AD (Albrecht Dürer)*, Little Sparta, 1975 (Photograph C. Jencks/Courtesy the artist)

slightly manic intervention is *Apollo in George Street*, 1982 (31), in which the Greek god is given a machine gun and the following explanation.

> The statue is stone, the sub-machine gun is only plaster. It was added by disillusioned Abstractionists, as a protest, but *looked* so acceptable that it remained unnoticed till the plaster was damaged by frost and the addition fell off. Apollo's emblems are the bow-and-arrow, and lyre; the gun is only the former, appropriately up-dated (though unlikely to be approved of by present fashion).

One of the enigmas of the 1970s and 1980s is the failure of pluralist democracy to produce a public art for itself. Where (except possibly in the new Sculpture Parks) is there any public celebration of radical secularism? Of ecological utilitarianism? Of caution-at-all-costs free conformism? Of Benthamite pacifism?[15]

This query explains Finlay's use of Nazi Classicism as a critique: by changing its labels and meanings it becomes a challenge to the present. The classical work and buildings that Finlay builds around his *private* home should be seen as a lyrical lament for the loss of the *res publica* (32). But it's also funny and mad. In fact, if one considers Finlay's continuous 'war' with the authorities then three historical parallels come to mind. First is the high-minded civil disobedience of Henry Thoreau and other figures now sanctioned by history as the heroes of democracy; the mythic protagonists of the French and American revolutions (whose real tawdriness Finlay is prepared to admit). Second there are the bitterly funny polemics of Jonathan Swift. And finally there is Monty Python's low comedy – the mad-cap antics of Finlay and his Saint-Just Vigilantes in setting up their 'panzer' divisions to repel the onslaught of the Scottish authorities (this battle was documented for the media in the style of a Python cartoon). But it would be wrong to think 'The Battle of Little Sparta' is just amusing, it's also very serious; like all good satire it brings out truths about everyday life. What his war has proved (if it needed proving) is that 'the law has been treated as the property of the class which holds power'.

This is not the place to recount the 'tempest in a cow-byre', which has been done many times and at length.[16] But the principle events are these. The Finlays had a semi-ruined cow-byre next to their modest cottage which they converted into a 'Canova-type temple', a 'garden temple'. Finlay contends that as a quasi-religious edifice, based on the precedents of eighteenth-century Neoclassical garden temples in Great Britain, the building should not have been taxed as a commercial building even though works of art were contained in it. Since 1978 Finlay and others have been trying to get the powers-that-be (The Scottish Arts Council and the Strathclyde Regional Council) to enter into a discussion of what a 'garden temple' is and whether it is liable for tax. This they have refused to do with a bureaucratic indifference that proves Finlay's major point: the law is used and defined most effectively by those who have power. Works of art have been confiscated from this temple by the authorities and the only time they took

3.31 Ian Hamilton Finlay, *Apollo in George Street*, 1982 (Drawing Ian Appleton/Courtesy the artist)

3.32 Ian Hamilton Finlay, *Temple of Apollo*, Little Sparta, 1978-84 (Photograph Andrew Griffiths/Courtesy the artist)

note of Finlay's objections was when an American owner of one of the pieces – the Wadsworth Athenaeum of Connecticut – asked the assistance of the US State Department to have it returned. The work was promptly released.

Clearly there are two sides to this story, but as told by Finlay and his supporters the Strathclyde Regional Council will never state its position on garden temples and their rating assessment: they just hold onto the confiscated art. As this 'war', or from Finlay's view 'legalised violence', drags on, he continues to build Little Sparta and it has now become quite an idyllic landscape of temples, votive columns, inscriptions, primitive huts and small lakes (33). It could almost be the Roman campagna of a Poussin or Claude except for the relentless Scottish mist. But it is a fitting, if modest, successor to eighteenth-century classical gardens, those at Stowe and Stourhead, which have their Temples of Ancient Virtue in the garden: quasi-religious structures intended to instil an *exemplum virtutis*. And the whole is dedicated to 'the neoclassical triumvirate of Robespierre, Saint-Just and J. L. David'; those who fought for a public, moral art. The last words in Finlay's booklet *Liberty, Terror and Virtue*, put his larger case succinctly: 'The war has produced a quantity of art; what it has not yet produced (in Britain as opposed to Europe) is serious didactic *thought* on its *causes* – the chief of which is, that where the Arts once overlapped with Religion, they now overlap with tourism and entertainment, and there is no form or mode for the non-secular in our society.'[17]

Embattled in his little patch of windy moor, which he never leaves, Finlay seems destined to prove his point even if it makes his life unpleasant. He has made Everyman's gripe over income tax into a larger cause, a question of religion and cultural definition. It might not be Solzhenitsyn fighting the Politburo, or Martin Luther King taking on Washington, but there is a public point to this battle and it gives his classicism a focus more defined than Robert Longo's: the definition and place of the 'non-secular' in our culture. We are here back to eighteenth-century didactic art.

3.33 Ian Hamilton Finlay, *The Present Order is the Disorder of the Future – Saint Just*, 1983, stone with Nicholas Sloan (Photograph David Paterson/Courtesy the artist)

CHAPTER IV
Allegorical Classicism

Implicit Allegory

Post-Modern painters characteristically approach allegory in an oblique manner, swerving away from the centre of traditional subject matter to catch it from the side. Their allegories are sometimes enigmatic and surreal – as we have seen in the case of Sandro Chia and Gérard Garouste – a pretext for a 'return to painting' and portrayal of a personal vision. The painters discussed in this chapter, for the most part Anglo-Saxon, are also subjective in their use of historical allusion, but their conventions are more recognisably part of the classical tradition. They adopt the familiar models and formulae of representation, emphasise human anatomy, and use many classical motifs such as the well-proportioned figure set in a timeless landscape.

Traditional allegory is the narrative description of one subject under the guise of another which is similar. Post-Modern allegory, however, is the implicit suggestion of a contemporary story under the guise of a historical narrative, and it is thus often unclear exactly what moral is to be drawn. In Swift's *Tale of the Tub*, or Bunyan's *Pilgrim's Progress* the allegory is clear and singular; with contemporary artists the allegory is often veiled and plural, allowing several readings. Many times it refers to the condition of art and culture today, a general rather than specific story. This paradox of Implicit Allegory is therefore a distortion since conventional allegory consists of an analogy between two identifiable stories whereas here there is only one plot: the historical subject matter. The contemporary story is missing or diffused in a labyrinth of speculation. But whether we decide to call this paradoxical genre 'allegory' or something else, it is still a most important mode of Post-Modern artists and writers. They have turned implication itself into the ostensible parable of their art.

Martha Mayer Erlebacher, wife of the sculptor Walter Erlebacher who has also explored contemporary allegory, is a master of anatomical painting. Human figures recline, leap and twist in all the standard positions, as if they were classical dancers, or models in a seventeenth-century studio. But she places these exercises of the body and brush against a strangely contrasting background, often a bleak, rocky mountainscape which seems as reminiscent of Mantegna's landscapes as the primeval world. The draped and nude figures of her *In a Garden*, 1976 (1), jump out from the landscape like well-nourished plants sprouting in the desert. Their faces and poses are as contemporary as the landscape is ancient. This incongruity is heightened by the fact that the 'garden' consists of a few leaves and a barren tree. It might just as well be titled *Not in a Garden*, or *Anatomical Lessons in Classical*

4.1 Martha Mayer Erlebacher, *In a Garden*, 1976, oil on canvas, 64x64in (Frances and Robert Kohler Collection/Courtesy Robert Schoelkopf Gallery, NYC)

101

Foreshortening and Contraposto with Acknowledgements to Mantegna's 'Dead Christ' and the Large-Format Camera. It is a contemporary interpretation of a mythological paradise, showing a Garden of Eden turned grey after an influx of well-fed Amazons. Hedonism and current technology have evidently violated nature.

This conjectural interpretation seems more plausible when one looks at two paintings made eight years later: *Scene from a Picnic I: Anger* and *Scene from a Picnic II: Sloth*, 1984 (2, 3). Here the allegories are much clearer and more melodramatic. In *Anger* (2), a well-endowed athlete turns towards the viewer as he threatens two recoiling women with a karate-chop. Other men stomp the ground or slump over in despairing rage. A figure in the background flees in the well-heeled manner of a Poussin, while a grimacing blond clenches her fist at the heavens. What, if we rule out ants, has caused this anger at the picnic? Several cues suggest the cause is contemporary culture. The fleeing hero in the background has an arrow shot through his cowboy hat, the sadistic athlete in the foreground sports a ridiculous 1970s moustache, and plastic plates and spoons are strewn around as on any suburban beach. The impulse to escape to an idyllic retreat has been ruined by the things people bring with them, above all themselves.

This is seen also in the next scene, *Sloth* (3), where the melodrama becomes quite droll. Our sadist, again exposing himself to admiration, looks out at the viewer with that brazen, vacant stare so typical of narcissistic culture. His headset is plugged in even if his mind is not. Empty beer bottles and bent ginger ale cans tell the story as much as the bloated *odalisques*, a story repeated again and again on every beach in the west: relaxation and indulgence have turned into the cult of the tumescent body, the triumph of consumption over the consumer. The snoring blond, with pursed lips and sunning goggles, sums up the ridiculousness of the whole scene.

These are not Bruegel's healthy peasants enjoying a drunken nap, although they recall both them and other classical bacchanals. Rather, they are a group of swinging singles who have found themselves repeating in a new key, and unwittingly, a great pastoral dream, the picnic in Arcadia. Through their expressions and trappings Erlebacher lets us know that she knows this tradition of idyllic communion is both dead and alive, a theme we shall see reiterated by many painters. It is a virtue of Erlebacher's skill that she can indulge in such obvious allegory without falling into pastiche. Because her irony is as controlled as her draughtsmanship we can read the allegory as both a form of social realism *and* as classical revival. She is saying, in effect, that we all enjoy a picnic with beautiful people in a beautiful place, but that this eternal impulse has to be enjoyed with the ambivalence of a culture that knows it is a cliché – and now even a polluting one. Erlebacher's irony allows both the ideal and the real to be expressed.

Claudio Bravo, a Chilean-born painter, is another skilled draughtsman who makes use of classical subject matter and motifs, but his allegories tend to be more naive and straightforward – that is not Post-Modern. He will paint

4.2 Martha Mayer Erlebacher, *Scene from a Picnic I: Anger*, 1984, oil on canvas, 64x103½in (Courtesy Robert Schoelkopf Gallery, NYC)

4.3 Martha Mayer Erlebacher, *Scene from a Picnic II: Sloth*, 1984, oil on canvas, 64x103½in (Courtesy Robert Schoelkopf Gallery, NYC)

4.4 Claudio Bravo, *The Temptation of St. Anthony*, 1984, oil on canvas, 94x66½in (Courtesy Marlborough Gallery, NYC)

4.5 Bruno Civitico, *Mars and Venus*, 1983, 54x63in (Courtesy Robert Schoelkopf Gallery, NYC)

4.6 Bruno Civitico, *Danae*, 1980, oil on canvas, 60x72in (Photograph Andy Edgar/Courtesy Robert Schoelkopf Gallery, NYC)

a classical *Crucifiction* or *Danae* with only the slightest indication that these allegories are implausible for us. But his work transcends a possible bathos because it is so well controlled and meticulously painted. His *The Temptation of St. Anthony*, 1984 (4), a rather heavy-handed allegory, is composed with such beautiful light, colour and shape that we can overlook the banal satire. It is so underplayed that only on second glance do we notice what the angel is carrying and what has happened to the lamb, or see the funny barbecued meat and climbing salamander, the earphones and excrement. These ironic details are meant to make the scene contemporary while remaining subservient to the overall theme of temptation. The danger of such genre painting, however, is that it becomes an old allegory reclothed in modern dress, rather than a fresh investigation of the subject. The contemporary touches then seem gratuitous. For instance, whereas Erlebacher uses hi-fi headphones to make a point about self-involved narcissism, Bravo puts them on one of his tempters simply because they're contemporary.

The greatest danger a Post-Modernist faces when he takes on historical allegory is incongruity. Bruno Civitico, an Italian-born artist who lives in New Hampshire, has been painting 'modern Classicist' works since the early 1970s. Inspired by his teacher Gabriel Laderman to look at Puvis de Chavannes, he found in this artist, as did many other New York artists at the time, a pre-Modernist who was both abstract and classical. Like Lennart Anderson and Milet Andrejevic he studied Puvis for his subtle use of colour and sculptural form as well as his Arcadian subject matter.[1] The latter has resulted in mythic pastoral compositions – bathers, musicians and children sporting in an unpolluted countryside. Civitico, looking for an allegory which is both fabulous and real, sets *Mars and Venus*, 1982-3 (5), in a Cape Cod seascape, a rather incongruous juxtaposition which is made stranger still by the way in which a Lolita-type with a gun regards the divine couple. Is she one of those prematurely knowing girls of Balthus, or some modern-day goddess about to level Venus with her double-barrelled Beretta? The conventions of mythology and *Playgirl* magazine seem to be consciously and somewhat confusingly mixed here, and Civitico has indeed explained this as an attempt at 'personal synthesis', the mixing of the 'abstractionist/expressionist/ naturalist lines of our tradition': 'The partial, mutually exclusive theories that we face present criteria that cannot accommodate acknowledged masterpieces of the past. In its incompleteness, it limits our own possibilities.'[2]

The desire for a personal synthesis may be exemplary, but it is achieved in only a few works by any Post-Modern Classicist. One early success of Civitico's was his *The Death of Eudamidas*, a new version of Lucian's story of the Greek who, on his deathbed, gives the care of his mother and daughter to his friends. Here the drama of parting is effectively translated to a spare New England bedroom, and the allegory attains more than a classical allusion. His *Danae*, 1980 (6), is another successful synthesis where the two stories of the allegory are plausibly fused. Danae, a comely nude, turns to the window, opens her bathrobe and exposes her body to the brilliantly enveloping

4.7

4.9

sunlight, a golden shower that sparkles over the houseplant while illuminating the distant landscape. In a contemporary context this might be an innocent act repeated a thousand times every spring in New England. The setting and classical composition seem entirely plausible; the handling of the figure and the frontal layering, while reminiscent of Poussin and Balthus, are unforced. The allegorical plot of Danae, locked up in her bronze house only to be impregnated by the golden light of Zeus, is kept on a secondary level, thus informing the primary meaning without disturbing it. Here is a rare case of synthesis without incongruity.

Lincoln Perry, who also studied with Gabriel Laderman, has, like Civitico, taken the large figurative composition from the classical tradition and applied it to contemporary life. Again the scene is New England, or rather New New England, a pastoral version of what the state would be like today *sans* megalopolis. The people, events and architecture depicted by Perry exist in a peaceful atmosphere without automobiles or a high divorce rate. It is an upper-class idyll of family and university life as seen by a nineteenth-century visionary and, not surprisingly, H. H. Richardson's buildings appear in the background. *Work*, 1984-5 (7), an allegory about creative labour, presents an architect's office as a smoothly run machine, showing a well-ordered sequence of discussions between architect and client, with a conscientious team led by a suave matron in a Laura Ashley dress making a presentation of drawings and sumptuous models. Woman and man, black and white, young and old, draughtsman and principal form the amicable brotherhood in this liberal atmosphere. It's all a bit unreal, flattering and nostalgic, although this is not necessarily a drawback since all Classicism has an element of historicist idealism in it. More disturbing is that the architecture and characterisation are left at the level of stereotype and Perry's admirable desire to reintroduce drama into painting has no actual subject. We feel that the protagonists are simply posturing, that their interest in the models they peruse is feigned.

More convincing are *Wedlock and Hierogamy*, 1983 (8) and *Afternoon, Plaza*, 1985 (9). Here the devices, reworked from Mannerist and Baroque *sacra conversazione*, draw us into the picture. The gaze of the artist out of the canvas catches our eye directly. The gestures of discussion, or a sudden awkward movement, engage our imagination. Perry has written of his attempt to involve the viewer, as the theatre does, by using the conventions of drama and everyday life; gestures, stances and clothing which have an implicit meaning.

> If there is a subject that runs through my work, it is the necessity and difficulty of making some sense of our world. In our attempt to find or create meaning, painting seems most right when it is metaphoric, when we can react to it on a number of levels. I have a tendency to think of spatial locations – left, right, up, down, forward and backward – as corresponding to choices or ironies in our lives, or as levels of conviction.[3]

4.8

4.7 Lincoln Perry, *Work*, 1984-5, oil on canvas, 7x12 ft (Courtesy Tatistcheff & Co. Inc., NYC)

4.8 Lincoln Perry, *Wedlock and Hierogamy*, 1983, oil on canvas, 52x42in (Courtesy Tatistcheff & Co. Inc., NYC)

4.9 Lincoln Perry, *Afternoon, Plaza*, 1985, oil on canvas, 50x62in (Courtesy Tatistcheff & Co. Inc., NYC)

Thus, in *Wedlock and Hierogamy*, where the allegory presumably concerns the relation between individuals and couples at an open house and at different stages of romantic and married life, all the points are conveyed through placement in space. 'Adolescent and sexual love' are presented near the open door and appropriately by the garden; 'union' is presented by the artist embracing his wife and sister (?); 'motherhood' stands silhouetted in front of a Palladian window, again gazing out at the viewer; and, on the same level, 'age' confronts 'childhood'. Perry has successfully interwoven the inherent drama of architecture and the stages of emotional life, although whether the contrast between real and ideal love is conveyed remains questionable. *Wedlock and Hierogamy*, or 'marriage and sacred union' is a powerful expression of antithesis rather than an accomplished drama.

Afternoon, Plaza, while highly theatrical, really does capture the quiet afternoon life of a New England campus (although Harvard Square and its *conversazione* are never quite so peaceful because of all the traffic noise). But the ideal presented here is both plausible and witty. A forbidding shadow, caused by an intruding skyscraper, cuts across this campus scene, menacing its composure. In the background is the ideal precinct of academia, a classical temenos of the type still found in many Ivy League colleges. In the foreground a fulsome co-ed drops a book awkwardly, a sitting figure (the artist?) turns to look, while a stylish student (?) holds her professor (?) at bay. Other conventions of dress and gesture classify the everyday drama in the midground and distance. There is probably no allegory intended here, but the daily life outside the Ivy Tower is given a peaceful dignity as if it were a lesson in urbane living. Lincoln Perry, like so many contemporary artists, prefers to leave the overall plot ambiguous and implicit.

An artist who, to my mind, achieves an extraordinary tension in his work through the use of implicit allegory is Stone Roberts. His painstaking realism, like that of a Dutch genre painting, always suggests much more than it reveals. The build-up of architectural detail, light, dress and symbolic flora and fauna is so exquisite that, apart from taking years to finish, it implies some disturbing significance beyond its modest appearance. Like the work of Jan Van Eyck it appears to contain some hidden Christian emblems. *Janet*, 1984 (10), portrays a girl disturbed while having coffee. Half her face starts to smile, the other half withdraws in apprehension. A dog sniffs a fallen lily on a Persian carpet. Light pours in through open windows and illuminates the pendant lamp, as in Van Eyck's *Marriage of Arnolfini and his Wife*. A glass is broken, shears lie open. Only the 1960s red steel chair displaces the sense of a timeless Dutch genre scene. But what do the clues add up to? Are the lily and cut pears and peaches on the table some comment on lost virginity, or expectant motherhood, or is this just a domestic portrait of Janet? Implications of meaning are here sustained at a very high pitch to suggest that the domestic realm is sacred.

The Conversation, 1985 (11), a larger canvas, sustains the same perturbing ambiguity with even more detail. There is so much going on that the unities of

4.10 Stone Roberts, *Janet*, 1984, oil on canvas, 60x54in (Photograph Robert Schoelkopf Gallery, NYC/Courtesy Metropolitan Museum of Art, NYC)

4.11 Stone Roberts, *The Conversation*, 1985, oil on canvas, 72x90in (Photograph Eeva Inkeri/Courtesy Robert Schoelkopf Gallery, NYC)

classical design and theme are pushed to breaking point. This, presumably, is life in the gracious American south, as opposed to Lincoln Perry's cultivated north-east. The manners, dress and gesture are much more specified here than in other contemporary paintings. *The Conversation* is close to a novel of Balzac or Mary McCarthy in its build-up of the implication of objects, and we must interpret this meaning as a detective reconstructs a crime. Evidently it is four o'clock on a winter's afternoon near some large southern city like Atlanta. After a late Sunday lunch the maid comes in to clear away the coffee, fruit and cheese. Guests continue to sip Sauternes. A couple to the left prepare to leave while behind them can be seen the threatening sky of the industrial city. The young son of the house precariously reaches up to steal some fruit while the daughter, with the aid of a curious light, reads an art book under the table. The hostess (?), Janet (?), listens with concern to a departing guest while the host, (the artist?), his jacket discarded, engages two *soignée* women on the chaise longue. His bow tie and wing collar contrast, rather pretentiously, with his suspenders and loafers. The pile-up of objects also tells a story of an eclectic, cultivated life: Neoclassical furniture is mixed with a Chinese coffee table, a 1960s brass light fixture and a discreetly hidden hi-fi speaker. If only it all meant something – if only an event equal to the setting would take place.

Perhaps it has. The expressions and drama across *The Conversation* suggest that it concerns some public event of significance to all the guests: the marriage of a friend is implied by the age and dress of the protagonists. Perhaps, as in T. S. Eliot's *The Cocktail Party*, the artist is trying to find some *sacra conversazione* or hidden ritual in the everyday life of the haute bourgeoisie. In any case the portentous mood is sustained at such a pitch that minor events take on an epic breadth. One is reminded of David Hockney's *Homage to Michelangelo*. This is contemporary allegory at its most a-allegorical.

Several American artists, who in 1985 exhibited in two shows of current classicism, have taken a more overt attitude to the past while being no less enigmatic about the intention of their references.[4] Their reuse of the past is the Post-Modern equivalent to the Modernists' reuse of the present. If the canonic approach for a 1960s Minimalist was to focus on the Tradition of the New and the specific technique of each art form as the subject of art, then the parallel course for the Post-Modernist is to focus on past styles and solutions. This has produced an equally hermetic and nostalgic tradition, although one which is wider in its references. Grant Drumheller, for instance, will recreate the pose of a well-known classical bronze, the Poseidon of Artemision, in his oil painting the *Lightning Thrower*, 1984 (12), partly to recall the past model through paraphrasing it and partly to challenge its meaning. Here Poseidon throws a lightning bolt while other streaks of light flash against a Mannerist heaven. Most of Drumheller's work is placed in the timeless evening of a brooding sky and one wonders just what this muddy atmosphere portends, combining as it does the conventions of mythic twilight with Cézanne and

4.12 Grant Drumheller, *Lightning Thrower*, 1984, oil on canvas, 76x92in (Courtesy the artist)

radioactive gloom. The incongruity of conventions reflects the uncertainty of thematic material; the desire to reanimate the grandeur of past themes fails through lack of a present subject adequate to the task.

This disparity haunts the work of all straight revivalists. Muriel Castanis, who also uses classical formulae, seeks a way around the dilemma by giving the archetypal forms a new material and construction, as if this twist of the medium might revivify the message. She also gives the traditional humanist message an agnostic surprise. Her *Standing Hooded Figure*, 1983 (13), is frozen Greek drapery minus the figure, an archetypal pose missing only its beneficent goddess. Made from cloth stiffened eternally by epoxy resin, this empty representation of the humanist ideal can be taken as either a conventional figure of Death coming to claim another victim, or as an allegorical comment on our time. When several such 'figures' are placed on top of a Johnson and Burgee skyscraper, they seem to imply the ultimate absurdity of our age: iconography without meaning, or agnosticism in search of the nameless and faceless hero (14). 'The presence of the absence' is such a well-known convention of both Late- and Post-Modernism today that it requires no elaboration. Sharron Quasius and Judith Brown, two Americans, also work with three-dimensional transformations of old themes into new materials. Where Brown uses smashed automobile fenders and steel frames to render the suggestion of Greek dancers, Quasius uses floppy polyester fibre on cotton duck for her versions of the historical epic. I suppose the inspiration must be Oldenburg's soft typewriter. Quasius' *Rape of the Sabine Women in the Manner of Poussin*, 1980, is an all-white travesty of its source, a parody which gains what dignity it has from the abstraction and reduction of this war to the condition of a pillow fight – or at least a pleasantly squashy tableau (15). Virtues of the original model are allowed to unfold through this pastiche. The parallel is with architects such as Philip Johnson who have also adopted previous models as 'ready-mades', only translating their scale and material, with the idea that this Duchampian act can confer a minimum form of creative beauty on the object. In some instances it also confers nostalgia on the object, a sentiment which can be positive when used in a critical manner as the French Revolutionists employed it, or negative, when used predictably.

Nostalgic Classicism

Nostalgia, a concept deriving from the Greek 'wishing to return home', usually means for us something pejorative, such as 'homesickness as a disease' or 'sentimental yearning for a past period'. There have been epochs, such as the Roman Republic and the American and French Revolutions, when nostalgia has taken on a paranoic strength and condemned the present in the name of an imagined past. Here one speaks not of an introverted mania, but of an extroverted, creative power, the past reformed as an ideal to criticise the present. In a period as fragmented and uprooted as our own, all

4.13 Muriel Castanis, *Standing Hooded Figure*, 1983, epoxy resin and cloth, 77in high (Courtesy OK Harris Works of Art, NYC)

4.14 Philip Johnson & John Burgee, *580 California*, and Muriel Castanis, *Figures*, San Francisco, 1984 (Photograph C. Jencks/ Courtesy the architects and artist)

4.15 Sharron Quasius, *Rape of the Sabine Women in the Manner of Poussin*, 1980, cotton duck with polyester fibre, 10x15x3ft (Courtesy OK Harris Works of Art, NYC)

sorts of nostalgia exist together and one must be careful to distinguish the types. The artists who will be considered next are, respectively, sardonic, naive and tragic in their use of a revived language and set of values.

Two Russian emigrés to America, Vitaly Komar and Aleksander Melamid, work together as an ironic collective of two. The subjects they paint – which have usually to do with the most important figure of their time, Stalin – are depicted in such a direct way as to be disarming. Komar and Melamid use the conventions of Socialist Realism, which have survived intact since Stalin's repression of the avant-garde, as a double critique of Russian neo-academicism and consumerist Pop art. Their own style they call 'Sots Art' and it is as literary and obvious as any historical painting of the nineteenth century or Great American Nude by Tom Wesselmann. It is also, in a sense, nationalistic or implicitly related to Russia as their mother country: it is in the tradition of *What is to be Done?* and the countless other polemical tracts and populist works which address a much wider audience than an avant-garde. One can't think of a western painter, or painting team, who would take on such a mixture of historical painting, populism, kitsch, literary directness and critical irony.

As Peter Wollen argues, their work is a Rabelaisian carnival, a gleeful parody which combines several preexisting genres to produce a sardonic humour.[5] In *Eggs, Coitus and Cicero*, for instance, these three subjects are placed in a literal, linear sequence in five separate frames. Broken shells and yellow yokes confront a Neoclassical pornographic set piece which leads to a pure Constructivist egg piece, then to the Platonic idea of an egg and finally to a frowning Cicero pondering the meaning of life (eggs). The narrative juxtapositions, like a Surrealist game of Exquisite Corpse, oscillate violently between high and low art, avant-garde and kitsch, abstraction and realism – the major antinomies of twentieth-century painting and those which Post-Modernists so often seek to merge.

Their 'history painting' started officially when they worked together at a Young Pioneers Summer Camp in 1972.[6] While collaborating on murals for the Alley of Heroes, it occurred to them that no one was using the heroic-realist style on unofficial paintings such as family portraits. Their ironic displacement of conventions dates from this point and ever since they have developed a literary, autobiographical, even confessional, realism that seems essentially Russian. An open-air show in which they took part was bulldozed by the authorities in 1974 and after emigrating to Israel they settled in America in 1977. Since then their 'Sots Art' has portrayed a bitter-sweet celebration of public figures and icons taken from Soviet history and consumer society. *Portrait of Ronald Reagan as a Centaur*, 1981, shows the President as this classical quadruped waving, as he often does, to a distant audience, but holding a red flag in his outstretched hand – to taunt the Russian bear? *Stroke (ca. Mar. 3 1953)*, 1982-3 (16), shows Stalin being found by one of his fearful inner circle, alone in contorted death. This momentous point in Russian history is obviously a suitable subject for traditional history

4.16 Komar & Melamid, *Stroke (ca. Mar. 3 1953)*, 1982-3, oil on canvas, 72x47in (Photograph D. James Dee/Courtesy Ronald Feldman Fine Arts, NYC)

116

painting and this is one of the few of their canvases that has a chilling dignity. Their best work, to my mind, is ambiguous and controlled, almost believable as traditional Neoclassical painting and not easily dismissed or consumed as a joke. Thus *The Origin of Socialist Realism*, 1982-3 (17), is a fairly competent new version of an old classical myth on one of the origins of art in which the Corinthian maiden Dibutade paints the silhouette of her departing lover that she sees projected on the wall. Here the young Soviet muse cups the chin of Father Stalin, who embraces her with one hand, as she traces his outline on the stone. The severity of the architecture recalls the background of David's *Death of Socrates*, while the treatment of the subject matter stems from the *Corinthian Maidens*, 1782-4, by Joseph Wright of Derby. These references, and indeed the *gravitas* of the work, give the ludicrous subject a much greater resonance than would its more obvious parody, allowing us to see the repressive act of Stalin – his destruction of the avant-garde and his creation of Socialist Realism – as believable and therefore more disturbing. When Komar and Melamid approach 'Sots Art' as a valid style and exploit the craftsmanship within its boundaries, their parody transcends the inherent limits of the one-liner and becomes both funny and sad.

That nostalgic genre can be used for libertarian and subversive ends is a point we have touched on in the previous chapter, but it can also, of course, be used for nostalgic ends. David Ligare, a Californian painter, adopts unadulterated traditional conventions, but puts them to non-ideological use. His polemic, if it can be called that, would change the beautiful rocky hills of northern California into a Greek landscape somewhere near Delphi. *Hermes and the Cattle of Apollo*, 1983 (18, 19), places the messenger god and the divine cows in the sunlit hills of Salinas, California. Late afternoon long shadows play across the rounded hillocks, accentuating the soft, sculptural boldness they actually possess. A meandering stream and heroic rock outcrop frame the idyllic resting place of Hermes, whose winged feet and caduceus can just be discerned. He sits on a stone, cocking his head impishly towards the viewer, proud of having stolen away the herds of Apollo. What can this allegory possibly mean applied to Salinas in 1983? The face and pose of Hermes seem adapted equally from the underworld of pulp magazines and Photo Realism and so one might guess at an ironic intention, but there are no other indications that this is so. In fact Ligare has spoken against irony as the facile orthodoxy of our time and instead sought a humanist 'purpose and wholeness of vision': 'I am first and foremost, then, a *retardataire*. I believe in looking backward as a means of going forward . . . we must search for a new ideal.'[7]

The obvious problem with this idealism, based as it is on Poussin, David and a transference of Greek mythology, is its narrow scope which is limited to the illustration of canonic young men and women placed against the clichés he is bold enough to recommend: 'sun-washed stone, and the "wine-dark" sea' (20). These formulae, however beautifully rendered, remain at the level of American naive painting, of Grant Wood and Grandma Moses, since they

4.17 Komar & Melamid, *The Origin of Socialist Realism*, 1982-3, oil on canvas, 72x48in (Photograph D. James Dee / Courtesy Ronald Feldman Fine Arts, NYC)

4.18,19 David Ligare, *Hermes and the Cattle of Apollo*, 1983, oil on canvas, 51x65in, detail below (Courtesy Koplin Gallery, LA)

tell us little about the painter's personal vision or the world we inhabit. Nostalgic Classicism has here yet to produce the challenging impulse of architects such as Leon Krier, or artists such as Ian Hamilton Finlay.

With the Irish born artist Stephen McKenna the situation is altogether more complex. Some of his work, such as *Jupiter and Antiope*, 1983, or *Europe*, 1981, is a straightforward historical mythology in a manner that combines Van Dyck, Titian and Courbet. There is not, it seems to me, much to be said for these exercises of style except that they have prepared McKenna's mind and vision for a deeper historical view of the present. McKenna, unlike Ligare, is primarily concerned with the fragmentation of classical culture in our century; the fact that our words and thoughts remain implicated in the ruins of a shattered Graeco-Roman and Christian past, while civilisation has marched on in disarray, holding up this past as its gold standard. For this reason the museum, with its neutral presentation of scattered and well-polished fragments, has become the revealing institution of our time.[8]

O, Ilium!, 1982 (21), is one of several historical paintings produced by McKenna, in the early 1980s, that deals with this catastrophic dissolution. It combines the institution of the museum with the Fall of Troy in a complex allegory about the present. Various recognisable fragments are littered about a battle scene that is at the same time a dense piling of sculptures in a classical sculpture court. A dead nude in the centre foreground pulls us into this spectacle, as does the bewildered child just above her. We see headless horses and decapitated temples standing erect. The eye moves in a classical progression forwards and back as if these frontally layered specimens were displayed in a proscenium space.

O, Ilium!, according to Jon Thomson, provides McKenna with the perfect vehicle for an allegory about the end of European culture, because the name refers to the Aeolian society, established briefly by the Romans, which plundered fallen Troy both as an act of cultural homage and for gain.[9] One is reminded of T. S. Eliot's *The Wasteland* – 'These fragments I have shored against my ruins' – and his characterisation of the twentieth-century artist as the uprooted Aeneas, fleeing the burning city of Troy while carrying over his shoulder his father and the remains of his culture. In the painting there is no attempt to make sense of the carnage, or provide a leading plot. Comic-like faces and crude renditions exist side by side with more lyrical inventions. The two protagonists of the drama – the barbaric Trojan horse (destructive technology), and the woman with outstretched arms (a force of humanist reconciliation quoted from David's *Intervention of the Sabine Women*) – are depicted and positioned in such a way as to express the unequal nature of the battle. The Trojan horse, the blind force of multinational materialism, according to one allegorical reading, crushes everything in its way.[10] It is based, ironically, on a primitive terracotta model from Boetia which now resides in the British Museum, a comment perhaps on the triumphant Modernist cult of the primitive. Sexuality, pride, fear and

4.20 David Ligare, *Woman in a Greek Chair (Penelope)*, 1984, oil on canvas, 40x48in (Courtesy Koplin Gallery, LA)

121

4.21 Stephen McKenna, *O Ilium!*, 1982, oil on canvas, 72x100in (Courtesy Galerie Isy Brachot, Brussels)

dismemberment are also presented as essential forces of our existence. In a companion piece, *The Age of Reason*, the 'Bacchanal of Rationalism' is portrayed as an orgy of food, wine, debauchery and modern buildings, as if this equation were a logical consequence of the lost centre. *O, Ilium!*, like these other historical paintings, is a tragicomic lament about this loss and, like the overstocked supermarket of classical busts and stelae lined up in the basement of the British Museum, it disturbs and alienates even while it engages. But the forces of cultural continuity, the Sabine woman and the horse with flying mane, are ultimately defeated by the black Zeus on top of the temple of war.

McKenna's bleak allegories of life are conveyed with a dark hazy technique that does not clarify form in the classical manner. And yet there is a very personal lyrical quality, perhaps derived from Courbet and Böcklin, which gives this work an ebullient undertone. *The Irish Coast*, 1981 (22), shows two tiny men fighting it out against a raging sea, sky and land. Watching over them, however, is a taciturn seagull which, like the frothy sea, undermines the mad frenzy of the scene with a playful irony. *The Italian Consulate in Berlin*, 1984 (23), another implicit allegory about the dilapidated state of classical culture, shows a cheerful cloudy sky and a flowering tree beside the heap of stones and crumbling palazzo. These images of ruin, recalling the Renaissance lament over the evidence of Roman destruction – *sic transit gloria mundi* –resemble not so much conventional evocations of the past, as Second World War photographs of bombed-out cities. If they have a nostalgia it is in their uncompromising belief that Modernism and materialism are in no way legitimate heirs of western culture, but rather barbaric intruders. This view, and the implicit allegories which present it, may be questioned, but McKenna works with a consistency and depth that have to be acknowledged as rare. A Post-Modern allegory of the stature of *Guernica* has yet to be produced, and one imagines that when it is, it will be a more equal confrontation between the past and present than we have yet seen.

4.22 Stephen McKenna, *The Irish Coast*, 1981, oil on canvas, 40x50in (Courtesy Ed Totah Gallery, London)

4.23 Stephen McKenna, *The Italian Consulate in Berlin*, 1984, oil on canvas, 80x110in (Courtesy Berlinische Galerie, W. Berlin)

CHAPTER V
Realist Classicism

Ideal Realism, the Forced Contradiction

Realism has always played a direct, but paradoxical role within the classical tradition. For the Greeks and Romans, as for the academies which revived their example, the representation of reality has always been a contradictory goal. The painter or sculptor would attempt an imitation of what he saw, and this *mimesis* would provide the direction for his efforts. But if he copied what he saw with too much rigour then his work would not be sufficiently unified and ideal. Rather it would wander into an endless enumeration of particulars, and these might not only be unsavoury and ugly, but destructive of the idea behind the appearances. Thus the unsteady hybrid Ideal Realism was formed, and there are many beautiful Greek athletes, warriors and *korai* to show how conventionalised it was. The sculptor was defined in Greece as one who, 'makes an imitation of the body'; but he would also select salient features that made the most of the particular subject in terms of ideal strength, beauty and expression.[1]

One ancient ideal, exemplified in the famous story of Zeuxis, was of an artist who made a simulacrum so convincing that a bird tried to pick a grape from the canvas. Myths of *trompe l'œil*, in one form or another, have always been at the heart of the classical tradition, even though they run counter to the demands of unity of theme and harmony of the whole. This inherent contradiction has been explored in the writings of Ernst Gombrich, particularly in his *Art and Illusion*, 1960, and we now understand why there are several different realisms based on different conventions of representation.[2] All pictorial illusions are based on a complex interplay between 'making and matching', 'schema and correction', or the traditions of the artist and the object to be captured. That this is true helps explain why there are always competing realisms, a pluralism which current writers on the subject have not only accepted but accentuated as the condition of Post-Modern practice.[3] Three fundamental types, evolving from the past, dominate the late 1960s and early 1970s.

Artists such as Lucien Freud and Philip Pearlstein reject the notion of the ideal human figure and portray the body in a limp and flaccid state, as much to make a social or psychological point as to provoke the viewer. The body as a metaphor of human existence, of our rather tired, distracted and melancholic age, is implied if never stated. A parody of sexuality is also suggested by the way vast stretches of the body are focused on, as in a *Playboy* centrefold, only to be turned into slabs of sagging meat. Philip Pearlstein, for instance, crops his paintings as a photographer would a

5.1 Philip Pearlstein, *Two Female Models on Bentwood Loveseat and Rug*, 1974-5, oil on canvas, 60x72in (Courtesy Allan Frumkin Gallery, NYC)

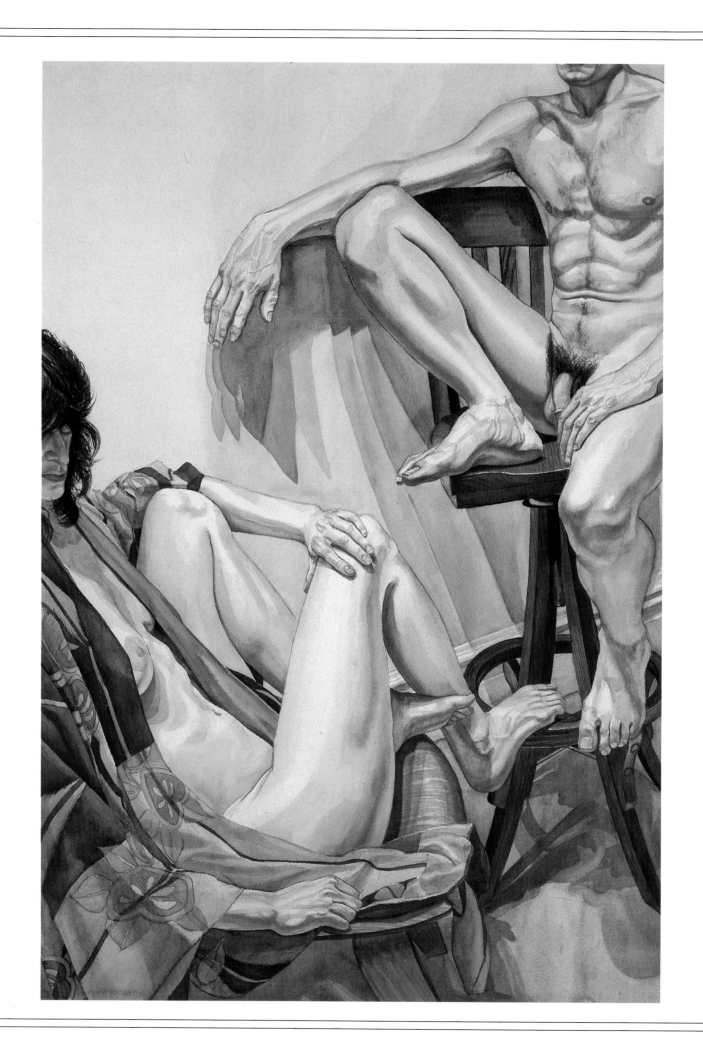

photograph and sets his mental camera at an oblique angle. *Two Female Models on Bentwood Loveseat and Rug*, 1974-5 (1), is characteristic of his work in its cropping, extreme foreshortening and off-centre viewpoint. Various Modernist devices that accentuate movement, transience and immodesty are set in counterpoint to the implied classical nude which is usually presented frontally, framed on a pedestal. Pearlstein's rotating and falling figures imply these counterparts so vividly that we begin to think of them as studio nudes caught between poses, in much the same way as Degas caught ballerinas off balance. The way parts of the body such as the ear are rendered in detail, or the rug and skirting board elaborated, suggests the endless, democratic empiricism to which some realists are committed. Linda Nochlin has shown how classicists and Modernists alike consider this lack of hierarchy and focus a 'crime'.[4] Looked at as a set of conventions, however, this type of realism is anything but unfocused – there is always a high degree of selection.

With Pearlstein the body is almost always shown at rest, so that breasts or arms and other limbs dangle without strength, without muscle tension (2). The characters portrayed are often past their prime, with double chins or bulging veins and their skin glistens with an unhealthy pallor. This psychological realism, deriving from literary conventions, is quite distinct from a genre that could be termed abstract or archetypal realism that had a wide following at the time of Pop Art. Alex Katz, for instance, takes figures from Long Island beach-life and essentialises their attributes. Thus heads become larger than life-size, hair falls in glistening plaits and skin takes on a graphic sheen, as much a sunbather's ideal as a Katz trademark (3). It is impossible at this level of abstraction to distinguish between social comment and idealism – to know whether these characters are being criticised for their hedonistic vacuity or celebrated for their eternal body worship – and it's no doubt an intention of Katz to remain studiously neutral, to present a minute of life in the Hamptons of Long Island as its essence.

A similar neutrality pervades the Photo Realist work of Richard Estes but it is much less abstract in its graphic reductions and much more committed to enumerating particulars. We can speak of his work as showing a third major genre, urban realism, which is no less related to classical conventions than the psychological and abstract realisms discussed above. An early painting, *Hot Foods*, 1967 (4), contrasts the reflection of centrally disposed architecture with an ephemeral background of lights, advertisement and urban squalor. An intense figure, dwarfed by the image of the Empire State Building, argues a point with someone who has disappeared, at least visually, because of the reflections. Perhaps this is an ironic illustration of 'Hot Foods', which can be seen in the background, and the overall meaning of this and other urban scenes is to emphasise the rather baneful triumph of monumentality over the contingent, of frozen beauty over life.

In *Alitalia*, 1973 (5), however, Estes treats the fleeting images of vehicles with the same concern as he does the classical column that can just be

5.3 Alex Katz, *Beach Scene*, 1966, oil on canvas, 64½x48in (Courtesy Robert Miller Gallery Inc., NYC)

5.2 Philip Pearlstein, *Female on Eames Chair, Male on Swivel Stool*, 1981, watercolour on paper, 60x40in (Courtesy Allan Frumkin Gallery, NYC)

5.4

5.5

5.4 Richard Estes, *Hot Foods*, 1967, oil on canvas, 48x30in (Courtesy Louis K. Meisel Gallery, NYC)

5.5 Richard Estes, *Alitalia*, 1973, oil on canvas, 30x40in (Stuart M. Spiesner Collection, Smithsonian Institution, Washington DC/Courtesy Louis K. Meisel Gallery, NYC)

glimpsed through the glass plane. This conjunction of the ephemeral and permanent was recommended by Charles Baudelaire as showing the 'heroism of Modern life', along with the 'eternal and immovable' in art. The antinomies must be given equal weight by the Modern painter in order, as Craig Owens has explained, to rescue modernity for eternity.[5] Here Estes has given an ultra-real New York airline agency a classical, frontal composition, a geometrically controlled layering and symmetry, one point perspective, and a host of traditional signs of stasis such as the column. These contrast with the transparency and fleeting images – a hybrid opposition typical of Post-Modern Classicism. In one sense, as the inheritor of Zeuxis and Apelles, it is typical also of canonic classicism: it would not only fool birds and horses but even the unwary urbanite who is always walking into glass ·walls. The urban realist accepts the ephemeral squalor of the city and presents this with monumentality, alienation and humour. Other American realists such as Ralph Goings, Duane Hanson and Robert Cottingham fail to achieve Estes' Baudelairean mixture of the transitory and classical, but two masters of realist sculpture, John De Andrea and Robert Graham, do achieve a similar stoic neutrality and, in different ways, are exemplars of the ideal realist contradiction.

If Philip Pearlstein knocks contemporary woman off her pedestal, then John De Andrea puts her right back on it, smoothes out the wrinkles, tones up the muscles, shampoos the hair and adds what appears to be a sheen of Pond's Ultra-Pink Skin Care No. 5 (6). This does not rescue suburban woman from enforced idleness, however, nor from the pensive melancholia which De Andrea makes her eternal state. Called by such abstractions as *Seated Blond with Crossed Arm* or *Seated Brunette on Pedestal*, these archetypes are just as sad and distracted as Pearlstein's. They inhabit a white minimalist space as stripped of time and culture as their pearly bodies. Often they are given a classical pose, which may recall Rodin's couples and nineteenth-century formulae (7). Their persona is thus arrested somewhere between an eternal ideal of bodily perfection and the kitsch of contemporary narcissism as purveyed through magazine culture. De Andrea presents the heroines of *Vogue, Harpers* and *Town & Country* as they must feel in their more lonely moments, just after the bath, when they ask themselves existentially – 'what are all the aerobics for?' These moments are not angst-ridden, this is not St. Augustine looking into his soul, or even the introspection of Norman Mailer, but rather that fleeting emptiness which comes to overtrained athletes between events.

The sculptures, as a group, have an uncanny presence. Being life-size they seem at first not only to be naked, living individuals trapped in their most flattering poses, but actually moving bodies. This illusion is sustained as one walks around them and they seem to rotate. Their presence, which owes much to the theatre and waxworks, plays on the deepest forces of perception as we quite naturally project animation into anthropomorphic images. Trompe l'œil, in this sense, finds its greatest realisation in illusions of the

5.6 John De Andrea, *Seated Brunette on Pedestal*, 1983, polyvinyl polychromed in oil, lifesize (Photograph D. James Dee/Courtesy OK Harris Works of Art, NYC)

5.7 John De Andrea, *Seated Man and Woman*, 1981, polyvinyl polychromed in oil, lifesize (Photograph D. James Dee/Courtesy OK Harris Works of Art, NYC)

5.8 John De Andrea, *Self Portrait with Sculpture*, 1980, polyvinyl polychromed in oil, lifesize (Courtesy OK Harris Works of Art, NYC)

132

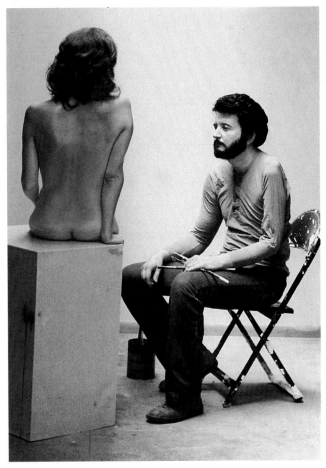

human body and one imagines that if Polygnotus or Lysippus could have used polyvinyl and all the latest technologies of cosmetic painting, they too would have created such virtuosic pieces of illusionistic skin. One has to admire the inventive use of all the current paints and plastics now at the artist's disposal. However, what makes De Andrea's sculpture so different from that of the Greeks is not the technology, nor the intentions of trompe l'œil, but the subject matter and mood of the portraits; the fact that these are the privatised idols of commercialised beauty, not the public statesmen or athletic heroes of the time.

When De Andrea places himself in opposition to his Pygmalion, he shatters the illusion of the *Vogue* beauty only to create a more disturbing image of sexuality. Destroying the convention of the 'artist and model', he casts himself, and thus by implication the observer as well, in the role of the 'dressed voyeur in the studio' (8). The blank, impassive stare of the artist tells us no more than does the stylised smile of a *kouros* – perhaps an indication that the artist sublimates his personality to the canons of craft as much as his anti-heroines do to the canons of fashion. In any case, the work is deftly ambiguous enough to mean opposite things to different people. To some it conveys a quiet dignity and respect for craftsmanship and sensitive detail, the closest thing to the antique combination of painting and sculpture that America produces; and it is true that the sculptures create an aura that forces the viewer to approach with a quiet respect. To others it conveys a neutral acquiescence to commercialism, a typical triumph of slick-tech over content. Both interpretations have validity since De Andrea obsessively idealises the upper-middle-class dream while at the same time attaining an exact 'copy' of reality, cast from life and polished to perfection.

Robert Graham's obsessively 'real' sculptures also seem as much Greek or Roman as Modern. Graham treats the human torso in its archetypal posture as part specimen and part ideal type. Since the measurement and understanding of the body – not to say the production of large bronze casts – is best achieved by a frontal positioning, Graham often uses an Egyptian or archaic Greek pose. The model is placed in a monumental position, legs slightly apart, arms at rest at the side, and in *Torso I*, 1974-5 (9), the gesture is repeated in the massive bronze base. It is of interest that Graham, like so many of the painters discussed here, uses geometrically defined architecture to underline his work.[6] (He has also designed and built the Doumani house in Los Angeles, a building which sets off the many collected art works with a very cool, white monumentality.)

There is, in addition to the architectural presence in his sculpture, a very sensual quality due partly to the age and physical grace of his models (10). A straightforward athletic sexuality – which has its inevitable classical counterpart – seems ready to burst out of these bronzes. Indeed in many respects Graham, a Mexican-born sculptor living in southern California, seems closer in spirit to the Greeks than De Andrea and this may result from the essential gravity of his works. They are real and ideal without being flattering; abstract

5.10 Robert Graham, *Cherie*, 1980, bronze, 71½x10½x6¼in (Courtesy the artist)

5.9 Robert Graham, *Torso I*, 1974-5, bronze, 22x9x4in (Courtesy the artist)

5.11 *Marble Female Figure*, 'Acropolis 686', early fifth century B.C., life-size (Courtesy Acropolis Museum, Athens)

5.12 Robert Graham, *Olympic Arch*, 1984, bronze and granite, Los Angeles (Photograph C. Jencks/Courtesy the artist)

5.13 Robert Graham, *Olympic Arch*, 1984

5.14 Robert Graham, *Olympic Arch*, 1984, close up of female athlete

5.15 George Segal, *Jacob and the Angels*, 1984, plaster, wood, plastic and rock (Photograph C. Jencks/Courtesy Sidney Janis Gallery, NYC)

and archetypal without being romantic. A frank honesty, archaic and even animalistic, is conveyed. Sometimes the head and legs are missing from the statue and these truncations serve to essentialise further the direct, wild sensuality, again like the broken, archaic *korai* that can be found in the Acropolis Museum (11). Indeed Graham's obsessive perfecting of his bronze craft, using the *cire-perdue* (lost-wax) casting method and several stages of remodelling, is the equivalent of the Greek emphasis on *techné*. His work is also more classical than De Andrea's because of its public intent, and not surprisingly he has begun to receive civic commissions: the Joe Louis Memorial in Detroit, a group set piece for the FDR Memorial, Washington DC (unfortunately celebrating, to my mind, rather private concerns) and the entry pylon for the 1984 Olympics (12). Here, the sensuality and the absolute truncations, along with the detailed genitalia, became too much for some of the public to bear. And before the Games, the athletes had to walk underneath this primitive totem – an overwhelming image of their brute power (13). But if this Olympic arch is a raw expression of the athletic animal, it is also heroically and unequivocally beautiful. This beauty comes from the reality of the content and the craft of making; the two opposing 'reality principles' which give art stable foundations. In the base columns and entablature are some views and reliefs of actual Olympic athletes. Here we can see their movements become the sculptor's exercises at the same time. Above this a long-armed woman starts to reach out as if she is getting set for a race, her masculine femininity, or muscle combined with grace, giving this votive statue a frightening energy (14). The reality of her body – photographed, video-taped, studied in model form at different scales – is turned into a form of super-reality and then abstracted by being cut off below the knees and placed on an Art Deco pedestal. If Ideal Realism was the unstable hybrid of fifth-century Athens, then it has found its present equivalent in this stark monument to the athletic body.

Monumentalised Mimesis and the Private World

Robert Graham's work, however large or small, tends towards the monumental, because of its frontality and relation to its architectural setting. The reduction of gesture and detail, the stiffness of pose and stoic expression, all add to the static posture, making it like an idea that has been frozen. Graham has spoken of the votary statuary from Egypt and Cambodia and the power that results from changing its scale: 'You have smaller votary figures to keep in your pocket and bigger things – civic – to scare you'.[7] George Segal, who occasionally displays an allegorical intention in his work, achieves a similar monumentality by abstracting very real, frail New Yorkers and placing them in archetypal settings. In his *Jacob and the Angels*, 1984 (15), for instance, Jacob's dream is reworked so that the disembodied spirits of people we all know are portrayed as ghost-like plaster figures in a timeless black space. This displacement of reality to an ideal cemetery inhabited by free roaming spirits gives a new twist to the classical canon of idealised beauty. Instead of

perfected white marble there is pock-marked, but abstracted, white plaster, a monumentalisation of the frail and bungled.

Penelope Jencks explores a similar connection between the real/imperfect and the abstract/monumental in her individual and group pieces. Leonard Baskin and Egypt are the two poles of this inspiration, as are everyday life and the demonic. In some of her work life-size terra cotta sculpture is coloured with clay slip to give a particular time, place and social existence to her characters (16). Monumental figures stand in mutual isolation, dignified characters who show not only the loneliness evident at a bad cocktail party, but a classical *gravitas* of calm introspection. Her public commissions are more directly allegorical and related to possibilities of the site which they characterise: *Samuel Eliot Morison*, 1983 (17), perched dramatically on a giant boulder, is characterised in sailing gear as he surveys the metaphorical ocean that he loved. Expression and gesture are reduced, as his costume is stylised, so that along with the rock he becomes a fundamental icon, a monumentalised piece of nature.

Here we are close to the classical notion of universal calm, the rational, still centre of a surrounding storm. Classicism plays with such oxymorons as the 'unmoving mover', 'controlled frenzy', 'passion recollected in tranquility' and one of its aesthetic ideals has always been, as it were, to freeze-dry emotion. Keats' *Ode on a Grecian Urn* is the classic expression of this paradox which many artists seek to capture. William Bailey, a New Haven painter in his fifties, is a case in point. His exquisite pencil drawings, recalling the delicacy of Clouet, have a life and conviction which put them in the centre of canonic classicism, while the expression on the subject's face is typically Modern (18).

Many may find his portraits and still-lifes stiff by comparison. A breathless air, verging on the claustrophobic, pervades the background of these paintings. But the intention of the flat blue-grey settings is to distance the subject, to make the particular woman or coffee pot look eternal. His *Fratta Still Life*, 1978 (19), treats a modest set of bowls and utensils as if they were pristine skyscrapers vying for space on a tight skyline, or a crockery San Gimingnano. Italian hill towns are a conscious source of inspiration and it is magically odd that rough, peasant construction is here turned into elegant china. The proportions, modelling, outline and colour-tone all combine to give the crockery a dignity and fabulous presence which it wouldn't have on a real table. One is reminded of Ozenfant's Purist compositions as much as of the more obvious classical sources, Chardin and Ingres. Bailey has mentioned that his limitation to still-life and portraiture springs from the agnosticism of the present age which has no 'shared myth'.[8] His cluster of bowls is meant, like Morandi's, as a substitute for the significant acts of great men, and in a sense to give to objects a dignity which the contemporary human presence does not have for him. Because of our agnostic age Bailey, like a Modernist, is almost forced into a form of elegant abstraction, although he uses realistic means.

5.16 Penelope Jencks, *Beach People*, 1977, life-size terracotta sculpture coloured with clay slip (Photograph P. Jencks/Courtesy Landmark Gallery, NYC)

5.17 Penelope Jencks, *Samuel Eliot Morison*, 1983, life-size bronze and boulder, Boston Common (Courtesy the artist)

5.18 William Bailey, *Reclining Nude*, 1970, pencil, 11¼x15¹⁵⁄₁₆in (Photograph John D. Schiff/Courtesy Robert Schoelkopf Gallery, NYC)

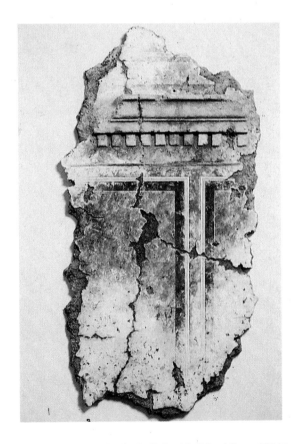

5.20 Peter Sari, *Relief with Moulding*, 1984, casein and gouache with plaster on canvas and wood, 94x48x8in (Courtesy OK Harris Works of Art, NYC)

When Realist Classicists lack a clear narrative script, or allegory, they will naturally tend towards a decorative treatment of themes, or a metonymic elaboration of elements. Peter Sari's reinterpretation of archaeological fragments illustrates the ornamental direction (20) and Richard Ryan's richly oiled still-lifes show the enumerative approach (21). Both could be interpreted, like Bailey's work, as allegories with no second text except an implicit one: classicism as the perennial return to ordered beauty. Neither nostalgic, nor polemical in intent, they ask to be evaluated as a form of realism applied to antique subjects. Sari has been inspired by Pompeiian fragments displayed in a museum setting, and he appropriates these dramatic elements to make a secondary illusion, an imitation of a cornice and a representation of a plaster fragment made in wood and paint. This trompe l'œil of a trompe l'œil is, like Andy Warhol's painting of a photo of a soup can, somewhat amusing in the way it forces a second glance. The surface is handled with a muted palette and a fissured, gritty quality that has been compared to contemporary colour-field painting, but, like this abstraction, the results do not make any demands on our sense of social and metaphysical reality. This is a realism, like that of the Modernists, of pure technique and beauty. With Ryan, however, the metonymic relations suggest a plot – *Still Life with Four Figures* suggests the four ages of woman – but this plot is not extended or contradicted by the attendant objects whether they are antique or contemporary. Thus any reading beyond the decorative will be forced and permissive.

Here we encounter one of the frustrations of contemporary realism. Although it implies that what is portrayed is meaningful in some way, it often suspends this next level of allegorical or narrative interpretation and throws us back to the object depicted and ultimately to the painting or sculpture itself. This inherent solipsism was made into a goal by Modernist critics such as Clement Greenberg and it has, not surprisingly, been taken up in a new way by Post-Modernists. William Beckman's superb landscape paintings of New York farms, or his portraits and self-portraits, look intensely into their subjects only to communicate, finally, the facticity of the subject. The farm landscape will show the effects of cultivating the land, the seasons and even, like a Constable, the current weather situation; the self-portrait with his wife will tell their age, that they are joggers and, with the hair combed this way and the face worn that way, they belong to a certain period. Interpretation beyond this point remains widely divergent. Is *Double Nude*, 1978 (22), a portrait of two latter-day puritans, or self-regarding narcissists? A straightforward Yankee couple of the eighteenth century, or one caught in the age of improvement cults? Such realism promises us an answer, then suddenly focuses back on the perfection of the medium itself.

What is being sought here is the the ever-elusive goal of absolute mimesis, or complete veracity. Two British artists, Michael Leonard and Ben Johnson, are, in this sense, traditional realists who nonetheless use modern equipment such as the camera, and current techniques of painting such as superimposition and layering. However, whereas Leonard will approach the

5.19 William Bailey, *Fratta Still Life*, 1978, oil on canvas, 45x58in (Courtesy Robert Schoelkopf Gallery, NYC)

5.21 Richard Ryan, *Still Life with Four Figures*, 1984, oil on canvas, 76x64½in (Courtesy Robert Schoelkopf Gallery, NYC)

5.22 William Beckman, *Double Nude*, 1978, oil on panel, 64x59in (Courtesy Allan Frumkin Gallery, NYC)

5.19

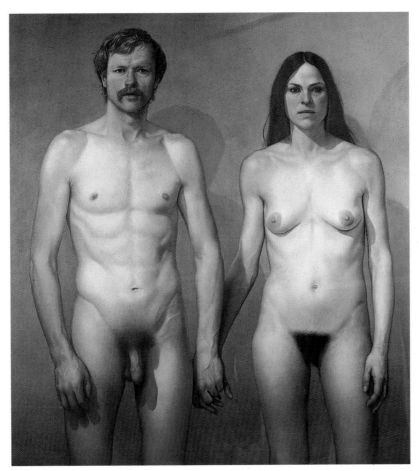

·5.22

urban landscape in an ad hoc manner, looking for an unposed view, Johnson, following the dictates of a formal architecture, will reshoot his positions endlessly until he comes upon the most monumental and composed view possible. And whereas Leonard is informal and episodic, Johnson is fastidious and categoric. Both, however, use Photo Realism and both desire to give monumental presence to the ordinary in life; recalling once again Baudelaire's stated goal to show the hidden 'heroism' of modern life.

Leonard will thus pick modest themes such as scaffolders at work, or a disregarded urban place such as the roofscape. *Like Upper Deck*, 1978 (23), reminiscent of Charles Scheeler's precisionist ship decks of the 1920s, has all the clear and healthy associations with which Le Corbusier imbued naval architecture, that seeming moral purity of the engineer. The work even recalls Le Corbusier's definition of architecture as being 'the masterly, correct and magnificent play of volumes seen in light'. It is only on second glance and when we reread the title, that we see that the ship stacks are just modest chimney flues held in place by wires. This double-take is as intentional as the subtle composition, using empty areas and a receding series of perspective lines formed by the cornices. Leonard paints with the conventions of both the Old Masters and the Modernists in mind, so when one sees his groups of happy scaffolders labouring on a roof, they are meant to recall not only the conventionalised noblehearted workman of the 1920s, but also Degas and Dutch group portraits. *Like Upper Deck* allows these double readings, being simultaneously a heroic ship's deck and a modest chimneyscape, a monumentalisation and a quick-snap view.

Except for one or two figural subjects, Ben Johnson has limited himself to portraying architecture and objects in the environment such as steel bolts, locks, elevator gates – all closely cropped to intensify and monumentalise the subject. Johnson has studied the effects of light in revealing the curve of three-dimensional objects and, like a Beaux-Arts epigone of the nineteenth century who would make virtuosic light and shadow studies of a column capital, he makes the highlighting of curved metal into an art form. Reflection, gleam and transparency are similarly means mastered as ends. But where a nineteenth-century renderer would draw stone buildings, Johnson is fascinated by steel ones. Hence his characteristic paintings concentrate on the early high-tech buildings of Stirling, or the continuing work of Norman Foster, and usually at the level of the revealing detail – the obsessive joint or window gasket.

The view of Foster's *Willis Faber Dumas' 'Poolside Reflection'*, 1984 (24), for instance, is a characteristic intensification of the architect's idea; what was actually intended before all the notice boards and clutter were added (which Johnson has subtracted) and what could have been achieved under ideal conditions. Thus Johnson takes a rarefied ideal and essentialises it even further. Where Foster is abstract and repetitive with his structure, Johnson is positively dazzling with his jazzy green coffers and staccato grid. The dance of these thin horizontal and vertical lines is an intense vibration contained

5.23 Michael Leonard, *Like Upper Deck*, 1978, acrylic on cotton duck, 25½x27in (Courtesy Fischer Fine Art Limited, London)

143

within a classical one-point perspective oriented frontally to the frame. It is as if Johnson is more and more intent on turning Foster or Richard Rogers, the exemplars of high-tech architecture, into super-cool classicists, so ordered and symmetrical does he make their work appear. For instance, the view of Rogers' *Inmos* building, 1985 (25), is taken down the central spine and at night, when all the spidery clickety-clack of the tendons and bones falls into a harmonious calm.

Edward Lucie-Smith has called Johnson today's equivalent of the great architectural painters Canaletto, Pannini and Pieter Saenredam, but unlike them he has not introduced the human subject, nor made some form of social comment on the use of space and buildings.[9] Rather his work remains determinedly focused on the beauty of mechanism *per se*, as if he were some sort of optimistic nineteenth-century engineer who not only believed in progress and the wholesomeness of polished machinery, but transcendental technology as well. Few will share these rarefied beliefs and inhabit the Elysium of the perfected machine, but those classicists of the eighteenth century who believed God was the perfect watchmaker have an heir in Ben Johnson. It seems to me his work implies more than a pragmatic outlook, that it rests on a metaphysical view of the way technical evolution reveals beauty. Whether this optimistic, indeed purist, view is wide enough, or even adequate to our condition, is open to question, but it has undoubtedly produced some of the most monumental realist works of the last twenty years.

Johnson, like many Photo Realists, is obsessive about making thorough photographic surveys of his subjects, but he follows up this empirical research with an investigation of the architect's working drawings and sketches. Having learnt both the idea of the building *and* the final result, he approaches his canvas just as meticulously, laying out perspective lines and diagonals. Then, over a three-month period, he carefully builds up the layers of colour, with the aid of a spray-gun. The obsessive intensity of this technique mirrors the fabrication of the architecture and can be seen as an underlying motive of all the realists. They give themselves to their craft, as a novitiate joins a monastery, and the commitment can become total.

This obsession with a virtuosic craft has been regarded suspiciously by the Modern Movement because it tends to supplant not only the ends of art but the free play of the symbolic imagination – the very power of the artist to transmute experience and to form an organic unity. Edward Lucie-Smith has written about this prejudice and the way the work of Steve Hawley, a young realist painter born in Brooklyn in 1950, challenges its assumptions.[10] Hawley, almost believing that technical mastery can lead to a new intensity of experience, achieves the richest luminosity of surface and texture by combining traditional and modern techniques.

Using the first technique, he draws in silver-point on a gesso ground,
then works up an elaborate imprimatura using a wax oil medium.
Over this goes a coat of clear alkyd resin, and this surface is worked on

5.24 Ben Johnson, *Willis Faber Dumas' 'Pool-side Reflection'*, 1984 (Photograph Prudence Cuming Associates Ltd./Courtesy the artist)

5.25 Ben Johnson, *Richard Rogers' Inmos Spine*, 1985, acrylic on canvas, 46x69in (Courtesy Fischer Fine Art Ltd., London)

further with egg tempera white and then repeatedly glazed. In the finished result, light strikes through the layers of glazing and is reflected back as glowing colour. Hawley's second basic technique is encaustic, a method using hot wax which goes back to classical times.[11]

The *Portrait of Regina in Black Kimono*, 1983-4 (26), shows the virtuosic effects these techniques and Photo Realism can achieve. The black silk kimono has a depth and texture which are tangible, the sheen and smoothness can be felt with the eyes. Furthermore, in this obsessive realism, the leaves of the bamboo can be distinguished as indeed can some of Regina's individual hairs. She looks at us like some *fin-de-siècle* aesthete startled, on her way to the bath, into a metaphysical truth. Her eyes catch ours like a hypnotist, and we keep coming back to them, after straying towards the objects behind her. There's an old conjunction of opposites here, as in David Salle's diptychs, except they are more literal: blank areas confront coloured iconography, Modernist collage is set off against traditional representation. Nothing much is made of these antinomies, but Hawley seems poised on the edge of a synthesis, or a dialectical interplay between them.

This can be seen in *Barbara Near Window*, 1983-4 (27), where the antinomies are played at even greater pitch, forcing us towards an allegorical reading. As in Stone Roberts' portrait of *Janet* we seem to be faced with a beauty isolated in a symbolic interior, now perhaps even trapped against the wall. The empty, fetishistic scribbles of Late-Modernism, collaged with Polaroid shots of the family, show the evanescent aspects of private life, to her left, while she looks longingly at public life through the window to her right. Her hair is made up, she wears elegant earrings, but perhaps she is incapable of dressing and leaving the studio – as is the artist? Or is she simply a *soignée* New Yorker entr'acte?

These paintings exude an air heavy with afternoon claustrophobia, as if the apartment, overstuffed in the nineteenth century is, even after cleaning out and repainting, still claiming its domesticated victims in the twentieth. In a sense, Hawley's work summarises the sadness and solipsism so evident in the realist tradition: the inwardness of Pearlstein's and De Andrea's women, the sepulchral light of Bailey's still-lifes, the inconsequential activities of Beckman's and Ryan's figures – the whole privatised world of the sensitive artist dedicated to the privations of technique. They remain haunting enigmas, monumentalised portraits of people who are about to abandon narcissism and melancholia, confident in their mature beauty, but still unsure of where to turn for engagement in the world.

5.26 Steve Hawley, *Portrait of Regina in Black Kimono*, 1983-4, oil, wax and alkyd on board, 60x48in (Courtesy Alexander F. Milliken Inc., NYC)

5.27 Steve Hawley, *Barbara Near Window*, 1983-4, oil, wax and alkyd on board, 60x90in (Courtesy Alexander F. Milliken Inc., NYC)

CHAPTER VI
The Classical Sensibility

Some artists capture the spirit of classicism while disregarding its letter. They may do this, as Ron Kitaj does, by treating significant historical subjects with a depth of understanding, or they may simply convey a classical feeling. A shared sensibility is difficult to define, but it is essential to any period, or to the maturity of any artist. Less than an ideology and more than a reigning style, it can be thought of as a sensitivity in conveying particular shades of feeling or attitudes to life. The classical sensibility has, characteristically, celebrated the sharp Mediterranean light and the clarity of volumes revealed by shadow, but it has also focused on a set of favourite subjects: the vernacular buildings of Italy and Provence, the burnt, rugged landscape of Greece and the tragic mode of portraying man's creations set heroically against an indifferent nature. Cézanne is the quintessential modern painter with a classical sensibility because, although he rarely painted an explicit classical subject, or used the Graeco-Roman style of realism, he nonetheless gave his subjects a simple dignity and *gravitas*. He also, of course, painted the archetypes of Provence: characters, buildings and landscapes.

Painterly Evocation

From the 1920s to the 1950s several important painters developed independently a very strong classical sensibility. Although eclipsed in art politics by the Modernists, Giorgio Morandi and Balthus in Europe, Rodrigo Moynihan in England, and Edwin Dickinson and Fairfield Porter in America all carried on exploring their personal visions through these years. While influenced by Modernist abstraction and Surrealism, they remained committed, to a degree, to the tradition of Realist Classicism. This evasive 'to a degree' suggests one of the problems of an art dominated by sensibility. In an age of changing ideologies and art movements, the more intelligent artists will retreat to their own visions which also tend to fluctuate, though usually not as violently as the art market. To an extent the artists considered here were conscious of this and thus sought the classical sensibility itself as the subject and stability of their art.

Edwin Dickinson was the master of painterly evocation. With a few brushstrokes or pencil lines he could capture the light of Cape Cod and turn its dunes into an Attic landscape. His *premiers coups* landscapes were, as Fairfield Porter has said, 'in touch with an elusive and fleeting essentiality . . . the presence of nature'.[1] His Cape Cod paintings would focus on beach grass or the porch of a house and give them the eternal stillness Cézanne gave

6.1 Edwin Dickinson, *Ruin at Daphne*, (detail opposite), 1943-53, oil on canvas, 48x60¼in (Edward Joseph Gallagher III Memorial Collection / Courtesy Metropolitan Museum of Art, NYC)

151

a dark pine tree. These fleeting moments are universalised to such an extent that although they convey the mood of Cape light, they remind one equally of Maine, or the Greek islands. Not surprisingly Dickinson returned several times to Greece at the end of his life and turned the Attic vision back on itself.

His particular style mixes the elusive with the clear-cut, the hazy atmospherics of Cézanne with crisp architectural drawing. *Ruin at Daphne*, 1943-53 (1), completed over a long period, is characteristic of this mixture. Semi-finished areas in a burning orange-red surround a central section of classical columns, broken vaults and open stairs. One's mind can wander around this architectural fantasy, taking in the mixture of Surrealism, Piranesi, Escher and Balbeck, and pondering what strange race could have used such suicidal monuments, but in the end one focuses on the melancholic sensuality of the place, its airy, dissolved presence. Dickinson uses a vapoury gloom and lyrical haze to such effect that he can turn these formal values into implicit allegories. Here the ruin becomes a slightly nightmarish speculation about heroic space and the travels of the mind through lofty constructions; this is an invented landscape rather than a nostalgic reconstruction of an actual site or a plausible Daphne.

Rodrigo Moynihan, who has painted in London and Provence for fifty years, is, like Dickinson, concerned with painterly values. One can feel his response to each brushstroke and the expressive potential of each hazy patch of colour. Again the empty and half finished area is as significant as the highly detailed part: like Dickinson, Moynihan relies on the suggestion of partially defined volumes and their contrast with areas of sharp focus. Thus *A Painter Holding a Canvas*, 1982 (2), is a serial interplay between strong framing elements and hazy infills. These are perceived to oscillate back and forth on interpretative as well as perceptual levels – the man holding the canvas and the canvas itself. Just as Dickinson favours a muted palette of suggestive greys, so Moynihan invariably returns to dust colours, the bone whites and creams he admires in the work of Pieter Saenredam and old photographs.[2] This chalky whiteness suffuses his still-lifes, the unarranged collection of objects he likes to come upon, and gives them a kind of frail timelessness like George Segal's plaster characters. In his universe, objects and figures are given the aged presence of ancient sculpture as if they were already ruins and part of history.

There are many painters who have developed similar aspects of this form of expression, notably the Israeli artist and curator Avigdor Arikha, the English painters Michael Andrews and Bill Jacklin, and the young Californian Richard Schaffer who seems close to Dickinson in sensibility if not technique. Michael Andrews can give a quiet dignity to a modest event. His portrayals of balloons and planes, or family relationships, have such a simple, humane air that one can overlook their complexity. In a series on deer hunting, for instance, he has explored one of the oldest classical themes – man attacking a wild animal – in a way which quietly suggests the moral dilemma involved. Should one shoot the animals to control the size of the

6.2 Rodrigo Moynihan, *A Painter Holding a Canvas*, 1982, oil on canvas, 24x19¾in (Courtesy Robert Miller Gallery, NYC)

6.3 Michael Andrews, *Peter's Day, Third Stalk*, 1979, acrylic on canvas, 72x72in (Private Collection, Paris/Courtesy Anthony d'Offay Gallery, London)

herds, to make their harsh winter easier? *Peter's Day, Third Stalk* implies this questioning by giving a strange tilt to the horizon and the stalkers, who seem to lean off the canvas to one side (3). The herd of deer runs across the painting and uphill at another angle. Foreground and midground thus take part in this quick and unbalanced action, a jarring moment whose essential truth was first captured by camera. The heroic landscape, the diminutive but deadly hunters, the rumps of fleeing prey that sparkle over the ground are set in a kind of dissociated and dissonant conjunction that is both very realistic and timeless.

Avigdor Arikha is another spare classicist who gives objects an understated and suggestive dignity. He deliberately sets up limits of time, subject and treatment – 'Everything I do is from life'[3] – in order to capture the essence of the object painted with minimal interference in mood. This method, which might be called Expressionist Classicism because of the importance it places on continuing immediate perception, produces haunting moments of insight and, like Dickinson's work, gives an essential dignity to place and object (4). Along with such painters, Arikha's brushstrokes possess an immediacy which serves to give a kind of sculptural permanence to the objects he depicts: a 'thingness' it has been called with more circularity than clarification.[4]

The painterly evocation of place and object is pushed in an even more Expressionist direction in the work of Paul Resika, so much so that many people would refuse to grant him a place in the classical tradition. But his sensibility, and occasionally his subject matter, clearly derive from this tradition. Once again, like Dickinson, he turns Cape Cod into the new Provence, or perhaps the sylvan glade of Olympia (5). Poussin and Cézanne, the lyrical tradition of the south and the 'return to nature' are all behind Resika's vision even if it is conveyed with a primitivist *impasto* and violent brushstroke. He sometimes uses paint as if it were a solid building material, attempting, apparently, to make his voluminous nudes more than statuesque – rather like huge Amazonian monuments left in a wilderness. These giant women are at one with nature, like Rousseau's noble savages, and the much more ancient classical myths recounted by Vitruvius and others.[5] Here by a brook, or 'primitive hut' dedicated to Venus, they sport, immersed in the trees, shrubbery and water as if they were a species of flesh-growing plant (6). One would imagine that Resika had invented this place in an Arcadian fantasy, except that several exist on Cape Cod and he occasionally inhabits a primitive hut in one of them.

His work derives from two Cape Schools, not only from Dickinson, but from the Expressionist teaching of Hans Hoffmann. The former influence explains his use of an Impressionistic haze and the latter explains his strong violent contrasts and use of fiery colour tones. Another influence, which he freely acknowledges, is the American Realist Classicist Edward Melcarth whom he met while working in Venice in the 1950s.[6] Resika pulls together these influences in a way which recalls yet other sources and ages: the nineteenth-century realist tradition of Corot and Courbet, the Expressionist

6.4 Avigdor Arikha, *August*, 1982, oil on canvas, 31¾x39¼in (Courtesy Marlborough Gallery, London)

6.5 Paul Resika, *Women and Pears*, 1981-4, oil on canvas, 51x64in (Courtesy Graham Modern Gallery, NYC)

symbolism of Edvard Munch and the aggressive use of colour of the Fauves.
All this anti-classicism is synthesised with a brutal force that could be termed
Primitivist Classical. His *Jacaranda Bull, End of the Day*, 1983 (7), shows a
truncated, dark force of nature grazing on a deep orange field in the late
afternoon sunlight. The field erupts with a burning red-orange – the violent
explosion of brushstrokes underscoring the content – while the mountain, the
tree, the bull and the tower assert their archetypal presence. All these are
classical forms, Platonic ideas, portrayed in their primal condition as if they
were before the classical tradition had started in Greece. Resika will rework
such a set of Ur-forms again and again until the brushstrokes, colour and
surrounding space cohere as an integrated symbol of expression and
meaning. In this respect he resembles the romantic artists and poets who
were always trying to achieve a resolution between medium, feeling and
meaning.

That Resika's erotic use of the medium is a Dionysian version of the
classical tradition can be doubted, but in two respects he is very much part of
this historical pedigree. His subject matter – the energised, personified forces
of nature – are directly Greek in origin, the bulls and trees are Provençal if
not Cretan. And the implied allegory is often of an ideal, undomesticated
nature – a kind of raw Arcadia before Poussin started tidying it up and the
garden brigade of the eighteenth century arrived. It's the wrong time in
cultural history to romanticise this primitivism, and Resika surely does not.

6.6 Paul Resika, *Temple of Venus (Dellbrook)*,
1979, oil on canvas, 40x30in (Courtesy Graham
Modern Gallery, NYC)

6.7 Paul Resika, *Jacaranda Bull, End of the
Day*, 1983, oil on canvas, 51½x64in (Courtesy
Graham Modern Gallery, NYC)

He simply prefers it to the more urbane and literary forms, or to the pastoral tradition which has, in America, recently been revived.

Arcadia Regained and Lost Again

It is sometimes said by scholars that one of the unique contributions America has made to the world of landscape design is the 1860s Cemetery Movement.[7] While this may be an exaggeration, it is no doubt true that by the end of the nineteenth century America had established a very real, living pastoral tradition which included, within its net, the City Park Movement and the National Park Movement, the Ivy League Colleges and campus planning, the City Beautiful Movement and the 'ideal suburb' (not to mention their mordant offspring the ubiquitous Forest Lawns). The so-called 'American Renaissance' of 1870-1910 had established so many living institutions of this type that during the twentieth century they simply became taken for granted. Only in the 1960s was interest in this period of the late nineteenth century rekindled, and such protagonists as Frederick Law Olmstead, the great park designer and planner, reassessed for their social and artistic idealism. The fact that Arcadia had been successfully planted in America started to be appreciated, as well as the fact that it was an alternative to the various forms of current thinking, whether artistic Minimalism, architectural Modernism or social radicalism. By the 1980s the Arcadian tradition in American painting, like the 'New Arcadians' in Scotland, was considered a critical enough force to be given an exhibition at the Robert Schoelkopf Gallery in New York.[8]

This development surprised many people, including one of the leading proponents of the movement, Lennart Anderson, whose slow conversion to using explicit images of Arcadia was made reluctantly.[9] The surprise lay in the fact that many critics had written off pastoral allegory as irrelevant and such conventional treatment of this subject as the worst form of academic escapism. The notion of Arcadia as both a real, isolated area of the Peloponnese surrounded by mountains (Arkady) and a myth of ideal rusticity seemed implausible, even for the Post-Industrial Age. Arcadia as a fictional realm celebrated by Virgil was a place where shepherds and huntsmen existed in a state of perfect bliss surrounded by a beneficent nature. This ideal existence went on, in literature and painting at least, until the seventeenth century when a disturbing notion was introduced. 'Death too dwells in Arcadia' – *Et in Arcadia Ego* – the famous lines treated by Poussin and many subsequent painters challenged the facile assumptions of the myth with a little social realism, a tradition brought up to date by the Scottish concrete poet Ian Hamilton Finlay.[10] Finlay shows how death, in the form of some beautiful instruments of war such as the tank, is a quite essential counterpoint in the land of idyllic peace. For the American artists, however, Arcadia is still a place of ideal virtue, and perfect harmony between man and nature, a more innocent place. The question is – how do Post-Modern artists treat this innocence in an 'age of lost innocence'?[11]

6.8 Milet Andrejevic, *An Afternoon of Acteon*, 1983, gouache on paper, 12⅝x19½in (Courtesy Robert Schoelkopf Gallery, NYC)

6.9 Milet Andrejevic, *Towards Bethesda Fountain*, egg, oil and tempera on canvas, 1978, 38x50in (Courtesy Robert Schoelkopf Gallery, NYC)

158

Milet Andrejevic, a Yugoslavian émigré living in New York, naturally locates Arcadia in Olmstead's Central Park (8). Here we can see typical New Yorkers engaged in athletic and cultural activities basic to Andrejevic's humanist ideals, disporting themselves with animals as they really do in the summer or at weekends. A skyscraper is seen in the background, neither Poussin's temple nor intrusive, but simply there. The characters wear contemporary clothing and engage in contemporary activities: Poussin's shepherd now has a tracksuit and eyes one of the jogettes while his dog chases a balloon. All of this very real, perhaps inconsequential, social life is abstracted, placed in a well-kept setting and suffused with a muted, pastel-like tone of grey and greens. The painterly atmosphere is a cross between Cézanne and his contemporary Puvis de Chavannes. The mood is calm, pleasant and voluptuous as Arcadia should be, and the date though 1983, is before the arrival of Death.

Andrejevic evokes this timeless vision of contemporary life again and again as if to say that it is just as significant and eternal as the more sensational forms of realism – the sex and violation that have today become so conventionalised. There is more observation than nostalgia in his realism, and it's suffused with a green-hued light – a cross between municipal lighting and that of Elysium. Thus in *Towards Bethesda Fountain*, 1978 (9), three boys are by the lake in Central Park engaged in typical activities: skyscrapers and telephone poles unobtrusively announce their abstract presence, a classical terrace is in the distance – and over all this peaceful spring activity plays a dream-like light, green and bright with promise.

A hint of irony occasionally breaks through this harmonious calm. In *Apollo and Daphne*, 1982 (10), we have what could be the moment of truth in this Greek tragedy of the gods: Apollo has chased Daphne to the river's edge and finally caught her, only to have her father (the river god Peneus) change her into a laurel tree. This inspires Apollo to promise her eternal life and (in the painting) break into song: whenever he sings a song and crowns a triumphant warrior or artist it will be with laurel. The scene of Andrejevic's reinterpretation could be any Ivy League college. Street-smart Vassar co-eds pretend not to listen to the lyre of this post-hippie, while in the background a skyscraper and other collegiate buildings are just discernible. The irony is gentle and subtle, but nonetheless present.

That Americans still pursue the Arcadian dream, along with modern life and technology, is perhaps the essential allegory of all Andrejevic's work. In *The Fountain*, 1981 (11), the archetypal family can be seen: the overworked father with drooping, depressed flesh; the mother, in slacks, helps her child get a drink at the fountain; an oversized, overdressed child turns with a cup of water while, in the background, Three New York Graces trip towards the shore. The gestures, faces and activities could occur in any American park, and the mood is entirely familiar. What is strange is the heightened, expectant atmosphere – the idea behind Central Park – as if myth might break into everyday life and challenge it. Andrejevic's virtue is that he can

6.10 Milet Andrejevic, *Apollo and Daphne*, 1982, egg, oil and tempera on canvas, 19½x28½in (Courtesy Robert Schoelkopf Gallery, NYC)

6.11 Milet Andrejevic, *The Fountain*, 1981, egg, oil and tempera on canvas, 36x50in (Courtesy Robert Schoelkopf Gallery, NYC)

convince us of the reality first and then allow the atmosphere and historical references – the oversophisticated Balthus girl, for instance – to come into play at a secondary level. Arcadia is thus regained as the discrete charm of middle America.

Lennart Anderson, like Andrejevic born in the 1920s, studied for a short time with Edwin Dickinson and, since the late 1970s, has taken up the theme of Arcadia. In a series of large canvases, *Idylls I-III*, he portrays an old bacchanal in modern undress. Next to a lake, amidst gentle, rolling landscapes that are at once the Peloponnese Arkady and the Roman Campagna, cavort dancing figures reminiscent of Degas' *Spartan Boys and Girls at Play* and the open-air scenes of Puvis de Chavannes. Giotto and the fresco painters have clearly influenced this work as much as the above-mentioned painters and Dickinson.[12] Hence the flat *impasto*, the mood of a fresco, and the feeling of a fresh nature conveyed through colour tones and clear outlines. A soft Attic light plays over the picnic scenes revealing the muscles and volumes of the bodies, but also, like Andrejevic's light, unifying the figures with nature.

Idyll I, 1978-83 (12), shows a laurel-wreathed Apollo playing a 1960s guitar while a small girl pushes a sailboat; one couple converse by a tree while another dance in front of a rock. In the background a shepherd tends his Arcadian flocks and a real boat sails in a very real lake – there are countless versions of this background to be found in upstate New York. In *Idyll II*, 1979-80, the scene is, as it were, rotated one-hundred-and-eighty degrees and there is slightly more activity as if the music is getting faster (13). The men remain undressed, while the women are mostly clothed. A tiny motor-boat and child's bow and arrow date it as 1980. In *Idyll III*, which Anderson continuously reworks as Dickinson did his large paintings, we return to the first scene except that now a bemused dog watches the dancers, two of whom are inspired to make love behind a rock. Except for this last touch and the shepherds, it could be any picnic gathering of a post-hippie clan from San Francisco to Woodstock, New York. Ultimately, however, in spite of Anderson's skill and sensibility, the atmosphere and theme do not convince us that this is the present because the attitudes of the characters seem forced.

More convincing, and no less theatrical, is his earlier *Street Scene* (14) painted in the late 1950s and early 1960s. Here the controlled composition, again a tableau of many characters, achieves an epic quality. The event is limited – a traffic accident and different people's reaction to it – but it has more weight and plausibility than the *Idylls*. Architecture and proportioned space provide a frame and contrast for the highly emotive content: the balanced tonal areas of paint give a controlled dignity to a chain reaction of events while the classical unities provide a stable context for contemplating the essential fragility of our time.

A street accident is not quite an Arcadian dream and it once again shows that a current artist may find urban calamity more real than pastoral harmony. Nonetheless a younger generation, following the lead of Andre-

6.12 Lennart Anderson, *Idyll I*, 1978-83, acrylic on canvas, 68x84in (Courtesy Davis and Langdale Co. Inc., NYC)

6.13 Lennart Anderson, *Idyll II*, acrylic on canvas, 1979-80, 64⅛x80⅛in (Courtesy Davis and Langdale Co. Inc., NYC)

6.14 Lennart Anderson, *Street Scene*, 1961, oil on canvas, 77x99in (Collection of Mellon Bank / Courtesy Davis and Langdale Co. Inc., NYC)

jevic and Anderson, have continued to explore this mythic land and give it, as Leon Krier does architecture, such attractions that it becomes a critical project, a Utopian prospect. Thomas Cornell, an artist born in the late 1930s, who painted an epic drama of death as a critique of the Vietnam war, had by the 1980s turned his polemical eye towards pastoral. The result, in a series of canvases celebrating the birth and early nurture of Dionysus, is an allegory about the continuing agrarian dream in America. *Utopian Landscape*, 1981, one of this series, shows an idyllic scene of dirt roads, a pleasant farm house, *déjeuner sur l'herbe* and the art of cultivating the land – all given a wishful promise through Cornell's characteristic use of bright colour patches (15). This Utopia looks like the nineteenth-century agrarian reality on a hot summer's day, before factory farming rendered it problematic.

The Birth of Dionysus II, 1980, shows a similar scene, again in iridescent blues and reds and bright flesh colours (16). Hermes arrives in the beautiful valley of Nysa, a mythologically lost paradise, carrying the baby Dionysus which he is presumably about to turn over to American foster parents. Whether this is an ironic gesture or pastiche is hard to tell. In any case, his winged hat contrasts, incongruously, with the red barn and nineteenth-century horse-drawn plough to say nothing of the blue jeans, T-shirts and Gauguinesque nymphs in the foreground, but curiously these intentional mixtures of time and place are not disturbing because of the overriding unities of mood and style. A lyrical celebration of the birth of wine – of strength, Eros, and the rebirth of nature – is convincingly portrayed in the gestures and glowing colours. One believes in the equation of sexual energy and nature's renewal. And since a contemporary audience is unlikely to know the particulars of Dionysus, and just associate him with wine-making and revelry, Cornell takes liberties with the myth and, like a latter-day structuralist, implies that all versions of a legend, including its interpretations, are part of the structure. Here the implication is that the agrarian dream of the settlers was a workable system that we could recapture: a *passéiste* Utopia.

In these Arcadian fantasies women are often dressed and men nude, as with Lennart Anderson's *Idylls*, or the relationship of work to play is changed to a more agreeable mixture: Utopia is here presented as a feasible alternative. That, by and large, it has remained a wistful dream can be seen in the work of two younger painters: James Lecky and Edward Schmidt. Lecky paints many pastoral scenes using an abstract, painterly manner reminiscent of Paul Resika and a brightness like Cornell's. These fantasies are again set in a timeless Mediterranean or Greece and given such titles as *Dorian Theme* – a harmless set of young male nudes and dressed lute players singing, presumably in the Dorian mode, next to a Doric temple. Lecky's *End of Arcady*, in progress, recalling Thomas Eakins' *The Swimming Hole*, shows the native hunters and fishermen of America Before the Fall – i.e. the advent of White Man and Industrialisation (17). Nature is unpolluted, men and women commune in unselfconscious nudity and a calm, fresh air pervades

6.15 Thomas Cornell, *Utopian Landscape*, 1981, oil on canvas, 38x54in (Courtesy G. W. Einstein Co. Inc., NYC)

6.16 Thomas Cornell, *The Birth of Dionysus II*, 1980, oil on canvas, 54x76in (Courtesy G. W. Einstein Co. Inc., NYC)

164

6.17 James Lecky, *End of Arcady*, 1981 (work in progress), oil on canvas, 60x94in (Photograph Erik Landsberg/Courtesy Tatistcheff and Co. Inc., NYC)

6.18 Edward Schmidt, *Departure*, 1981-2, oil on canvas, 40x50in (Courtesy Robert Schoelkopf Gallery, NYC)

6.19 Edward Schmidt, *Figures in a Forest*, 1981-2, oil on canvas, 36x60in (Courtesy Robert Schoelkopf Gallery, NYC)

the landscape. What makes this the 'End of Arcady' is its cloying treatment of innocence, the unlikely happiness it depicts and the little contact it makes with the dark side of Arcadia. The painting is still 'in progress' as is a lot of other work in this genre, and one feels this is a telling hesitation. It is also, clearly, not the end of the tradition.

Edward Schmidt, who has worked with Michael Graves on several architectural murals and sculptures, can give a Poussinesque dignity to the same set of Arcadian subjects. He has repainted Milet Andrejevic's *Towards Bethseda Fountain* as a mural and developed several generic subjects such as *Figures in the Forest* and *The Destruction of a City* –archetypal situations in search of contemporary relevance. His *Departure*, 1981-2, perhaps the most successful of these perennial themes, shows a young man leaving his father as his family weeps in the background (18). This Greuze-like melodrama is given an epic treatment which is more convincing at the level of composition and mood than the period costume. The space, divided down the middle just as the lives are depicted dividing, plunges off to one side – the point of departure – and then marches up an arid hill to a ruined stone building. The portrayal of grief thus relies as much on landscape as it does on gesture. It's a plausible integration of concept and expression.

Figures in a Forest, 1981-2, returns us via historical quotation to the land of Arcadian sweetness where all ages and conditions of men and women can coexist in peace (19). Reclining nudes, lovers, waking and sleeping figures (some hooded), and the classical runner pulling a streaming cape, animate this lost Elysium like alienated figures lifted from different myths who've been forced together in a primal forest. The setting is unknown, the text missing and we're unsure whether this masterful young painter intends his tragic portrayal of paradise lost, or is being directed by the conventions. He does not, like Andrejevic, locate this drama in the present tense. The plausibility it has comes from the way figures are used metaphorically: the contrast of Eros and Thanatos, the rippling of human activity set against a melancholic forest of solemn trees – once again the grand contrast of Death in Arcadia.

The Arcadian tradition also continues outside America, in Britain with the New Arcadians, and on the Continent with Ivan Theimar. As an ideal polemic it sets primary relationships of play, work and sexual potency in a wilderness which knows little conflict except, latterly, death. That this ideal is, thanks to the proliferation of leisure and travel, today accessible to large parts of the population in both a debased and elevated form is obvious, as is its continued existence in many American parks and European havens of rest in the south. But its continuing validity is best shown in art and act, and here the most persuasive example is that of Ian Hamilton Finlay. He has created the idyllic garden of Little Sparta in Scotland and sometimes associates with and writes for the Yorkshire group of New Arcadians led by Patrick Eyres.[13] Finlay and his wife Susan have, as mentioned in Chapter III, built up an Arcadian landscape on the treeless moors using cow byres for temples, model

6.20 Ian Hamilton Finlay and the Saint-Just Vigilantes, *Monument to the First Battle of Little Sparta*, 1983, bronze and brick (Courtesy the artists)

tanks for tombs and the mausoleum whose inscription so fascinated the shepherds: *Et in Arcadia Ego*. In fact this theme is a constant subject of his concrete poetry and emblematic constructions: it appears in lithographs, based on Poussin and Panofsky's exegesis, which are given accompanying interpretive texts; it appears on his sundials, panzer tanks and *Monument to The First Battle of Little Sparta* (20) – the machine gun. It is Finlay's insight, following Panofsky, that Arcadian innocence, beauty and virtue always entail, or bring into being, their opposite, like some Hegelian demon. In America, he notes ironically, the Arcadian wilderness and frontier theme are now best personified in this ambivalent dialectic by Clint Eastwood.[14] For him it is Puvis' *Inter Artes et Naturam* which summarised the tradition, and he has transplanted several objects from this painting into his garden, including a guillotine. Virtue begets terror in the French Revolution as surely as Arcadia begets death: the dialectic is the essence of the myth.

The Representation of Order

Deep within the classical sensibility is an attachment to paradoxical order. This motive pervades all classicism and it has been perverted, or exaggerated, in our century particularly by fascist and Nazi architects. While they produced an impressive order it was inevitably over-regular, overscaled and oversimple, lacking precisely that inherent antithesis, that paradoxical contradiction, which has been the hallmark of true classicism. With the Egyptians, at the start of the tradition, one finds entasis and many other distortions and refinements introduced into a governing order, and these subtle variations have always served to give metaphorical life to an otherwise stale formula: hence the terms 'elasticity', 'tension' and 'dynamic' are often used to describe inanimate objects that are given slight variations from the norm. 'Asymmetrical symmetry' is, for instance, one of the current tropes of Post-Modern architecture. But all such refinements may also become sterile if they are predictable and done to no purpose: hence the constant struggle of the classicists to find new ways of making an order surprising and the frequent change of the rules for entasis in ancient Greece. Three current artists who take as their goal the representation of order, and are aware of these issues, use architecture as their principle geometrical or compositional means.

William Wilkins, the London-based artist who studied architecture for a while, often organises his spaces so that they are frontally layered to the picture plane. As in Balthus' work one can be sure of finding the skirting board and wall line parallel to the frame, and a series of further horizontal and vertical subdivisions. This frontal layering serves to divide up the canvas into a series of receding space cells which, characteristically, pull the viewer in by perspective and then force the eye to wander around the subject. In *Figures with a Landscape* (21), 1978-9, Wilkins uses an ordering device to make one's mind jump back and forth between the three perplexing subjects: the dressed musicians, the nude who is lost in thought and the artificial landscape hanging on the wall. We begin to realise that we are faced with a set of paradoxes here, as subtle as the geometrical grids which leak off to the right. Apparently it's an evening, indoor concert whose subject is a daytime, outdoor *Déjeuner sur l'herbe*. The men are clothed, as in Manet and so many previous *déjeuners*, but are transformed into barefooted musicians playing by an anglepoise light. It could be any dormitory bedroom with its tawdry bed, but then there's the voluptuous odalique and the rather grand canvas on the wall.

The trompe l'œil of a trompe l'œil, with all its double meanings and allusions to history is a piece of classic Post-Modernism. If the subject of Modern art, according to one oversimplification of Clement Greenberg, is the perfection of its medium, then the subject of Post-Modern art is about past art which acknowledges its artificiality.[15] This cliché lets us look at Wilkins' and so much other historicist work without regarding it as cynical: the presence of quotation marks, the self-conscious artificiality, make it instead ironic. Thus we enter Wilkins' sparkling world of daubs, of *pointillisme* à la Seurat and *déjeuners* à la Manet, as we would a theatre with painted screens and stage. Each level of reality is a perfectly plausible representation of the present, but it also alludes to a previous world of painting or myth.

In *Picnic* (22), 1981, Wilkins carries his theatrical layering and allusions a stage further. Giorgione's pastoral equation of music, nudity, nature and architecture is now turned towards the other Arcadian tradition of men and

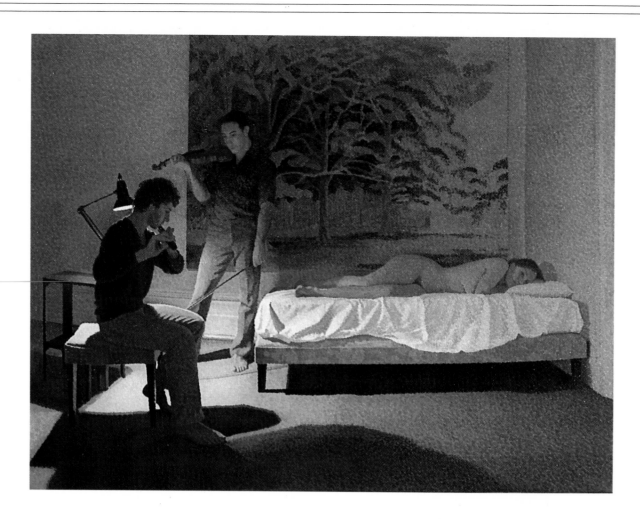

women eating in a pastoral landscape. Here, however, the woods are a stage backdrop and the *l'herbe* a crinkly sheet painted as grass. The group could be either actors, enjoying a work break, or two couples who live in a trompe l'œil; both equally plausible, contemporary situations. As we explore this ironic but voluptuous world further we can see the opposition sustained. The blond woman lays a comforting hand on her companion as he gazes at her, but her eyes are averted from his glance; the balding man opens a beer can, disconsolate perhaps, as his companion moves away to dress. A hesitant mood pervades the scene as if the actors were unsure of their script and the picnic about to break up. The wintry trees in the backdrop, unfinished as a trompe l'œil, underscore this ambivalent mood. But the chromatic sparkle – even dance – of luminous dots, and the bright grass and flesh colours reestablish the ideal of pastoral delight, just as the architectural control lends an air of serenity.

In these works Wilkins makes the stage as real as the pastoral ideal and the everyday picnic, and, by presenting these as various conventions, he equates real Arkady with Poussin's reinvented Arcadia, Manet's *Déjeuner* and subsequent idylls. Each convention is signalled and distinct, rationally adopted without the comforting illusion (more possible for Giorgione) that a particular Arcadian landscape, or even the Italian countryside, will remain untouched by progress and fashion.

Alan Feltus orders his paintings not with actors and distinct interpretative conventions, but with previous paintings, particularly those selected from within the classical tradition: Giotto, Piero della Francesca, Paolo Uccello and Balthus.[16] He does not work from life or with models in the studio, but rather from photographs of Greek and Roman statuary and the Italian painters. Thus he combines, for instance, a turban from Uccello with a face from Balthus. This eclecticism may sound unpromising, a recipe for the incongruous mélange, but the results are thoroughly worked out in feeling and theme. In *Another Summer* (23), 1984, a dignified serenity pervades the room. Two dancers wait, perhaps between exercises; one has removed part of her leotard and is smoothing her hair under the turban; the other is distracted in thought. Outside the window is part of a vernacular house, the type of building Edward Hopper painted to suggest similar moods of contemplation. Muted Post-Modern colours in flat geometric areas underscore this calm scene where almost nothing is happening: it's just 'another summer' of practising dance for two young women: a still moment captured by the harmonious composition.

Alan Feltus orders his controlled world as the painters Ozenfant and Le Corbusier ordered their Purist canvases. A predetermined geometrical pattern, usually a grid, generates well-proportioned areas full of both objects and empty space. *After the Event* (24), 1978-9, shows just such a harmonious space with all the variants, distortions and refinements which give a subtle movement to the grid. What might have been 'Three Graces' frozen in a claustrophobic studio has become a moving triangular composition that

6.21 William Wilkins, *Figures with a Landscape*, 1978-9, oil on canvas, 24x31in (Courtesy Robert Schoelkopf Gallery, NYC)

6.22 William Wilkins, *Picnic*, 1981, oil on canvas, 30x30¾in (Courtesy Robert Schoelkopf Gallery, NYC)

171

6.23

6.24

6.23 Alan Feltus, *Another Summer*, 1984, oil on canvas, 48x36in (Courtesy Forum Gallery Inc., NYC)

6.24 Alan Feltus, *After the Event*, 1978-9, oil on canvas, 70x85in (Courtesy Forum Gallery Inc., NYC)

approximates a time-lapse photo of one woman. What 'event' is this 'after'? If we read the painting from left to right we might assume that the demure lady has just emerged from a minor crisis. She plays with a ribbon and suspiciously shoots out a look; in the centre, more relaxed and now dressed, she ties the ribbon in her hair thus regaining composure and finally, hiding her sex, recollects the 'event' in tranquility.

There are other plausible readings since Feltus intentionally pursues the state of uncertain mystery by combining latent and opposite narratives. Thus his tightly ordered worlds convey a quiet suspense, the anxiety and promise that lie between times of resolute activity. If they have an obvious problem it is their alienation from the public world, that airless solitude which also pervades the work of Balthus, William Bailey and so many other contemporary painters. The monumentality of the space and characters seems to mock the extreme privacy of their moods.

Whereas Wilkins and Feltus impose a compositional order only to vary it in small ways, John Nava, the Californian artist who is also interested in architectural ordering, makes the process of representation the pretext for his ordering devices. The process of painting is sometimes even adopted as the subject of his work. Thus in *D.A.K. Standing*, (*Diptych*) (25), 1984, we see, reading from right to left, the stages of representation emerging in ever greater clarity. First is a quick sketch of the Platonic idea, then come pasted up sections which form a ghosted figure and then finally D.A.K. emerges in colour, youthful and over-relaxed. The matter-of-fact pose and lack of idealisation are reminiscent of Philip Pearlstein's nudes and the 1920s *Neue Sachlichkeit*, where objects and figures are portrayed in the aimless ambiguity of modern life. But here the implicit vitality of the figure and the abstract conventionalization set this representation apart from social realism. This complex collage is partly about attitudes towards Modernism and partly about its goals of simultaneity, process and abstraction.

This commentary on previous tradition and the explicit representation of artifice is characteristic of Nava's work, as it is of Post-Modernism in general. For instance, *Asymmetrical Diptych* (26), 1984, takes the same set of conventions and combines them with ghost-like classical formulae: a Doric arcade, a Corinthian capital and various proportioning systems. This diptych, as its title suggests, is broken up into various harmonic fragments which can be read in several ways. From left to right we have the major rhythm Ab which is the diptych itself; or, possibly, if we read the major areas, abc; or ABcd if we subdivide them. Horizontal divisions are a somewhat simpler basic triad.

Just as the geometry is an ordered variation, so is the subject matter. The woman, to the left, is at first a gridded ghost and then, further left, an almost finished representation. To the far right she is rotated twice – upside down and frontally – while the kitchen chair and umbrella are also ghosted and rotated. This strange reminiscence of Surrealist beauty ('the fortuitous encounter of a sewing machine and an umbrella on a dissecting table') is balanced by, and blends with, traditional notions of beauty and classical associations. The umbrella becomes the structure of a dome, or in another similar painting, the plan of the Campidoglio, just as the Doric and Corinthian orders are shown as different ratios of beauty.

This representation of feminine and architectural harmony is abstract and matter-of-fact. It is played out in the muted tones and dry, *impasto* patches that are so consistently reused by those with a classical sensibility; from Dickinson to Resika to Anderson and Cornell. The imperfections and the antiquity implied by these areas of eroded paint are self-conscious conventions which symbolise the continuity of effort across time – the painter's tradition as well as the tradition of rediscovered truths. Against these signs of age and the archetypes such as the Doric column, is set a sharp grid and a carefully observed woman in contemporary dress. Everyone can recognise the artifice and quotation marks – they are presented neutrally as an essential part of the subject matter. The conventions of beauty are made explicit, thus forcing the viewer to become as self-aware of his reactions as the artist is self-conscious of his artifice. Self-consciousness is thus, once again, a consequence of 'lost innocence', the typical Post-Modern psychic state of an age which knows that its myths and conventions are freely adopted. For Nava, as for the other Post-Modernists, this self-consciousness is something to be enjoyed.

6.25 John Nava, *D.A.K. Standing (Diptych)*, 1984, acrylic, oil and collage on canvas, 1984, 6x8ft (Courtesy Koplin Gallery, LA)

6.26 John Nava, *Asymmetrical Diptych*, 1984, acrylic, oil and collage on canvas, 6x10ft (Mr. & Mrs. Jeffrey Berg Collection/Courtesy Koplin Gallery, LA)

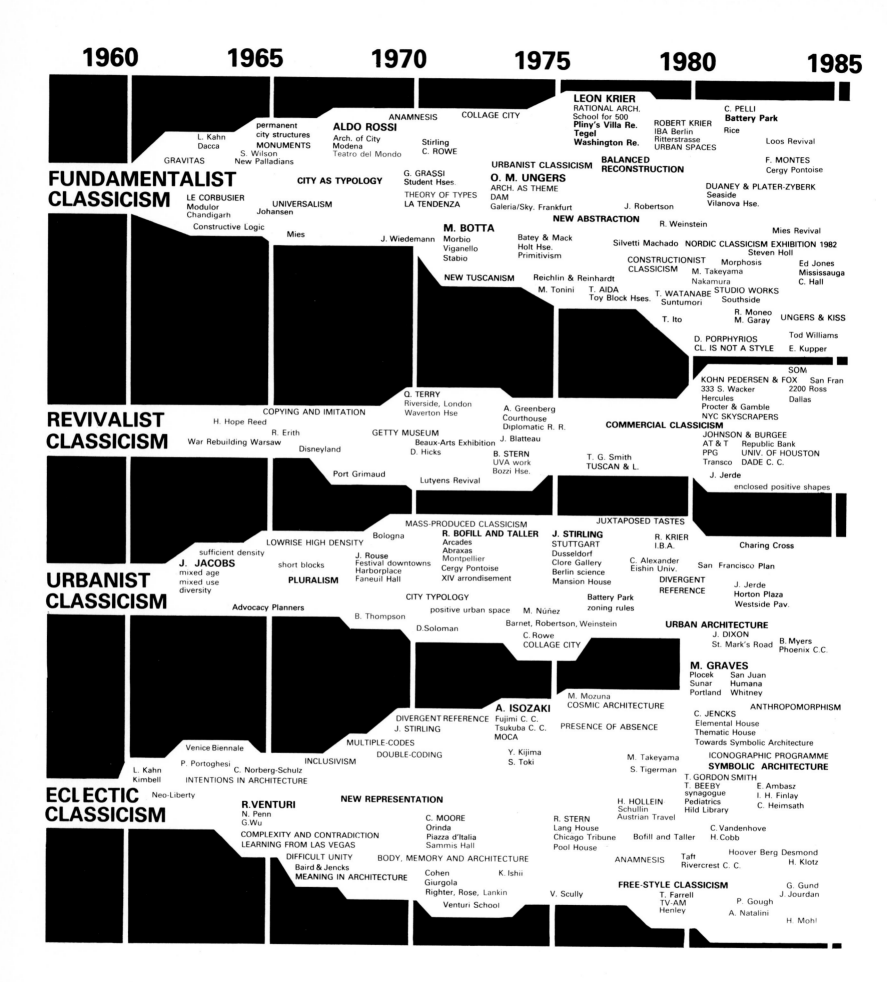

1960 **1965** **1970** **1975** **1980** **1985**

LEON KRIER
RATIONAL ARCH.
School for 500
Pliny's Villa Re.
Tegel
Washington Re.

C. PELLI
Battery Park
Rice

ANAMNESIS   COLLAGE CITY

permanent
city structures
L. Kahn   **MONUMENTS**
Dacca   S. Wilson
GRAVITAS   New Palladians

ALDO ROSSI
Arch. of City
Modena   Stirling
Teatro del Mondo C. ROWE

Loos Revival

URBANIST CLASSICISM   **BALANCED
                        RECONSTRUCTION**

F. MONTES
Cergy Pontoise

FUNDAMENTALIST
CLASSICISM

CITY AS TYPOLOGY

G. GRASSI
Student Hses.

O. M. UNGERS
ARCH. AS THEME
DAM
Galeria/Sky. Frankfurt

ROBERT KRIER
IBA Berlin
Ritterstrasse
URBAN SPACES

DUANEY & PLATER-ZYBERK
Seaside
Vilanova Hse.

LE CORBUSIER
Modulor
Chandigarh   **UNIVERSALISM**
                Johansen
Constructive Logic

THEORY OF TYPES
LA TENDENZA

J. Robertson

NEW ABSTRACTION

R. Weinstein

Mies Revival

Mies

M. BOTTA
Morbio
Viganello
Stabio

Batey & Mack
Holt Hse.
Primitivism

Silvetti Machado NORDIC CLASSICISM EXHIBITION 1982
                  Steven Holl
CONSTRUCTIONIST   Morphosis
CLASSICISM   M. Takeyama   Ed Jones
Nakamura   Mississauga
                                    C. Hall

J. Wiedemann

NEW TUSCANISM
M. Tonini

Reichlin & Reinhardt

T. AIDA
Toy Block Hses.

T. WATANABE STUDIO WORKS
Suntumori   Southside

T. Ito

R. Moneo
M. Garay   UNGERS & KISS

D. PORPHYRIOS   Tod Williams
CL. IS NOT A STYLE E. Kupper

SOM

KOHN PEDERSEN & FOX San Fran
333 S. Wacker   2200 Ross
Hercules   Dallas
Procter & Gamble
NYC SKYSCRAPERS

REVIVALIST
CLASSICISM

Q. TERRY
Riverside, London
Waverton Hse.

A. Greenberg
Courthouse
Diplomatic R. R.

COPYING AND IMITATION

H. Hope Reed

R. Erith

War Rebuilding Warsaw

Disneyland

GETTY MUSEUM
Beaux-Arts Exhibition
D. Hicks

COMMERCIAL CLASSICISM

J. Blatteau

B. STERN
UVA work
Bozzi Hse.

T. G. Smith
TUSCAN & L.

JOHNSON & BURGEE
AT & T   Republic Bank
PPG   UNIV. OF HOUSTON
Transco   DADE C. C.

J. Jerde

Port Grimaud

Lutyens Revival

enclosed positive shapes

MASS-PRODUCED CLASSICISM   JUXTAPOSED TASTES

LOWRISE HIGH DENSITY

Bologna

R. BOFILL AND TALLER
Arcades
Abraxas
Montpellier
Cergy Pontoise
XIV arrondisement

J. STIRLING
STUTTGART
Dusseldorf
Clore Gallery
Berlin science
Mansion House

R. KRIER
I.B.A.

Charing Cross

sufficient density
J. JACOBS
mixed age
mixed use
diversity

short blocks

J. Rouse
Festival downtowns
Harborplace
Faneuil Hall

C. Alexander
Eishin Univ.

San Francisco Plan

URBANIST
CLASSICISM

PLURALISM

CITY TYPOLOGY
positive urban space

Advocacy Planners

B. Thompson

D.Soloman

M. Núñez

Barnet, Robertson, Weinstein

C. Rowe
COLLAGE CITY

Battery Park
zoning rules

DIVERGENT
REFERENCE

J. Jerde
Horton Plaza
Westside Pav.

URBAN ARCHITECTURE
J. DIXON
St. Mark's Road   B. Myers
                   Phoenix C.C.

M. GRAVES
Plocek   San Juan
Sunar   Humana
Portland Whitney

M. Mozuna
COSMIC ARCHITECTURE

ANTHROPOMORPHISM

C. JENCKS
Elemental House
Thematic House
Towards Symbolic Architecture

A. ISOZAKI
Fujimi C. C.
Tsukuba C. C.
MOCA

PRESENCE OF ABSENCE

DIVERGENT REFERENCE
J. STIRLING

MULTIPLE-CODES
DOUBLE-CODING

Y. Kijima
S. Toki

M. Takeyama
S. Tigerman

ICONOGRAPHIC PROGRAMME
SYMBOLIC ARCHITECTURE
T. GORDON SMITH

Venice Biennale

INCLUSIVISM

L. Kahn
Kimbell   P. Portoghesi
             C. Norberg-Schulz
Neo-Liberty INTENTIONS IN ARCHITECTURE

H. HOLLEIN
Schullin
Austrian Travel

T. BEEBY   E. Ambasz
synagogue   I. H. Finlay
Pediatrics   C. Heimsath
Hild Library

ECLECTIC
CLASSICISM

NEW REPRESENTATION

R.VENTURI
N. Penn
G.Wu
COMPLEXITY AND CONTRADICTION
LEARNING FROM LAS VEGAS

C. MOORE
Orinda
Piazza d'Italia
Sammis Hall

R. STERN
Lang House
Chicago Tribune
Pool House

C.Vandenhove
H. Cobb

Bofill and Taller

DIFFICULT UNITY
Baird & Jencks
MEANING IN ARCHITECTURE

BODY, MEMORY AND ARCHITECTURE

Cohen   K. Ishii
Giurgola
Righter, Rose, Lankin
Venturi School

ANAMNESIS

Taft
Rivercrest C. C.

Hoover Berg Desmond
H. Klotz

FREE-STYLE CLASSICISM
T. Farrell
TV-AM
Henley

G. Gund
J. Jourdan

V. Scully

P. Gough
A. Natalini

H. Mohl

176

CHAPTER VII
The Fundamentalists of Architecture

Post-Modern architecture inherited from Modernism two character traits: irony and classicism. But it displayed these characteristics rather than repressed them. Where Mies van der Rohe and Walter Gropius were cryptic classicists, hiding their entablatures and axes behind technical necessity, their followers such as Aldo Rossi and Mario Botta are candid about these influences. Where Le Corbusier was implicitly ironic at Ronchamp, his follower James Stirling consciously uses irony at Stuttgart.[1] As has often been noted,[2] Modern architects had a subconscious strongly attracted by classicism, but for various reasons – primarily social guilt and the commitment to a changing technology – they suppressed this traditionalist urge.

Yet at times they did consult the past. When, for instance, Le Corbusier was troubled by the state of architecture, he would return to the Parthenon as a standard to emulate, he would mentally 'start again at zero'. The return to fundamentals was both the primitivist reflex of Modernism – of Picasso and so many recent artists – and the result of a preference for ascetic, tragic forms.[3] Le Corbusier loved Greek temples for their *gravitas*, their heroic contrast with a 'Homeric landscape' and their simplicity. At heart he was, like Louis Kahn, a Fundamentalist. The return to the fundamentals of building – structure, space and light – guaranteed a poetry of truthful building. Like Abbé Laugier, the father of Modern primitivism, he might aver, in moments of self doubt: 'one should never lose sight of our little hut', because its simplicity is a check on subjectivity. Primitive huts, *gravitas*, the minimal ascetic style, truthfulness accompanied by a raw awkwardness – these are the hallmarks of the Fundamentalists. With Post-Modernists this tradition takes on a different coloration, a new interest in the city as the basis for architecture and a commitment to anamnesis (i.e. the memory of past forms). Both goals are given ironic twists and disguised deflections, the typical displacement tactics of Post-Modernists.

Louis Kahn's Dacca Assembly Building is a case in point. Designed in 1962 and finished in 1983 after Kahn's death, the building is a powerfully incongruous version of Ledoux's classicism (1). Where Ledoux might have used concrete and marble, Kahn would reverse the proportions of these materials, or invert the customary relations between background and adornment. No doubt Kahn's mouldings are ultra-thin to save money, but their strange size, especially when contrasted with the monolithic walls, is as much a mannerism as the voided pediments and gargantuan circles. In plan

Opposite:
The Four Traditions of Post-Modern Classical Architecture, 1960-1985

one finds more Ledoux-like forms, such as the interlocking of primary shapes, again expanded in scale and given a haunting *terribilità* beyond anything that Michelangelo would have attempted. It's interesting to turn such Fundamentalist Classicism mentally back into the canonic norm to see what is missing: the cornices and domes which would crown these drums, the bay rhythms and base mouldings which would give them scale. Clearly Kahn, like Le Corbusier, displaces classicism by distorting its elements to create a new feeling of the sublime. His primitivism is the acceptable face of classicism for a western building in an underdeveloped or newly rich Middle Eastern country, and indeed, this lead has been followed not only by the large American offices but by sensitive designers such as Jorn Utzon.

One can't help viewing these developments with mixed feelings: convincing as monuments, they are questionable in terms of local building materials and culture. India has constructed vast cemeteries of such public buildings, emulating Kahn and Le Corbusier, which a younger generation of architects is already beginning to regret. Hot, dark, monolithic and no doubt sublime, these works miss the delicacy of the previous colonial classicism. Their primitivism is meant, however, to compensate for the pretence and political control of the colonial mode: one understands the motive of social guilt in keeping the Fundamentalists' style pure.

The Types and Morphology of the City

Aldo Rossi, whose work Vincent Scully has proclaimed 'the most moving and haunting being done today', is also the most resolutely anti-bourgeois.[4] Like Kahn's it is stripped to the fundamentals and built from rhetorically proletarian materials: raw concrete, bare faced wood, and steel. It always has an urban genesis and attempts to gain validity through embodying city archetypes such as the perimeter block or centrally planned building (2). These constitute, like Laugier's primitive hut, the basis for an abstract and social order. In the Post-Modernists' appeal for authority such city building ranks, along with history and symbolism, as a prime justification.

Rossi's *L'Architettura della Città* published in Italy, 1966, was translated into several languages and appeared in English in 1982.[5] By that time its arguments had become widely disseminated and overlapped with those of other Post-Modernists. They promoted three different values: the analysis of the city in terms of typology versus a 'naive functionalism', the permanence of city types throughout a series of functional transformations (such as the coliseum at Arles being turned into housing and shops) and the importance of monuments and 'primary areas' for preserving the collective memory of cities. These arguments gained support by analogous ones promoted by O. M. Ungers, Colin Rowe, Kevin Lynch, the 'Contextualists', Robert Venturi, Robert Krier and my own writings.[6] In short, they were part of a broad movement towards reasserting the importance of urban constants.

Their main contribution was the way in which Rossi illustrated his notion of type. Returning to nineteenth-century theoreticians such as Quatremère

7.1 Louis Kahn, *Dacca Assembly Building*, Bangla Desh, 1962-83 (Photograph James Dunnett)

7.2 Aldo Rossi, *Il Teatro del Mondo (Floating Theatre)*, Venice, 1979 (Photograph courtesy the architect)

de Quincy, he defined the type as a principle or rule of structure and form, rather than a model to be copied. In returning to this abstract level he effectively adopted the notions of the Platonic idea, and the classicist distinction between imitating and copying.

The idea that one could creatively imitate a type allowed him to refashion the norm and cliché with surreal displacements, rather than, as preservationists were arguing, replicate existing urban fabric. The striking results are more apparent in his drawings (3) than executed buildings, but they're evident in both. For instance some of his conceptual sketches for an IBA project in Berlin (a competition he won), show invention within the urban type he is proposing: the perimeter block (4). This favoured city form is mixed with his characteristic repertoire of archetypes – the truncated tower, chimney, church, crane and blank white column. All of these elements are presented with a sad, stark boldness, reminiscent of de Chirico, and the lament for a lost culture also derives from this painter. So indeed do many of the actual elements and motifs, such as the empty piazza and the window made more melancholy by the stark shadows. Even the abrupt chimney, symbolising industrialisation and paternal authority, is adapted from de Chirico. In effect these de Chirican drawings and buildings compress time as much as they do space. Past and future are collapsed into a standardised present which is shorn of stylistic specificity – Rossi spurns 'the styles' as much as did Le Corbusier and Kahn. All ages are one in this dream world; a world which would be nostalgic if it weren't so remorselessly dour. This sadness, which Peter Eisenman and other critics equate with a portrayal of death,[7] might, I think, be equated just as well with the neutrality of the archetype.

Aldo Rossi loves buildings that are generic, ascetic, modest and relatively unknown. His taste for the timeless and abstract – for the type shorn of all individuality – lends his work a haunting memory which is reminiscent of the cemetery. The burnt-out look, used in the 'House of the Dead' at Modena and ironically on houses of the living in Berlin, derives from the motif which Boullée and Adolf Loos used so effectively: the black shadow cast against a windowless wall (5). This stark figure immediately reminds us of destroyed buildings, ones that have been bombed and show no signs of life: no mouldings, glass, vegetation, written inscriptions, or any other variation of rhythm. They are absolute monuments of the sublime, of eternity and its terror, or, as Rossi dubs them, the essential types of architecture.

His cemetery of San Cataldo at Modena, without doubt the most basic of the Fundamentalists' work, is made from the following Neoclassical or Phileban primary forms: a surrounding wall with pitched roof, a cube, an 'abandoned' house with voided windows and, on axis, the communal grave. Between the cube and the cone is another wall building and then a triangularly disposed ossuary. So triangle, cone, cube, rectangle and pitched roof – the classical repertoire – are reduced to essentials and dramatised by Boullée's 'architecture of shadows'; the very recipe this eighteenth-century architect recommended for portraying the finality of death. 'Nothing is

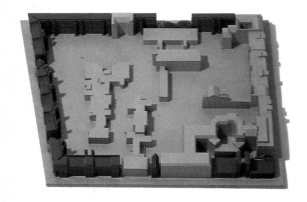

7.3,4 Aldo Rossi, *Sudliche Friedrichstadt*, block 10 model, 1982-5, and study for a column at the corner, 1981, Berlin (Photographs IBA)

7.5 Aldo Rossi, *'House of the Dead' or Ossuary*, cemetery of San Cataldo, Modena, 1971-84 (Photograph C. Jencks)

7.3

7.5

gloomier', he said of his projected *Monument Funéraire*, 'than plane surfaces, bare . . . light-absorbing materials stripped of detail'. Boullée's design has that same sublime massing and ratio of solid to void that have become Rossi's trademarks: wide expanses of masonry punctuated by very small holes. When Michael Graves started using a similar syntax in the Portland Building, the client quite naturally asked him to enlarge the window size for both functional and semantic reasons. The small black void on a wide white wall has since become a fashion and one the more powerful for its sinister overtones.

Here we touch a nerve ending of the Fundamentalists which its supporters, such as Vincent Scully, are loath to admit or deal with adequately. Convincing as painting, heroic as concept and model, the austere *gravitas* of this kind of building has unpleasant associations for many. Rossi and Manfredo Tafuri would deny these associations, particularly those with fascist architecture, but stubbornly people continue to read architecture through related imagery.[8] No doubt Rossi is sincere in designing this cemetery based on the typology and associations he perceives: the arcaded path, the courtyard and archetypal house and tomb. But there are other, equally plausible, meanings associated with the concentration camp, prison and mental hospital. I have often criticised this aberrant signification, not as Rossi avers because I believe a cemetery should always be happy, but because of its lack of multiple coding and irony.[9] The problem with the Fundamentalist style is precisely its virtue – its simplicity. When every form has a dignified *gravitas*, one asks for a contrasting elegance and humour. That Rossi can produce buildings which are witty and colourful is clear from his spry cabins of Elba, his Teatro del Mondo and Friedrichstrasse housing. And latterly his work has become more complex and mixed in genre, so the promise of his urban typology may indeed result in the most poetic architecture of this century. It's just premature for Scully to announce its existence.

O. M. Ungers, who deserves equal credit with Rossi for having reintroduced an urbanist typology and the idea of its transformation, actually uses opposition as an integral part of his design method. What he terms *'coincidentum oppositorum'* after medieval rhetoric results in the extreme contrast of pure types: in the Frankfurt Fair Hall, for instance, where the galleria of glass is set against the red masonry shed (6, 7). This last is further articulated into two types – the stepped platform and rooftop parking lot. In each case there is a reduction to the abstract idea, the basic ordering principle, which is then manipulated or transformed. He has written about this method as both 'The New Abstraction' and 'Architecure as Theme'.[10]

The New Abstraction in architecture deals with a rational geometry, with clear and regular forms in plan as well as in elevation. In this context, the plan is not the result of a literal interpretation of function and structural conditions but rather of logical, geometrical systems. It is based on proportional relationship and coherent sequences – as was the case in the 'bound system' of medieval architecture, in the

7.6,7 O.M. Ungers, *Frankfurt Fair Hall*, exterior view and interior of galleria, Frankfurt-Am-Main, 1979-82 (Photographs C. Jencks and the architect)

Palladian plan, and in Durand's lessons on architecture – rather than on the empiricial results of programmes or functional organisation.[11]

In arguing thus Ungers is, like Rossi, stressing the autonomous nature of architectural ideas and organisation, their independence from local context and history, and also the architect's duty to use them as the creative 'themes' of a building. This method, exemplary in so far as it goes, also like Rossi's, fails to deal with changing styles, symbolism and the 'taste-cultures' of those for who the design exists. But, more positively, it focuses on several essences of architecture: space, geometrical organisation and the transformation of types. Because Ungers reduces architectural ideas to these types, his work is characteristic of Primitivist Classicism.

We can recognise Laugier's primitive hut – the fundamental house and temple – inside his German Architectural Museum, 'the house within a house' (8). Originally conceived to break upwards out of its nineteenth-century shell and announce its new presence to the city of Frankfurt, it could, if carried through, have been a striking *coincidentum oppositorum*. As it is, floating in pure, white, transcendental abstraction, this house-temple conveys the sacred notion of architecture as pure idea. The whole museum is a masterful opposition between the existing and the new, incorporating, among other antinomies, the contrast between white grid and masonry (9). With the collection of Post-Modern drawings and models which Heinrich Klotz has built up, it has now become a fundamental shrine of the movement. It's a beautiful and successful building. Many regard it as Ungers' finest, and the only doubts concern its denial of representational and local symbolism.

At the most abstract level Ungers will incorporate representational signs into his *bricolage* of types. Thus his Frankfurt skyscraper, near the Fair Hall, mixes the two Frankfurt codes in striking contrast: the all-glass skyscraper and the red masonry cube (10). The interpenetrating opposition of these pure forms is, like the work of Arquitectonica, taken to a rhetorical extreme to accentuate the underlying idea and, like all such reduced Platonism, it may suffer in several years time from seeming too diagrammatic. But at present, surrounded by dull one-liners, it is refreshingly tough and witty.

Ungers taught with Colin Rowe at Cornell University for several years and, perhaps because they shared many ideas on city building, their small differences became pronounced and they continuously quarrelled. Rowe was evolving his idea of Collage City which, along with Rossi and Ungers' ideas, must be taken as the third cornerstone of urbanistic thinking. Unlike these other two, Rowe is not so much a Fundamentalist as an eclectic and his ideas of collage necessitate a stylistic pluralism. Yet because of temperament and sensibility – his affinity with Le Corbusier – his writing tends to promote the Primitivist Classicists and he has influenced work in this school. For instance, James Stirling's first essay in Collage City, his design for the Düsseldorf Museum, keeps the pure classical forms – the positive cube and negative circle – at a very basic level (11). Classical ornament is reduced to the expression of masonry joints and the presence of one pediment. These forms

7.8,9 O.M. Ungers, *German Architectural Museum,* 'The House Within a House' and gallery space, Frankfurt-Am-Main, 1982-5 (Photographs C. Jencks)

7.10 O.M. Ungers, *Skyscraper,* Frankfurt-Am-Main, 1983-5 (Photograph Dieter Leistner)

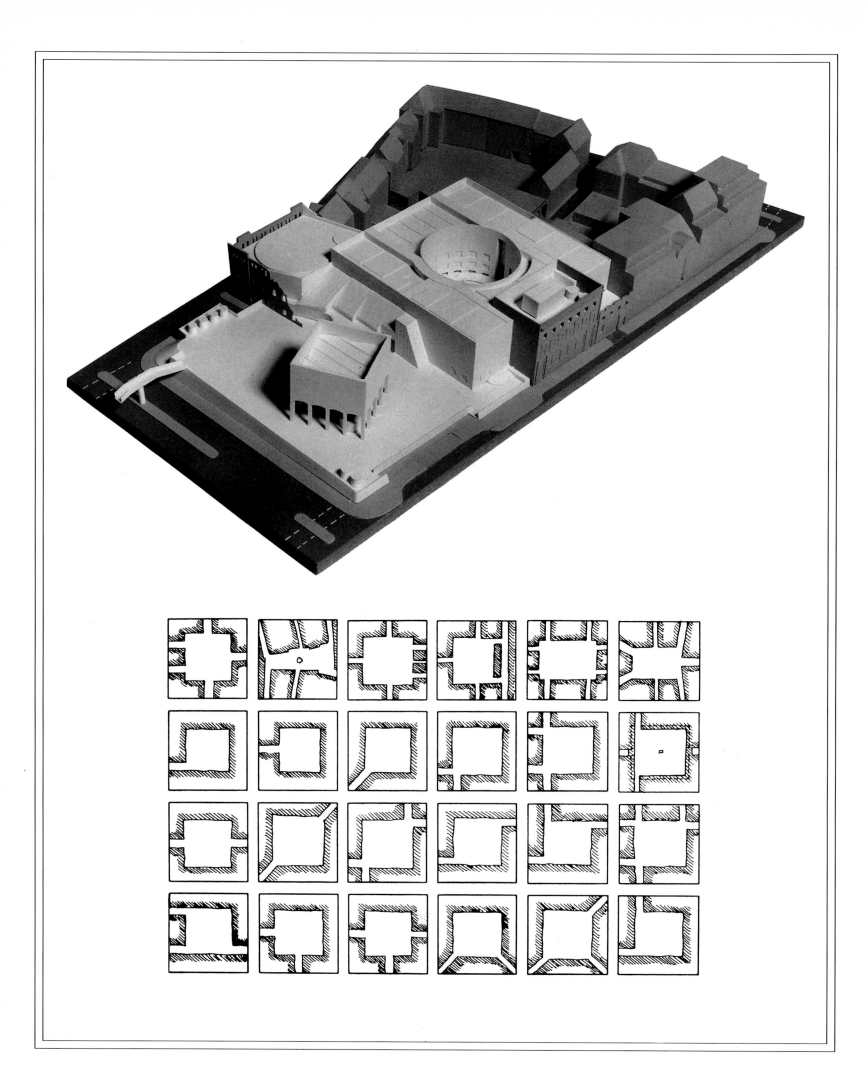

are collaged into the existing fabric – nestling at the same height – and with Modernist technologies such as the warped glass canopy. This project, unfortunately not built, led directly to his later Stuttgart addition which will be considered later as the canonic example of Eclectic Classicism, but is here included because it shows how both he and Colin Rowe keep one foot in the Fundamentalist tradition.

Rowe's theory and book on *Collage City*, 1978, has had as great an impact as Rossi's *Architecture of the City* and Ungers' *Architecture as Theme*.[12] Unlike these two, however, Rowe is committed to the juxtaposition of 'utopian' fragments as a political as well as a formal strategy. His philosophy favours a democratic pluralism, the competition of small groups, the decentralisation of decisions, as against the more totalitarian planning theories whether Marxist, Modernist or, to give it the unhappy label it deserves, Consumerist Monopolist. He foresees a new city and a planning strategy based on vest-pocket utopias, which recognise 'both the demands of the ideal and the needs of the *ad hoc*'. These latter needs, it should be stressed, are precisely the kind of contingent things which Rossi and Ungers explicitly deny. While Rowe, like them, wants the beauties and clarities inherent in a conceptual approach to architecture, he also wants to include elements which are ephemeral and conventionally symbolic. Needless to say I find this approach more developed than the former two – indeed on the level of politics and formalism, *the* most developed theory of urbanism to date. Its reliance on a series of antinomies – primary among which is the figure/ground dichotomy – uses dialectic as the agent of urban meaning. Thus monument is consciously set against a background tissue, not left free-standing in a park as it would be according to Modernist theories; positive urban space is formed – squares, arcades, curved circuses – against the background of wall-buildings, or tissue of infill. Urban space and enclosure are conceived as an equally valid and necessary pair, to be shaped together.

Such truisms need to be reasserted after the one-sided exaggerations of Modernist redevelopment. Modern architects sought to get rid of the urban 'room' and succeeded; commercial development worsened the situation by creating three current anti-spaces: the sprawl, the strip and the haphazard scatter-shot. The younger group of Post-Modernists, following on from Rossi, Ungers and Rowe, in counteracting these trends has been more doctrinaire in this reassertion of traditional types of organisation. Robert Krier, for instance, in his book *Urban Space*, returns to a classical typology which is explored systematically through a series of conceptual sketches (12). Positive and negative space is designed together to create enclosed urban places that lead dramatically on from one another. The all-important relationships between figure and ground, monument and infill, public and private are worked out in a classical balance. It was, of course, this balance which was lost in the Modernist emphasis on the free-standing block.

Robert Krier, as well as Rossi, Ungers and several other architects, has had the opportunity to build new versions of this traditional typology in

7.11 James Stirling, *Düsseldorf Museum Project*, 1975 (Photograph John Donat)

7.12 Robert Krier, *Typology of Squares*, from 'Urban Space', 1979

Berlin, under the direction of Paul Kleiheus and IBA. This organisation has provided a unique opportunity, over five years and more, for major international architects to try out this new urbanism, 'the reconstruction of the European city' as it has come to be known. Not only do such architects design whole perimeter blocks, but they collaborate with others on a particular street so the resultant urban texture has the same 'unity in variety' of a classical city built over time (13). The result, while modest as architecture, is much more effective urbanistically than the work of a single architect. In Block 31, for instance, something like seventeen architects have orchestrated the overall perimeter composition. Thus the unity of the street theme is kept in height and surface while it is varied by window details and materials. The space flows continuously in curve and straight line to come to climactic enclosure on Robert Krier's 'palazzo' at the end of a square (14). With such overall control the inherent symphonic organisation of a city again becomes possible and we can experience the equivalent of the sonato-allegro form while walking down the street. A musical theme is stated, inverted, modulated and finally brought to a climax at a public space and building.

In this sense the new classical urbanism is not, as its critics sometimes aver, nostalgic and reactionary, but rather a precondition for meaning. Only in cases where some public ground rules have been laid down – mostly about the classical archetypes of street, perimeter block and monument – is this symphonic and social meaning possible. Post-Modernists have begun to face the inherent paradox which Modernist urbanism has bequeathed them: the emphasis on creativity with the freestanding monument destroys the impact of that creativity. Only by locating the figural building in a stronger background fabric can it gain significance.

Understanding this contextual level of meaning, Robert Krier has, since the early 1970s, designed many urban set pieces which stitch together a fabric eroded by Modernist planning. This work requires patience, time and political willpower, three things in short supply in an era of transition. Nevertheless, his vision has been taken up on several sites in Berlin. An early example, the 'white house' on the Ritterstrasse, is another abstract palace type, an H-shaped block with classical symmetries that focus on a figural sculpture and the communal front door (15,16). Here there is a very interesting mixture of the white International Style with the classical palazzo style, particularly its recurrent aBa motifs. The more we analyse the building, the more dichotomies we discover. For instance, the secure, massive fortress shape with its large archways recalls the Karl-Marx-Hof and other housing projects of the Vienna which Krier inhabits, while the eroded body recalls *The Victory of Samothrace* and mutilated classical sculpture. No doubt the project is meant to tie the social Utopianism of the 1920s with the broken humanist tradition and this explains the melancholic erosion of the sculpture as well as the obvious double-coding, both of which define it as Post-Modernist (16). A caryatid or herm is often traditionally placed by the front door next to a column, and this anthropomorphism is here treated in such a

7.13 Robert Krier et al, *Block 31*, Linden-Ritterstrasse, West Berlin, 1984 (Photograph courtesy the architects)

7.14 Robert Krier, *Block 31*, palazzo at the end of a square (Photograph courtesy the architect)

7.15 Robert Krier, *'The White House'*, Ritterstrasse Block, Berlin-Kreuzberg, 1977-80 (Photograph Gerald Blomeyer)

7.16 Robert Krier, *Sculpture*, Ritterstrasse Block, Berlin-Kreuzberg, 1981 (Photograph Gerald Blomeyer)

haunting way that it suggests another significance – Berlin as the city of hope and continuous human mutilation, the city of victory and destruction.

Leon Krier Discovers the Proper Balance

Leon Krier, Robert's younger brother, has been equally influential in formulating the new classical urbanism, perhaps even more important in crystallising its particular small block morphology. The key project, which shows the breakthrough in all its salient points, is the school for 500 children which was to be located on an artificial lake at St. Quentin in Yvelines, next to Ricardo Bofill's first Post-Modern Classical housing (17). Unfortunately it wasn't built because Krier refused to compromise on the construction, which came in over double the budget.

Nonetheless this project was seminal and has influenced the work of most Post-Modernists, notably that of Michael Graves, Jaquelin Robertson, Fernando Montes, Ed Jones, and Andres Duany and Elizabeth Plater-Zyberk. What were its chief characteristics?

First of all the scheme broke up a large-scale urban function into a cluster of village-like volumes connected by a public way. Let us call this method 'syncopated variation', the compositional method of the Roman colonial town. As a result the school is grammatical, unlike the superblocks or megabuildings with which Leon Krier contrasts it. This point should be underlined, since these megastructures include those of Herman Hertzberger who is usually thought to be the most humanist of Modern architects. Krier's point is that even these articulated superblocks don't break down into a readable and enjoyable scale: only such types as the vernacular-classical village or Roman *insula* can provide the right syntax. In the school project a tissue of pantiled rooms forms the peripheral background for a public core of monuments: the octagonal library on one end of the main axis leading to the general assembly building and then the public space and restaurant overlooking the lake. Public and private areas are intermeshed by tight walkways and squares (18). A foursquare belvedere dominates the scheme, but, like the other monuments, it is subtly and informally placed off-centre. A series of refinements and distortions are introduced to humanise the grid and give the classicism a life it lacks in the schemes of Albert Speer – which Krier perversely defends.[13] Here, part and whole, repetition and variation, square and deviation from the square are used in a proportion which, unlike Nazi Classicism, does not intimidate. This balance of elements reminds one of a monastery, the plan of St. Gall for instance, except that it has a more lively and varied harmony. With this scheme Leon Krier comes closer than any other current architect to capturing the spirit, if not letter, of classical urbanism.

As a polemicist Krier has been compared with Schinkel, Poussin and Serlio by Colin Rowe, who also calls him a 'mini-Mozart'.[14] Jaquelin Robertson compares him to Le Corbusier and Piranesi, and has proclaimed him 'the most curious, potent and significant force in architecture today'.[15] Andres Duany, at an architectural conference in London, 1985, referred to

7.17,18 Leon Krier, *School for 500 children,* axonometric and plan, St. Quentin-en-Yvelines, France, 1978 (Photographs courtesy the architect and the Canadian Centre of Architecture, Montreal)

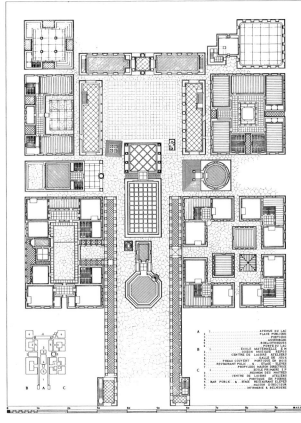

him simply as 'The Unattainable Master'. These superlatives and comparisons are well deserved if one focuses on his urbanistic schemes, and not on the semantic drawbacks of his language.[16] For what he has managed to do is take Aldo Rossi's idea of city typology and Ungers' idea of urban morphology, combine the two, look at the European city as an archetype and come up with the ideal balance between the small urban block and the square, the private realm and public monument. In effect he has produced the ideal harmony between competing values, avoiding the boredom of repetition inherent in the Baroque palace, the nineteenth-century perimeter block and Modernist sprawl (19).

His critique of these oversimplified monoliths obviously has a social and political dimension, although this aspect remains relatively implicit. Presumably Krier, a Post-Marxist, favours a decentralised organisation, or something like the small-scale economic units of the New England township. He is certainly against all forms of overcentralisation whether socialist or capitalist, and his return to an *insula*-type fabric implies a mini-capitalism of small businesses and shop-owners. At a certain level of abstraction, it is quite true to say that these ideas were not original, having been very much in the air since Jane Jacobs published *The Death and Life of Great American Cities* in 1961. Her emphasis on the essentials of urbanism – the small block, diversity of age, mixed use and pedestrian streets – all find confirmation fifteen years later in Krier's designs. What makes his contribution important then is not the abstract theory, but its architectural derivation; the particular artistic form he has given to these principles.

Leon Krier's most developed urban scheme is for the Tegel area in Berlin, an IBA project ultimately won by Moore, Ruble and Yudell. Krier proposed a much denser tissue of buildings than the other competitors, one that relates to a large Renaissance town (20). His 'tourist map' view of the scheme shows the way the existing boundaries – river, forest and autobahn – are accentuated. Small-scale *insulae*, with many pedestrian routes leading to a shared courtyard with shops below apartments, form the secluded background realm (21). The combinations, scale, and name – *Insula Tegeliensis* – make explicit Krier's polemical point: that in terms of urban blocks, no European organisation has ever improved on the Roman prototype. Within this ideal pedestrian environment are a series of public buildings – the cultural centre called for by the IBA – which are turned into Roman building types such as theatre and public bath. The most imposing building, in the middle of this 'town within a city', is the covered square, a powerful mixture of vernacular and Imperial Classicism (22). Here Roman cross-bracing is repeated so often that it resembles a steel truss. A heroic Doric order of paired columns opens out to the lake and streets on either side. This grave, explicit classicism is as close as Krier has come to seeing the consequences of his position carried through to the details, and the result is an awesome display of elements – perhaps too many. However the overall balance of public building and housing, street space and square, courtyard and housing,

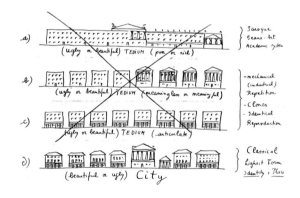

7.19 Leon Krier, comparison of Baroque, mechanical and classical city building, circa 1984 (Photograph courtesy the architect)

7.20,21 Leon Krier (assisted by Francisco Sanin), *New Hafenviertel*, masterplan, *Insula Tegeliensis*, axonometric, Berlin-Tegel, 1980-3 (Photographs courtesy the architect)

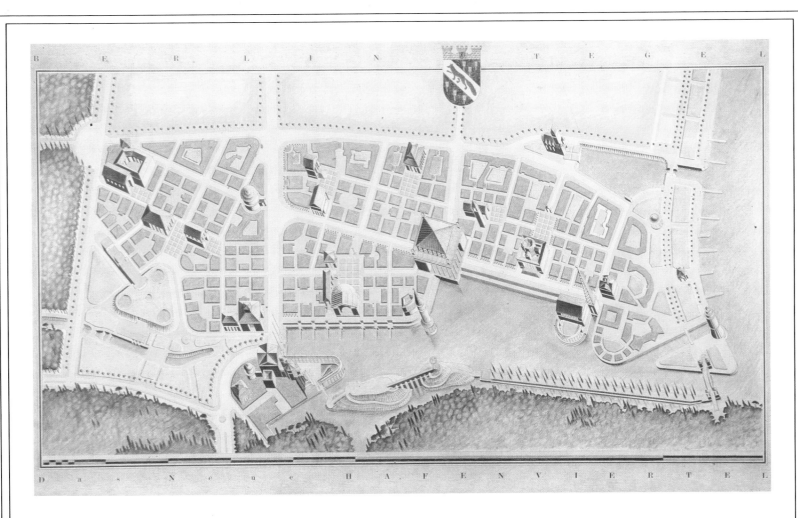

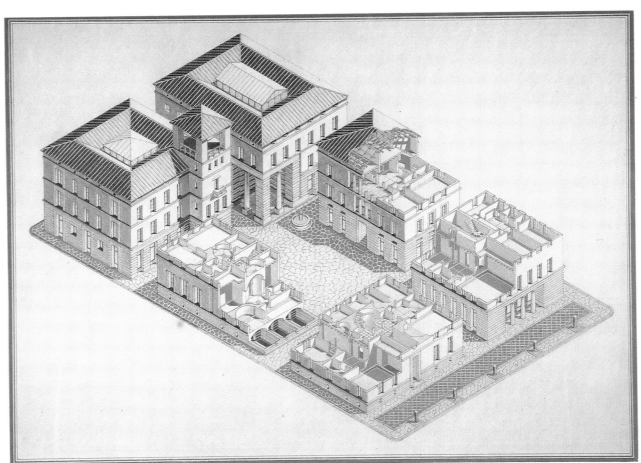

7.22 Leon Krier, *Belvedere and Covered Res Public*, Berlin-Tegel, 1983 (Photograph courtesy the architect)

7.23 Leon Krier, *Pliny's Villa Laurentium*, reconstruction, 1982 (Painting courtesy Rita Wolff)

7.24,25 Leon Krier, *Completion of Washington DC*, aerial perspective and plan, 1985 (Photographs courtesy the architect)

7.26 Leon Krier, *Capitol Building Redesigned*, Washington DC, 1985 (Photograph courtesy the architect)

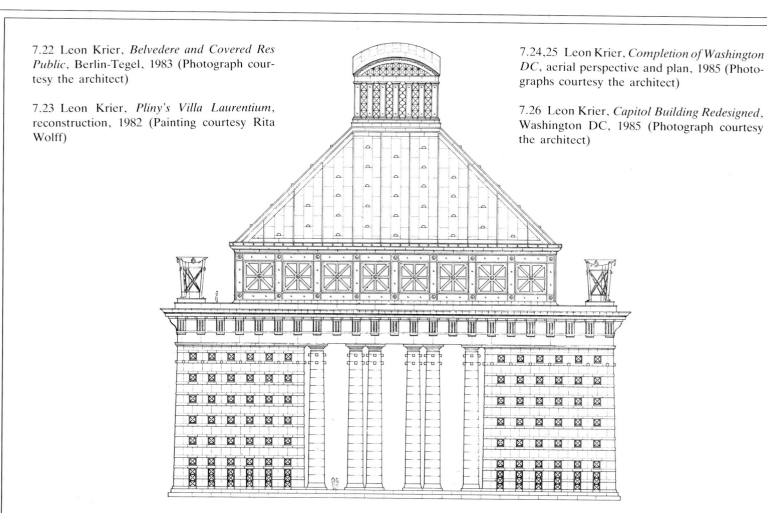

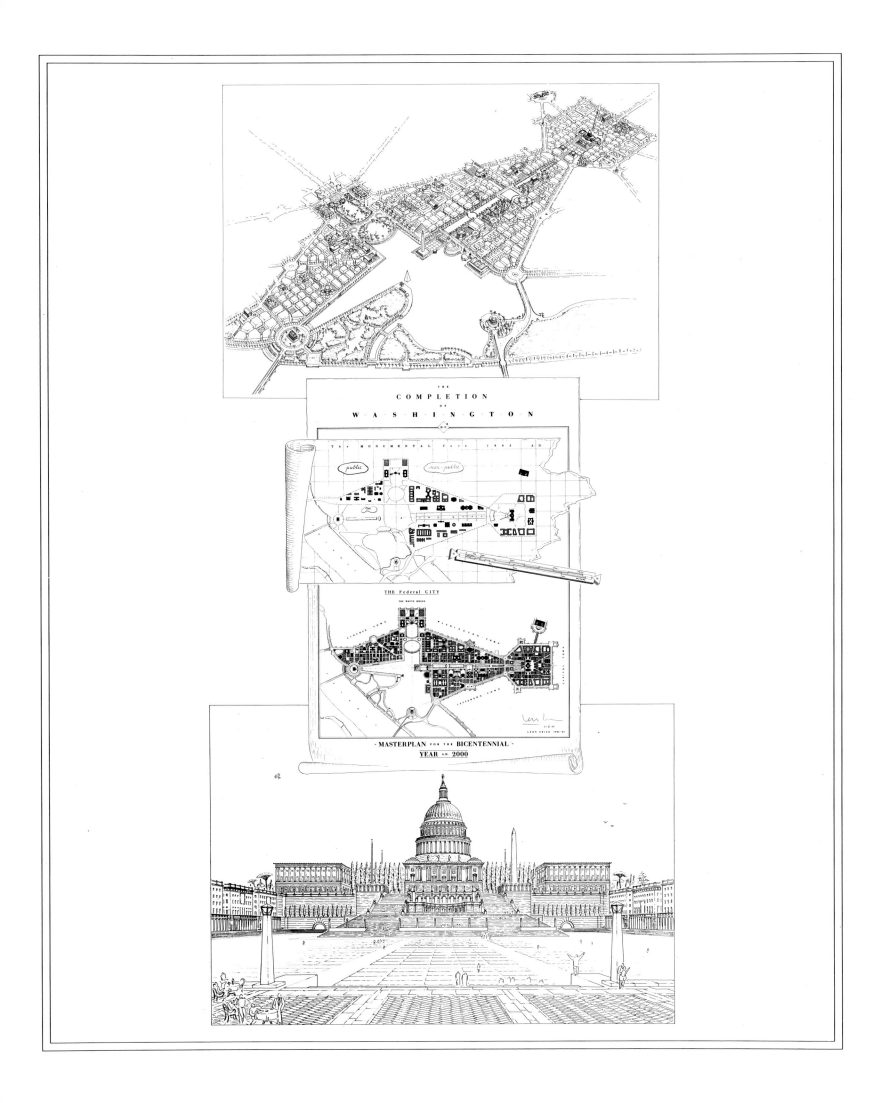

THE
COMPLETION
OF
WASHINGTON
D.C.

public   non-public

THE Federal CITY

· MASTERPLAN FOR THE BICENTENNIAL ·
YEAR A.D. 2000

is once again near perfect: that is if one wants the best type of urban morphology that Europe has produced.

No doubt these schemes are feasible from an economic and social viewpoint and, as we'll see, they're even being built in an American context where there are more cars. Their importance lies however in being critical propositions in favour of the small urban block. Small block planning, to give this *insulae* type its generic name, shades nicely into acropolis/village planning, and here we touch upon a related schema Leon Krier has revived for the architectural world. In his reconstruction of Pliny's Villa, a speculative exercise that has intrigued architects for several hundred years, Krier could play with his typology of collaged set-pieces in a more lyrical manner than his urban 'reconstructions' allowed (23). Here we have a vision of village planning as if the twentieth century never happened (which indeed it hadn't when Pliny described his retreat), an Arcadian ideal that has influenced painters as well as architects (see Chapter VI). There is no compromise here and none of the ironies or complexities of reference which are the defining characteristics of Post-Modernism. Rather the scheme has a heroic straightforwardness, a positive nostalgia which illustrates the advantage of dividing up a large functional programme into small, room-size elements, which are then juxtaposed in plan. Frank Gehry and others have used the same typology in a completely different style.[17]

Krier applied similar principles to his Utopian design for the completion of Washington DC. Here we find the wide open spaces of this Capitol city finally filled up with an urban tissue that gives the monuments a scale and purpose. Presently the centre of Washington suffers from the kind of agoraphobia which besets many suburbs: the large buildings are much too far apart and separated by dull municipal planting. Their scale belongs not to the pedestrian, but the helicopter. So Krier proposes dividing the federal area into four new towns, called after the presidents Lincoln, Washington, Jefferson, and the Capitol, and these form a small city of 80,000 with the kind of density one finds in neighbouring Georgetown (24). This reuse of 'small town American' models, of Savannah and Williamsburg, as the guide for the future is made without Post-Modern irony. They are combined with the 'small urban block' of his European prototypes to create that dense urbanity which is the ideal of any pedestrian area. Monuments, lakes and a Grand Canal punctuate the fabric and give it life, removing the classical pomp and circumstance which is now overbearing (25). Indeed the Capitol Building itself is cut down to size and redesigned so it too becomes comprehensive and grammatical (26). New monuments are added, paid for by the private building, such as the new stylobate under the Washington Monument and Constitution Square in front of the Capitol. Krier, not surprisingly, compares his masterplan to the American constitution, as a set of benign principles which mediate between public and private interests: 'A good masterplan will allow man to satisfy all his material and spiritual needs within walking distance. It will not promote any one of them at the expense of the others.'[18]

7.27 Leon Krier, *The Market of Antiquities*, Berlin-Tegel, 1982 (Photograph Der Scutt Architect Collection)

The heroism and courage of this plan are astounding: it really does complete L'Enfant's initial sketch in the most rational and lyrical way. One can, however, raise doubts about the paternalism needed for its realisation, one can carp at some of its nostalgic masonry (which has effectively shut out the twentieth century), but fundamentally it is a rational scheme based on such ideal urban proportions as the sixteenth-century ratio of street to square, of monument to background, and of the ten-minute walk to various urban functions. Because Krier has patiently built up his knowledge of the proper balance between city archetypes, he can offer them to a Late-Modern culture without equivocation. Hence his disarming simplicity; the past has effectively challenged the present, the nostalgia is used as creatively as it was in the American and French Revolutions.

Leon Krier has underscored his polemical position with a paradoxical aphorism: 'I can only make Architecture because I do not build. I do not build because I am an Architect.' The contradiction can be unravelled once we understand that he means the Architect cannot build under the present technical and social circumstances which force him to produce instant megabuildings constructed of flimsy materials: the billion dollar monolith of glass and steel. Thus he has had to live by selling his drawings – not to the English collectors as Piranesi did, but to the Americans. His quick sketches and tourist map views, his coloured axonometrics and melancholic perspectives, mix the conceptual drawings of Le Corbusier with the haunting classical paintings of Paul Delvaux (27). Massive forms seen in light and shadow remind one of Le Corbusier's Utopian drawings, whereas the odd disjunctions and combinations, the occasional black sky and dreamlike atmosphere, remind one of the northern Surrealists. Rita Wolff, Leon Krier's wife, also paints like a Belgian Surrealist and, as we have seen in Chapter II, is also influenced by de Chirico. This mixture of genres might be explained partially by the fact that both Leon Krier and Rita Wolff come from Luxembourg, a tiny country where surreal distortions of classical models are to be found. Whatever the explanation for their powerful mixture, it has had an enormous influence both on architectural drawing and urban practice.

The young husband and wife team of Andres Duany and Elizabeth Plater-Zyberk has translated Krier's ideas into an American context, building several sections of new towns and small villas in the stripped classical style. The Vilanova House, built on the principles of the Erechtheum on the Acropolis, illustrates their classical ideas (28). Here we find a picturesque massing, meant to be perceived from an oblique approach as indeed the Erechtheum is first seen. A tetrastyle porch, leading off the main bedroom, is the main focus, rather like the Temple of Nike first seen from below the front of the Acropolis. Another small tetrastyle 'megaron' marks the side entrance and gives the rest of the building a gigantic scale. It's hard to believe this is not a small village designed by Schinkel, which was perhaps the image intended. The playful, small scale also derives from Leon Krier's small-block planning,

7.28,29 Andres Duany and Elizabeth Plater-Zyberk, *Vilanova House*, Florida, 1984, *Charleston Place*, Florida, 1983 (Photographs courtesy the architects)

as does the combination of classicism and simple vernacular: the white walls, tiny windows and pan tiles. The big/small scale is heightened by the introduction of a dark cream entablature – 'the datum of earth at a different level' – which effectively divides the building into a massive base and tiny village of one room temples. Another reason they give for the picturesque massing is that an irregular envelope can accommodate the changing requirements of domestic life; it can be modified with ease.

Duany and Plater-Zyberk have extended their classicism to the urban scale in several low cost developments. One, called 'Charleston', reuses southern building types which its name implies (29): here the 'megaron' alternates in elevation with a low garage to make a pleasing Ab rhythm down the street, which is then unified in a line at cornice level. It's Jefferson's University of Virginia at twenty-eight dollars per square foot; an extraordinary price, and, in terms of value for money, not only a developer's dream but an urbanist's delight. The architects characteristically turn functional requirements to their advantage. The mandatory jogging track, for instance, becomes a pretext for creating a pleasant system of walkways behind the housing.

Such practical idealism has led to the new town of 'Seaside' in Florida, the first of what may become a long line of such sensible developments. Duany and Plater-Zybeck were given a unique opportunity by the developer Robert Davis, to put their and Leon Krier's urban ideas into practice. The result is a pleasant southern town which has the kind of 'American Constitution' that Krier called for in Washington DC; that is, a masterplan with a set of zoning laws that create comprehensible streets and squares, a strong centre focusing on the town hall, a clear distinction between private and public buildings, and a variety within the overall classical vernacular (30). Following Rossi and Ungers, a basic urban typology is generated by the zoning laws, which create eight different town types, varying from the denser inner town and arcaded buidings to the grander villas on the road to the tennis club ('Type IV . . . The prototype is the Greek-Revival mansion of the Antebellum South'). The proportions of the squares come from southern examples and even the suburban prototype is found in nearby states such as Georgia (31). But the strength of the approach lies in its sensitive flexibility; in the architect's realisation that the zoning laws should establish positive urban continuity – street lines, roof heights, building out to plot lines – which can then be interpreted by different designers.

A study of towns throughout the American South indicated that a community of genuine variety and authentic character could not be generated by a single architect. Building is, therefore, given over to a multitude of designers [including Leon Krier] (32). The public buildings are to be freely designed by architects selected for their sympathy with the regional vernacular. The private buildings will be commissioned by the individual citizen/buyers subject to the provisions of a Master Plan and Zoning Code. These documents are

7.30 Andres Duaney and Elizabeth Plater-Zyberk, *Town of Seaside*, plans, Florida, 1978-83 (Photographs courtesy the architect)

7.31 Andres Duaney and Elizabeth Plater-Zyberk, *Town of Seaside*, suburban section type VI houses, Florida, 1982-5. The zoning generates picket fences, a street line, free-standing houses, small out-buildings at the rear etc. (Photograph Steven Brooke)

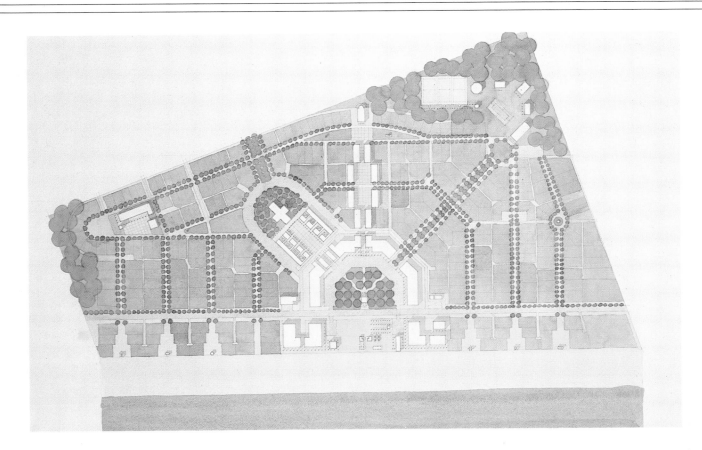

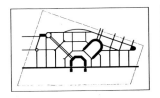 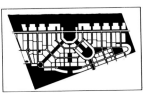   

intended to generate an urban environment similar to that of a small Southern town of the period prior to 1940.[19]

The short document that Duany and Plater-Zyberk have produced on Seaside provides a model of concise, classical urbanism. The developer's success with this prototype – houses are selling at three times the expected amount – promises the model will be taken up elsewhere in America.

In Europe, as one would expect, with less car ownership and more emphasis on the communal block, similar ideas are carried out at greater density. For instance Fernando Montes has applied the new classical urbanism to a part of the French new town Cergy-Pontoise and come up with large-scale primary forms that surround open public space (33). Ricardo Bofill and Manolo Nuñez have done the same, but in a more historicist manner, as we shall see in Chapter IX on the Eclectic Classicists. In the European examples, as with both Krier brothers, the emphasis is more on the public, shared nature of architecture than in America, and so the schemes always remind one of the monastery and Roman castrum, the medieval commune and hill town which are the ultimate roots of this tradition. Fernando Montes characteristically has a Fundamentalist belvedere overlooking the heart of his scheme, reminiscent of the church bell-tower and medieval lookout.

Given the basic antithesis between America and Europe, it's interesting to see the Argentinian-born Cesar Pelli building synthetic versions of both traditions in New York and Texas. Pelli does not belong exclusively to any single tradition, be it Fundamentalist, Eclectic, or even the Late-Modernist from which he springs.[20] Rather he's an architect who has developed coherently from one school to the next, keeping aspects of his approach as it becomes more complex. In the huge Battery Park 'city within the city' in downtown New York, there is the kind of multi-billion dollar concentration which Leon Krier and Jane Jacobs attack as the death of urbanism. But it is carried out in an abstract classical manner with primary forms, major and minor axes, and public and private articulations which ultimately stem from the classical tradition (34). The zoning laws formulated by Cooper, Eckstut Associates after Richard Weinstein also generate the small-scale, street architecture which is the hallmark of this tradition (35). Furthermore the emphasis on constructional realism is the essence of classicism. And the emphasis on establishing a system of rules for coherent urban development is consistent with Rossi and Krier's approach.

If there is one obvious stylistic way Pelli differs from these Fundamentalists it is in his more eclectic approach which, like the Collage City of Colin Rowe, appropriates various languages from different typologies. Thus at Rice University in Texas he adopts a version of the preexisting brick vernacular, but combines this with a Modernist emphasis on horizontality and what must be called an intellectualist display of structure and construction (36). For instance, the diaper patterns of the end walls are shown to be non-structural by the random punctuation of the pattern and ever-so-slight

7.32 Leon Krier, *House at Seaside*, Florida, 1985 (Photograph Abdel Wahed el Wakil)

7.33 Fernando Montes, *Public Area*, Cergy-Pontoise New Town, France, 1981-4 (Photograph courtesy the architect)

7.34 Cesar Pelli and Associates, *World Financial Centre*, Battery Park, New York, 1981-5 (Photograph courtesy Wolfgang Hoyt Esto)

7.35 Charles Moore, *Housing Layouts,* Battery Park, New York, 1982-6 (Photograph courtesy the architect)

protrusion of the side walls. The architectural expression is thus a collage of rational decisions and historicist patterns. Pelli allows himself only the license of blending the different red materials – the copper clad roof, the pink St. Joseph brick and the burgundy-coloured glazed brick (37). These form regular rhythmical patterns that are broken up into staccato beats to announce a change in function, or an entrance. Because Pelli keeps so literally to such juxtapositions, and eschews handicraft (for ideological reasons) his buildings have both an integrity and awkward straightforward-ness which, as mentioned at the outset, are the hallmarks of the Fundamen-talist tradition. For instance, the Reading Room is placed under an oddly truncated arch. On the inside it has an overall decorative pattern of yellow and turquoise checks which, like the outside diaper pattern they resemble, express their non-structural role. This is all very pleasing to the mind and it is carried through with a dead-pan seriousness that is the essence of classical *gravitas*. It is a mark of Pelli's structural classicism that it can be modified to suit a Beaux-Arts complex of loggias, arcades and terraces without becoming hackneyed or deferential. The scheme could also be said to mark the point at which the urban theories of Rossi, Ungers, Rowe and the Kriers have penetrated into mainstream practice.

The New Tuscanism and Constructionist Classicism

At several periods in its history classicism, like Catholicism, has claimed to be universal. Like the Modernism of Mies van der Rohe in the 1950s, this 'universalism' is really the abstraction of form to its most archetypal level: invariably today the rectangle, column and grid. Modernists pursued this abstraction either because of its supposed affinities to the machine, or for its Platonic beauty, but there was also another, hidden reason: abstract form was neither tainted by specific historical association nor contaminated by the bourgeoisie. Tom Wolfe explored this notion in his entertaining and over-simplified book, *From Bauhaus to Our House*; but it's not necessarily wrong because he discovered it everywhere. It has a limited truth; the Modernists, like so many others in this century, wished to suppress their economic roots and social dependence on the bourgeoisie. Hence the taste for the primitive and rustic, a desire to emulate a classless style, which can be found in the work of Le Corbusier, Mies, Kahn and all of the contemporary Fundamen-talists. This proletarian style has become so ubiquitous today as to be completely conventional. Like the blue jean, its sartorial equivalent, it's adapted from a supposed necessity of cost and function and, also like the blue jean, it's rejected by the very working class it was originally intended to serve. Rather, abstract Modernism is promoted by a professional elite for its moral probity and, ironically, for its aristocratic restraint. Like the Tuscan style, which Sebastiano Serlio recommended in 1537, it is the 'solidest and least ornate', a simple style of walls, cornices and undecorated columns.[21] In fact Modernist abstraction has evolved into the New Tuscanism, a style which the Fundamentalists tend to use on all their buildings, regardless of function

7.36,37 Cesar Pelli and Associates, *Herring Hall*, Rice University, Houston, 1983-5 (Photographs Paul Hester)

and context, as if it were the only proper style. Contrary to Serlio they don't regard it as one genre among others to be used where appropriate on modest building types. But, in a bid to establish its universality, they cite its constructional expression and timeless quality. Constructional Classicism has thus become a leading mode of Post-Modernism.

Mario Botta, the Swiss architect influenced by Louis Kahn and Le Corbusier, developed beyond these two Fundamentalists in the late 1970s as he became more explicit in his use of classical organisation. Four houses, produced from 1979 to 1981, show his new interest in using a Palladian plan in conjunction with the canonic Modernist material, the concrete block. At Pregassona, in the Ticino part of Switzerland where he usually builds, a classical cube with a nine-square Palladian plan is violently fractured on two sides to allow in light and articulate the space and view (38). The tiny glass and steel skylight contrasts aggressively with the white-grey box, just as the uncompromising geometry does with the site. The chiaroscuro is as extreme as the other mannerist contrasts, as one perceives the flattest of facades gouged out by the darkest of voids. That the mannerism is intentional might be denied by Botta since he tends to present his buildings as *necessary*, a consequence of constructional reality. However there are too many strange shapes and disproportionate contrasts to deny its presence. For instance, virtually all his houses look like heavy rusticated bases awaiting their *piano nobile* and roof. Conceptually they are all foundation or bottom floor.

Nowhere is this clearer than at Massagno where he has constructed another 'one-family house' with a banded rustication of light red and grey concrete (39). Here the 'foundation-house' has a miniscule skylight contrasting with a huge round window of the late Kahnian variety, the whole building perfectly illustrating the mannerist trope of oxymoron: giant/midget, voided/solid, open/closed and round/square are just some of the more obvious paradoxes that are here slammed together. When the diagonal glass mullions slide apart, the 'eye of the camera' focuses on the dramatic view, while on the back/front of the house two tiny portholes provide the inscrutable visage. Here the opposition is similar to Japanese houses of the period and the Batey and Mack villas which follow the ancient Roman type.

More relaxed is the house at Viganello – a little temple with its giant fanlight and sunken keystone (40, 41). These classical distortions again order the view over the Swiss hills and are now more successfully proportioned one to another. A centrally placed giant column in grey block gives a social rootedness to this mini-fortress while the same block skewed at forty-five degrees adds scale, and at the top becomes a refined cornice. It's a measure of Botta's control of his minimal means that he draws every salient constructional element in plan, section and axonometric so the fabric is rendered totally familiar (42). This knowing control makes Botta's work comparable to that of Mies, and marks him as a leader of the Constructionist Classicists. It also suggests why his approach is perhaps too architectural, and too reverberant: anything which is not architecture (such as fabric) tends to be disregarded if

7.38,39 Mario Botta, *One Family Houses*, Pregassona and Massagno, Switzerland, 1979 (Photographs courtesy the architect)

7.40,41 Mario Botta, *One Family House*, Viganello, Switzerland, 1980 (Photographs courtesy the architect)

not actively denied. Yet spatial logic and constructional beauty – two of the oldest classical qualities which Palladio and Ledoux accentuated – are his virtues and as his work matures perhaps it will become wider in range and more refined (43, 44). The fundamentals are deeply thought through and lovingly detailed, something one would expect from a Fundmentalist.

The same is true of the work of Andrew Batey and Mark Mack, a firm of architects that practised mostly in California's Napa Valley until it broke up in 1985. Mark Mack, an Austrian-born designer, has written extensively on the new Primitivism which he polemically places opposite the more flimsy type of Post-Modernism characterised (for him) by Robert Venturi and Charles Moore: 'it is the ruins of Pompeii rather than Las Vegas that inspire us'. The sentiment is partly shared by Andrew Batey and hence their work, like Botta's, is archaic – full of concrete block used as an honorific proletarian material – and as strong and defensive as a Pompeiian house. The Holt House, in the Bay of Corpus Christi Texas, typifies sophisticated Primitivism as it does the New Tuscanism in general. On the bay side, where storms from the Gulf of Mexico periodically destroy buildings, the main axis of the house flows right down into the sea. Its travertine piers act like breakwaters and pre-emptive ruins – characteristically they lack a capital (45). These are the Primitivist 'Sixth Order of Architecture', a type of ultra-Tuscan without any mouldings; the kind of thing Prince Charles would label a 'travertine stump'.

However, for Batey and Mack and Fundamentalists generally they have a heroic presence, an archaic, solid honesty which stems from their constructional and spatial logic – specifically here a twelve inch square pier on a thirty-six inch bay module which is ordered on major and minor cross-axes (46). The plan *is* most elegant and open, as if Mies were doing Early Roman, and is, in spite of the designer's protestations to the contrary, absolutely typical of the Post-Modern hybrid between new and old. Every detail is ordered to the grid and then executed with consummate finish, from the rosy Mexican ashlar to the light coloured travertine, microzinc roof and cornice of grey cross-braces (47). Here again the feeling of the Tuscan order is evoked without being used literally. Wall, pillar, absent capital, trussed architecture – a sonorous ensemble full of *veritas* and *gravitas*. Indeed, the gravity is so grave that at times the 'ruined' structure seems beaten into the ground, the expression so restrained as to break off in mid-sentence.

As with Botta we are tempted to ask: 'But where is the roof?' The presence of the absence of this member is so emphatic that it is clear we are on to one of those emergent types that constitute a new convention, like the flat roof of Modernism from which it stems. To be aware of such absences, to give up the superfluous and concentrate on essentials, is what the architecture demands. When they are so beautifully crafted and set against an archetypal nature of sand and sea, as here, these denials succeed in focusing the mind on the basic generalities.

For urban buildings this Fundamentalism is less plausible because of the variety of tastes which have to be accommodated. One can't be reductive in a

7.42-44 Mario Botta, *Office Building*, up axonometric and views, Lugano, Switzerland, 1981-5 (Photographs courtesy the architect)

Following pages:
7.45-7 Andrew Batey and Mark Mack, *Holt House*, view, plan and detail, Gulf of Mexico, 1979, 1981-4 (Photographs courtesy the architects)

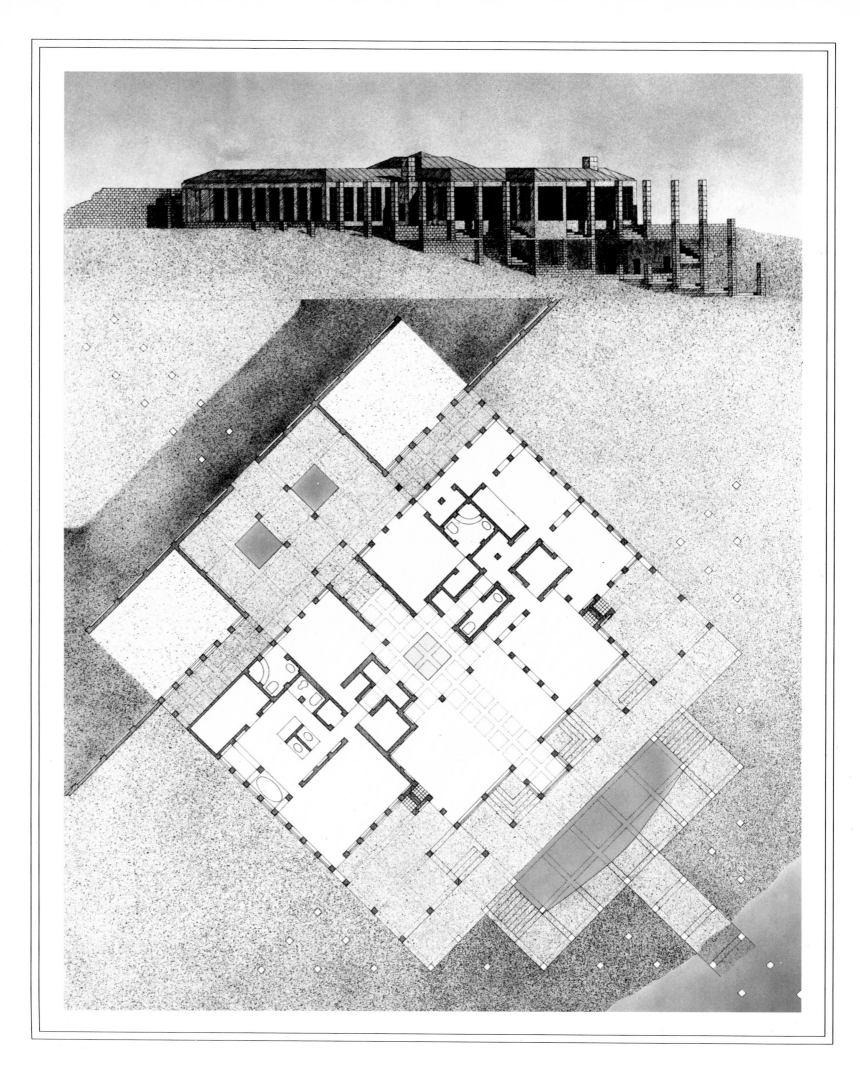

7.48 Toyokazu Watanabe, *Sun-Tumori Building*, near Osaka, 1979 (Photograph courtesy the architect)

7.49 Minoru Takeyama, *Nakamura Memorial Hospital*, Sapporo, 1978-80 (Photograph courtesy the architect)

7.50,51 Takefumi Aida, *Toy Block House I*, Hofu, Japan, 1979, *Toy Block House III*, Tokyo, Japan, 1980-1 (Photographs courtesy the architect)

city without conveying the feeling of deprivation. Nevertheless several adroit Japanese architects have adopted the mode for urban structures. Toyokazu Watanabe uses flat Tuscan wall architecture for an office building where Serlio himself might have recommended it. He proposed the Tuscan order for use on fortified palaces, prisons and 'similar structures used in war', and a modern office is conceived as both an economic fortress and upmarket prison. Watanabe has, like Botta, created a mannerist version of this style contrasting black voids with pink ceramic, an oddly shaped 'pediment' with classical 'arches' (48). This pediment, a kind of useless canopy, recalls pitched roofs and the reverse perspectives of Japanese paintings, whereas the flat, rigid symmetries of perfect geometrical shape recall the work of Adolf Loos which has influenced Watanabe in this and many other Minimalist works.

There are quite a few Japanese architects who occasionally work in this mode, among whom one should mention Arata Isozaki (discussed later), Shin Toki, Toyo Ito, and Minoru Takeyama. Takeyama adopts the Tuscan style partly for economic reasons, as do the others, but also because it is appropriate for such neutral and functional buildings as hospitals. His Nakamura Memorial Hospital in the northern city of Sapporo has a noble, dignified presence, with its arch forms and repeated windows towering over the now ephemeral urban background (49). Perhaps the new Tuscan order will become conventionalised for offices and hospitals as did the International Style of the 1950s: in a way it is the natural successor to this style. Takefumi Aida has used it in a series of 'Toy Block Houses' as he calls them or 'Building Block Offices' (50, 51). In nearly every case the Tuscan emphasis on the heavy wall, the undecorated pier, the minimal ornament which appears only at the joints, again define this work as Neo-Tuscanism. The blocky aspect is Aida's particular addition to the mode and it makes his buildings toy-like, in this respect similar to the Froebel Block Games that influenced Frank Lloyd Wright, and very understandable in terms of construction. One must never forget that the style recommends itself to designers because of its visual logic, because it dramatises the 'how' of building.

This is the main point of Constructionist Classicism and helps explain why it is so appealing to a professional elite: the architect can master this aspect of his art a lot more easily than he can control the actual formation of the building. Constructionist Classicism is thus becoming a main genre of Post-Modernism and cynics would say this is because it is the easiest to understand, copy and build. The arguments which used to justify the International and Miesian styles are now used to recommend the New Tuscanism. There is, however, a completely different defence mounted by Demetri Porphyrios in his monograph *Classicism is Not a Style*.[22] Attacking Post-Modern Eclecticism in general and my writings in particular he makes 'an urgent plea for closing architectural discourse towards the constructional logic of vernacular and its mimetic elaboration: classicism'. His argument, stemming from Leon Krier's, dismisses the vulgar reasons that have led to the

7.52 Rafael Moneo, *Roman Museum*, Mérida, 1980-3 (Photograph courtesy the architect)

7.53-5 Edward Jones and Michael Kirkland, *Mississauga City Hall*, Canada, 1982-6 (Photographs courtesy the architects)

success of Constructionist Classicism and proposes in their place a completely fresh justification. Fundamentally, Porphyrios wants to restore the 'mytho-pœic power' of architecture and he believes that this can only be done, in consumer society, by returning to constructional logic. This is then represented, or mythologised, at the level of architecture, much as the Greeks transformed wooden construction into a stone art. His argument is reductive and wrong-headed as far as Post-Modernism is concerned, but nonetheless admirably illustrates the high-minded idealism of these European architects – and classicism would be very little without idealism. Our argument is really over whether it should be limited to a constructional art.[23]

The architects that Porphyrios placed in his canon are nearly all part of the group I've considered as Fundamentalists, with the addition of a host of Spanish architects: Iniguez and Ustarroz, Miguel Garay, Jose-Ignacio Linazasoro and Rafael Moneo (52). Most of them, like Moneo, have been greatly influenced by Aldo Rossi who had an exhibition in Barcelona during the late 1970s called 'Aldo Rossi and 21 Spanish Architects' – a fair indication in its title of how tradition is sometimes carried on by a group which seeks anonymity. Moneo's work has all the aristocratic abstraction and constructional purity one would expect from this school.

Owing more to Krier than to Rossi is the work of Ed Jones and Michael Kirkland. In fact their Mississauga City Hall, built after a competition in 1982, can be considered a compilation of Leon Krier, James Stirling and Michael Graves: the School for 500, Stuttgart and the Portland Public Service Building (53-55). Unfortunately the scale of the urbanism still suffers slightly from Modernist overconcentration into large chunks, but in other respects it is a commendable essay in what had by now become a common international style. Clearly identifiable functions are placed behind Platonic solids while a vernacular background of repetitive windows is placed above a modestly rusticated base. Truss and Roman cross-braces are expressed as is the small attic window (something of a Fundamentalist hallmark). The ensemble has grace, wit and urbanity. One proceeds up stairs to an open podium, an outdoor public room, and then on axis to the cylindrical council chamber, identified as the most important section by its shape and banded granite. The high clock-tower acts as steeple and emblem to identify this suburban city hall, dropped somewhere between urban Toronto and the Canadian farming community, and the architects have consciously sought to represent these opposites. Strong, severe in its emphasis on constructional mimesis, and dependent on Louis Kahn as well as the previously mentioned architects, it is a good example of what the Fundamentalist tradition can produce both monumentally and urbanistically. For other values such as humour, symbolism and ornament one has to turn to traditions which the Fundamentalists often disdain, that of the revivalists and Post-Modern Eclectics.

CHAPTER VIII
Revivalist Classicism

Copying, Imitation and Transformation

The modern artist has laboured under the romantic injunction: 'make art original'. This onerous duty created the 'Tradition of the New', as Harold Rosenberg called it – that oxymoronic entity which is at once a historical continuum and set of discontinuous acts. In the 1960s its inherent contradiction became more apparent as artists started devising variations of previous movements such as Dadaism and architects began elaborating the early work of Le Corbusier. These 'neo' styles showed not only the exhaustion of the avant-garde, but, even more importantly, the arbitrary nature of choosing any preexisting convention as a departure point. If all invention depends on creating from past ideas and imagery, then which movements should be revived?

The various answers to this led to the pluralism which is still a defining aspect of Post-Modernism, but also to another query: what value should be given to repeating past formulae, to copying and imitation, in comparison to the rarer event of a significant breakthrough? How far should an architecture seek to fit in with a preexisting urban fabric; when should it contrast with a previous street facade, when repeat it? A major goal of Post-Modernists has been to formulate new attitudes towards such perennial concerns, attitudes which allow a certain amount of convention and yet also demand invention. For this complex goal the Modernist notion of creativity *ex nihilo* is of no use. More fruitful are other critical ideas which also stem from the Romantic movement; those distinctions – formulated by Joshua Reynolds among others – between copying (necessary for the student) and imitation (the goal of the mature artist).

To paraphrase this argument: one has to first master copying before creative versions of past models can be produced. Thus the ultimate goal of the artist is to find new uses for those traditional formulae whose worth has been tested by time. This ensures the continuity of culture and allows the really new to emerge. To this old idea and distinction Post-Modernists have added a third term, transformation, to refer to a more radical form of imitation: the modification of a preexisting type in its structure.

In addition to these critical norms, Post-Modernists have adopted another distinction from the Romantic period – Coleridge's opposition between fancy and imagination. The fancy aggregates ready-made formulae, whereas the imagination assimilates parts into a new whole. The former produces striking but identifiable signs, the latter creates symbols which are strange and new because so many meanings are tied together. The difference

Opposite:
Philip Johnson and John Burgee, *Republic Bank*, interior, Houston, Texas, 1981-4, *see fig.23* (Photograph Richard Payne)

217

8.1 Dr. Norman Neuerburg (Historical Advisor); Langdon, Wilson and Mumper (Architects); Stephen Garrett (Consultant), *Getty Museum*, inner peristyle garden with replicas of ancient bronzes, Malibu, 1970-4 (Photograph C. Jencks)

8.2 Dr. Norman Neuerburg (Historical Advisor); Langdon, Wilson and Mumper (Architects); Stephen Garrett (Consultant), *Getty Museum*, peristyle garden from the south, Malibu, 1970-4 (Photograph courtesy J. Paul Getty Museum)

parallels that between copying, at one extreme, and transformation, at the other, and it allows the critic to make distinctions concerning invention without falling into the progressivist trap, the Tradition of the New. This critical apparatus is helpful at a time when, for instance, some Post-Modernism is being condemned as 'xerox architecture' or 'flashcard design' and some Late-Modernism is reviving Futurism, Constructivism and the white architecture of the 1920s. With all invention necessarily linked to the past, the focus shifts away from some abstract notion of the avant-garde towards more relevant criteria. The questions become: what is the relevance of any particular style to the job at hand, and how many imaginative links are made within a particular work?

Pragmatic Replication and Automatic Eclecticism

Such issues were raised for Post-Modernists when the Getty Museum was opened in 1974 to a shower of both critical abuse and public acclaim. Damned as 'fraudulent', 'recreated by inappropriate technologies', 'too vivid', 'too harsh and too bold', it was seen by the *Los Angeles Times* critic William Wilson as a 'camp' folly in the tradition of Disneyland and dubbed 'The First Real Plastic Museum'.[1] Those, like Reyner Banham, who dismissed this imitation of a Pompeiian villa, were condemning its lifeless air, its 'bureaucratic precision', in short, its mechanical copying.[2] Apparently it was everything Modernism fought against – luxuriance, vulgar display, cliché – such was the virulence with which it was met. And yet, on closer examination, the Getty Museum was not the revivalist sham which these stereotypical views imposed on it, but something more modest and subtle. As its chief designer, the archaelogist Norman Neuerburg, insisted in defence, the building was 'a legitimate scholarly adaptation' of several buildings from Pompeii and Herculaneum: adaptations of old forms to appropriate new purposes, that is, the display of Greek and Roman artefacts.[3] It was, as he put it, a 'recreation rather than a reproduction', an eclectic mix that was given a new museum function (1). The notion of designing a period room to display objects from the same period is as legitimate as the Modernist counterproposal for a 'museum of our time'. The second Getty Museum, now being designed by Richard Meier, will probably house Renaissance and eighteenth-century objects in a Modernist Revival building. Whether the former or latter approach is more valid *per se* (ultimately the undecidable argument between fitting in and contrast) is of less interest than determining the type of creation. The first Getty Museum is not an imaginative transformation of Roman architecture, but a pragmatic adaptation of archaelogical fragments.

Nearly every part of the museum has an ancient precedent except for the underground parking garage, where a great opportunity was missed for celebrating arrival by modern chariot. Here the Romans clearly would have modified one of their heroic engineering types – the aqueduct or giant sewer – to create a dramatic and pleasant point of arrival. However, above this

218

twentieth-century hole (and failure of imagination) is a grand peristyle garden which is not only a faithful compilation of Roman prototypes, but a very pleasantly scaled, sun-filled space that mixes sculpture, herbs, hedges, pergola and painting in a complementary way (2). The individual elements are not very distinguished (nor were the 'originals'), but the ensemble, which becomes mellower every year and melts the parts together, takes on an aura which a Roman emperor, or the patrician owner of the Villa Papyrii, would have envied.

A curious consequence of this reconstruction, which has been missed by most commentators, and one that helps explain the negative reaction to the building, is what it reveals about Roman architecture, both its ostentation and its freedom in combining classical motifs. The Getty is more creative than we'd like it to be. It does not show the Vitruvian decorum we associate with the antique, nor the Palladian and Neoclassical restraint, nor even the academic, Beaux-Arts version of the past. Rather it displays a Free-Style Classicism. In its entrance vestibule, for instance, a licentious mélange of green marble Solomonic pilasters, oversized Corinthian capitals, painted ceilings, polychromatic walls and polished, visually vibrating, geometric floor patterns all compete for our attention (3). Absent is the high-minded idealism and intellectual rigour which, for two thousand years, we have been taught, constituted the essence of Graeco-Roman architecture, and present is a compensating vigour, sweetness and imaginative pragmatism.[4] If the stereotypes about academic architecture are upset by this shock of realism, then so too are assumptions about classical taste. On this evidence it looks rather middle-class and vulgar, as if a Roman patrician hording his copies of Greek sculpture were no better than a present-day oil man collecting fragments of a tired culture four thousand miles away. As J. Didion puts it, the Getty Museum is a grim reminder that 'we are now and will never be any better than we were'.[5] It 'depresses many people, strikes an unliberated chord' and looks 'as if dreamed up by a mafia don'. In effect it tells us that kitsch is a constant in western culture, that *Dynasty* and *Dallas* are the longest running epics, and why the Royal Family can continue to watch and be fascinated by such trash.

This interpretation perhaps loads too much on the back of the poor Getty, but it does clarify why so many intellectuals dislike it and why, for instance, Norman Neuerburg had to tone down the real Roman colours, make them more subdued and less typical of ancient fresco than his scholarship advised him: our notions of classical good taste couldn't tolerate the glitz. Happily it has begun to fade and another form of antique realism, the presence of a nearby fault in the earth's crust, has introduced fissures and cracks in the stucco. The building, as it ages and slowly becomes a venerable ruin, responding to earthquakes and its own internal history, will become archaeologically more correct in a different way.

In sum, the museum is not only appropriate to the Graeco-Roman artefacts it will finally hold in its entirety, but suitable to the climate of

8.3 Dr. Norman Neuerburg (Historical Advisor); Langdon, Wilson and Mumper (Architects); Stephen Garrett (Consultant) *Getty Museum*, entrance vestibule, Malibu, 1970-4 (Photograph courtesy J. Paul Getty Museum)

southern California. Mediterranean architecture works well here. What lifts it above pastiche is its obsessive scholarship, its literalness about precedent that gives each part the completeness of detail. When the designer, with little creative pretension, applies twentieth-century techniques of reproduction – available through photography, xerox, travel and organised scholarship – the language of the past can speak creatively and with conviction. Our time, like no other, can use exact historical simulation to create living wholes out of dead parts. Thus for the Modernist notion of 'anonymous architecture', the background office building of Mies and his followers, we have the Post-Modernist rejoinder of automatic eclecticism – the building which is generated almost autonomously by patching together features taken from Herculaneum and Pompeii.

No doubt this genre of pragmatic replication is a modest one, if not as base as its critics would contend. It provides a suitable ambiance for period artefacts, an educational function, and is a serviceable example of Coleridge's notion of the fancy at work, aggregating together recognisable ready-made parts. One should place it above pastiche and copying and below imitation and transformation. The tendency of the genre is, however, towards the facile accommodation of prevailing tastes, towards Neo-conservativism and the easy answer. Allan Greenberg has adopted it for public commissions in America, such as a courthouse, and in Washington DC (where it has virtually moth-balled a generation of architects) for diplomatic reception rooms (4). Quinlan Terry uses it on country houses and in traditionally sensitive areas such as the Thames-side embankment in London (5). Here again it is the anonymous, automatic revivalism, a language, as semiologists would say, without speech and as successful as its detail and overall appropriateness. No one will censure it for exaggeration, or creativity.

One way of avoiding the pretentious stolidity of the genre is by adapting it to realistic building types, such as the suburban detached house. Thomas Gordon Smith, the San Francisco based architect, has used saturated colours, reminiscent of Pompeii, in combination with the pastel blue, rose and yellow prevalent in these suburbs (6). He will reuse existing Doric columns, copy a Doric frieze (returning to the original, shocking colour) and then compose an informal path through the building which combines Baroque space with open, Californian living. The mixture of quotation with the regional conventions shows a modest wit and although the brash colours and incongruous proportions will offend the revivalist, they keep the work from becoming smug and predictable: they continue the spirit while distorting the letter of classicism.

Robert Stern has made much use of the adapted quote. Indeed, much of his work fits precisely into the category of pragmatic replication since various styles are quickly researched and modified to suit a volume of different work which would otherwise require an invention beyond the capacity of any individual. Like Philip Johnson, who he emulates, Stern works fast with a

8.4 Allan Greenberg, *Diplomatic Reception Room*, Washington DC, 1984 (Photograph courtesy the architect)

8.5 Quinlan Terry, *Richmond Riverside Development*, London, 1984 (Photograph courtesy the architect)

8.6 Thomas Gordon Smith, *View from Tuscan to Laurentian House*, Livermore, California, 1979-80 (Photograph Douglas Symes)

team of fifty to a hundred associates and draughtsmen. Since his commissions vary in size and meaning, he quite rightly rejects the Modernist alternative of a single style for all jobs while still accepting the modern imperative to build fast and in volume. Thus his pragmatic replication tends, like other work in the genre, to be anonymous and diagrammatic, what, borrowing from the nineteenth century, he has called 'scientific eclecticism', and what I would call 'automatic'.

Stern's Bozzi House in Long Island is a professional version of the Shingle Style houses of the nineteenth century and it has some refreshing touches (borrowed from different sources) such as a gridded, shingle verandah and a large/small turret reminiscent of the scale distortions of Ernest Coxhead (7). Eyebrow windows peer cautiously over a large expanse of roof, while an exterior chimney jumps up pertly on the end, serving both to anchor the building and, on the inside, to focus the ambiguous, flowing space. The Hamptons, where this is built, has a long tradition of Shingle Style buildings and hence the mode was predictable; but it's brought off here with conviction and knowledge partly because Stern, like his mentor Vincent Scully, has been studying the style for many years (twenty in Stern's case[6]).

Another successful example of automatic eclecticism is his modification of a Modernist dining hall at the University of Virginia (8). Here the brick and white trim of Jefferson's campus has been combined with Modernist windows and classical lanterns to provide a dignified repetition and a solid background for student life. Chippendale balustrades are quoted, as indeed are the paired Tuscan columns set above heavy piers, but this quotation avoids banality by being incorporated into a new system of repeated huts. It is basically Louis Kahn's typology of the centralised, primitive temple which includes a complex AB rhythm (he used this type first on the Trenton Bath Houses) but now fleshed out with classical trim rather than concrete block. The rhythm allows Stern to divide the interior into a sequence of tall pyramidal spaces separated by low ceilings, a rhythm which is effectively underlined by paired columns on the inside (9). He calls these additions 'metaphoric "porches" intended to camouflage the existing facility' because it was discontinuous with the existing Jeffersonian campus. One virtue of his scheme is that the camouflage isn't complete and parts of the old Modernist building, its pitched roofs and amoeboid centre, are allowed to contrast ironically with the end pavilions and give them a crowning role.

Robert Stern has attempted an ambitious Post-Modern hybrid in a speculative office building on the outskirts of Boston, Point West Place (10). Here he has combined the horizontal office block (Mies' concrete project of 1922) with a palazzo *and* a temple front to produce, as he says, 'a palace of work that is both "traditional" and "modern"'. Kohn Pedersen and Fox attempted similar collages a bit earlier. The problem here is not with the intention of contrast, but rather with the way the quotation marks hang around afterwards, self-consciously underlining the main point. Nothing illustrates Coleridge's notion of the fancy more perfectly: the parts are not

8.7 Robert Stern Architects, *Bozzi Residence*, East Hampton, Long Island, 1982-3 (Photograph Langdon Clay)

8.8 Robert Stern Architects, *Observatory Hill Dining Hall*, UVA, Charlottesville, Virginia, 1982-4 (Photograph Tim Hursley)

8.9 Robert Stern Architects, *Observatory Hill Dining Hall*, interior, UVA, Charlottesville, Virginia, 1982-4 (Photograph Whit Cox)

assimilated by the imagination, but left as stereotypes (partly, no doubt, because of the budget) which knock against each other with a certain daft rigidity. It's the type of clash which Robert Venturi described as 'the ordinary and ugly', the 'decorated shed', and which undoubtedly has the conviction of its own ill proportions: squat corner podia (awaiting their fountain bowls), senseless acroteria and a voided keystone, a centre pier and oculus window (where they shouldn't be according to classical grammar), a bloated curved pediment, a maladroit rhythm of black windows – etcetera. The ugliness is charming and as knowing as that of the nineteenth century. But there is an unresolved contradiction here. Stern seems to have been caught between his intention to produce an ironic hybrid and the desire to make a grandiose statement with a 'lavish entrance sequence', a 'tree-lined Court of Honour' and a 'balcony of appearances'. All this for a spec office with perfunctory Modern spaces! With such mixed intentions the result probably had to be banal, an intersection of the sublime and ridiculous. Looked at as self-conscious parody however, the building shows a certain integrity since no one can deny that the grammatical mistakes are consistently underlined. In the squashed entrance hall, for instance, giant architraves (not the usual one, but *four*) and bulbous globes push into a constricted area to show how mean the budget really is (11). When Post-Modernism fails as serious architecture it sometimes succeeds as critical humour, something Stern is always quick to exploit.

8.10,11 Robert Stern Architects, *Point West Place*, general view and interior, Framingham, Mass., 1983-4 (Photographs Peter Vanderwarker)

Wrestling with Mega-Build

Stern's mentor in architecture, Philip Johnson, has, since the early 1970s, focused his efforts quite clearly on the speculative office block, after having practised for twenty years on more architecturally malleable building types. The switch of the elderly Johnson was quite conscious. First, after teaming up in 1967 with John Burgee, a partner who had experience with commercial clients through working at C.F. Murphy in Chicago, Johnson set his sights on prestige high-rise. An early success with the IDS Center in Minneapolis, a Late-Modern skyscraper with a pleasantly jazzy 'atrium', led to further commissions and the all-important association with Gerald D. Hines, the 'mega-developer'.[7] Together Hines and Johnson/Burgee opened a new stage in commercial architecture, what might be called the High-Rise Icon Style, or the Instant Image Mode (there are other less flattering epithets).[8] Picking up and popularising Post-Modern ideas they produced one iconic image after another, in twelve or so historicist modes. The result was highly abstract, predictable and, like the Pop Art that influenced it, different from its sources in scale and material. By 1985 they had finished thirteen mega-projects and had in hand two-and-a-half billion dollars worth of work. The speed of building and the amount of architecture to be designed, if nothing else, guaranteed that the work would be anonymous and stereotyped. Naturally, it was condemned by Ada Louise Huxtable in the *New York Review of Books* as 'fancy dress' and 'flashcard architecture'.[9]

Some obvious points should be made about this genre of building before we look at the results, since the constraints of the building type are rather severe. Fundamentally there are five realities to commercial high-rise or mega-building: it must be produced quickly at a relatively low budget by a large firm in a style which is acceptable to the public (and this means familiar) and hung on a steel frame. These realities have the force of a social law which means they could, theoretically, be challenged, but in practice hardly ever are. They explain why most recently built cities are so unutterably boring, in spite of the good intentions of architects, and they explain why cynics, opportunists or else convinced Minimalists dominate the skyscraper business. One may fight these realities, one may deplore their existence as many do, but in a mass culture they won't go away.

The Modernist approach to this problem, the Miesian and Huxtable approach, is to opt for a Minimalist style which, virtually ignoring the demands of stylistic pluralism and public symbolism, celebrates the hard facts of technology and organisation; thus Mies' oft-quoted aphorism – 'I'd rather be good than interesting'. This was answered recently by Johnson, as he turned to one style after another, 'I wouldn't know how to be good'.[10] Clearly this form of realism, cynical in its high-minded concentration on technique, has been rejected by Johnson in his return to the older pattern of stylistic eclecticism and 'the style for the job'. But in returning to McKim, Mead and White and Raymond Hood, as Johnson explicitly does, a new issue is raised, because these pre-Modernists worked with more highly developed traditions, at a slower pace and on fewer styles. They were not, to misquote Mies, forced 'to change style every Monday morning', nor to fly all over America and come back with instant solutions to regional contexts. The reality for any successful practice like Johnson's is a San Francisco tower on Monday, a Denver high-rise on Tuesday, an office cluster in Boston on Wednesday, a Trump Castle in New York on Thursday, a Los Angeles skyscraper on Friday and the weekend in New Canaan putting the finishing touches to other jobs in Honolulu, Dallas and Washington DC.[11] Inevitably, a single Modernist style for all of this would be repressive and reductive. And yet the attempt by Johnson to give each commission a separate style is reductive in another way, towards the stereotype of Pop Art.

Of course this modern reality, what I'd call fast-food mega-build (until I can find a worse label), is firmly entrenched, for architects are not, in spite of Leon Krier's and Christopher Alexander's protestations, going to give up their commercially successful practices.[12] Johnson, understanding this quagmire, is quite candid in saying frequently and publicly on TV and elsewhere, 'I'm a whore, all architects are whores, I just admit it'. Critics and journalists who quote these remarks don't know quite what to make of America's premier architect calling himself a prostitute, and assume he must be joking. But he's not – he knows to what extent one must go to get the prestige commissions and, just as importantly, keep them coming in to feed the large office. For only large commissions beget other large commissions and if one isn't large one isn't on the corporate lists. When this isn't a vicious circle it's extremely entertaining and Johnson has decided to enjoy it: it confirms his Nietzschean view of the world as founded on power relations and the will to art and immortality.

The AT&T Headquarters was commissioned by its chairman John de Butts, a strong-willed individual who, with his corporate board, demanded of the architects an alternative to the glass box. To build on a large scale in Manhattan at this time of real estate depression was something of a rarity and to build the first Post-Modern skyscraper took a calculated nerve, although given the five-year preexistence of this architectural movement, it was not as surprising or heroic as the press later made out. Rather, like a well-timed advertisement or shift in corporate policy, it was a judicious anticipation of greater trends already underway. Johnson, with his philosophy of constant change, was well placed to switch direction again, for the third time in his career. From Miesian structuralism to the formalism of the 1960s to the Post-Modernism of the 1970s, his modes shifted while his underlying approach remained the same: aestheticism combined with a Nietzschean view of cultural politics, the competition of elites and the survival of the strongest image. The AT&T, like his other corporate headquarters, PPG (Pittsburgh Plate Glass), or the Transco Tower in Houston, reflects this philosophy of unmitigated power and was an appropriate commission for what was then, with over two million stockholders, the largest public company in the world.

It rises sheer from Madison Avenue, nicely holding the street line, up thirty-seven storeys in pink granite to its celebrated split pediment – a Pop icon of a 'Chippendale Highboy' as it was termed by *The New York Times* critic Paul Goldberger. The image was familiar but, at this five-storey scale, a giant amplification (12). Claes Oldenburg's urban monument of an ultra-large lipstick or clothes pin were urban prototypes of the 1960s which anticipated this gesture. Other images were accredited as possible sources and symbolic references: a grandfather clock, a Neoclassical icon based on Ledoux from which smoke rings would be blown (the mechanical equipment is behind the pediment and, when the temperature is right, clouds of vapour emerge), a gravestone and the front end of a Rolls Royce or Lincoln Continental.[13] Robert Venturi and Denise Scott Brown even suggested the top was based on Venturi's Chestnut Hill House for his mother which is, in effect, a whole building as a giant split pediment. The potential heaviness of Johnson's fifty-foot version is mitigated by a top moulding which has gently upturned ears, a characteristic eighteenth-century gesture of refinement.

If the top is an effective piece of divergent symbolic reference, then so too is the base although most meanings evoke sacred building types: the Pazzi Chapel by Brunelleschi, and San Andrea in Mantua by Alberti (13). Behind this 'church front', to either side of the lobby, is an open sixty-foot high loggia which alludes to an Egyptian hypostyle hall (and is almost as dark as one), while to the back is a rather gloomy version of Milan's Galleria. The entrance lobby itself mixes the sacred overtones of the front with new religious meanings – gilded cross-vault, 'rose' windows without their roses, Romanesque capitals – and a few secular references to Lutyens. Most audacious of all is the gilded statue, *Genius of Electricity*, rescued from the top of the former AT&T and placed inside this Pazzi Chapel on a very high, polished black altar (14). The luminous non-rose window lights up the lightning flashes of the *Genius*, a suitable icon for the new secular religion that Henry Adams predicted for America: energy equals power equals money. Ironically, this Nietzschean superman, who has in this chapel displaced the suffering Christ, is a fey Golden Boy, an overgrown *putto* with wings. How conscious is this blasphemy, this 'transvaluation of all values' that Nietzsche recommends? Probably not entirely, as it looks more the result of a method of *bricolage* and borrowing than a contemplated symbolic act. Since Johnson's eclecticism extends to any period, both present and past, it is bound to produce by its inherent variety a strong set of images that are only partly understood. In effect the multiple languages themselves manufacture the meanings. For instance, the sculpted figures on top of a San Francisco office building were commissioned as aesthetic crowns; only retrospectively do they imply the figure of death. The symbolism results automatically as a consequence of latent meanings inherent in the different conventions (15). As a method of accidental creativity it bears comparison to the Surrealists' game of Exquisite Corpse, in which turns are taken to draw different sections of the human body on a piece of paper folded in such a way as to prevent collaboration: the

8.12,13 Philip Johnson and John Burgee, *AT&T Corporate Headquarters*, New York, 1979-84 (Photographs C. Jencks)

8.14 Philip Johnson and John Burgee, *AT&T Headquarters*, lobby and 'Genius of Electricity', 1979-84 (Photograph C. Jencks)

8.15 Philip Johnson and John Burgee, *580 California*, San Francisco, 1981-4 (Photograph C. Jencks)

8.16 Philip Johnson and John Burgee, *AT&T Headquarters*, entrance under construction, 1982 (Photograph C. Jencks)

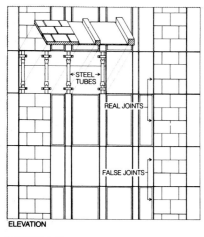

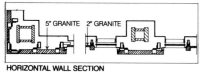

ELEVATION

HORIZONTAL WALL SECTION

8.17 Philip Johnson and John Burgee, *AT&T Headquarters*, analysis of facade structure (Drawing D. Wedlick)

8.18 Philip Johnson and John Burgee, *AT&T Headquarters*, Sky Lobby (Photograph C. Jencks)

result is a whole figure which no one intended. The credit for invention there must go to the resources of the language rather than the mind of a single *originator*.

In a similar manner Johnson produces buildings, although of course he coordinates the ready-made motifs so they form a whole, indeed, a very fastidious unity. At AT&T the exterior granite panels, clipped to the steel frame, are unified visually in two systems, either as traditional masonry architecture, implying thick stone and compression (hence the mouldings near the base), or as a curtain wall in tension (the building's true nature). Johnson and Burgee do not play this truth against falsity, as for instance James Stirling does at Stüttgart, and they thereby miss a great opportunity for representing the actual cross-bracing which ties the vertical loads into the piers (16, 17). Unlike the Greeks and Romans who made a symbolic art of disguise, the camouflage is here offered straightforwardly as the truth.

What is at stake here has little to do with the Modernist goal of structural honesty; rather it concerns the questions of representation and consciousness. It implies, as in the earlier tradition of Madison Avenue, that appearances are the truth, that advertisement is based on fact; a slightly anachronistic position today when so many ads enjoy the *double entendre* of conveying both a fantasy and the artifice behind it. An audience brought up on advertisements is now quite sophisticated and has a taste for ironic double meaning: in this respect the building's naivety is more nineteenth century than it is Post-Modern.

In the Sky Lobby, sixty feet above the entrance and where only AT&T personnel are allowed, another opportunity for symbolic expression is missed (18). Here some quite beautiful black veined white marble, Breccia Strazzema, is used to cover virtually every surface, while, again in the manner of Ledoux, classical forms are amplified and cut out. At first sight it is impressive, a dazzling array of nervous lines dancing against a creamy background. The interior of the Taj Mahal, the sublime? But then the reality of the uniformed guards protecting the personnel, and the echoing emptiness intrude on this fantasy and the allusions, as it were, switch gear to become the blank walls of a reverberant abbatoir or, more simply, the inside of a king-size bathtub. What has gone wrong? It's not, I suspect, the aesthetic control which is, as usual, meticulous, but rather the absence of any iconography, or symbolic programme which could make sense of all the buzzing marble. Or, again, a bit of structural representation to contrast with the covering, to let us appreciate the mastery of illusion.

Admittedly the AT&T executive is not in the least interested in such matters and it is mostly architects who debate these sort of things; but there *is* some popular curiosity about skyscraper building and a genuine interest in understanding professional expertise, the mystique of the well-turned corner. One needn't show the insides of every escalator, as Norman Foster likes to do, in order to play on the subtle interaction between revealed and hidden function. It's an obvious question of balance between aesthetic

8.19 Philip Johnson and John Burgee, *AT&T Headquarters*, view from Citicorp Building (Photograph C. Jencks)

covering and technical revelation, a balance which Michael Graves comes closer to achieving at the Humana Building (see Chapter IX), as Johnson and Burgee do on the outside of the AT&T.

Here, the building, when seen from a distance, looks well-proportioned and noble (19). Set against so many silent rectangles, it has the presence of a dignified monument, yet it isn't solemn because of its upturned ears, or depressing, because of its pink granite. Visually one can understand how it relates to the surrounding International Style boxes, and conceptually see it as a vertical steel frame holding out its clip-on granite mullions and horizontal floor panels. The logic is both witty and pleasing to the mind. We understand that it's a typical modern skyscraper corsetted inside a classical skin which carries forward an Old New York mode: the tripartite organisation of base, middle and crown, but now supplemented with extra articulations at the top

233

8.20 Philip Johnson and John Burgee, *College of Architecture*, University of Houston, Texas, 1983-5 (Photograph courtesy the architects)

8.22,23 Philip Johnson and John Burgee, *College of Architecture*, plan and section, University of Houston, Texas, 1983-5

and rhythmical bays in the shaft. In overall image it opens up the discourse – with its neighbours, the past, and the grid of New York – that was a traditional goal of urbanism before the Modern Movement. It may, in its structural representation and symbolism, 'strike an unliberated chord', as J. Didion says of the Getty, but it has a dignified urban presence. Its lobby and galleria may not be the public realms that they should, but the skyscraper has once again returned to its role as a definer of regional place: in sum, it's a very New York building.

I have dwelt on the AT&T at some length, not only because it has been considered the first major monument of Post-Modernism, but also because it remains, after five years and with all its flaws, one of the best examples of the genre: more detailed than Johnson's Transco Tower in Houston, which is diagrammatic by comparison, less of a one-liner than the PPG and less embarrassing than the Times Square Centre (which if it is built will do more to damage Johnson's reputation, not to mention the area, than all his fast-food buildings put together).

Johnson has undoubted intelligence and wit as a designer, but every so often he lapses into the most banal corporate corn. 'If we had our portrait painted', a public relations executive of AT&T suggested to the designers, 'it should be by Norman Rockwell', Luckily, they didn't take the hint.[14] However, the College of Architecture at the University of Houston did not escape so lightly (20). Mimicking Ledoux's design for a House of Education in nearly every way, they managed only to thin out the original, in appearance at least, by subtracting its base and adding extraneous windows that lessened its *gravitas* (21). The architectural students protested, calling the design a 'blatant copy' made by 'Xerox Inc.', but the Dean and Assistant Dean came to its defence, arguing that the Ledoux-Doppelgänger would put this provincial school on the map.[15] 'I think it is important that we gain some degree of notoriety', the Assistant Dean said, and he wasn't alluding to a Business Degree. The students lamented such fame at their expense: 'You almost feel like he's mocking our school. It's like he's saying our school's not worth even sitting down (*sic.*) and thinking up a new design.'[16]

As a result of this controversy the architects had a sudden reconversion to Mies' theory of excellence through imitation. Johnson answered *à propos* his replication: 'It's better to be good than original'. And Burgee added: 'The only complaint we're hearing is that it looks like Ledoux's design. Well, so what? The question should be whether you like what the building looks like.'[17] These statements bring us back, again, to those fundamental distinctions of the eighteenth century. A good copy of a good prototype is an acceptable, if modest, goal. An imitation which extends an original design is more worthy, and an imaginative transformation of a type is the ultimate aim of the mature artist.

Using these axioms to grade would make the Houston School a borderline C-minus because, as one professor noted, Ledoux's colonnades and platform 'created a better transition from the ground' and the 'round

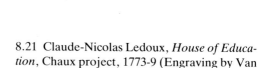

8.21 Claude-Nicolas Ledoux, *House of Education*, Chaux project, 1773-9 (Engraving by Van Maelle and Mailla)

8.20

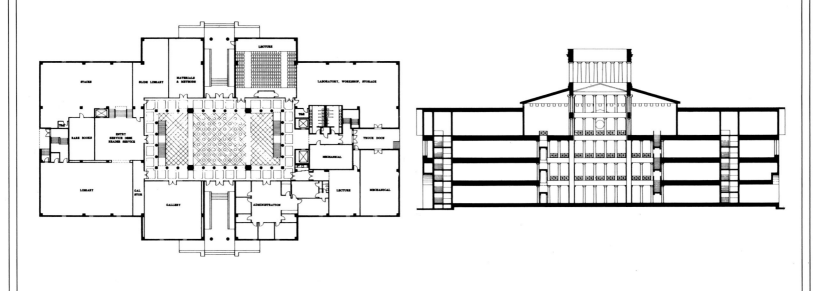

8.22   8.23

cupola was better suited to the round arches of the windows than is Johnson's square one'.[18] When the copy is nearly exact, the few differences can be compared on a one-to-one basis to see whether there has been an improvement; in these respects, at least, it's a clear Fail. Johnson and Burgee might answer, however, that it is not their design which should be under scrutiny but the original type: does the organisation of design studios around a classical, central well, lit from above, provide good social interaction and a pleasant space to use (22, 23)? We await the professors' and students' marks on this score.

In other cases, Johnson and Burgee go up and down the scale between fair copies and inventive imitations. Judged against spec offices by other large firms in America their Republic Bank Centre in Houston must be given an A, for it is a far more interesting imitation of unlikely building types (the Dutch guild hall, German Rathaus, nineteenth-century galleria) than anyone else is producing at this scale (24). Judged against nineteenth-century commercial eclecticism, however, its fantasy lacks depth and thoroughness – and is probably worth no more than a B.

Corporate Professionalism and Industrial Craftsmanship

Fast-food mega-build poses this problem for Post-Modernists: how can one create an inexpensive illusion without looking thin and cheap? There are several answers to this rhetorical question, none of which is entirely satisfactory. Arguing that we lack craftsmanship, Robert Venturi has advocated an architecture of appliqué which is mass produced – a 'simplified, repetitive and depictive approach to ornament'.[19] The problem with this position is that it results in an ornament which is too stereotyped and diagrammatic, a caricature of the care which ornament should possess. More fruitful is a mixed system which combines a repetition on the mass of the building with a variable, careful detailing on the smaller, public parts. This hybrid approach, which can be faulted theoretically for its impurity and schizophrenia, is in many ways more realistic because it acknowledges contradictory requirements and the fact that, *pace* Venturi, craftsmanship still exists, as well as the desire for it. By balancing the crafted with the mass produced the quality of each is brought out, while the notion of quality itself is reaffirmed. In the late twentieth century the antithetical arguments about ornament forwarded by Traditionalists and Modernists appear equally simplistic, since there are different parts of the building task which are incontestably best pursued with different strategies. Small-scale fittings and ceremonial objects are still best treated as things requiring extra design and expenditure, while in large, repetitive parts of a building the quality control is actually increased through mass production – an old truth of the Modernists. Although no architect, or firm, has yet operated perfectly at these two extremes, one can still imagine the possibility and see that some firms are evolving towards this dual approach.

The most commercially successful Post-Modern practice is Kohn,

8.24 Philip Johnson and John Burgee, *Republic Bank*, Houston, Texas, 1981-4 (Photograph Richard Payne)

Pedersen and Fox, started in New York in 1976. Made up of seven partners, twelve associates, a supporting staff of one hundred and sixty, and divided organisationally into a group of architects and a group of interior designers/planners led by Patricia Conway, it combines the skills of a large firm with the flexibility and horizontal structuring of a small one. As a result it turns out commercial Post-Modernism with a professional competence second to none (at least at the level of detail and urban appropriateness), becoming in effect the Skidmore, Owings and Merrill of the movement (and indeed SOM, in some of its work, has followed its lead). KPF's leader is A. Eugene Kohn who, like a few of his colleagues, was formerly a principal at the mega-firm of John Carl Warneke. Kohn may seem like a venture capitalist invented by the architectural profession to create bigger jobs. No one is so tireless in working through the corporate lists, arranging marriages between local opportunities and big business, and interviewing directors about their real needs – which not surprisingly turn out to be a 'desire for partner attention, design consciousness and a deep respect for budgets'.[20] 'Partner attention' is an apparent rarity in the world of mega-build and it's KPF's attention to such niceties that has recommended them to major companies such as the American Broadcasting Corporation, who often come back with further commissions. Although the practice treats architecture as an art, it sees itself fundamentally in the 'service profession' of providing a professional product. Thus, in terms of the distinctions we have been considering, while its work does not often aim at imaginative transformation, it nevertheless fulfils, at a very high level, the ideals of imitation as distinct from copying. Taking as goals the notion of urban assemblage and collage, it completes the urban fabric with outdoor rooms and a language derived from the site.[21]

One of its first notable achievements was the spec office designed for the Urban Investment and Development Corporation, known by its curious sounding address, '333 Wacker Drive' (25). This building, in the shape of an eroded and pointed ellipse, takes as its cue the bend in the Chicago River and the neighbouring commercial classicism – the first Chicago style. The curving green river provides the pretext for the highly reflective curving green glass which seems to sparkle sympathetically in geometric waves of viscous colour and a white foam created by the metal mullions. Conceptually then, the river facade is a Pop icon of frozen water which sits on a classical base of banded stone and is topped by a crown of mitred slots and flat profile. This tripartite organisation, formulated by the chief designer William Pedersen, is an imitation of an Art Deco classical skyscraper. But it's an imitation with a difference: the violent contrast of its decorative base.

Here we see the dualism of approach very clearly. Above, the skin of glass is stretched tight and repetitive as an obvious sign of economic sheathing (and profit). Below, bands of green marble and grey granite shoot around the curve, urging on the high-speed traffic, before stepping down towards the central entrance, an equally obvious sign of public space (and pleasure). The interior lobby develops these themes with an impersonal expertise as the

8.25 Kohn Pedersen Fox Associates, *333 Wacker Drive*, Chicago, 1981-3 (Photograph Barbara Karant)

8.26 Kohn Pedersen Fox Associates, *333 Wacker Drive*, interior, Chicago 1981-3 (Photograph Gregory Murphy)

239

terrazzo floor, taking up the curve, fans deftly into the horizontal rhythms of stainless steel trim and green marble (26). Doors, handrails, column capitals and even mechanical grills are convincingly transformed into stainless steel decoration – a clear indication that one can have one's ornamental cake today, if not eat it everywhere. Inevitably this ornament, a result of industrial craft, is abstract and not sustained by works of art or an iconographic programme; but the building was designed in 1979-80.

More developed, along the same dualistic lines, is their headquarters building for one of America's most successful mega-companies, Procter & Gamble.[22] A leader in the consumer marketplace with its collective brand names and annual sales of over thirteen billion dollars, it is now the largest advertiser in the US. But whereas its commercial policy has been adventurous, its architecture has been *retardataire*. A giant slab block of 1957, the kind that gave both Modernism and fascism a bad name, a block that refused to disappear in spite of its underwhelming understatement, forms the unlikely pretext for KPF's new design. Picking up its lines and materials, the designers take this unpromising grammar of grey granite and dark windows, stretch it along a line and then turn it upside down at the corner – into monumental gateways marking the expressway entrance to the city (27) – and bend it sideways to form a public park and border to the city grid (28). These urban moves, working both ways at once, now look inevitable because they are so logical, but they were, of course, exceptions to the Modernist way of planning a skyscraper in a park.

This is a modest yet monumental expression of the corporate power that runs America – the Nietzschean equivalent to the Church, but one that extends the public realm and city space in interesting ways. Conceptually, there is not *one* single sacred space as in the AT&T lobby, but rather *two* connected on the diagonal, each given a truncated spire (29). These take up the octagonal themes of the plan and, through a series of setbacks and articulations with white marble, turn the geometry into pyramidal crowns. The clever massing makes use not only of Art Deco precedents in Cincinnati, but Baroque belltowers as well. It's a professional version of academic invention and as such is reminiscent of the best nineteenth-century practice when architects adapted traditional forms without losing their inherent logic.

This logic runs throughout the public spaces and fixtures, uniting both the whole and its parts. For instance, the 'rose' windows of the 'chapel', apart from being, like the fountain, irregular octagons, relate well to the octagonal spires (30,31). Stainless steel, harmonising with the grey granite and marble, acts like punctuation marks as it does in KPF's other buildings, but here it is used with a greater linear elegance; wandering over surfaces in the same way as Frank Lloyd Wright made his ornament roam in the Unity Chapel, to keep the eye constantly moving. The light fixtures are also of Wrightian conception, glowing warm cylinders held in a geometrical cage that conceals the wiring (32). These tectonic shapes, used to define the piers, run dramatically into the structure overhead thus also serving to define the whole space.

8.27,28 Kohn Pedersen Fox Associates, *Procter & Gamble Headquarters*, views from expressway and park, Cincinnati, Ohio, 1982-5 (Photographs Jock Pottle)

8.29 Kohn Pedersen Fox Associates, *Procter & Gamble Headquarters*, plan

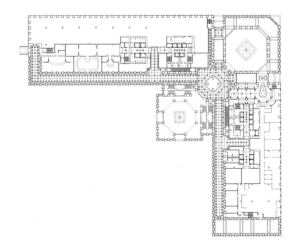

8.30,31 Kohn Pedersen Fox Associates, *Procter & Gamble Headquarters*, exterior and interior of lobby (Photographs Jock Pottle)

8.32 Kohn Pedersen Fox Associates, *Procter & Gamble Headquarters*, lighting fixtures and mouldings (Photograph Jock Pottle)

8.33 Kohn Pedersen Fox Associates, *Procter & Gamble Headquarters*, lighting colonnettes (Photograph Jock Pottle)

Playing against these thin lines are flat, stainless steel mouldings which elsewhere are used as lighting sconces (33); these are Art Deco inventions, by way of Michael Graves, but the theft is not upsetting because it is so thoroughly assimilated into the grammar as a whole. Finally, what is impressive is the comprehensive design itself, the *Gesamtkunstwerk*, which interweaves the themes of urban form, interior design and the objects of everyday use. The Procter & Gamble Headquarters is not a greatly imaginative building and it lacks a symbolic programme and works of art, but it does teach two important lessons: industrial craftsmanship *can* pull together the two extremes of mass production and handcraft ornament, if the design is thought through; and fast-food mega-building *can* reach a high professional standard if done by a coordinated team sharing the same style. Perhaps the two lessons are really one.

CHAPTER IX
Urbanist Classicism

If generals are always fighting the last war, then urban planners are always designing with theories that are twenty years old. In both cases professional frustration is the result. It takes roughly a generation for new urban ideas to filter their way into mainstream practice and by the time they finally reach the hands of developers, mayors and official planners – those able to realise them – they are usually so distorted by commercial realities as to be unrecognisable. So it is with Post-Modern urbanism. First formulated in the early 1960s by theorists such as Jane Jacobs and Herbert Gans, the new planning ideals of historical and functional diversity are now the basic assumptions of many successful developers.

The Rouse Corporation in America, one of the largest urban speculators, has made a billion dollar business out of Jacobite formulae, transforming old and decaying downtowns into commercial festival centres. Boston's Faneuil Hall Marketplace and Baltimore's Harborplace are James Rouse's two most convivial, surgical operations; saving traditional buildings, creating open public space on a Roman scale and generating a great deal of money, recreation and employment for everyone in the vicinity (1,2). The formula has been repeated throughout America and Europe, from Horton Plaza in San Diego to Covent Garden in London, and the urban decline, which seemed the inexorable result of suburbanisation and the motor vehicle, has thereby been checked in a few key areas. But a price has been paid. Traditional monuments have been changed in use and pickled in glitz (or at least masonry preservative) while second-rate designers, chosen for their skill at accommodation, have dominated an activity necessarily founded on compromise. In true Mephistophelean fashion, we have gained back a few old hearts of the city only at the cost of finding them instant tourist centres – Disneylands crossed with shopping arcades made up of a thousand speciality stores catering for the middle-class. The new Faustian urbanite is a distractedly affable Yuppie strolling across recycled cobblestones in his Bass Weejun loafers and Bermuda shorts in search of designer spaghetti and today's equivalent of the *passegieta*. He's not a native of the area, nor a poor member of an ethnic minority, but surprisingly, in a few cases, his presence has benefited these other citizens. In Rouse's schemes, for instance, blacks and other minorities are given a certain percentage of the jobs and store locations. The results thus constitute a mixed blessing; an improvement on Modernist notions of total clearance and superblocks – of functional separation and streets-in-the air – but still far short of either historical

9.1,2 Ben Thompson and the Rouse Corporation, *Faneuil Hall Marketplace*, restoration, Boston, 1972-8 (Photographs C. Jencks)

245

continuity or the Post-Modern ideal. An ironic assessment of this evolution is possible and indeed necessary, one that acknowledges the progress made while remaining critical of the architectural and social results.

Urban Pluralism

The key ideas that Jane Jacobs defined in her 1961 manifesto, *The Death and Life of Great American Cities,* concerned city diversity and economic health. She proposed four conditions which, acting in combination, would generate this diversity: multiple functions, short blocks, a mixture of old and new buildings and a 'sufficiently dense concentration of people'.[1] Her devastating attacks on Modernist planning, especially Le Corbusier's Radiant City with its pointless open spaces ('so that Christopher Robin might go hoppety-hoppety on the grass') was the first salvo of what became a literary bombardment over the next twenty-five years (including of course, in time, the very real monthly blowing up of useless housing estates). Polemic preceded dynamite in this war of theories. *Defensible Space,* 1972, by Oscar Newman followed Jacobs' lead in showing the correlations between Modernist slab blocks, streets-in-the-air, space that was not owned and that which might jolt the authorities into action: crime. Further polemical tracts by academics in America and Britain continued throughout the 1970s – Peter Blake, Malcolm McEwen, Brent Brolin, Colin Ward, John Turner – with widespread support from journalists and TV reporters. By the early 1980s the death of Modern architecture and planning was no longer a secret. Thus it came as something of a surprise when, as late as 1984, Prince Charles added his royal firepower to a battle that appeared to be already over; attacking bureaucratic planning in general, the Mansion House scheme of Mies van der Rohe as an inappropriate 'glass stump', and the Late-Modernist addition to the National Gallery as 'a monstrous carbuncle'. These attacks were picked up in the popular press and supported by a groundswell of reaction led by the conservationist lobby and traditional architects. The passion against Modernism ran unchecked in England for the next year until it was finally exhausted and the two schemes which Prince Charles had criticised were shelved (see below). Alice Coleman in her *Utopia on Trial: Vision and Reality in Planned Housing,* 1985, used statistics to prove, once again, just how deleterious were the ills of Modernist council housing: litter was found in 86% of the blocks, graffiti in 76%, vandal damage in 39%, urine in 23%, and faeces in 7.5%.[2] Twenty-four years after Jane Jacobs' demolition job, fourteen years after Pruitt-Igoe was blown up, ten years after such estates stopped being built in England and with royal sanction, we could safely say that mainstream planners had got the message. And yet for all this, there is not much to be shown for it. Such is the scale of the problem that there are still only imperfect fragments of the counter-urbanism, the Post-Modern solution. One has to look selectively all over the globe to find the few good examples.

246

In San Francisco the failure of Modernist planning led to 'neighborhood preservation' becoming a political issue in the mayoral election of 1972. Various groups were formed in the mid 1970s made up of politicians, planners and students from the University of California at Berkeley. They produced typological studies which showed how the traditional patterns of San Francisco could be made to work with the new town planning requirements, such as the automobile. One such group, led by Daniel Solomon, published reports on this typology and built several small infill blocks to show what could be done. His 'little village' of seventy-two houses is typical of these developments (3). It has the short blocks that Jane Jacobs and Leon Krier recommend, and holds the old street line and scale of surrounding buildings while pushing back the garages and parking lots into the inside of the block. The typology of street, courtyard, passage and garden is reaffirmed while the white architecture of Le Corbusier, its logic and economy, is also discernible. This mixture, typical of Post-Modernism, is consciously sought by Solomon: 'For ten years now my intent has been to take Corbusier's athletes and make them into urbanites'.[3] The white cubic architecture also has a few San Francisco touches added to it, such as the clapboard, indented facade and roof trellis.

Predictably, as San Francisco is a mature European-type city with a small block system (laid out along Spanish lines in rectangles of 275 by 412 feet) and many pleasant urban features worth preserving, it became the first American city to adopt Post-Modern planning legislation. This was the result of twenty years of agitation followed by the arrival on the scene of Dean Macris, a Chicago-trained planner who took over the city's Department of City Planning in 1981. By September 1985, after striking many bargains between competing districts and interest groups of San Francisco, he managed to push through the 'Downtown Plan'. This plan is extraordinary not so much for what it envisions – which is standard Post-Modern theory – as for its enactment. It's virtually the most comprehensive urban development plan ever conceived in the United States. Fundamentally it entails that office development be cut down in size and shape to smaller, thinner towers than prevailed in the International Style blocks of the 1960s, and that speculators will put aside part of their investment to pay for public open space, works of art and public transport. Specifically it calls for seven main guidelines. The allowable building height of skyscrapers is reduced by almost fifty percent. New high-rise construction is limited to 950,000 square feet per year – the equivalent of one Empire State Building – an extraordinary limitation for this booming, financial centre. Every new tower must incorporate design criteria which entail setbacks; the visual division into base, middle and top and interesting articulation (4). Older buildings and districts are to be preserved, mixed use incorporated, housing for secretaries, janitors and executives provided (those who work in the new office space), one percent of the budget made over to public art works, money put aside for child-care funds and five dollars per square foot of new construction put towards the cost of public

9.3 Daniel Solomon, *Amancio Ergina Village*, 72 affordable houses, San Francisco, 1982-5 (Photograph C. Jencks)

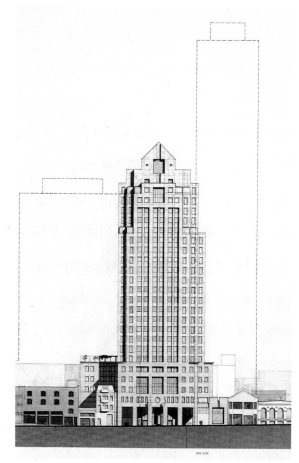

transport. In effect Dean Macris has managed to pass legislation that favours the public over the private realm, and communal open space over the automobile. In America this reversal of prevailing values is unique, at least on such a scale.

A skyscraper designed by Kaplan, McLaughlin and Diaz before the Downtown Plan was approved anticipates most of its demands (5,6). Here we can see the vertical mass of a tower diminish towards the top and end in a distinctive pitched roof point – a shape influenced by local towers of the 1920s and the recent work of Aldo Rossi and Diana Agrest. The street wall of Stevenson Street is maintained and the base of the building matches the scale of adjacent structures both in height (eighty-foot cornice) and detail. John Ellis, the chief designer, has also adapted Philip Johnson's notion of dramatising the escaping steam at the top, where he has placed a mechanical room behind a split pediment – the AT & T solution. The base, banded in red granite, opens onto an arcade that leads to a plaza – an example of the private office providing a public amenity and open space.

The architecture of such towers, while modest, is already beginning to enhance the urban realm and it bodes well for San Francisco that there are so many firms adopting this approach with a certain flair – SOM, KMD, Heller & Leake, and Fisher-Friedman. The latter in particular has specialised in a type of low-rise, high density housing which is a prime example of the new urbanism. Admittedly this movement inevitably favours the middle-class and white collar workers and, as critics point out, has not done enough for housing the poor. Nevertheless, Dean Macris' Downtown Plan did win the approval of different districts and ethnic groups – for instance the very strong Chinese community – because by controlling growth it also protects their interests. The consequence of enlightened urban pluralism, a reflection of American democracy in general, is that the benefits of middle-class city building can be shared in part by the rest of society. This is not quite the 'social responsibility' – worker's housing and comprehensive redevelopment – for which the Modern Movement fought, but it has so far proved far less injurious to the urban fabric than the Radiant City and its form of idealism.

Urban pluralism exists both as a social goal and stylistic strategy and it is in this latter role that it has provoked such a response in the mass media, not all of it positive. As Post-Modernism has been disseminated through mass culture it has become a leading approach which has, like Modernism before it, come to be built quickly at low cost, and likewise taken on diagrammatic qualities. An architect based in Los Angeles, Jon Jerde, has been the most commercially successful in extending this pluralist urbanism to shopping malls and city centres such as Horton Plaza in San Diego – a Caesar's Salad of clichés (6). Nevertheless, these have revitalised the downtown area with a mixture of activities that Rouse and other developers have shown to be so effective. Jerde's Westside Pavilion, for instance, has a brightly coloured facade of light pinks, blues and orange highlights that blends in well with Los Angeles and is appropriate to its sunny climate (8). Semi-classical motifs are

9.4 SOM (Houston) and Heller & Leake (Design Consultants), *100 First Street*, San Francisco, 1985 (Photograph courtesy Heller & Leake)

9.5 KMD (John Ellis Project Designer), *71 Stevenson Street*, north elevation, drawing, 1983 (Photograph courtesy the architects)

9.6 KMD (John Ellis Project Designer), *71 Stevenson Street*, elevation, 1983 (Photograph courtesy the architects)

9.7 John Jerde Partners, *Horton Plaza*, San Diego, California, 1984-6 (Photograph Dhana Solish)

9.8 John Jerde Partners, *Westside Pavilion*, Los Angeles, 1985-6 (Photograph C. Jencks)

wrenched from several sources leading some critics, such as Douglas Davis of *Newsweek,* to condemn it as 'a Michael Graves showroom gone mad'.[4] It's true the graphic language is a polyglot, based mostly on Graves' motifs and colours, but it's nevertheless vastly superior to previous shopping centres – 'Mies van der Rohe boxes gone mad' – precisely because of its bubbly eclecticism, more suitable to commerce and shopping than the customary monoliths dumped across America. The genre desperately needs the articulations and colour which Jerde has given it; the festive canopies, portals and banners. On the outside its long length is divided up into six visually comprehensible, discrete sections, while the inside galleria is also broken up by various elements, including palm trees, escalators and current versions of Victorian structure (9). The designer, inspired by disparate sources, has spoken of mixing the active surfaces of Egyptian architecture with the delicate frame of the GUM department store in Moscow.[5]

Most importantly the parking is to the rear, while the street line and scale of the area is held, with the result that this gigantic volume works as a piece of contextual urbanism. Judged as high architecture or, as Davis does, as a portent of where Post-Modernism is heading, the building must be considered mediocre; but judged as an urban shopping centre it is a step forward. This double judgement is, once again, necessary for a historical appreciation of Post-Modern urbanism – necessarily a more compromised genre than that of the individual building.

Berlin's International Building Exhibition (IBA) shows the same ambivalent results. Worthy for its urban intentions – reasserting the basic city grammar and pluralism – it has failed as yet to produce major architecture; nor has it attempted to. Rather, within very restricted budgets, a variety of architects have each built small sections of a city next to each other, following common rules. The basic typology of the Rauchstrasse section, for instance, follows the 'urban villa' type, which is appropriate in scale to the adjacent Diplomatic Quarter. Most of the nine architects involved break the five-storey villa into four squat parts centring on a relatively large informal space (10). The idea of this space, like that of the courtyard which unites the villas, is to create a public realm full of activity, where neighbours can meet and drink in the pubs, children can play and even, in Robert Krier's sketches, communal dancing can take place. Alas for this fraternity, IBA and the developers did not come up with the money and so the public space, while built, ended up as yet another Modernist garden of token greenery without a clearly defined social use.

With all its inadequacies – no fault of the architects who lost money on the design – the Rauchstrasse group of villas still has to be considered a step forward. It has a pluralism of style and layout – two brick buildings, three white villas and three decorated ones – a common height and street morphology and is, in Robert Krier's eastern most 'palazzo' of flats, a noble monument of social housing (11). On one side two stairs come up from a central arch and monumental bust (Krier is a sculptor as well as an architect)

9.9 John Jerde Partners, *Westside Pavilion*, galleria, Los Angeles, 1985-6 (Photograph C. Jencks)

9.10 IBA, *Rauchstrasse Development*, Block 109, axonometric, Berlin, 1985 (Photograph courtesy the IBA)

9.11 Robert Krier, *Rauchstrasse Flats*, east convex wall with bust, Berlin, 1983-5 (Photograph courtesy the architect)

9.9

9.11

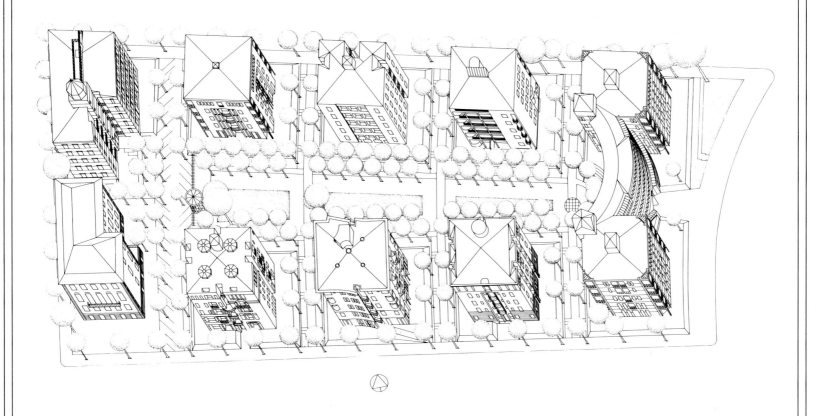

9.10

and on the other, two banded brick towers punctuate the three sections. The variety of interior room layouts, like the exterior variation, is restrained and urbane, even grand and noble in the best classical sense. And the formal language, while familiar, is fresh because continually varied and combined with the Berlin grammar of brick and concrete. Robert Krier has had a running battle with the developers here and elsewhere at IBA and this resulted, finally, in his withdrawal from social housing and a bankrupt practice in Vienna. But his and many other IBA schemes, however compromised, still set a standard for urbanism, especially because they show the virtues of many architects working together with shared assumptions.

There are other fragments of an urban pluralism worth mentioning: the infill buildings of Bologna promoted by that city's communist administration; the projects of Jaquelin Robertson under construction in Washington DC and elsewhere; and the infill housing of Jeremy Dixon around London, which adapts an existing typology in a lively, eclectic language to the new exigencies of denser living (12). In these projects Dixon has even managed to reintroduce an element of traditional craftsmanship and refinement. There is also the sensitive reinterpretation of Japanese traditions made by Christopher Alexander for the Eishin University in Japan, and the extension of the Montreal urban tissue by Peter Rose. All over the world architects are trying, with the meagre mandate they have, to stitch together parts of cities that have been eroded either through neglect, Modernist planning, zoning codes of the 1960s and/or aerial bombardment.

Much of this work can be characterised by two schemes of Terry Farrell and the values of the association he heads in London, the Urban Design Group. This pressure group, founded in 1979, rewrote the influential Athens Charter of 1933, a Modernist treatise which for thirty years had greatly influenced zoning law and development. The Urban Design Group, in setting forth guidelines for creating the 'good city', touched on some familiar points of Jane Jacobs and Oscar Newman – the formulae of mixed use, easy access, increased communication, defensible space – as well as reasserting the Post-Modernist's trust in personalisation, legibility and city memory.[6] It constitutes more a summary of current wisdom than an addition to it. Terry Farrell has managed to disseminate these values to a wide public while at the same time convincing large developers to put them into practice. The groups of buildings that result from this conjunction of large-scale building and 'think small' have a pleasant contradiction of scale – the result of the process of 'mega-infill'. One scheme for the Old London Wall area, and another for development in the air rights above Charing Cross station, estimated at £65 and £100 million respectively, are much larger than the usual infill projects and comparable in size to Rouses's schemes. Piecemeal growth in a city, drawing on the work of both architects and non-architects, inevitably takes years to achieve and is, by definition, incremental. Farrell, in systematising infill, has attempted to create a process which conforms both with current economic growth and the more usual package development. If 'small is

9.12 Jeremy Dixon, *Lanark Road Housing Project*, London, 1986 (Photograph Martin Charles)

beautiful' but uninteresting to those who shape the city with big movements of capital, then perhaps 'a lot of small is beautiful', or at least preferable to one megastructure.

Farrell's London Wall scheme proposes the demolition of a Miesian 1960s office tower and its replacement with two Gravesian/Art Deco towers, complete with large glazed areas and semicircular tops designed to break up the huge mass (13,14). One tower straddles both the London Wall and the road, thus bridging two areas that have previously been divided by these physical barriers. Above pedestrian arcades are seventeen storeys of offices with large spans and deep floors which it is anticipated will be required by London's 'Big Bang' – the deregulation of the Stock Exchange. Thankfully, low-rise housing is provided that fronts on two squares, so the area will have some activity in the evening. The set backs, squat shapes and mixture of granite and glass are reminiscent of Graves' Humana Building as well as Farrell's own previous schemes and, with their axial symmetries and ABA rhythms, they are unmistakably part of the Post-Modern Classical language in general. Indeed, in programme and style the scheme would well qualify for San Francisco's Downtown Plan.

It is obviously too soon to say whether this mixed development will be successful at ground level, but what gives life to the overall design is the way in which highly ordered masses have been juxtaposed to take up the two city axes. Each facade is composed as a centred whole with heavy, banded corner elements incorporating a glazed central section. Pediments, or their semi-circular equivalents, are split and pulled back at the top to give visual variety and accommodate large outdoor balconies (again reminiscent of the Humana Building). Functional flexibility is thus underlined by varying the classical language at an amplified scale. The resultant aesthetic can be gauged by Farrell's completed bank at Fenchurch Street in the City of London which has a related grammar of granite and glass (15). Here, an abstracted classicism, with banded masonry base, similiarly leads up in setbacks to a top with more glazing.

Architects such as Ricardo Bofill and James Stirling have been playing with similar amplifications of classical columns, splayed cornices and large glazed areas, and it is these combinations that constitute one of the emergent canons of Free Style Classicism: the figural part, or small iconic shape, used as the ordering principle for a large whole. Thus the London Wall scheme is ordered effectively as two giant Edwardian pylons or two Art Deco radios.

Farrell's 'Air Rights Building' for Charing Cross is designed as a gigantic split pediment with corner towers, or as a huge face motif with upturned ears (16). Whatever image we can discern in this scheme, the monolith has a striking presence appropriate for its urban role as one among a number of festive palaces that overlook the River Thames. Farrell has studied the history of development along the river and rightly argues that tradition favours buildings which face the water with towers and a strong stature.[7] The buildings thus combine these oversize images with the familiar ABA rhythm

9.13,14 Terry Farrell Partnership, *London Wall Scheme*, axonometric and model, London, 1985 (Courtesy the architect)

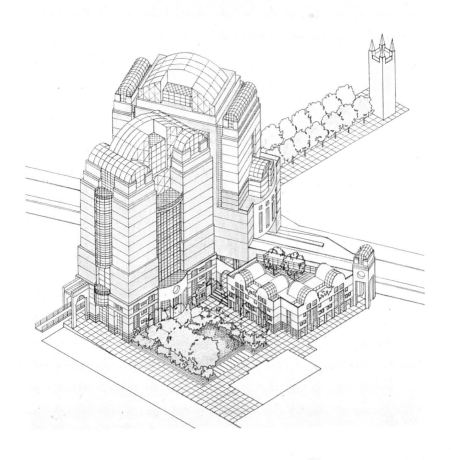

of the classic railroad station and the curved shape of a bowtruss arch, from which the office floors are slung. So in effect we have four simplified images moulded together, the first three of which are gigantic amplifications of classical motifs.

No doubt Pop Art of the 1960s made room for this Post-Modern trope but its main point of interest is the way in which it is combined with small-scale changes to the urban fabric. Thus Farrell's Air Rights Building blends into the existing patterns of movement – a footbridge over the Thames to the south, Trafalgar Square to the north and a redesigned garden to the east. Adding arcades and proposing piecemeal changes to shops, theatres and garden, he manages to mediate between large images and the intricate grain, the big and small scale, which is one reason why his 'mega-infill' has become so popular with both developers and conservationists.

An American counterpart of Farrell who has been promoting the new urbanism since the late 1960s is the Virginia-born Barton Myers. His commitment to democracy and pluralism reflects, in a sense, his varied background: part southern gentleman with a slight Virginian accent, he is also part intellectual Jew, an émigré to Canada for several years and former air force pilot who looks as if he were chosen for a lead part in Tom Wolfe's *The Right Stuff*. He actually studied historic sites in Europe, among other ways, by flying over them several times. And this method of aerial reconnaissace is perhaps one reason why his designs combine a traditional urban scale with a light-weight, high-tech imagery. Along with his former Canadian partner, Jack Diamond, Myers built several urban schemes, such as York Square in Toronto, which not only carried out many of the ideas of Jane Jacobs, but even managed to win her approval.[8] Slowly he built up experience at filling in old parts of the city, rehabilitating existing buildings, adding arcades, changing uses and, along with George Baird, formulating a philosophy they termed 'Vacant Lottery'.[9] This theory, as its title suggests, emphasises the consolidation of the existing urban fabric and the importance of mixed use, low-rise building in stitching together a city: the intelligent use of vacant lots, instead of the usual opposition between an ultra high-rise centre and a shallow surburban periphery. Many of his schemes – such as the completed Sherbourne Lanes infill housing in Toronto or the unbuilt Grand Avenue in downtown Los Angeles (which, like the IBA work in Berlin, involved a number of architects working together on a single site) – show the wisdom of his synthetic approach; a wisdom he credits as much to a growing tradition as his own perspicacity.

In 1985, competing against such architects as Michael Graves and Arata Isozaki, he won the commission for the government centre in Phoenix, Arizona (17). This project, to be built in stages, illustrates many of his basic tenets. The central foreground buildings are surrounded by a dense texture of background fabric; low-rise office blocks connected by sheltered passages (necessary because of the extreme summer heat) which, modifying the classical cornice, are cooled by hightech sunshades. This small block

9.15 Terry Farrell Partnership, *Bank on Fenchurch Street*, London, 1983-7 (Courtesy the architect)

9.16 Terry Farrell Partnership, *Air Rights Building I*, Charing Cross Station, London, 1986 (Courtesy the architect)

planning, the Jacobite and Leon Krier formula, uses existing passages of Phoenix to produce repeatable systems of major and minor pedestrian routes. Set in contrast to this, and one reason Myers won the competition, is a civic centre which captures the essence of American democracy.[10]

The mayor of Phoenix, Terry Godard, asked for a solution which would express open government and the accessibility of elected officials. Myers answered this call by providing a civic plaza – a three hundred foot square piazza – containing a City Council Chamber that is clearly open to public access. Cafés, restaurants and slow-moving traffic furnish the everyday life of this 'great public room', while on special days it can be closed off to make a congenial space for outdoor concerts, markets and conventions. Toronto's Philips Square, next to its City Hall, was an influence Myers cited, and one that has two-hundred-and-fifty scheduled public events per year. Covering the Civic Plaza, at times of extreme heat, will be a velarium suspended on catenary cables from the four towers. Symbolising city democracy will not only be the abstraction of the phoenix – an obvious totem – but a mixture of functional civic forms: courtyard, arcade, council chamber and other public amenities realised in the reddish-brown earthcolours of the south-west and desert. Spikey tensile members and sunshades contrast with the monumentality. Here is the current paradigm of pluralist urbanism realised in an eclectic style.

The High Game of Architecture - Ricardo Bofill and James Stirling

The truth of city building today is that good architecture and good urbanism are opposed. This is not how it should be according to theory, or anybody's wishes, but rather a natural result of the way large areas get built and the values it takes to build them. Good architects, like good artists, are primarily

258

concerned with the language of form, while good urbanists must have an equal commitment to the things that erode such a language: compromise, democracy, pluralism, entrepreneurial skill and patience. It's very unlikely that a single person or architectural firm will combine these opposite skills and values and even when they do the results are likely to be flawed. Nevertheless, the attempt at a fusion will be made by a few intrepid and romantic individuals – characters such as Ricardo Bofill and James Stirling – who have spent their careers rebelling against convention and believe they can overcome the usual opposition between the two fields.

Bofill and Stirling are very different architects, but, in some respects at least, bear comparison. Both developed away from a Late-Modern practice in the early 1970s to formulate their distinctive styles of urbanist classicism, the former influenced by Palladio, Ledoux, Durand and the techniques of heavyweight construction, the latter by Le Corbusier, Colin Rowe's *Collage City* and Schinkel. Both rejected the International Style while retaining many Modernist attitudes towards construction, and both were influenced by the urbanist theories of Aldo Rossi, Leon Krier and the Rationalists, without subjugating their own identities. By 1975, very early in the development of Post-Modern Classicism, they had both produced urban schemes in the new style – Bofill's Arcades du Lac and Stirling's Düsseldorf project.[11] In most other ways, however, these two architects are quite different.

Ricardo Bofill and his Taller de Arquitectura produce buildings which are, in effect, Modernist ones in classical garb. Their large housing projects, like Le Corbusier's *Unités d'Habitations,* go back to the social utopianism of Charles Fourier and his *Phalanstères* of 1820 – large palace complexes which combine the Baroque style of Louis XIV with the latest facilities of modern technology in attempting to build new communities of a manageable size. Bofill (or really his Taller which deserves equal credit) mix precast concrete elements of one colour and set them off against in-situ concrete elements of a lighter shade, just as Le Corbusier, at the *Unités,* achieved similar contrasts but with rougher textures and finishes. The Taller product is superior, not only to Modernist work – which often crumbles, stains, discolours, moves, leaks and generally looks like abandoned bunkers – but to other contemporary use of the material. This is because the Taller experiment with concrete methods until they achieve a smooth surface that resembles stone or marble, and use precise steel moulds to give a crisp finish (18). Ironically the results are close to what Le Corbusier (speaking of the mouldings of the Parthenon) described as exemplary architecture: heroic profiles, 'naked and polished like steel'. Bofill and his group have brought off, with their well machined concrete, a major turnabout in style; they have shown that the machine aesthetic need not look like an Eiffel Tower, or an oil refinery, or a lightweight Fuller dome. It can also be fashioned to resemble an architecture of mass and *chiaroscuro,* going back to ancient Egypt; or in the words of Peter Hodgkinson, one of the Taller's leaders, 'the Mediterranean Graeco-Romanic heritage or, as I call it, the Memphis, Athens, Rome axis'.[12] To this

259

heavyweight and hieratic tradition of monument building with massive compression members, Bofill adds the further influences of Michelangelo, Borromini and Ledoux.

Les Arcades du Lac, being near Versailles, takes its cue from this Baroque palace by incorporating a giant rhythmical bay system of precast pilasters (19). Diagonal *allées* flare out, as they do at Versailles, over flat green lawns, but now there is parking underneath the *parterres*. Following the dictates of the new urbanism, perimeter blocks and arcades enclose positive figural shapes given over to the pedestrian (20). But their overbearing scale and single use – for housing – go against the paradigm formulated by Jane Jacobs. Indeed if there is an obvious criticism of Bofill's work it lies here more than in the alleged fascism or Stalinism of the style. What is missing is the urban fabric, the old buildings, historical and functional diversity – all the background which would give his foreground more meaning. The problem with his schemes is that one can't escape Architecture; there is no complementary building.

This is of course a problem Bofill likes: 'I am the greatest architect since Michelangelo', he has said and certainly, given his hairy drawings which sometimes, like Michelangelo's, compare on the same page the musculature of a nude with the *modenature* of a cornice, we can see direct parallels in approach. Building elements break out in a sensual way all over the surface, casting sharp shadows (21), while broken pediments, pilasters and balconies are jammed into each other with a vigorous force, if not with the *terribilità* of the Renaissance sculptor-architect. Michelangelo believed that the study of human anatomy was essential for the architect and it's an obvious feat of Bofill that he can achieve this body language using only the recalcitrant medium of prefabrication. However, if there is this parallel and a shared architectural preoccupation with the human anatomy, there is also a difference. Michelangelo could gradually mould the sensuous parts together to form a whole, responding to the interrelationship of parts as he worked, whereas Bofill has to prefabricate the parts separately and resolve them in drawing.

Bofill's work thus exhibits a paradoxical flavour typical of Post-Modernism, blending the mechanical with the voluptuous, the unyielding with the sensual. *Les Espaces d'Abraxas*, a gigantic development of six hundred apartments near Paris, illustrates well this characteristic opposition. On the outside of the curved 'Theatre of Abraxas', where the cars speed by, a heroic Doric order shoots up ten storeys, only to be contrasted, in Michelangelesque fashion, with paired Tuscan columns of three storeys (22). The tough, masculine robustness of these contrasting orders is appropriate to their place beside a traffic intersection. Their precise machine finish, more controlled and 'perfect' than could be achieved by handwork, lends the rustication great elegance. Here again we touch upon the paradox mentioned in connection with Kohn Pedersen Fox (Chapter VIII), that some ornament is actually better made by industrial methods. In this case the recurring sharp

9.18 Ricardo Bofill and Taller de Arquitectura, *Les Echelles du Baroque*, Paris, 1983-6 (Photogaph courtesy the architect)

9.19 Ricardo Bofill and Taller de Arquitectura, *Les Temples du Lac*, St. Quentin-en-Yvelines, near Paris, 1972-83 (Photograph C. Jencks)

Following pages:
9.20 Ricado Bofill and Taller de Arquitectura, *Les Arcades du Lac*, central piazza, monument and arches, St. Quentin-en-Yvelines, near Paris, 1972-83 (Photograph C. Jencks)

9.21 Ricardo Bofill and Taller de Arquitectura, *Les Arcades du Lac*, Le Viaduc, St. Quentin-en-Yvelines, near Paris, 1972-83 (Photograph C. Jencks)

9.22 Ricardo Bofill and Taller de Arquitectura, *Les Espaces d'Abraxas*, theatre from the highway, Marne-la-Vallee, near Paris, 1978-82 (Photograph C. Jencks)

9.23 Ricardo Bofill and Taller de Arquitectura, *Theatre of Abraxas*, Marne-la-Vallee, near Paris, 1978-82 (Photograph C. Jencks)

9.24 Ricardo Bofill and Taller de Arquitectura, *La Place du Nombre d'Or*, plan of Antigone, Montpellier, France, 1978-84 (Courtesy the architects)

9.25 Ricardo Bofill and Taller de Arquitectura, *La Place du Nombre d'Or*, 288 apartments and shop, Montpellier, France, 1978-84 (Photograph courtesy the architects)

9.26 Ricardo Bofill and Taller de Arquitectura, *La Place de Nombre d'Or*, city-side of apartments broken into pavilions and columns, Montpellier, France, 1978-84 (Photograph courtesy the architects)

outlines are more standardised and continuous because they are produced by steel moulds. Gavin Stamp faults Bofill for 'ignoring the rich possibilities of textures and craftsmanship suggested by other European building traditions'.[13] But this misses the point. One should rather applaud him for inventing a new kind of concrete texture and industrial craftsmanship. It results in flat, staccato finishes and chunky outlines which no doubt look crude to the eye trained on handwork ornament and the refinements of entasis, but which have a sharp beauty all of their own. Perhaps only an eye trained in twentieth-century architecture can fully discern this charm.

On the inside of the theatre, the masculine Doric character is transformed (as it should be according to Vitruvian decorum) into a lighter version of the Corinthian (23). Here fluted, engaged columns of reflective black glass, shielding the living rooms from gaze and glare, shoot up to a triple-level crescendo of mouldings, and the new acanthus leaf – an entire cypress tree! This incredible conceit characterises the whole, slightly mad, method of Bofill: take a normal element – a capital or triumphal arch – and, like a Pop artist, blow it up ten times in scale; turn columns into lift shafts and metopes and triglyphs into a complete apartment floor (Thomas Jefferson did this at Monticello but it was for his *children's* floor). The amplification and displacement of elements are methods shared by the Surrealists and Le Corbusier as much as by Pop artists, and their presence here again shows how Post-Modernists owe as much to Modernism as they do to the classical tradition.

Bofill, coming from Barcelona, has naturally been influenced by Salvador Dali and Antonio Gaudi. In fact he once told me, in a modest moment, that after trying to do a modern version of Gaudi for a few years, he gave up in despair realising that he could never be as creative as this Catalan Prometheus.[14] Instead of competing with this 'the greatest architect' (he was divided between Michelangelo and Gaudi) he decided to strike out at a new scale of creation where no one had ever operated before and therefore new standards could be set: the gigantic, urban level. In effect, by increasing the size of the designed unit ten times, he would expand the realms of creativity. And that's exactly what he has done.

The *Antigone* scheme in Montpellier, France, is a good example of this amplification. Here the cross-section of a Gothic pier (and Bramante's plan of St. Peter's Cathedral) has been expanded several thousand times to form a ring of apartments (24). This form – a Baroque quatrefoil – is also influenced by Gabriel's urban plans and ordered by golden section proportions, hence its name *La Place du Nombre d'Or*. The number of references, like the formal determinants, are eclectic and divergent: they don't, as in the Renaissance, add up to an integrated system of metaphysics. Why Baroque, why golden section; indeed why St. Peter's, a Gothic pier and precast stone? And, to ask further questions which show the divergence of traditions, why did a socialist mayor commission this inner-city redevelopment? Why is the Taller's work the most popular form of mass-housing in France? Why does

Bofill's architecture overcome the great dichotomies of left/right wing, classicism/Modernism, bourgeois/industrial, clichéd/inventive, individual/mass-produced? To pose these rhetorical questions is to answer them, because the work is so clearly conceived in terms of polar opposites.

At Montpellier, for instance, the curve of apartments and their streamlined cornices whip around the site like so many precise electrons anchored in orbit by a linear accelerator. This machine-age image is also tied to a classical conceit, insofar as the mouldings curve out, like those of the Roman Pantheon, 'to hold the dome of the sky' (25). On the inner side of the piazza, the prefabrication of pediments and pilasters is rather cold and severe, but the careful attention to contrasting finishes (darker precast concrete set against lighter in situ concrete) is touching and thoughtful. Again the omnipresence of Architecture is one-dimensional if not totalitarian, whereas the break-up of mass into columns and pavilions is humane (26). This is not to say that every fault is cancelled by a virtue, but rather that one admires the work in spite of the faults. It creates a forceful, sometimes heroic, public realm in an area – housing – where it had ceased to exist in this century. It opens up a new chapter in prefabrication, showing how Post-Modernism can produce the equivalents of marble, limestone and *stucco lustro* (itself false marble) using controlled and oxidised concretes set in machined moulds. Bofill's Michelangelesque urbanism could be improved upon if it were to be embedded in the old, botched tissue of the city and if it provided functional flexibility, instead of sticking out like 'an advertisement of someone's ego' (as Jane Jacobs said of Le Corbusier's urbanism). It's not asking too much of Bofill that he add the final touch of background fabric to his polarities. Indeed, given his intelligent swerves of direction in the past, he might do it. What he and the Taller have already accomplished shows, in spite of its shortcomings, a heroic willpower in overcoming the clichés, compromise and bureaucratic planning of our time. In a sense their creations are *petites citiés ideal*, cities of the Renaissance, but built by spec developers instead of gentry; monuments which occupy a category somewhere between the bombastic, the amazing and the sublime.

When the same ideas are pushed further by Manolo Núñez, a disciple of Bofill, the amplification of forms returns them to their origins in Pop caricature. *Les Arenes de Picasso,* Núñez's answer to the *Palace of Abraxas* (and just one giant step away) is a huge bull-ring of housing with Ledoux-like scoreboards placed on either side (27, 28). The exaggerations in scale and the prefabrication of classical allusions in concrete, seem to be a conscious parody and critique of Bofill, as if this designer were settling an old score with his former mentor. On the negative side, the juxtaposition of styles is often gratuitous. For instance Art Deco lighting details are crossed with Gaudiesque buttresses to form arcades that lean into housing, thus providing a nice visual rhythm but no real protection from the sun and rain. On the positive side, this is a refreshing combination of classical mouldings and rustication with computer graphics – a symbolic indication of the fact that this classicism was

9.27,28 Manuel Núñez, *Les Arenes de Picasso*, Marne-la-Vallee, 1980-5 (Photographs C. Jencks)

conceived and built partly by machine. And the arena space is well scaled with respect to the surrounding walls. But, in the end, this mixture of the sublime and the idiosyncratic is unconvincing.

The urbanism of James Stirling, by contrast, weaves quotes from the ideal city into a more complex and dialectical pattern. There are elements of the sublime and perfect geometries in his work, but these are culminating incidents set in relief against a more generalised background. This mixture, formulated by Colin Rowe in *Collage City*[15] as a proper balance between figure and ground, reaches its highest expression in the work of Stirling and Wilford, who have developed progressively, synthesising most of the key Post-Modern ideas.

Responding to Jacobite planning and the demands of social pluralism, they have evolved a hybrid aesthetic that accepts both old and new buildings within the existing urban context. From Le Corbusier and latterly Schinkel and Leon Krier, they have formulated a Free-Style Classicism that mixes ideal shapes with vernacular construction, while from the Modernists they have derived a taste for industrial beauty, dissonance and contrast. From Robert Venturi they have learned how to use outline shapes, or 'ghost-buildings', to refer to previous architecture and from the Post-Modernists in general they are beginning to learn the virtues of symbolic ornament. Listing these influences does not detract from the synthesis, but rather makes it more impressive, partly because what we value in urbanism is a balance of opposite goals and partly because competition within a tradition sets new standards.

Stirling and Wilford's first synthesis was in the Düsseldorf Museum project, although their first completed compound was the Neue Staatsgalerie in Stuttgart (29). Here we have not so much a single building as a series of fragments placed on an acropolis (or car park) which attracts the pedestrian either into the museum or over the site. One arrives on the Konrad-Adenauerstrasse, a high-speed road that divides this part of the city, at a red and blue steel temple – the taxi drop-off point. Echoing Venturi's ghosted buildings, this symbolic ornament, like the other high-tech attachments, provides an entrance focus but also tells us something about a new attitude to the past. For it refers both to the primitive hut – underlying the temple and classicism – and to the modern past, when the straightforward use of steel I-beams was considered beautiful (30). This complex, even divergent, message is placed above the entrance to the car park – which is given the battered profile of an Egyptian pylon – and underlined by the dayglo handrails that hold lighting fixtures. These high-tech cylinders are themselves given a divergent role inasmuch as they function both as the cornice to the banded rustication and as a traffic sign indicating where to walk (31). At first glance, and in a Neoclassical or Modernist reading of the building, these blue and pink fixtures look extraneous: 'punk clip-ons' according to the former view and 'high-tech costume jewellery' according to the latter.[16] Post-Modernism poses the same threat to both these integrated aesthetics because of its radical pluralism and hybrid language.

9.29 James Stirling and Michael Wilford, *Neue Staatsgalerie*, view of site and Konrad-Adenaeurstrasse, Stuttgart, 1977-84 (Photograph C. Jencks)

When I first saw these strong colours they did seem extraneous and overdone. If the lighting and handrails had been more delicately hidden – for instance behind an Eygptian cornice used on the galleries – then the complex would have been more formally integrated. However, when I became familiar with the contrasts and saw how consistently they were used elsewhere and how they conformed with the colourful clothing of those using the building, I came to understand the logic of this mixed aesthetic. The overall compound is actually used in a variety of ways, some of which are not connected with art at all. Since it forms very pleasant outdoor rooms which are open to the public, it attracts the kind of spontaneous behavior one finds in a bazaar. On the day I visited it, the building provided a bustling spectacle which presumably, since it has become one of the most popular museums in Germany, it still does. The young I talked to compared the building to the Pompidou Centre – a valid comparison only if one subtracts all the classical masonry, but nevertheless an interesting reading of certain technological images such as the extract units to the rear, or the elevator within (32). The older people – a group of *plein air* painters and some businessmen – also liked the building but gave completely different readings. One group saw the complex as a Graeco-Roman ruin, another as a typical German institution in the tradition of Schinkel's *Altes Museum*.

Pompidou Centre, Acropolis, Neoclassical gallery – each of these divergent interpretations has a plausibility that stems from the different tastes or 'language games' of the observers. As Jean-François Lyotard has defined it, *The Post-Modern Condition* evolves from the battle between such different language games, none of which has absolute authority.[17] Since our metaphysics is not shared, since, as he puts it, 'the grand narratives' of religion, social emancipation, progress and science have been relativised, there is no possibility of a shared world view. The implication of this for aesthetics, and particularly urban aesthetics, is a plural language. And here the arguments of Jane Jacobs and so many Post-Modern theorists, including myself, come into agreement with Lyotard. The most feasible style for an open society is not the integrated ones of Modernism and Neoclassicism – nor even the monolithic mode of Ricardo Bofill. Rather it is one that acknowledges our fragile position of departure, where we have left the certainties of an integrated Christian culture, where we gain a certain identity from the past but are dependent on, and enjoy the fruits of, a fast-changing technology. Our sensibilities have been formed by these fragmentations and discontinuities but, far from disliking the heterogeneity which they entail, we enjoy the resultant hybrid aesthetic for its continuity with our daily life. By contrast, integrated systems can seem artificial and constricting.

It is to this Post-Modern condition that the Stuttgart Museum speaks directly and with a kind of fractured beauty. On the main street side the classical harmonies prevail as they are enveloped within a Schinkelesque wall architecture of sandstone set against travertine – and concrete (33)! Romanesque arches and windows, Egyptian cornice, rustication and the

9.30 James Stirling and Michael Wilford, *Neue Staatsgalerie*, taxi drop-off point and steel temple, Stuttgart, 1977-84 (Photograph C. Jencks)

9.31 James Stirling and Michael Wilford, *Neue Staatsgalerie*, rails and lighting elements, Stuttgart, 1977-84 (Photograph C. Jencks)

9.32 James Stirling and Michael Wilford, *Neue Staatsgalerie*, elevator to gallery level, Stuttgart, 1977-84 (Photograph C. Jencks)

classical set of motifs – rectangle and circle – are so subtly absorbed into the overall grammar that we hardly notice the eclecticism. A particularly strong opposition emerges – the essential dichotomy between Traditionalism and Modernism – which Stirling dramatises without attempting to resolve. For if one conclusion is drawn throughout this site it is that both positions are legitimate and partial. Neither can win, nor can there be a transcendent Hegelian synthesis. There is simply the juxtaposition of two world views with the ironic reversal of both: the Modernist high-tech mode has been used as symbolic ornament, while the traditional rustication functions to clothe the volumes.

To underscore this ironic dualism Stirling has removed several blocks of masonry from the parking garage, allowing them to fall in front of the building like ruins set in an eighteenth-century landscape (34). Yet when we sit on these blocks and scrutinise the construction carefully, we realise that the holes in the wall are functional – that they serve to vent the garage – and that the fallen blocks are a sham. The sandstone and travertine of the building are only an inch thick and are suspended from a steel frame – the reality of construction today. This amusing detail, as much as the gallery lighting and doors within, shows the way we can have it both ways; beauty and stone detailing, as long as they are skin deep; technology and automobiles, as long as they can be hidden.

The centre of the Neue Staatsgalerie is the outdoor sculpture court which is insulated against noise and traffic on all sides. Here is the public realm, the contained piazza which Bofill, Charles Moore and every Post-Modernist except Robert Venturi incorporate in their schemes. Its round shape and curve against the sky turn it into a sacred form, a rotunda complete with 'domeless dome' (35). The shape is reminiscent of the Pantheon and its Christian successors. Stirling also intends affinities with the ruins of Hadrian's Villa where weeds and trees sprout in a similar manner from the top of fractured vaults. A sunken Doric portico, based on Weinbrenner's design of the eighteenth century, is on one side facing a modern staircase on the other, while a pedestrian ramp curves through and climbs up the drum. Given the beauty, associations and placement of this rotunda, I naturally thought it would have some symbolic significance and that the centre, where an altar might be (or at least the emperor's throne at the time of Hadrian), would be its culmination. Stirling quashed this assumption – 'The centre is a drain and the three circles represent not the Trinity, but the cross-section of an electric cable'.

This quick response was an amusing rebuff to my question. It recalls Henry Adam's prediction that in our century the dynamo would replace the Virgin, or the pursuit of energy and power would replace the Church. But it also reveals a characteristic problem for so many Post-Modernists who design centrally planned buildings and piazza: what should occupy the centre? What should culminate the walk through the site and make sense of all this heterogeneity? For where collage is accepted as an end in itself, where there

9.33 James Stirling and Michael Wilford, *Neue Staatsgalerie*, sandstone, travertine and concrete cornice, Stuttgart, 1977-84 (Photograph C. Jencks)

9.34 James Stirling and Michael Wilford, *Neue Staatsgalerie*, 'Ruins' which reveal the true steel structure, Stuttgart, 1977-84 (Photograph C. Jencks)

9.35 James Stirling and Michael Wilford, *Neue Staatsgalerie*, 'Domeless Dome', the sculpture court, Stuttgart, 1977-84 (Photograph C. Jencks)

is no overall plot to a building, no concerted symbolic programme, then the ornament and formal motifs will tell only a confused and disjointed story. Stirling and Wilford originally wished to house the old art in the new part of the building and the contemporary art, which is not to their taste, in the old Staatsgalerie. They were not, in the event, allowed to make this extreme contrast of form and content.[18] But neither did they work out a sequence connecting space, ornament and the new art collection. Thus, one now travels up in the elevator only to arrive at the most recent art, that is the end of art history.

If this, undoubtedly the most impressive building of Post-Modernism up to 1984, shows the limits of collage used as an end in itself, it still reveals its virtues as an urban strategy.[19] For the Neue Staatsgalerie is both a very popular and a profound building. It appeals to many different tastes, the prime if not the only goal of Post-Modern architecture, and illustrates many of its strategies, including ironic representation and contextual response. Stirling and Wilford have built on the strengths of Post-Modernism and applied the lessons of urban pluralism elsewhere in Germany and England.

In Berlin, next to a palace and the River Spree, they have juxtaposed a series of 'type-solutions' for a Science Centre: the castle, odeon, octagonal tower, stoa and cathedral (36). This collage of abstracted plans is given a common facade and a medieval site plan, the combination creating many picturesque left-over spaces which make up for the relatively dull window treatment. In London, for an addition to the Tate Gallery, they have transposed their eclecticism from plan to elevation, literally changing style every time they reach the corner and a new type of adjacent building (37). In both cases the eclecticism is extreme – an interesting intellectual pursuit of a valid requirement – but more notable as a demonstration of method than as a perfected result. More successful, to my mind, are the schemes Stirling and Wilford propose for the Mansion House Square in the financial centre of London.

These two projects were commissioned by Peter Palumbo after the Miesian office tower, criticised by Prince Charles and others, was rejected. Palumbo's choice of architect was a wise one, not only because Stirling has proven his ability at handling difficult urban sites, but also because the polarisation of debate within England between conservationists and Modernists has reached such a deadlock and Stirling, with his eclectic approach, could incorporate arguments from each side. This he has done skilfully. Keeping the nineteenth-century facade of the site designed by Mappin and Webb, which anchors the prow-like corner, Scheme A rises up in measured rhythms to a splayed tower (38). Scheme B, which fills out the entire site with lower buildings, also breaks up the horizontal expanse into chunky blocks (39). Both schemes thus retain the small block image of a traditional city which belies the different reality hidden inside. Thus one of the buildings incorporates large, open floor spans, again designed to cater to the requirements of the so-called 'Big-Bang'.

9.36 James Stirling and Michael Wilford, *Science Centre*, model, Berlin, 1980-7 (Photograph John Donat)

9.37 James Stirling and Michael Wilford, *Clore Gallery Extension to the Tate Gallery*, London, 1982-7 (Photograph C. Jencks)

This difference between external appearance and underlying reality has come to be a hallmark of Stirling's work and a means of accommodating contending requirements. Since the City of London is a patchwork of odd shapes, alleyways and classical structures, a monolithic solution would be unsuitable. Stirling and Wilford have therefore broken up the mass of both schemes into vertically proportioned bays. This gives the overall volume an episodic quality as if it were built over time, a quality the designers have reinforced by incorporating fragments of the preexisting buildings into the stuccoed walls. However, it avoids becoming chaotic because of the variation on a similar theme. In fact one could analyse the rhythmical and thematic structures in terms of the classical symphonic form, with a clear beginning, middle and end. As at Stuttgart a sequence of spaces culminates in a centralised rotunda: here a drum surmounted by a triangular void open to the sky (40). This is hardly hinted at by the exterior, although the large round arch is meant to suggest a collective, public area. Colonnade, bowed facades, rolled mouldings, splayed window – all these enliven the street front and welcome passage through the site. Again it's a question of the contextual dominating the literal, the needs of the pedestrian and shopper overriding the Modernist injunction to reveal the inside on the outside.

In the Secretary of State's report on, and rejection of, the Mies building, an emphasis was placed on the way the scheme might harmonise with the buildings of the City. In conforming with this guideline Palumbo's project aspired to be 'both modern and monumental'.[20] These divergent requirements were effected quite literally in the oppositions between large glazed areas and articulated masonry. A traditional hierarchy and gradation of stonework is envisioned, starting with granite at the base and then moving up from deep cut Bath stone to more finely articulated Portland stone. As in an Italian palazzo, from which this method stems, the delicacy and apparent distance of the top floors is here emphasised; but, unlike a palazzo, the discontinuity of layers is stressed. Such discontinuity, typical of Post-Modernism in general, is of course a conscious choice since it would have been much simpler to make the covering continuous.

Particularly impressive is the way in which Stirling has used monumental forms without being either predictable or pompous. Although the shapes have a familiar classical feeling, there are no obvious precedents he follows. And the variety of rhythms and chunky volumes is an appropriate representation of urban pluralism. To see how far Post-Modern urbanism has come in twenty years, we have only to contrast these schemes with those of Mies. Whereas Mies gave the client one perfected box, Stirling and Wilford offer the client and public two alternatives; where before there was a free-standing tower dominating a square compromised by cross-traffic, there are now several infill shapes containing a sheltered piazza. Lively historical ornament is substituted for deadpan structure, colour for monochrome darkness, and the mixed use and age of buildings for a single office function. Evidence to the contrary notwithstanding, there *is* progress in Post-Modernism.

9.38 James Stirling and Michael Wilford, *No. 1 Poultry, Scheme A*, model, London, 1986 (Photograph courtesy John Donat)

9.39 James Stirling and Michael Wilford, *No. 1 Poultry, Scheme B*, model, London, 1986 (Photograph courtesy John Donat)

9.40 James Stirling and Michael Wilford, *No. 1 Poultry, Scheme A*, up axonometric, London, 1986 (Courtesy the architects)

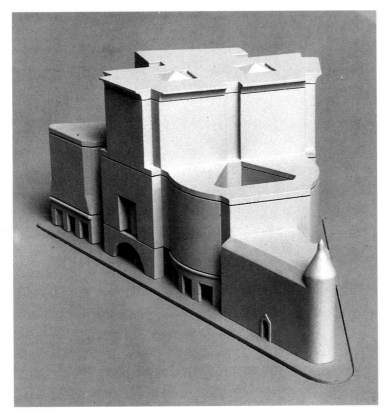
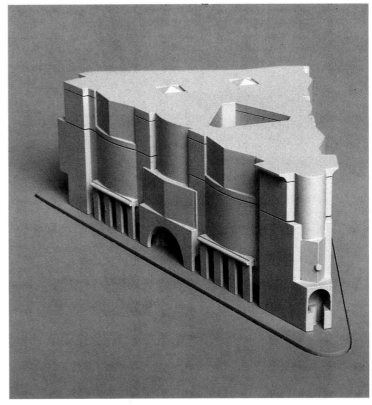
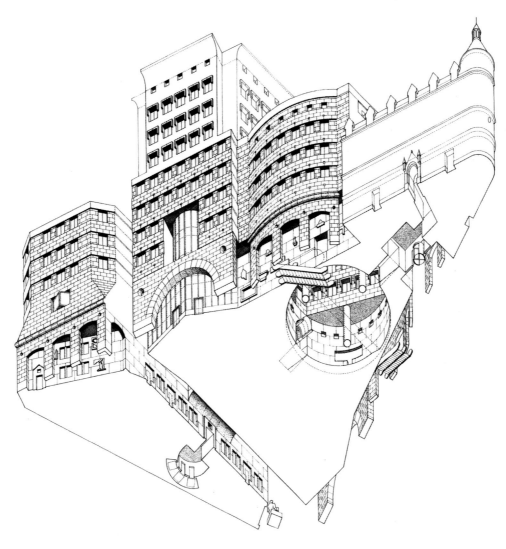

CHAPTER X
Eclectic Classicism

Modern architecture and its International Style enjoyed a long and prosperous reign. From 1927 when it was publicly launched at a building exposition in Stuttgart, to 1960 when it became the style followed by design students all around the world, it dominated all other approaches. It survived vicious attacks by reactionaries, suppression by the Nazis and even unpopularity, but was ultimately killed off, like so many nineteenth-century styles, by too much success. In flourishing, not only did it become instantly unfashionable among the avant-garde, but its limitations as a language became obvious. There was little variation, no colour or ornament to speak of, hardly any symbolism and only one basic image – the grid. It made a virtue of absence, or 'almost nothing' as Mies termed it, and professors could teach this Quaker doctrine quite effectively. But it had one overwhelming advantage envied by competitiors: it was easy to mass-produce.

Thus the first attempts to modify the International Style in the 1950s by the Italians, Japanese and Americans, were revisionist in aim. Mass-production and fast-track building were accepted, but architects hoped to turn these intractable realities towards more poetic and regional ends. The first wave of revisionist architects – Franco Albini, Eero Saarinen and Kenzo Tange – were quickly followed by others, which soon grew into a flood of Post-Modernists of all sorts. Their only similarity was the point of departure, their training in Modernist practice and belief that the modernisation of building production was irreversible. Hence the definition of Post-Modern architecture as partly Modern and partly 'something else', a hybrid mixture which can be loosely described as 'double-coding'.

Sometimes these architects were misnamed anti-Modern, a misunderstanding containing a small degree of truth. For they were indeed critical of the International Style and the preceding ideology, but aimed to transform these orthodoxies rather than return to a pre-industrial culture and closed society. Robert Venturi's 'gentle manifesto' of 1966, *Complexity and Contradiction in Architecture*, typifies this critical attitude. It attacked 'orthodox modern architecture', the simplicity and boredom of the reigning language, but simultaneously sought to enrich it with other languages – those of Pop Art, Route 66 and Sixteenth-Century Mannerism. Charles Moore, at the same time and in a similar vein, extended the Modernist style with vernacular elements and Supergraphics. Both architects shared a great respect for the work of Louis Kahn and his influence is discernible in their style – lean, flat and classical in an abstract way. In effect they mixed

Opposite:
Hans Hollein, *Austrian Travel Bureau*, Vienna, 1976-8, *see fig. 6* (Photograph J. Surwillo)

abstraction with representational languages to accommodate the realities of American life – its pluralism and commercialism. By 1970 this double coding produced the first messy amalgamation of language games – adhocism – and by 1980, as the architecture had gradually become more popular and public, and architects had begun reflecting on the notion of a language *per se,* the style evolved into a shared eclectic Classicism.

The New Representation and Difficultà

In his manifesto Venturi emphasised a series of rhetorical tropes that were opposed to those of the International Style: hybrid rather than pure elements, 'messy vitality' rather than 'obvious unity', complexity and ambiguity rather than straight-forward simplicity. Many of these stylistic figures could be summarised by the sixteenth-century Mannerist conceit of *difficultà* – solving difficult problems through virtuosic display rather than attempting to suppress them. The most fundamental statement of Venturi's method concerns his commitment to the 'difficult whole' – 'But an architecture of complexity and contradiction has a special obligation toward the whole; its truth must be in its totality or implications of totality. It must embody the difficult unity of inclusion rather than the easy unity of exclusion. More is not less.'[1]

This attack on Miesian simplification ('Less is not more, less is a bore') well illustrates the High Church creed of Modernism and explains too the austerities of Venturi's own style. His house for his mother, for instance, shows the flat, planar style of Louis Kahn with its punched out voids then subtly enriched by mouldings, oversize windows and a symbolic (broken) arch (1). That it is basically the International Style, with thin linear attachments, explains why it was so much more shocking to the Modernists than outright eclecticism. For these attachments and its overall form represented the type of complexities which Mies might have suppressed behind a flat roof and curtain wall. The central void, broken arch and pediment marked the main entrance (in Miesian architecture usually hard to find), the small ribbon windows to the right indicated the kitchen, the pitched roof represented 'house' while the off-centre chimney and giant square window signified that 'this is a strange home'.

Indeed the stringcourse, surprisingly positioned between the floor lines, also represented this arbitrary *manièra*. These distortions and amplifications were used by Venturi like the giant shifts in scale of the Pop artists. They made the house seem 'too big' or 'too small' depending on perspective, just as did the amplifications of Warhol and Oldenburg, or the out-of-scale drawings of a small child. Later, in 1982, Venturi was to see this building as a giant pediment, a precursor to the AT&T and a harbinger of Free-Style Classicism – a large weight to place on so small a structure.[2] But, like many inclusive buildings, it does contain different implications – in particular inclusiveness itself. Its virtue is the way in which a variety of representational elements are finally resolved into a whole.

10.1,2 Robert Venturi, *Vanna Venturi House,* general view and plan, Chestnut Hill, Penn., 1963-5 (Photograph Architectural Association)

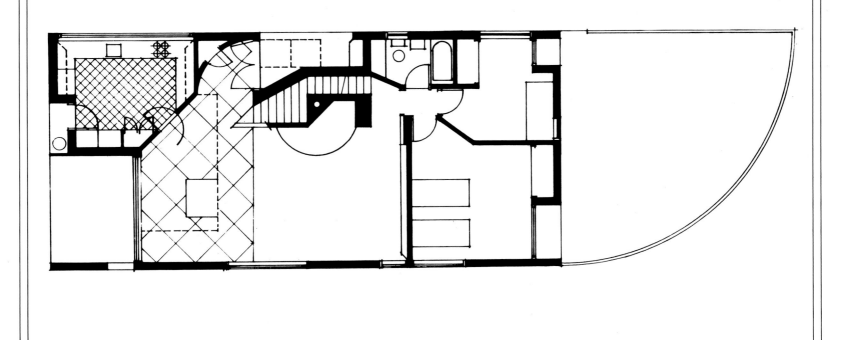

This 'difficult unity' is achieved in plan, section and elevation where different functions are dovetailed together in the most inventive and concise *manièra*. The entrance, shifted stair and fireplace are successfully interwoven as a strange and difficult whole (2). The public front, conveying the overall pitched shape, shows also how the symmetries just dominate the punctuated voids and asymmetries. It is from such work as this (as well as the Queen Anne Revival from which it derives) that the Post-Modern convention of 'asymmetrical symmetry' comes.

While Venturi and then Robert Stern were, in the late 1960s, advocating inclusiveness, other Post-Modern architects and writers were emphasising the related notions of pluralism and architecture as a symbolic system. These ideas were first summarised by Christian Norberg-Schulz in *Intentions in Architecture,* 1963, and then further developed, along with the additonal notions of semiotics and mutivalence, and used as an argument for *Meaning in Architecture* (the title of both a magazine and book which George Baird and I edited in 1967 and 1969).[3] We attacked modern architecture because it was impoverished as a language and too unconventional: to put it in semiotic terms, the International Style, like Esperanto, was concocted from neologisms outside the 'codes of the users'. Semiotics, the science of signs, emphasised that architecture was a language with multiple interpretations and this idea became key to the development of Post-Modern theory. Firstly, it identified the two major audiences the architect addresses; the general public and other architects, and from this developed a futher reason for double-coding: the idea that a building should be accessible to different groups in different ways with various types of architectural sign.[4]

These ideas were then taken up by Robert Venturi in *Learning from Las Vegas* where 'decorated sheds' (conventional signs), were distinguished from 'duck buildings' (iconic signs) and the architect encouraged to apply symbolic ornament to his buildings, just as a billboard artist might paint a message. Venturi's argument at this point, in 1972, was liberating because it revived yet another communicative mode that had been purged by Modernism – the false-fronted facade. Yet soon its limitations became obvious, the chief one being the dissociation between signifier and signified, form and content. This led to an architecture which failed to marry its visual language to the space, function and associations of a building. Effectively Venturi was advocating a 'signolic not symbolic architecture', signs which clashed rather than symbols which had a common resonance.[5] The 'decorated shed' was ultimately as barren and univalent as the Modernist building it sought to replace.

The virtue and vice of this method are apparent at the Gordon Wu Hall on the Princeton campus in New Jersey (3,4). This acknowledges its academic context of Neo-Gothic and Elizabethan revival building by its use of limestone and brick elements. Altering its shape and volume it ties together different buildings and passages using traditional bay windows, Palladian

10.3,4 Venturi, Rauch and Scott Brown, *Gordon Wu Hall*, Princeton, New Jersey, 1982-4 (Photographs Tom Bernard)

motifs and marble ornament. Modernist sensibility and a tight budget are apparent in the ribbon windows, while informality is acknowledged by the odd downpipe cutting across the last bay. Visually complex and inclusive of different tastes and uses, this building is a textbook example of Venturian theory. Furthermore, it is vastly superior to the Modernist campus buildings of Walter Gropius at Harvard and Mies van der Rohe at IIT. But (one could hear it coming) too much is made of the stuck-on symbolic ornament, particularly the marble and grey granite Serliana around the front door which shouts, 'here is the entrance'. The implicit face motif, with its cheerful ABA rhythm, is most welcoming, but its discontinuity and lack of relation to any other such motif – or space, or function, or sign – make it shallow. Since there is no symbolic programme which would make sense of this applied ornament, it is reduced to a mere sign signifying entry.

Post-Modernists have faulted Modernists for suppressing this, the most inviting part of a building. George Baird in *Meaning in Architecture* showed how Eero Saarinen did away with the rite of passage in the CBS Building; Michael Graves pointed out the same suppressions in Le Corbusier and the Modern airport with its sliding doors, and I have repeatedly shown how Late-Modernists get their exits and entrances all tangled up in a cacophony of beautiful, absurd form. Nevertheless all these weaknesses fail to justify the primary role which the followers of Venturi have given to the single sign. In this work it has become almost the equivalent of a church steeple or dome, suggesting that 'entry' is the only thing worth symbolising in an agnostic age.

Venturi, of course, symbolises more – at the Gordon Wu Hall the communal space is represented by large bay windows – and he and his wife Denise Scott Brown have been tireless in advocating the representation of different tastes. Their theory of pluralism has been a constant force in Post-Modernism since the late 1960s and is as important a contribution as their specific rhetorical inventions. But it is Charles Moore who has been more successful in carrying this pluralism into practice. His Piazza d'Italia, designed in 1976 and built in 1979, was for its time the most radical example of demonstrating different tastes and functions by using ornament(5). The Five *Italian* Orders, boot of Italy and fountain set in a piazza are all symbols and functions originating directly from the programme given to Moore and his collaborators: to provide identity to the Italian community in a city dominated by other ethnic groups.

'Italianess' is inevitably a conventional fabrication and it's a mark of Moore's realism that he represents this convention in a consistently dualistic way, blending the serious with the ironic. The Five Orders are thus partly constructed from water and neon, but to lend a certain dignity are also given canonic proportions and a stainless steel and marble finish. Abstract planar elements and black and white paving pull in the Modernist sky-scraper to one side, showing that the pluralism can even include reductivism. The fountain was designed in consultation with the Italian community and

10.5 Charles Moore, Perez Associates and UIG, *Piazza d'Italia*, New Orleans, 1976-9 (Photograph Norman McGrath)

285

its rhetoric is designed particularly to support the St. Joseph's Day Festival, when the mayor addresses an audience from a podium placed most cleverly on top of a representation of Sicily! With systematically divergent references – to Vignola, Schinkel, and Hadrian on the one hand and Italy, commerce and the citizens of New Orleans on the other – this fountain successfully establishes the public realm through multiple-coding. It was meant to be supported by a strong background of urban buildings which would make sense of the foreground shapes, and until this fabric is completed the fountain will look rather lonely and out of place – no fault of the architects.

The next stage of representational architecture was reached by Hans Hollein who, in his several travel bureaux for the Austrian government, imagined a scenario of individual signs (6). These suggest travel to different places (palm tree, pyramid, ruined column), travel by different means (ship, rail, bird flying), and different forms of entertainment (box office, chess boards, sun glasses). Hollein constructed a conceptual grid of thirty such signs, or clichés, and then, depending on the particular travel bureau, selected the appropriate set. In most cases he transformed the cliché from kitsch stereotype into a fresh sign by transforming the material and patiently detailing it. The Austrian flag, for instance, is made of alabaster and the palm trees of brass and steel. Without the irony (one pays for the vacation at a cashier's desk set behind a Rolls Royce radiator grill) and without the craftsmanship, this collage of signs would be banal. Indeed it is quite a feat of imagination that these bureaux have a fresh, almost innocent, air as if travel were still an adventure and we lived before the age of package holidays. The tourist, as many critics have pointed out, is kitschman triumphant. Building temples for him might not seem a very promising way of practicing authentic architecture, yet Hollein has taken this, the ultimate commercial task, and made it playful again. Some of his other notable commissions – candle shops, prestige jewellery boutiques (7) – are equally devoid of redeeming social virtue, but he has also found in them a hidden integrity. He does this by combining and inverting the customary relationships between materials – by treating plastic like onyx and burnished bronze like cardboard – and by transforming ephemeral functions into permanent monuments.

A collage of different signs has become the standard method of Post-Modern representation, and while this fails to achieve resonant symbolism, it does have some obvious advantages over the Modernist abstraction. The followers of Venturi and Moore, the younger generation of American architects, have absorbed some of the lessons of ornament and semiotics and now customarily incorporate a plurality of signs in their work. Robert Stern, for instance, has borrowed the palm column from Hollein (who in turn took it from John Nash) and appropriately used it in a swimming pool, along with other signs of luxuriant pleasure associated with bathing. His 'skycolumn' design for the Chicago Tribune Tower is a very

10.6 Hans Hollein, *Austrian Travel Bureau*, Vienna, 1976-8 (Photograph J. Surwillo)

10.7 Hans Hollein, *Schullin Jewellery Shop III*, Vienna, 1984 (Photograph courtesy the architect)

10.8 Robert Stern, *Late Entry to Chicago Tribune Tower Competition*, 1980 (Drawing courtesy the architect)

forceful mixture of eclectic references and one that has influenced the recent development of the polychromatic skyscraper (8). Adolf Loos' famous solution to the same problem is turned from masonry into coloured glass, partly because Chicago is the home of the Miesian glass and steel tower. The glass is here fashioned to represent stone pilasters. This 'sign of a sign' is made relevant to Chicago not only through use of realistic glass, but also through the imperial red colouring which Stern uses ironically to refer to the civic function of the newspaper 'column'.

> The signboard is intended to refer to the cultural condition of the Midwest which in earlier days gave rise to the urbanism of the false front, a cultural condition whose nostalgia for the somewhat grander things from other places gave rise also to the rather pompous name 'Chicago Tribune' with its self-righteous overtones of Roman morality. The red and gold colour scheme of the Roman emperors therefore seemed appropriate to our proposal.[6]

The layered pilasters, adapted from Michelangelo's top storey of the Palazzo Farnese, would give a sparkling light as the excess of corners reflected off one another. For its inventive use of coloured glass this scheme remains an important icon of Post-Modern Classicism and, along with a diminutive skyscraper by Kazuhiro Ishii in Tokyo, represents a step forward in the development of the historicist tower.[7]

Some of the most accomplished work in this genre is of a more modest nature. Ornament and representation are often most satisfying when understated and subordinate to other things, although examples of Baroque and Rococo building show this need not be the case. Still, when an agnostic society does not offer a pretext for rhetoric, designers can often achieve the most powerful result by playing it straight and dumb. H.H.Richardson showed this in several commercial buildings, notably the W.H.Fields warehouse in Chicago, a stripped palazzo with nice, blocky proportions and obvious, but generous, details. Today, the firm of Hoover Berg Desmond achieves something of the same, simple grandeur with their horizontal civic building in the small Colorado town of Castle Rock (9). Part palazzo with rusticated base, middle section and false attic windows, it is also in a sense the 'decorated shed' of Venturi – the decoration consisting of a masonry skin that is either ground smooth, or split to give a rough texture. Stringcourses and bay rhythms run on, ungrammatically according to the rules of Canonic Classicism, with the fresh rigour of modern prefabrication. The designers could of course have articulated these parts but, as with the blank square windows, have chosen not to. The flag and clock over the main entrance are also clear signs that the references are intended to be realistic, 'dumb' and in keeping with the everyday life of a small town.

Equally impressive for its bold straightforwardness is the River Crest Country Club in Fort Worth Texas by the Taft group from Houston (10). These young architects were asked to design a replacement for a clubhouse that had burned down. The directives were that it be 'classical' and

10.9 Hoover Berg Desmond, *Douglas County Administration Building*, Castle Rock, Colorado, 1981-3 (Drawing courtesy the architect)

10.10,11 Taft Architects with Geren Associates/CRS, *River Crest Country Club*, perspective and west facade, Forth Worth, Texas, 1981-4 (Photographs courtesy the architects)

appropriate to its role as an enlarged country house. Their departure point was the nine-square plans of Palladio which focused on the four horizons, and the chunky Palladianism that has so influenced Charles Moore – in particular Stratford Hall in Virginia, with its towering chimneys set in foursquare relation to the plan. Here in Texas these massive stacks carry the twentieth-century equivalents of smoke: i.e. the mechanical, electrical and plumbing runs, exhausts and elevators. They boldly incorporate these services in bands of brick and terracotta which also serve to visually orientate the building to the four main views (11). To make these elements less monumental, the architects have combined them with domestic forms such as the low pitched roof and the repetition of French doors. The building thus has a 'big/smallness' found in other Post-Modernism, but it is here underlined by the repetitive use of horizontal banding in the concrete basement and four facades.

As one might guess, the underlying reality of the masonry facade is a steel frame, a fact hinted at in the dark coloured parts of the fabric. But this representation, like that of the entrance, is thankfully underplayed and absorbed into the overall grammar. The *porte-cochère* tells you where to drive in but, in spite of its heaviness, doesn't overstate its case. The generous route through the building culminates in a vaulted ballroom – setting for Fort Worthian cotillions – that confirms the view of the four horizons promised at the beginning (12). Here, a central planned church and secular Villa Rotonda combine their plans to represent the Hearth of Society, which is illuminated at the centre by the standard crystal chandelier. If the iconography of this culmination is unsure – the green acoustic coffers and column capitals are left dumb – at least the hall has a meaningful division into lofty communal space and small-scale aisles appropriate for intimate conversation. Representation thus occurs not in the ornament but, at an abstract level, in the combination of conventional spaces and building types.

Symbolic Architecture and the Iconographic Programme

The difference between a collage of signs and a symbolic architecture is partly a matter of degree and partly a matter of intention. A sign is a ready-made convention, a word, traditional form or object. Thus, the umbrella is a sign of rain, but when it's very hot it has the potential to become a sign of sun. Furled up it's a phallic symbol and in ancient, desert cultures it signified kingship or power. Signs, or clichés, denote a series of specific meanings, while symbols both denote and connote a wider set of meanings and pull them together into a significant cluster. Thus the pyramid denoted the specific life and society of the Pharaoh but also connoted such concepts as the 'stair-way to heaven', 'shaft of sunlight', 'order of the four cardinal points', 'desert and Nile' and ultimately 'death and rebirth'. Bridging the everyday to the eternal (a characteristic role of potent symbols) it thus had a resonance or multivalence of connecting links.

10.12 Taft Architects with Geren Associates/ CRS, *River Crest Country Club*, ballroom (Photograph Paul Warchol)

Architectural signs, by contrast, may not relate to each other or an overall plot and thus remain univalent. They convey information and certainly provide more interest than abstract forms alone, but they can lead to a dissociated architecture, as in the 'decorated shed' for instance, where the signifiers and signifieds have no point of contact.

Post-Modern theory and practice has developed along these divergent paths. The majority of architects are content to adopt references appropriate to the context, function and tastes of their clients and let the signs interact as they may – a creative approach in the hands of a Stirling or Hollein, and even the method of Le Corbusier in his late period.[8] As long as the architect attends to the interactions, a *bricolage* of meanings can create its own dynamic. The danger of this for architecture (but its virtue for Surrealism) is the wild association, the inappropriate metaphor, as with the sacred structure that looks like a cooling tower (in the case of Le Corbusier's church at Firminy). More fruitful and difficult than *bricolage* is the synthesis of signs, or symbolic architecture, which is usually achieved by a dialectic process combining collage with an iconographic programme. The architect may tinker with his references until they point in some direction and then consciously reinforce that tendency with a programme to which all the signs must partly relate. The iconographic programme is no longer imposed beforehand by a client or tradition, nor is it entirely the creation of the architect. It is something he finds through historical precedent, researching the building task in hand and discovering the interaction of the signs themselves.

A primitive example of this is Arata Isozaki's Fujimi Country Club, one of the first essays in Post-Modern Classicism, 1972-5 (13). As he describes its genesis, the final form of a curving barrel vault was chosen because its simple shape would contrast with the rolling hills, and frame the long, horizontal views.[9] In the early stages of design this curve doubled back on itself and quite naturally took the form of a question-mark, which Isozaki retrospectively turned into a symbol by providing a 'period' to its shape in the form of a flower bed. It thus asked the question 'Why do the Japanese play golf?' The answer to this, left to the viewer but implied by the architecture, concerns westernisation and trade on the golf course, an implication suggested by quoting Palladio at both ends of the question mark: the curved forms borrowed from the Villas Malcontenta and Poiana. These forms were not copied but transformed, partly because the new material, reinforced concrete, allowed a new system of structured support; now, as in the Mannerism of Venturi, the columns could be placed acentrically. Here then is a primitive form of symbolic architecture which, without the support of ornament, written inscription or artworks, integrates the view, the function of playing golf, and ironic social comment.

The next, slightly more explicit, stage of symbolism was reached in Isozaki's Tsukuba Civic Centre, a commission to provide the 'heart' of a Japanese New Town. This obligation was crucial because such new towns so

10.13 Arata Isozaki, *Fujimi Country Club*, Fujimi, Japan, 1972-5 (Photograph Masao Ara)

10.14 Arata Isozaki, *Tsukuba Civic Centre*, aerial view, Japan, 1980-3 (Photograph Satoru Mishima)

conspicuously lack a social centre and also because Tsukuba, dedicated to innovation in science and technology, is to be a symbol of Japan's new determination to lead, rather than simply copy, the west. Isozaki, with extraordinary courage and not a little perversity, has chosen to represent the lack of a heart in Japanese culture, the 'presence of the absence' of leadership, the void at the top. One of the inspirations for this nihilistic act, he told me, was an observation of Roland Barthes on the curious 'presence/absence' of the emperor and Imperial Compound in the life of Tokyo – the way life in this teeming metropolis revolves around an invisible palace and manicured landscape. When one tries to track down this supreme power one sees only a hole in the city.

Isozaki was asked to give an image of centrality and authority to the Tsukuba civic centre, something equivalent to the monument or steeple. Instead he has taken the Roman symbol of the *res publica* – Michelangelo's Campidoglio which surmounts a hill – and sunk it under a plaza (14). So no one will miss the point of this inversion, water is run from a broken cascade down into the centre, producing a kind of anti-fountain or visual black-hole where Mother Earth 'devours' all meaning.[10] Around this anti-monument he has strung a series of quotes from western sources, among them the Piazza d'Italia of Charles Moore. There is also a bronze laurel tree wrapped in a gold tunic (symbol of Daphne's transformation near a river and a theme recurring in Post-Modern art, see page 161). This was no doubt inspired by Hans Hollein's bronze palm trees. The borrowings continue across a spectrum of elements, from the fat columns of Michael Graves to the overlaid grids of a Scottish tartan. There are fragments taken from 'Otto Wagner . . . Richard Meier, Aldo Rossi, Peter Cook, Adalberto Libera, Philip Johnson, Leon Krier, Laurence Halprin, Ettore Sotsass and', Isozaki assures us, 'many more'.[11] In particular the 'many more' consists of quotes from Ledoux such as the banded hotel columns and the concrete rustication (15). Pastiche, *haute vulgarisation* and inventive transformation are all mixed up in this *mélange* of a non-centre. As it was being designed Isozaki slowly began to understand the anti-plot of his 'novel': the fact that by giving the fragments their own independence, they would not 'converge on one point'. This non-covergence and non-hierarchy – design by preexisting language games – was of course instantly interpreted as the essence of French Post-Modernism as found in the theories of Lyotard, Kristeva and Derrida.[12]

This interpretation of Isozaki's eclectic design method makes sense and was also inspired, he told me, by an article I wrote on his work in 1977 called 'Isozaki and Radical Eclecticism'.[13] But of more interest is his own comparison of the Tsukuba Centre with Velasquez's non-portrait of the royal family, *Las Meninas*. In this painting it is the ladies in waiting, a dwarf, dog and courtiers who take centre stage along with the painter himself, so that we are seeing in effect a small slice of court life as perceived through royal eyes. Only when we look carefully at the background of this

10.15 Arata Isozaki, *Tsukuba Civic Centre*, banded rustication of hotel (Photograph courtesy the architect)

294

canvas and see the reflected gaze of the king and queen in a mirror do we fully understand this 'presence of the absence'. Isozaki notes the parallel with his creation:

> The architect has been hired not by a king, but by a state, and requested to produce a portrait of the state. And yet the countenance of the state is not as clear as that of an existing ruler, and even if it were, I feel ambivalently that I would rather it didn't emerge too clearly. In order to deal with this ambivalence, I made the centre simply a space – a void; I portrayed a metaphor in which all the usual spatial arrangements are reversed or inverted. Everything is situated around a void, descending and then vanishing into oblivion at the centre. This is Michelangelo in reverse.[14]

This is interpretation in reverse – like 'why do the Japenese play golf?' – a symbolic programme imposed retrospectively and a somewhat nihilistic one at that. But it is also latent within Isozaki's method of eclectic design and his belief in the heterogeneity of life. Since he, like Stirling and other Post-Modernists, believes that creativity in architecture must come from several, discontinuous sources, he does not impose a single aesthetic nor does he seek to recreate a new, integrated style *ex nihilo*. The creation by autonomous language games was thus a conscious choice during the design and only later became incorporated within the symbolic programme itself.

This way of proceeding is, as it sounds, rather facile since it evades a prior commitment to the 'difficult whole' which Venturi rightly claims should be the ultimate goal of design. Unless there is some narrative beyond the non-plot, there will be little connection between the language games. To lend his work some unity Isozaki has provided a common syntax of squares repeated at different scales and in shades of grey and silver. These are superbly detailed and even quite beautiful in their juxtaposition (16). Glistening ceramic tile is set against precise aluminium, roughly textured rock and smooth marble – all related in hue. The outline of shapes is continuously varied and thus the eye moves quickly from a chunky hotel to the concert hall. Because of this picturesque eclecticism many critics have asked: 'Are all these western quotes really suitable for the most Japanese of building tasks?' Kisho Kurokawa and the majority have answered negatively, but there is an ironic, positive answer as well: 'Where else, except in Japan, would they do high-tech Ledoux, aluminium Rossi and "many more"?' More than fifteen western architects are invoked by Isozaki to tell the Japanese they are at their most national when learning from others and then refashioning this information in their own inimitable style. And western nihilism? It comes of course from Zen Buddhism.

Isozaki's next significant building, the Los Angeles Museum of Contemporary Art (MOCA), continues this juxtaposition of language games (17). Here, a series of rectangular masses are broken into two main sets, one dominated by a barrel vault, the other by pyramids. These two sets, we're told, represent east versus west or Yin/Yang versus Golden Section.[15] The

10.16 Arata Isozaki, *Tsukuba Civic Centre*, Daphne statue and waterfall (Photograph Yasuhiro Ishimoto)

10.17 Arata Isozaki, *Museum of Contemporary Art*, forecourt and library, Los Angeles, 1982-6 (Photograph C. Jencks)

problem with this symbolic programme is that it is purely architectural and hidden from view, embedded in the plans and spirals of space. However, what one can see is the very strong Palladian motif – almost the face of a sprightly animal – confronting a western pyramid. This canine image marks the entrance and orients the visitor towards the galleries down below. It is sheathed in the marvellously burnt red sandstone of Fatehpur Sikri which contrasts with the green metallic skin, providing perhaps the most noticeable clash between east and west. Again, the control of different shapes and materials is virtuosic (except for the claustrophobic library trapped in the barrel vault behind a dead screen of onyx) and the detailing of the sandstone is subtly controlled with contrasts of texture. If I have reservations about the symbolism, they concern its lack of explicitness; the absence of ornament, writing and art works that could tell the story that Isozaki claims is embedded within the plan.

Roland Barthes has described Japan as an 'empire of signs' and there are quite a few Japanese architects intent on making this characterisation come true. Minoru Takeyama, Shin Toki, Takefumi Aida, Hiroshi Hara, Kazuhiro Ishii and Yasufumi Kijima are all Post-Modern Classicists who are developing a hybrid language by the manipulation of architectural signs.[16] But it is Monta Mozuna who has explored symbolic architecture most directly. A typical house of his design will have five or six different levels of symbolism bound together by a Jungian system of archetypes. Buddhist and Shinto are combined with Platonic and Christian metaphysics and all is resolved, so far as it can be, at the level of abstract geometry. The method has produced some bizarre and striking results, as Mannerist in their own way as the work of Venturi, and as eclectic as that of James Stirling. So far the most developed example of this compound (and divergent) symbolism is Mozuna's Kushiro City Museum.

This sits as a heavy brooding form on a hill above a lake (18). U-shaped tiers cascade over the central entrance and symmetrically to either side embracing the arriving visitor. What he makes of these enigmatic, inward-looking curves is open to question, although he may guess the solid forms contain a museum. Characteristically Mozuna's symbolism is more esoteric than accessible.

The embracing curves refer to two kinds of birds – the red-crested crane which is the symbol of Kushiro and the Golden Hen which, with her outspread wings, is an ancient symbol for the oriental art of divining. The crane actually appears in a literal form painted on the interior of the dome, but it seems to me doubtful that the unsuspecting visitor will make the connection before exploring the museum. Mozuna has missed an opportunity of using sculpture, ornament and writing to bring out and underline the meanings. As a result they remain abstract, like programme music, a score in need of an accompanying text.

He has provided this, in a book at least, and it explains some of the latent symbolism. The museum is divided into three vertical sections. The

10.18,19 Kiko Monta Mozuna, *Kushiro City Museum*, view from south and double spiral staircase as a sign of DNA, Kushiro, Hokkaido, Japan, 1982-4 (Photographs courtesy the architect)

ground level holds archaeological artefacts such as excavated pottery and dinosaur bones ('earth'); the middle level has exhibits relating to industry, fishing, mining and current history ('man'); the top level with its flying cranes and paintings of the sky represents the cosmos ('heaven'). Past, present and future are thus also signified by this sequence which is connected by a double spiral staircase, a symbol of time and the double helix of DNA(19). This form, adapted from Renaissance stairways, becomes an obvious symbol connected to the other meanings once one knows them; but again the significance could have been brought out with ornament. Mozuna mentions further references – the structure as a three-dimensional mandala, the embracing arms of Bernini's piazza at St.Peter's, and the earth's layered strata. It is the last meaning which is most apparent to the westerner familiar with stepped pyramids and ziggurats. The museum weighs on top of its mound like an eternal monument, a memorial to the Ainu people for whom it is built.

Mozuna's commitment to symbolism *per se* is most exemplary, especially in the field of architecture which naturally tends towards abstraction and practical necessity. In traditional societies such commitment could be taken for granted, but in modern cultures it is thrown into doubt, because of the pervasive agnosticism and pluralism. This is why I support explicit iconographic programmes from which the symbolism emerges as a conscious product of the dialogue between designer and client. In a public art such as architecture there are good political and artistic reasons for this: if the symbolic meanings are made explicit then the architect, in collaboration with the client, can develop his expressive art more freely. Thus, in *Towards a Symbolic Architecture* I argue that an iconographic programme makes design more enjoyable for both parties because it gives a rationale to expressive form and helps pull the variety of meanings and building trades together.[17]

My own work, carried out in collaboration with other architects and based on symbolic programmes, is intended as multivalent design. Whether it is in fact successful is for others to judge, but my aim is to work out the links between function, space, ornament, inscription and theme so that a coherent scenario runs throughout the building. The Thematic House in London is structured around ideas related to time and change along with a set of main themes focusing on the seasons, sun and moon, spiral galaxies and cultural history. Various signs recur throughout the house which is also unified by a Free-Style Classicism. In many spaces the structure, space and ornament are related to the governing idea of cosmic time. The spiral staircase, for instance, designed as the 'Solar Stair' with treads undulating as sun rays, focuses upwards towards a bright disc of sunlight (20). The spiral is not only a natural structural shape which, tied to the cylinder, holds up the adjacent chimneys, it is also a representation of cosmic time: spiral galaxies, DNA helixes, the spiral motion of water running out of a drain, and, most importantly of all, the shape we describe when climbing stairs in a cylinder of

10.20 Charles Jencks and Terry Farrell, *Thematic House*, Solar Stair, London, 1978-82 (Photograph Richard Bryant)

10.21 Charles Jencks, *Thematic House*, Sun, Earth and Moonrail Zodiac Discs, December 1982 (Photograph Richard Bryant)

10.22 Eduardo Paolozzi, *Black Hole Mosaic*, 1983 (Photograph Richard Bryant)

space. Several of these meanings are taken up in the stainless steel ornament and railings, which also mirror the spiral motion of sun, earth and moon (21). Small round discs with stylised zodiacs on the side of each step cluster into threes or fours to make a month, so one ascends from January at the bottom, towards December at the top. Since there are fifty-two steps and the front of each one is articulated into seven parts we have three-hundred-and-sixty-four days in all, which is *almost* a solar year. In most cultures descending is associated with darkness and decline, the netherworld and mystery. Here we have pulled together these conventional and natural meanings with a mosaic, 'The Black Hole', designed by Eduardo Paolozzi following a symbolic programme conforming to that of the Solar Stair (22). This mosaic picks up the spiral motion and the sun rays of the stairs in its curving tesserae, pulling them into a dark, multicoloured vortex. Thus, looking down one sees the natural symbols of entropy and despair, while above are the natural symbols of light, hope and energy.

I have focused on this one space to show the difference between symbolic and 'signolic' architecture. Whereas the 'decorated shed' is based on discontinuities between structure, meaning and ornament – the breaks necessitated by commerce and constant change – multivalent architecture is based on the linkage between meanings. To reiterate, symbolic architecture links the everyday necessity (here the reinforced concrete structure), the function (ascending and descending), the ornament (globes and etched zodiacs), the art (mosaic), the space (light and dark), the articulations (rays of the sun and days of the year), with the metaphysics (cosmic time, hope and despair). A symbol is resonant because it pulls together microcosm and macrocosm; a sign is not resonant because it has a single isolated meaning unrelated to other possible frames of reference.

These distinctions parallel those we discussed in Chapter VIII between the imagination and fancy, transformation and copying, and they continue to divide Post-Modernists. While Robert Venturi emphasised the 'difficult whole' in his writings of 1966, his later work has tended towards heterogeneity and an emphasis on discontinuity. A few Post-Modern theorists such as Hal Foster see dissociation itself as a fundamental reality, and argue, following Derrida, that languages, or texts, have their own inbuilt creativity and autonomy.[18] The notion of intertextuality with its attendant 'death of the author' is helpful in explaining much current work, particularly that of Isozaki, but it tends to overemphasise the role played by traditions and dissolve the synthesising power of the individual. We can see this power operating most clearly in small buildings, where there is some degree of individual authorship and control.

Thomas Gordon Smith, for instance, has built several modest houses around themes he has chosen. One for himself and his family, in Richmond California, focuses on a communal space which symbolises both local and timeless themes (23). Thus, the black Pompeiian colouring of the main room refers not only to the classical past, but to the particular view from these hills

10.23 Thomas Gordon Smith, *Richmond Hill House,* cut-away perspective, California, 1981-3 (Drawing courtesy the architect)

10.24 Thomas Gordon Smith, *Richmond Hill House,* living room, California, 1981-3 (Photograph Henry Bowles)

10.25 Tom Beeby, Hammond Beeby Babka, *American Academy of Pediatrics,* Chicago, Illinois, 1982-4 (Photograph courtesy the architects)

in Richmond where 'black gold' – petrol – can be seen arriving by oil-tanker. Different American gas stations are painted on the bottom sections of the frescoes, above which is an inscription on the subject of Richmond Hill (put to music by Henry Purcell in 1692) and then, crowning this, a classical frieze. The frieze depicts, at entablature level, scenes from the myth of Persephone and, on the ceiling, various stages of life from birth to death (24). Diagonal views are accentuated by paired windows and a Baroque floor plan ornamented in marble and terrazzo fragments which Thomas Gordon Smith picked up as off-cuts from a stone mason. The overall contrasts between gold and black, vernacular and classical, real and painted architecture, work to make this a lively but unified space. Although the architect has sought a literalness of classical reference, it is the juxtaposition of this with modest elements that makes the architecture so convincing. Thus the simple curved windows define a yellow space which, apart from focusing the view and corner light, bites into the rich pervasive darkness, as do the corner bookshelves. Without the conflict of language games, or intertextuality, the themes would be one-dimensional and predictable. But they are also carefully interconnected in both colour and iconography to create a dissonant unity, a resisted whole, a disharmonious harmony.

The Chicago architect Tom Beeby achieves a wry juxtaposition of similar languages, but the classicism is now set against the glass and steel vernacular of Mies van der Rohe (25). These languages are used straightforwardly without much flourish, as one would expect in the city of High Modernism. The rhythms and proportions of steel framing, its slender ratios and wide intercolumniations, are allowed to set up their own severe discipline. But the plan, volumetric organisation and articulations nonetheless constitute a primitive form of classicism, with the entablature subdivided on column centres, and the capitals given a tough Tuscan-like abacus. The drama comes from playing the two different games with equal rigour. It's as if Beeby has discovered the common descent of Modernism and classicism in structural expression, no doubt an ancestor which they do both share.

The Hild Library in Chicago takes the kind of linear, palazzo shape that Henri Labrouste used on the Bibliotheque St. Genevieve and encases it in hard engineering brick and black steel (26). Large windows for the reading room are set above arches as in the Paris library, and there are fragments of a symbolic programme similar to that which Labrouste developed; even the plan and sequence of space go back to this key nineteenth-century building. One enters at the centre of the long facade and notices the strangely proportioned steel Neo-Grec slightly protruding from the brick skin, while both glazing and brick are fashioned as curtain walls hanging from a steel frame (27). The structural 'honesty', or rather the symbolic logic, of these articulations has a tough intellectual beauty underscored by the dour colouring. The ordering stems from the way Mies symbolised internal structure and brick covering at IIT although now such motifs as the acroteria and pediment are added to the repertoire.

10.26,27 Tom Beeby, Hammond Beeby Babka, *Hild Library*, general view and entrance, Chicago, Illinois, 1982-5 (Photographs courtesy the architects)

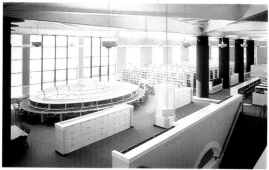

10.28,29 Tom Beeby, Hammond Beeby Babka, *Hild Library*, entrance oval with view to library floor, and stairs and stacks on library floor (Photographs Hedrich Blessing)

10.30 Michael Graves, *Plocek House*, Warren, New Jersey, 1979-82 (Photograph Proto Acme)

10.31 Michael Graves, *Domaine Clos Pegase Winery*, elevation, front entrance, 1984 (Photograph Proto Acme)

After entering through the Romanesque brick arch one arrives unexpectedly at a cheerfully lit Mannerist oval of space framed by a Tuscan Order and punctuated by metope lights made of half globes (28). The sunburst motif overhead affords views into the reading room above and the exposed structure – a system which both the Greeks and Mies used in a straightforwardly expressive way. The fact that this structure is painted white and left raw on the floor above symbolises Beeby's intention of showing the parallels between these two rationalist languages, while the addition of a row of high dark columns down the centre is again a reference to the Paris library (29). Where Labrouste used a row of thin steel columns to refer to the basilica at Paestum and thereby the Graeco-Industrial ideal, Beeby uses fat, purple columns with a suggestion of air-vent capitals to extend the tradition to the Graeco-Industrial-French-Chicago ideal. In short, his architecture symbolises the historical continuum and the idea that meanings from different periods can be related and integrated, a key notion of Post-Modern Classicism as we shall see in the last chapter. That these syntheses occur more at the level of structure than iconography is partly due to Chicago building regulations and partly to the fact that Beeby's programme for mural paintings has run into political trouble. But his symbolic intentions are clearly developed and since he has become the head of Yale's School of Architecture we might see more multivalent work emerge from his office in the future.

There are a handful of designers committed in part to symbolic architecture (and gardens) among whom we should mention Clovis Heimsath in Texas, Emilio Ambasz in New York City, Thomas This-Evenson in Oslo, Charles Vandenhove in Brussels and the poet-polymath from Scotland, Ian Hamilton Finlay, who we have already come across several times in the chapters on art. The scattered heterogeniety of this list is enough to suggest that we are considering here a broad tendency, a trend in the direction of multivalent architecture, rather than a conscious movement. The work of Michael Graves shows this tendency, but he stops short of using explicit symbolic programmes. Rather, he incorporates fragments of signs where they suit his intentions and integrates them with his distinctive Post-Modern Classicism, the language he more than anyone else has synthesised.

Graves' first real essay in the genre is his Plocek House designed in December 1977 and constructed several years later (30). Here we find all the elements of his mature style pulled together on a dramatic hillside site: the abstraction of classical and vernacular elements influenced by Aldo Rossi and Leon Krier (the latter taught at Princeton with Graves at the time); the emphasis on symbolic features such as keystone and column used in several different ways, partly due to my own writings and critiques of his work; the use of repetitive grids at different scales stemming from Josef Hoffmann, a pre-Modernist and major influence; and finally the planning ideas of French eighteenth-century architects who tie building and site together with similar shifted axes. The references are thus extremely wide, extending to Lutyens, Asplund and Aalto, and show the way Graves designs with other architects'

10.32 Michael Graves, *Public Library*, general view from south, San Juan Capistrano, 1981-3 (Photograph Maggie Keswick)

solutions in mind.[19] But he transforms rather than quotes these solutions, abstracts and uses them to rethink a problem and thus his work is synthetic, rather than a compilation of distinct language games.

For instance, the classical tripartite division of a palazzo – basement, *piano nobile* and attic – is explicitly reinvented to anchor the building firmly in the hillside and relate it to the sky. The keystone is suggested by the massive front pylons, the plan of the entrance walk and also the culminating chimney. Because Graves suggests all sorts of historical references, but leaves them abstract or incomplete, his work has a resonance of meaning that cuts across time and culture. They seem to belong to several periods at once and evoke half forgotten memories.

This rhetorical device of anamnesis is the acceptable face of Post-Modern historicism (as opposed to nostalgia) and stems from Venturi and Moore's work. But Graves, to my mind, is much more effective in his use of memory than these other archiects, at least when he alludes to rather than quotes the past. This is because of his masterful skill at drawing together these memories in a new way. His notebooks, like Le Corbusier's, are full of sketches which transform a historical idea through a series of changes; through coloured design drawings and gouaches the sequence finally becomes a controlled synthesis (31). His best work thus achieves a visual wholeness unequalled in Post-Modern architecture.

Particularly successful is the San Juan Capistrano Public Library, a modest building in size and cost ($1.5 million), which alludes to the surrounding Mission Style without apeing its manner. For this building Graves looked at Mexican and Guatemalan wall architecture, sketching its strangely proportioned ziggurats and sun temples, until he understood this language which was related to the Spanish Mission Style. Other architects, who lost the competition to Graves, quoted this style directly, whereas he found a synthetic equivalent: something with flat, heavy walls divided in colour, with pantiles on tiny roofs, shrunken obelisks and black-green trellis work (32). It is an odd, idiosyncratic synthesis, but a wonderful one for a small, municipal library. It provides the nooks and crannies and endless changing vistas so appealing to children, who use half of the building, and its illuminated stencil patterns symbolically mark the reading area for them (33).

Because Graves designed the furniture, lighting fixtures and wall patterns, they reinforce the overall scenario of the library as a tiny village and give the long passages and many subdivided spaces an identity. Strangest of all is the 'big/smallness' of the building, a contradiction in scale which Graves learned from Venturi and uses here in a fresh way. Indeed the stringcourse cutting through the square windows is pure Venturi, although the break up of mass into many small 'light monitors', obelisks, chapel-like rooms and gazebos is Graves' own contribution to the same rhetorical idea. All these incidents are organised around a courtyard, while major and minor axes are layered up against each other to produce a dense grid of differentiated space (34). Here is one of the key plans illustrating Post-Modern space and some of

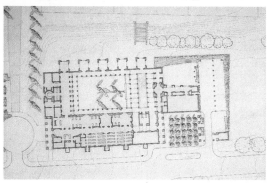

10.33 Michael Graves, *Public Library*, story-telling nook (Photograph Proto Acme)

10.34 Michael Graves, *Public Library*, detail of site plan (Photograph courtesy the architect)

10.35 Michael Graves, *Public Library*, court-yard (Photograph Proto Acme)

its characteristic qualities – ambiguity, complexity, layering, asymmetrical symmetry and the combination of Modernist flow with classical containment. Again, Graves didn't invent these figures; in fact he arrived at most of them rather late as he only discarded his Late-Modern Style in 1977. But he pulled the ideas together more convincingly than others by drawing out and resolving their implications.

In terms of symbolic architecture the San Juan Capistrano Library is a moderate but undeveloped success. The signs of the locale and Mission Style are inventively acknowledged and serve to enhance the function of reading and browsing in differently scaled spaces – one goal of a good library is to provide such secretive space where one can hide with a book. The light monitors, clerestory lights and rhythm of shadows and light in the courtyard begin to establish a metaphor of light as literary enlightenment, although this is not fully developed and made into a programme (35). Compared to the iconographic system that Bertrand Goodhue and others developed for the Los Angeles Public Library in the 1920s, a comparable building in some ways, the one here is primitive.

Graves' most ambitious completed building in terms of cost ($60 million) is the tower for Humana Inc., the health-care conglomerate whose home is in Louisville Kentucky. Like other corporate headquarters – the AT&T Building and Hong Kong and Shanghai Bank – it's an exercise in the difficult art of spending a lot of money well and, to my mind, does this more wisely than the others. Here the shapes, masonry and setbacks relate partly to the surrounding context (36). The nineteenth-century street scale is held to one side, while the twentieth-century Miesian box, to the other, is acknowledged with glass and steel curtain walling (Graves refers to this adjacent, taller piece of packaging as 'the box the Humana came in'). The building accentuates the views out to the four horizons with four little temples placed above the twentieth floor and gives a dramatic accent to the wide expanse of the Ohio River by its curving roof garden (37).

On the twenty-fifth floor the little temple, with Hoffmannesque gridded windows, is cantilevered way out so that patients in the Humana hospital can get a framed view of the river and steel bridges crossing it. The cantilevered trusses directly recall these bridges and this provides a fresh and relevant image. Without the contrast of this engineering realism with the classical idealism the latter would have become oppressive. Equally as important is the ritualised function of the outdoor rooms. Often visiting patients are brought up to the large terrace to enjoy the sun and air (38). They enter the space through battered Egyptian pylons and are surrounded by a rhythm of classical piers with gold-leaf flutings, suspended out over a view two-hundred feet above the ground. When they go from the curved garden to the greenhouse/temple they suddenly enter a celestial elevator flying over buildings and the street below. It takes one's breath away, like the sharp immersion in the ice-cold baths at Lourdes, a physical shock which may have a beneficent healing effect. In any case the signs of health and recuperation –

10.36 Michael Graves, *Humana Building*, view from Main Street, Louisville, Kentucky, 1982-5 (Photograph Paschall & Taylor)

10.37 Michael Graves, *Humana Building*, roof garden and belvedere (Photograph courtesy the architect)

10.38 Michael Graves, *Humana Building*, twenty-fifth floor balcony (Photograph Paschall & Taylor)

310

10.39 Michael Graves, *Humana Building*, model from north-east (Photograph courtesy the architect)

10.40,41 Michael Graves, *Humana Building*, south facade and entrance (Photographs Paschall & Taylor)

the sun, space and greenery which Le Corbusier recommended to cure the city's ills – are used to create a ritual and symbol appropriate for Humana.

Less successful is the way too many materials and colours break up an already articulated volume. The coloured drawings and model show a unity which the finished building, with its discord between red granite and greenish glass, lacks in the centre sections (39). The polychromy which Graves is trying to reintroduce into the skyscraper has yet to reach the subtle modulation of his drawings.

Nevertheless the volumetric articulations work well to break up the box and give it an animal, or human, presence. In his initial sketches we can see the two fundamental ideas: a basic tripartite division into a base loggia, middle section of offices and top belvedere; and the symmetrical visage, or body, that confronts the river. The anthropomorphism of this latter image is clearly felt, but abstract and never explicitly stated – an apposite humanisation of the Humana Corporation. The subtle use of canted 'brows' on the loggia front, or suggested 'eyes and nose' of the cantilevered garden, hint at the body image underneath. The side views of this inherent metaphor are more austere with shoulders tilting in to a neck and small head. On the south face, overlooking the city, the image is changed to that of a classical temple of healing as a giant red column of 'sun rooms' curves out, framed by a symmetrical grid of Art Deco forms (40). Here, as opposed to the street front, the facade of pink and red granite is unified into a strong vertical image which is twenty times the size of the usual engaged column.

Access from two street sides (41) under a colonnade leads to a public loggia with waterfall and fountains, which are intended to recall the dam architecture of the 1930s and the Falls of the Ohio where the city started. The covered space is rendered in richly coloured granites and dramatically lit like a shrine, thereby emphasising the connection between water and the gods of healing, or the River and the Temple – a theme reiterated in the roof garden. As in a Constructivist building, the letters 'Humana' are canted out on a pediment for easy viewing, although the Roman lettering and heaviness unfortunately convey affinities with fascist architecture of the 1930s. Sadly this feeling follows one into the marble lobby and then to the Rotonda in the centre where lavish white, green, beige and red marble bedeck the walls, and a Roman torso crowns the view (42). However beautiful and well executed, this climax is an expensive disappointment, an opportunity lost. While the surrounding space, a shopping area and bank, rightly give this public realm a bustle and *raison d'être*, there is no ceremonial activity to this centre, nothing that ties the civic consciousness of Humana to the city in a symbolic way and makes the space come alive.

Nevertheless, in its entirety, this is one of the first skyscrapers in which there are a variety of pleasant and unusual spaces to discover. Most tall buildings suppress the drama of movement behind the elevator and the repetition of identical floors. In the Humana Building there are three key areas which come as a welcome surprise: the belvedere and roof garden, the

curved sun rooms on each floor and the terraces and atrium within the low street section (43). These last interpenetrating spaces, reminiscent of Le Corbusier's dream that one could recapture domestic life even when suspended ten storeys up, are both dignified and lively; like the front of the building, a combination of Modernist space and classical *gravitas*. They give to this tall building a changing experience, an unfolding drama usually reserved for horizontal movement through a low structure. Norman Foster's Hong Kong and Shanghai Bank achieves a similar sequence, but less expressively and with a more indulgent budget. The Humana has to be seen, along with Foster's building, as the beginning of a new stage in skyscraper evolution, with communal spaces and changing incidents occurring every so often within a repetitive structure. It alludes to the adjacent buildings and the historic fabric of Louisville; it breaks down the huge scale into abstracted images of face, shoulder, eyes and body; and, through its roof garden and fountains, it hints at the restorative powers of nature – the programme behind this health-for-profit company.[20]

Along with Stirling's museum at Stuttgart it has to be seen as culminating the first phase of Post-Modern Classicism and, like this other monument, raises unanswered questions about symbolic architecture. The gains of a shared, public language have been realised in both buildings – which are popular yet esoteric, widely understood yet also read as complex texts. But in both buildings there is finally a crisis of content which leads to a confusion of form and expression: the lack of a credible symbolic programme which could pull together all this art, ornament and money and give it some greater sense. It is as unfair to fault the architects for this failure as it is the clients or contemporary society, but it helps explain why, in the end, these great and partly beautiful buildings leave something to be desired.

Nevertheless, Post-Modern work shows some very real gains over Modern architecture. With Venturi, Moore, Isozaki and Stirling it has returned to a representational language which uses various, even divergent, codes to appeal to different tastes and to send different messages. This variety recognises in a positive way the pluralism of an agnostic culture and yet still seeks a 'difficult unity' in attempting to synthesise such commonly held values as the continuity of history and urban context, the anthropomorphic image and the sensual reponse to form and colour. With Graves it has once again become a complex language under the control of a painterly art; while multivalent symbolism and political significance are still very much on the agenda as they are for commercial society as a whole.

10.42,43 Michael Graves, *Humana Building*, Rotonda and terraced atrium (Photographs Paschall & Taylor)

CHAPTER XI

The Emergent Rules

As we have seen throughout this book, the third phase of Post-Modernism, from the late 1970s to the present, has returned to a classical language with a difference. For it is a wider tradition than Canonic Classicism – more eclectic, hybrid or Free-Style – and is based on different assumptions than other classical revivals of the past. Nonetheless it uses almost all the elements of the canonic language in architecture and art, and even shares some of the traditional assumptions. Most important are the ideas of relating our efforts to those of the past, and using universal figures of representation, or previously discovered constants of a language. The portrayal of the human body in art and the figurative use of the column in architecture are the two most obvious constants to have reappeared under new guises, but one could easily extend this list to cover twenty or more similar elements, compositional rules and qualities. Thus the new classicism has appeared partly because those creating it have rediscovered necessity: the fact that if archetypes and universals are inevitable, they might as well be consciously articulated or turned into a representational art. Alternatively, of course, they can be suppressed – it's a matter of choice. Late-Modern architects, for instance, deal with such universals as the column and street by underplaying them or reducing them to utilitarian abstractions (which may occasionally be quite beautiful). Post-Modernists, by contrast, choose to celebrate these perennial concerns, thereby creating a dialogue with history.

The motive for this may vary. In the case of Michael Graves and James Stirling it is to develop a richer resonance of language, one which exploits both local and historical associations. For more Neoclassical artists, such as Stephen McKenna and Carlo Maria Mariani, the motive may be to revive a cultural era and set of values, while Leon Krier favours classicism because it took out the best patents for city building. Yet underlying all these motives is the idea that, in its continuous evolution, the classical language has been transformed over time and ties generations together in a common pursuit. Artists and architects who work on archetypal problems will naturally come to related solutions, which serve to pull history together into a continuum and even, on a cultural level, make history reversible.

The Reversible Historical Continuum
The revival of classicism has often been accompanied by personal testament, or a description of a private endeavour between friends. Indeed one of its most surprising aspects is this expression of self-disclosure and individual

11.1 *Hatshepsut's Mortuary Temple* at Deir el-Bahari, circa 1500 B.C. Many Free-Style Classical motifs and principles can be found here varying from anthropomorphic piers to Proto-Doric columns to symmetry, proportion and a procession across a gridded, axial space (Photograph C. Jencks)

11.2 *Anubis Shrine*, Hatshepsut's Temple, circa 1500 B.C., with its classical architecture of continuous stone, cavetto moulding and Proto-Doric columns (Photograph C. Jencks)

commitment. This was particularly true in the Renaissance which, as its root-meaning suggests, was always concerned with spiritual rebirth. Antonio Filarete, the architect and sculptor, describes the characteristic experience of conversion, quite naturally using the metaphor of personal, spiritual reawakening. He writes in 1460:

> I, too, used to like modern [scil., Gothic] buildings, but when I began to appreciate classical ones, I came to be disgusted with the former . . . Having heard that the people of Florence had started in this classical manner [a questi modi antichi], I decided to get hold of one of those . . . and when I associated with them, they woke me up in such a way that now I could not produce that smallest thing in any manner but the classical . . . I seem to see, my lord [in the new structures built according to the *modi antichi*] those noble edifices that existed in Rome in classical times and those that, we read, existed in Egypt (1,2); I appear to be reborn when I see these noble edifices, and they seem still beautiful to me.[1]

Filarete is describing his conversion in the first person singular, using a confessional, private tone of voice. As Erwin Panofsky points out, the renaissance of classicism is associated with a personal 'reawakening', a 'restoration', *'rinascita',* 'resurrection' or 'second birth'. This ultimately goes back to the Gospel of St.John: 'Except a man be born again, he cannot see the kingdom of God'. The Born-Again Christian of today has his secular counterpart in the Born-Again Classicist. The implications are interesting. When a painter or architect suddenly recognises the western tradition as a *living alternative* to the Modernist notion of the 'tradition of the new' and realises that his efforts can play a part within it, he can experience a rebirth similar to that felt by the Born-Again Christian. This is one idea of classicism which links artists, architects and writers today. Such an insight leads to a personal disclosure because it is self-conscious: the painter and architect suddenly understand the classical tradition not merely as an endless set of forms and motifs, but as an idea that is alive. The consciousness of this idea leads to a personal challenge.

Again, the testimonies from the Italian Renaissance bring out this challenge. 'After I had returned from exile', Alberti writes in his preface to *Della Pittura*, 1435, 'I recognised in many, but foremost in you, Filippo [Brunelleschi], and in that very good friend of ours, Donato the sculptor, and in . . . Massacio, a genius for all praiseworthy endeavour not inferior to that of the famous ancients . . .'[2] The friends of Alberti are being called together on a first-name basis ('you, Filippo') to challenge the ancients in a way that will not only revive these dead artists, but revivify those living ones.

When the moderns are put on the same level as the ancients, two things happen. Firstly, time becomes reversible and historical figures live and become equal with contemporary ones. Secondly, this equality between old and new artists soon leads, as it did in the seventeenth century, to protracted comparisons and then finally to an attempt to find winners and losers in the

11.3 Roland Freart de Chambray, *Parallel de L'Architecture Antique Avec La Moderne*, Paris, 1650. Callimachus deriving the Corinthian Order beside an Egyptian pyramid. This treatise compares new and old versions of the Orders and thus heightens the competition between the present and past

318

competition for ideal classical form (3). The famous Quarrel of the 'Ancients' and 'Moderns' which took place within the French Academy in the 1670s led to the later 'Battle of the Styles', a struggle between Modernists of all brands that is still with us today. But the positive aspect of this struggle should be stressed – the notion of the classical tradition as an organic continuum, a living whole.

Partly, this idea is nothing more than a practical insight: each generation learns from preceding ones, taking some of its values and formal solutions and passing them onto the future. Hence the pedigree, or provenance, always entailed in the classical idea. Hence the disputes as to what should be included. Where did the form come from, who developed and perfected it, what are its historical meanings? Classicism is always involved with a heightened historical consciousness. The Greeks knew Egypt well, and we may term their transformation of Egyptian architecture 'the first classical revival'. As Filarete reveals, the Renaissance also recognised its debt to Egypt.

The concept of an artistic community in continuity has led some writers to follow the extreme formulation of this idea by T.S. Eliot, an author who regarded himself as a classicist in literature. He also saw the western tradition as an organic continuum – a reversible, living entity whose *past* could be changed by the introduction of a new link in the chain. It's a potent idea and one that has deservedly changed the way we think about the classical tradition and its necessary dependence on true innovation.

Tradition is a matter of much wider significance. It cannot be inherited, and if you want it you must obtain it by great labour. It involves, in the first place, the historical sense. . .the historical sense compels a man to write not merely with his own generation in his bones, but with a feeling that the whole of the literature of Europe from Homer and within it the whole of the literature of his own country has a simultaneous existence and composes a simultaneous order . . .

No poet, no artist of any art, has his complete meaning alone. His significance, his appreciation is the appreciation of his relation to the dead poets and artists. You cannot value him alone; you must set him, for contrast and comparison, among the dead . . . what happens when a new work of art is created is something that happens simultaneously to all the works of art which preceded it. The existing monuments form an ideal order among themselves, which is modified by the introduction of the new (the really new) work of art among them. The existing order is complete before the new work arrives; for order to persist after the supervention of novelty, the whole existing order must be, if ever so slightly, altered; and so the relations, proportions, values of each work of art toward the whole are readjusted; and this is conformity between the old and the new. Whoever has approved this idea of order, of the form of European, of English literature, will not find it preposterous that the past should be altered by the present as much as the present is directed by the past . . .[3]

This organic tradition certainly does work on a metaphorical and perceptual level: we change our view of the past through new creations in the tradition and by new interpretations. In these two ways it makes sense to talk of an organic continuum, or the continuing life of dead artists, and this discovery of cultural immortality has often led to a sudden personal insight. We have already seen the testimony of Filarete and Alberti, but there are present day versions where an artist simultaneously discovers the past and his contemporaries' relation to it (4). Evidence can be gathered from all quarters – not just from those 'revivalist' Born-Again Classicists, in whose impassioned words the sudden inspiration is most evident, but also from committed 'survivalists', defenders of the faith whose ideals have not diminished even in the Modern epoch.

The art historian E.H. Gombrich has attempted to formulate a creed for such survivors as himself, heirs to the western tradition. He acknowledges the way in which 'The Tradition of General Knowledge' is more an ideal than a current reality: the actual continuum of events, the number of significant individuals who make up its history, are much too large to be known, even by the specialist in cultural history. So another attack is called for, that adopted by the Church.

> The classical tradition was only kept alive throughout the Dark Ages because a few learned churchmen such as Isidore of Seville were not ashamed of writing simple compendia to which they committed those few ideas about the universe and about the past which they considered indispensable . . . I have been toying with the idea of secular creeds, as brief and concise, if we can hammer them out, as the Athanasian Creed . . . It is with some trepidation that I submit for your criticism the first untidy draft of such a creed . . .
>
> I belong to Western Civilisation, born in Greece in the first millenium B.C. It was created by poets, philosophers, artists, historians and scientists who freely examined the earlier myths and traditions of the ancient Orient. It flourished in Athens in the fifth century, was carried East by Macedonian conquests in the fourth century . . .[4]

And there follows a concise history of the transformation of the classical tradition, 'biased, subjective and selective' as Gombrich is at pains to emphasise, but also cogent for what it intends and includes. If one were to modify it, as he asks, the most obvious additions would be at the beginning and end – Egyptian culture and the Modernist 'experiment' are the two most surprising lacunae.

There have been several times when the idea of a continuum has been expressed in art, notably during periods of revivalism when a strong historical consciousness is crossed with a sense of imminent creativity. Raphael's *School of Athens*, the *locus classicus* of classicism, is the best known version

11.4 Peter Blake, *The Meeting or Have a Nice Day, Mr Hockney*, 1981-3, detail, oil on canvas, 39x49in. Blake's new version of Courbet's painting takes place in Venice California and contrasts the two British Post-Modern painters with their ephemeral setting, the heroic with the banal, the present with the past (Courtesy Tate Gallery, London)

320

of this reversible history.[5] Here the present and past are interwoven pictorially and symbolically as if all time were present at a single moment. Plato (with the visage of Leonardo) points up to the heavens, the realm of ideas and, by analogy, at the very real, unfinished Cathedral of St. Peter. Aristotle, to his side, points downwards towards the things of the earth, towards matter, multiplicity and everyday reality; and thus the dialectic starts which pulls into its systematic opposition many artists and philosophers of note including Michelangelo as Heraclitus, Bramante as Euclid and Raphael as himself. This collapse of space and time represents in an immediate way the continuity of traditions, the past alive in the present and the present reanimating the past.

A later, more elaborate version of the reversible continuum is painted by Paul Delaroche in the *Salle des Prix* at the Ecole des Beaux-Arts (5). Here four main periods of history are pulled together and united allegorically on the curving wall of an amphitheatre. Athens, Rome, the medieval period and the Renaissance are personified as elders who sit, life-size, in judgement on the Beaux-Arts student as he presents his efforts to the real jurors below.[6] Palladio talks to the Gothic architect Robert de Luzarches, while another group of architects from different countries listen attentively to the medieval designer Arnolfo di Cambio. Thus these two periods and types of design, Gothic and classical, which are generally seen as engaged in a 'battle of the styles', are here more accurately portrayed as related by blood type and endeavour. The synthesis of the tableaux takes in not only the nineteenth-century professors and students but, above in the half dome, the Ecole Flamande, Ecole Hollandaise, Ecole Allemande and so on – that is the plurality of European schools which stem from the Graeco-Gothic continuum. As in Raphael's *School of Athens*, the implicit valuation of the designers and culture portrayed in this mural is one of a broad-based hierarchy stemming from a shared classical centre. And this hierarchy and centre are analogous to the later position of T.S. Eliot's 'ideal order'.

In nineteenth-century England a similar idea is expressed by Gilbert Scott's Albert Memorial in London. Here western culture is again seen as a hierarchical evolution and the representation mixes a view of quality and worth with a more neutral historical narrative so that one writer leads to another, one artist to the next, both polemically and logically, both in terms of judgement and canonic history. Here a certain optimism places Shakespeare next to Homer and, on another panel, current architects next to their more renowned predecessors. This challenge thrown down to the past by the present typifies the hubris of contemporary culture, and is a direct consequence of regarding the past and present as a whole. After all, if both are part of the same continuum then the 'Moderns' can summarise and transcend the 'Ancients' in both quality and technical skill, as long as these aspects are narrowly defined.

Whatever goes into our collective view of western culture as a living continuum, the very idea of it has key relevance for our subject. In so far as

11.5 Paul Delaroche, *Salle des Prix*, Ecole des Beaux-Arts, Paris, circa 1849 (Courtesy Ecole des Beaux-Arts)

11.6 Robert Longo, *Corporate Wars: Wall of Influence*, 1982, centre section detail, cast aluminium, 7x9ft. The convention of Roman battle scenes and sarcophagi are here transformed (Courtesy Metro Pictures, NYC)

classicism is alive today it entails disputed interpretations and differing values. The subversive work of Robert Longo, for instance, while outside the canonic definition is nevertheless a part of the wider tradition in its appropriation of Roman forms for contemporary myths (6). The protagonists of current classicism are no more likely to agree on every article of faith than are politicians as to the essence of democracy. In fact this debate, essential to the health of classicism, springs from ethical positions which are as fundamental as political and social ones. Any living tradition must challenge its roots, especially when they are so venerable, and this leads to minor battles. However, as we shall see, the disputes are not just within the family.

Style Wars – The Battle of the New Classicism

In the summer of 1977 a new architectural campaign emerged in Stuttgart and I had the good fortune to arrive there one week after James Stirling had won a competition for the design of a state theatre and museum. As we have seen in Chapter IX, it showed affinities with Schinkel's work, but also various eclectic elements such as Egyptian cornices, Modernist steel canopies and vernacular masonry walls (7). This stripped classicism led, however, to something of a public outcry. Students, generally siding with the foreigner who had brought such invention to the city, were delighted but confused; older architects who had lived through the Second World War were perturbed by what they took to be a recrudescence of Nazi classicism; while the press, as usual, was enjoying this new style war. To mark Stirling's acceptance of the commission there was a large public meeting of designers, politicians, representatives from the art world, and, most significantly, his architectural competitors. Gunter Behnisch came up to the podium to give Stirling what was expected to be a quick vote of thanks and congratulations. Instead it turned into a thirty minute diatribe against Fascist Classicism: 'Why Mr. Stirling, do you use this circle? It's a Nazi form.' Stirling rose to his feet, walked over to the designs of Behnisch which were pinned on the wall – he had finished third – and countered: 'Why do you repeat the square so often? That's fascist.'

This confrontation was notable more for its bitterness than for its intellectual subtlety. When I arrived to lecture on Post-Modernist architecture, the issue was even hotter. Those favouring the new style were still the perplexed young, who may have been partly convinced by Stirling's argument that the Bauhaus style was now becoming repetitive; those disliking all forms of historicism were, generally, over fifty. The generation gap signified by this controversy was nothing new, but the debate did pose the illuminating question: what kind of classicism should we have today?

If all architectural meaning necessarily has an associational component, then those who associated the stripped classicism of the 1930s with the regimes that supported it had a good case for rejecting Stirling (8). If, however, many of the classical forms he was using were more universal, then

11.7 James Stirling and Michael Wilford, *Neue Staatsgalerie*, the sculpture court, Stuttgart 1977-84. An Egyptian cornice in concrete above a rusticated base and Modern door (Photograph C. Jencks)

11.8 Albert Speer, *Zeppelinfeld*, Nuremberg, Germany, 1934 (Courtesy Library of Congress)

surely, as he responded 'the Nazis didn't ruin Schinkel for all time'. One could argue, as I did, that classical forms, with an ornament and style far removed from stripped Neoclassicism, would be more appropriate in Germany; this would avoid the still comparatively raw association with fascism, which in time will fade. But Stirling rejected my arguments because for him classicism is associated with the designer Thomas Hope and his Deepdene. There are, however, no eternal associations connected with classicism. Based on different memories, people have been accepting and rejecting the style for three thousand years. Christians, for instance, changed their mind several times concerning the propriety of using pagan basilicas and secular forms for their sacred buildings. Only a fanatic would reject classicism *in toto* because of some bad historical connections.

And yet such blanket rejections occur all the time and are made especially by older Modern architects and critics who have lived through the Second World War. Bruno Zevi, for instance, equates classicism with symmetry, and both of these sins with the fascist personality. In his polemical book *The Modern Language of Architecture* (1973), an answer to Summerson's *The Classical Language of Architecture* (1963), he states the case this way:

> Symmetry is one of the invariables of classicism . . . Symmetry = a spasmodic need for security, fear of flexibility, indetermination, relativity, and growth – in short, fear of living. The schizophrenic cannot bear the temporal aspect of living. To keep his anguish under control, he requires immobility. Classicism is the architecture of conformist schizophrenia. Symmetry = passivity or, in Freudian terms, homosexuality.[7]

According to this reasoning, asymmetry should promote heterosexuality. The discussion later goes on to articulate a widely held prejudice (or, should we say, plausible association of ideas?): '. . . symmetry is the facade of sham power trying to appear invulnerable. The public buildings of Fascism, Nazism and Stalinist Russia are all symmetrical. Those of South American dictatorships are symmetrical. Those of theocratic institutions are symmetrical; they often have a double symmetry.'[8] Therefore, presumably, they are doubly repressive. However unlikely this argument sounds, it results from Zevi's experience under the Mussolini regime and has at least a modicum of statistical truth: insecure regimes probably do favour an architecture of control and Neoclassicism, like the International Style, lends itself to this use.

Indeed the French Academy, supported by the centralised state, almost killed classicism as a living tradition precisely as it was formulated into a system under Louis XIV. Colbert (Controller-General of Finance) consolidated his control over art and the economy by centralising all the academies concerned with the arts and imposing a uniform and integrated state style. This style, under the tutelage of Charles Lebrun, was essentially an Eclectic Classicism of a Baroque type, which integrated not only the obvious areas such as painting, sculpture, furniture, tapestry and architecture, but even food, fireworks and flowerpots (9). Classical taste was in a sense mass-

11.9 Julie Hardouin Mansart, *Versailles,* garden front and urn, 1678 + (Photograph C. Jencks)

11.10 Michael Graves, *Portland Public Services Building*, Oregon, 1980-2 (Photograph Proto Acme)

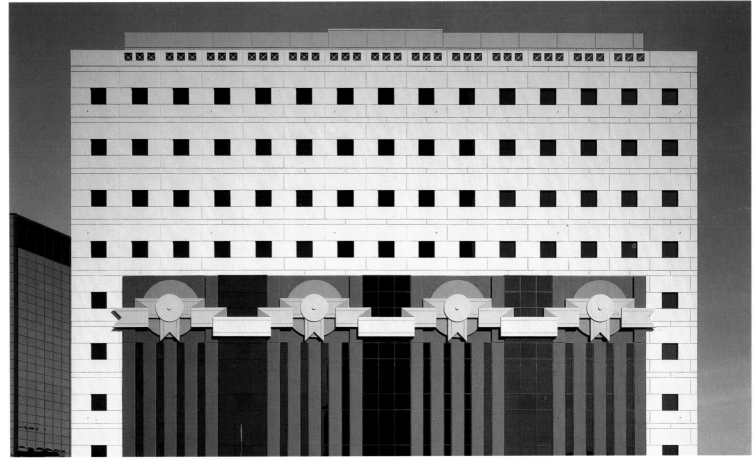

produced by state fiat and from this mechanical reproduction comes not only the modern distaste for monotonous classicism, but also the contrary Modernist ideal of repetition and celebration of multiplication. Versailles as an institution anticipates this ambiguous love of endless production: 'I want to be a machine', announces Andy Warhol, 'machines have less problems'. This ironic statement suggests an aesthetic delight in repetition and predictability, just as it elucidates the new emerging regard for Albert Speer's architecture. Furthermore, we cannot deny that classicism as a language has been perverted by megalomaniacs such as Peyre and Boullée, even if we deny Zevi's equation of the style with repression. All languages can express nasty sentiments.

The way Modern architecture grew in the nineteenth century with its 'call for morality', as Siegfried Giedion has described it, parallels the anti-classical trends in Modern art.[9] 'Pompier' architecture and salon art were perversions of the spirit of ancient classicism, and produced reactions which resulted in the wholesale rejection of that style. The rejection was turned into a myth to be taught in all the schools, and its ideology is so much a part of recent Modernism that its story hardly needs repeating today. Every student of architecture knows that Le Corbusier spurned the Ecole des Beaux-Arts and that Frank Lloyd Wright damned the insipid revivalism of the 1930s as 'deflowered classicism'. Every student of art knows the heroic stance the Impressionists, Fauves and Expressionists took against academic art and its worst excesses of commercial kitsch. Indeed the whole myth is epitomised in Clement Greenberg's influential essay of 1938 – 'Avant-Garde and Kitsch' – which argues that current art has to be either one thing or the other: the Modernist 'Tradition of the New', or commercial cliché. Modernism could be defined most clearly by what it was against, and the enemy, as if to prove one's worst suspicions, duly arrived in the 1930s and 1940s espousing Fascist Classicism.

So ingrained did this ideology become that it created the kind of taboos which Bruno Zevi, architectural critics and especially journalists could exploit. Thus when Charles Moore designed the Piazza d'Italia, using an industrial version of the Five Orders, he could be compared with the arch-villain of the moment, the Shah of Iran.[10] Michael Graves received an even greater shower of abuse for his Portland Building, in spite of the fact that its classical elements were transformed. His stylised garlands led to the building being labelled a 'beribboned Christmas package', his square front and large black window led to the epithet 'enlarged juke box', puffed-up 'turkey' and, again, fascist monument (10). Wolf von Eckhardt, a German-born critic who supported the Modernists and obviously finds classicism repugnant because of its Nazi overtones, called the building, in *Time* magazine, everything from 'Sarastro's Temple' to 'rubbery ET' and 'Mickey Mouse Classical', while Graves himself became 'A Pied Piper in Hobbit Land'.[11] In the Style Wars no image is too far fetched to pin on the enemy.

It's interesting that one origin of stylistic categories lies precisely in such abuse, and starts with the main definer of Canonic Classicism, Vitruvius. In a well-known passage in his seventh book of architecture, written at the time of Augustus, he attacks what we could call the anti-classicism of current fresco painting, the fashion for 'monsters' and impossible structures, both of which can be seen in Pompeiian wall painting of the second style.

> On the stucco are monsters rather than definite representations taken from definite things. Instead of columns there rise up stalks; instead of gables, striped panels with curled leaves and volutes . . . slender stalks with heads of men and animals attached to half the body . . . Such things neither are, nor can be, nor have been. On these lines the new fashions compel bad judges to condemn good craftsmanship as dullness.[12]

How many times will we hear this complaint? E.H. Gombrich has shown how this attack on 'irrationality' was transformed within the classical tradition by so many critics – St. Bernard, Vasari, Bellori, Winckelmann – into an attack on 'expressionist' aesthetics.[13] Furthermore, he shows how Vitruvius' strictures form the basis of stylistic terms such as Gothic, Baroque and Rococo, which started life as derogatory labels condemning 'anti-classicism'. This might lead us to believe that these styles are indeed against classicism, but in fact, with hindsight, we recognise them as transformations of the classical language according to new canons – fresh forms of Free-Style Classicism. And this should warn us about the supreme irony of the present Style Wars. For what do the attacks on Stirling, Moore and Graves amount to? Their work is condemned for being too close to, or too far from, Canonic Classicism; the former when it is thought too reminiscent of fascist repression: the latter when it is thought too irrational and surreal, like Vitruvius' despised frescoes. In the latter case, current classicism is being criticised for being anti-classical by the Modernists – who actually hate classicism, and in the former for being too ordered. Irony upon irony, absurdity upon absurdity. From such mad logic we might conclude that Modernism was actually related to classicism – its despised opposite. As we have seen in previous chapters, there is a little truth in this paradox: Post-Modern Classicism evolved out of the Modernist Classicism of Le Corbusier, Mies and Louis Kahn; Carlo Maria Mariani evolved from de Chirico; Kitaj and Hockney owe a debt to the cubism and classical work of Picasso; and the work of Lennart Anderson and Milet Andrejevic springs from Morandi, Balthus and other Modernist painters.

Post-Modern Poetics and The New Rules
Often in history there is a combination of continuity and change which looks perplexing because our view of both the old and the new is altered. Thus, with Post-Modern Classicism the meanings, values and forms of Modernism and classicism are simultaneously transformed into a hybrid combination. The present mode looks disturbing, partly because it is both strange and yet very familiar. Previous rules of decorum and composition are not so much

disregarded, as extended and distorted. Indeed, the very notion of designing within a set of rules, which has been anathema since the Romantic age, takes on new meanings.

Now, rules or canons for production are seen as preconditions for creativity, a situation caused partly by the advent of the computer, which makes us conscious of the assumptions behind a building. Analytical scholarship within the art world has also increased this consciousness, as students are now forced to become aware of the conventions behind such seemingly spontaneous twentieth-century movements as Primitivism and Expressionism. The only escape from rule-governed art is to suppress from consciousness the canons behind one's creativity – hardly a comforting liberation. And it's practically impossible to remain ignorant of these, at least of antecedent ones, in an age of constant communication and theorising. Thus, consciousness of rules, conventions and canons is thrust upon us.

To conclude this survey of Post-Modern Classicism we might summarise a few of the more outstanding canons that lie behind the new art and architecture. These canons are not universally held by Post-Modernists and some are contingent upon the momentary historical situation arising after Modernism. They thus contrast with the older notion of classical rules in being understood as relative rather than absolute, responses to a world of fragmentation, pluralism and inflation rather than formulae to be applied indiscriminately. The following list is a selection, from the many emergent precepts we have discussed throughout this book, of eleven of the most significant.

1) The most obvious new convention concerns beauty and composition. In place of Renaissance harmony and Modernist integration is the new hybrid of *dissonant beauty*, or *disharmonious harmony*. Instead of a perfectly finished totality 'where no part can be added or subtracted except for the worse' (Alberti), we find the 'difficult whole' (Venturi) or the 'fragmented unity' of artists like the Poiriers and architects like Hans Hollein (11). This new emphasis on complexity and richness parallels the Mannerist emphasis on *difficultà* and skill, but it has a new social and metaphysical basis. From a pluralist society a new sensibility is formed which finds an oversimple harmony either false or unchallenging. Instead, the juxtaposition of tastes and world views is appreciated as being more real than the integrated languages of both Exclusionist Classicism and High Modernism. The new taste for disjunctions and collisions is apparent in such popular films as *The Gods Must Be Crazy* which alternates frequently between the world view of a scientist, drop-out journalist, Kalahari Bushman and a revolutionist, yet manages to create from these a coherent drama. Significantly it appeals to different tastes and ages.

'Disharmonious harmony' also finds validity in the present consensus among scientists that the universe is dynamic and evolving. In the past, classical revivals have been associated with a presumed cosmic harmony. Vitruvius equated the 'perfect' human body with the celestial order and then

11.11 Hans Hollein, *Städtisches Museum Abteiberg*, Mönchengladbach, 1976-82, fragmentation of the office block (Photograph C. Jencks)

justified the perfected order of the temple on these assumptions. The Renaissance, with its well-proportioned buildings and sculpture, followed these equations between microcosm and macrocosm. Today however, with our compound and fragmented view of a Newtonian/Einsteinian universe, we have several theories of the macrocosm competing for our acceptance, none of which sound wholly plausible, complete or harmonious. Any scientist who has listened to the supposed origin of the universe – the noise of the Big Bang that apparently is still reverberating – does not speak only of 'the music of the spheres'; the 'violent universe' is as good a description of exploding supernovae as the eternally ordered and calm picture behind classical and Christian art of the past.

Inevitably art and architecture must represent this paradoxical view, the oxymoron of 'disharmonious harmony', and it is therefore not surprising that we find countless formal paradoxes in Post-Modern work such as 'asymmetrical symmetry', 'syncopated proportion', 'fragmented purity', 'unfinished whole' and 'dissonant unity'. Oxymoron, or quick paradox, is itself a typical Post-Modern trope and 'disharmonious harmony' recurs as often in its poetics as 'organic whole' recurs in the aesthetics of classicism and Modernism. As we have seen, the Japanese architect Monta Mozuna is characteristic of many architects in combining fragments of previous metaphysical systems into his buildings: Buddhist, Hindu, Shinto and western. My own attempts at cosmic symbolism, realised in collaboration with the painter William Stok, mix twentieth-century cosmology – the Big Bang theory, the concept of evolving galaxies and nebulae – with traditional views of morality and the idea of a cultural continuum (12). The heavens are traditionally represented by circles and spirals, the earth by squares or rectangles, and here this symbolism is reused on the ceiling (*coelum*) and floor (*terra*).

A suspended 'dome' hangs precariously from above with layered ovals and rectangles diminishing one above another towards the spiral centre which pulls these visual forces together. While these forms are, according to the conventions of Guarino Guarini, a harmonious representation of infinity they nevertheless contrast with other forms, just as our different cosmologies conflict with one another or precariously coexist. For instance the mural of William Stok can be read as illustrating both the Big Bang and Oscillating views of the universe. His painting starts with the cosmic egg and explosion, and ends with an implosion leading to another cycle (13). But below this, and discontinuous with it, is a representation of cultural time, suggesting how one period may be transformed by another, such as Egypt by Greece and Italy. And below this in turn are the stencilled themes of the house, again partly discontinuous and partly harmonious with the forms and themes above. The layers of architecture and art thus revolve around this oval space, consistent within themselves but occasionally out of phase with each other. Sometimes they are synchronised, sometimes they conflict, just as the various levels of our existence do: the everyday, the cultural and the cosmic. It is the eternal hope of religions and secular creeds such as Marxism that the macrocosm and

11.12 Charles Jencks, *Dome*, William Stok, *Mural,* Thematic House, London, 1983. The 'dome' represents the cosmos with circles, ovals and spirals. The mural shows the Cosmic Egg (Big Bang) and the evolution of the galaxies (Photograph Richard Bryant)

11.13 William Stok, *Mural* , Thematic House, London, 1983. This section shows cosmic evolution above historical figures: Erasmus, a Jesuit missionary in China, John Donne talking to Francesco Broomini and, to the far right, Prince Ito from Japan. Below this are stencilled themes of the house (Photograph Richard Bryant)

microcosm interact and reflect each other. This is symbolised here by the similarities of ornament: the spirals and nebulous shapes of the wood grain, for instance, are juxtaposed with the spiral galaxies and nebulae of the mural. But the usual situation is one of discontinuity, signified by the separation and syncopations between the three layers.

2) As strong a rule as 'disharmonious harmony', and one which justifies it, is *pluralism*, both cultural and political. As we have seen, the fundamental position of Post-Modernism in the 1970s was its stylistic variety, its celebration of difference, 'otherness' and irreducible heterogeneity. Feminist art and advocacy planning were two typical unrelated movements which helped form the tolerance of, and taste for, variety. In architecture, the stylistic counterpart of pluralism is *radical eclecticism* – the mixing of different languages to engage different taste cultures and define different functions according to their appropriate mood.

James Stirling's addition to the Tate Gallery is undoubtedly his most divergent creation to date, a building which changes surface as it meets different buildings and defines different uses (14). Where it attaches to the classical gallery it continues the cornice line and some of the stonework, but where it approaches a preexisting brick structure it adopts some of this red and white grammar. Its main entrance is different again, a formal grid of green mullioned glass which reappears in another main public area, the reading room. As if these changes were not enough to articulate the changing functions and mood, the grammar becomes Late-Modern to the rear – a style suitable to the service area – and more neutral on the other side so as to be in keeping with the back of the Tate. To pull this heterogeneity together is a grid frame, presented as something analogous to a classical order. A square wall pattern, like the Renaissance application of pilasters, reappears again and again, inside and outside, to form the conceptual ordering system. But it is used in a dissonant not harmonious way – broken into quarter rhythms around the entrance, hanging in fragments over the reading room, and marching down part of the side facades (15). Thus Renaissance harmony is mixed with Modernist collage even in the background structure that is supposed to unify the fragments. While such extreme eclecticism may be questioned for such a small building, it does serve to characterise the heterogeneous functions, such as accommodating groups of schoolchildren, for which this building was specifically designed. Stirling speaks of it as a garden building attached to a big house, and this helps explain the informality, the lily pond, trellis work and pergola. It also underscores why this eclecticism is radical: because, unlike weak eclecticism which is more a matter of whim, it is tied to very specific functions and symbolic intentions. Another motive for the heterogeneity is its communicational role – the idea that an eclectic language speaks to a wide and divergent audience – something of a necessity for a public art gallery.

David Salle is an artist who adopts an analogous approach in his divided canvases. Mixing different styles, as does Stirling, which vary from the

11.14,15 James Stirling and Michael Wilford, *Clore Gallery*, addition to the Tate Gallery, London, 1982-6 (Photographs R. Bryant)

11.16 David Salle, *Midday*, oil and acrylic on canvas and wood, 1984, 114x150in (Courtesy Mary Boone Gallery, NYC)

popular and banal to the sophisticated and classical, he achieves some of the same wry clashes and mutual cancellations. In *Midday*, 1984 (16), a secretary ambiguously wards off the effigy of her boss as she falls back onto a sleazy office floor. This potential narrative is juxtaposed with a Modernist colour field painting and other signs of abstract art, while the conventions of journalism, TV and graffiti cancel to a degree the classical and Modernist conventions. Although the eclecticism reaches out to various audiences, the message it sends is disturbing and unresolved.

Enigmatic allegory and suggestive narrative are two Post-Modern genres, as we have seen, which try to make a virtue of ambiguity and in this sense reflect an open, plural metaphysics. When several possible readings are presented simultaneously, it is left to the reader to supply the unifying text. This also entails frustration – the Post-Modern counterpart to the classical canon of 'withheld gratification'. Both Stirling's and Salle's work is frustrating in the sense that it avoids a hierarchy of meanings. One has to look elsewhere to find a clearer expression of a unified view.

3) The most commonly held aim of Post-Modern architects is to achieve an *urbane urbanism*. As we have seen in Chapters VII and IX, urban contextualism gains near universal assent. New buildings, according to this doctrine, should both fit into and extend the urban context, reuse such constants as the street, arcade and piazza, yet acknowledge too the new technologies and means of transport. This double injunction amounts to a new rule, as clear and well defined as any tenet of Canonic Classicism. Furthermore, there are those such as Leon Krier who would argue for an optimum relationship between all the parts of a city, what I have called the 'proper balance' between essential elements: public to private, work to living, monument to infill, short blocks to city grid, foreground square to background housing. If one focuses on this balance, rather than any particular set of dualities, then one will achieve the urbane urbanism of the Roman *insulae*, or the traditional eighteenth-century European city, or nineteenth-century American village (17). Small block, mixed-use planning thus amounts to an urban absolute for convivial living. In Krier's schemes the physical and functional hierarchies are clear. There's no ambiguity, irony or juxtaposition here, which is why they seem at once so powerful and nostalgic. The urbane way of life is simply better than is the dissociated and overcentralised city.

4) Almost as favoured as contextualism is the Post-Modern trope of *anthropomorphism*. Almost all of the new classicists incorporate ornament and mouldings suggestive of the human body. Geoffrey Scott in the *Architecture of Humanism*, 1914, applauded classicism because it 'transcribed in stone the body's favourable states'. Its profiles, as Michelangelo emphasised, could resemble silhouettes of a face; its sculptural mass and chiaroscuro could echo the body's muscles. Such architecture humanises inanimate form as we naturally project our physiognomy and moods onto it. This empathetic response is most welcome on large housing estates, or in a context which is fundamentally alienating or over-built. Jeremy Dixon,

11.17 Leon Krier, *Spitalfields Market*, aerial view of redevelopment project, London, 1986

11.18 Michael Graves, *Plocek House*, detail of rear elevation, Warren, New Jersey, 1978-82 (Photograph C. Jencks)

11.19 Charles Jencks and Terry Farrell, *Thematic House*, garden elevation, London, 1978-82 (Photograph C. Jencks)

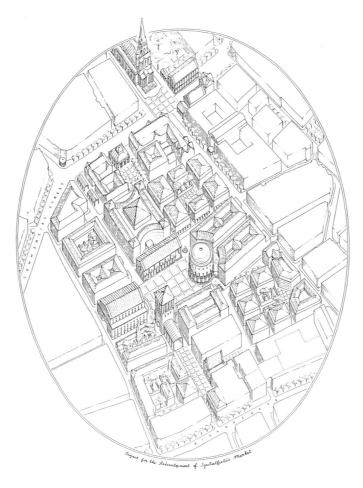

Project for the Redevelopment of Spitalfields Market

Robert Krier, Hans Hollein, Cesar Pelli, Kazumasa Yamashita and Charles Moore among others have developed this anthropomorphism, just as Michael Graves and I have tried to make abstract representations of the face and body in our work (18). The explicitness of the image varies from the obvious caryatid, or herm, to the hidden figure and seems most successful when combining these extremes. At a large scale the figure is best incorporated with other motifs and meanings, so it is not overpowering: in the Thematic House, for instance, head, shoulders, arms, belt and legs are as much arches and windows as they are anatomical parts (19). The general rule favours a subliminal anthropomorphism, but promotes an explicitness in detail and ornament. In an age when architects and artists are often at a loss for legitimate subject matter, the human presence remains a valid departure point.

5) Another credible subject is the historical continuum and the relation between the past and present. This has led to an outbreak of parody, nostalgia and pastiche – the lesser genres with which Post-Modernism is equated by its detractors – but has also resulted in *anamnesis*, or suggested recollection. In a Post-Freudian age the unconscious is often invoked as the source of anamnesis, and it works characteristically with the juxtaposition of related and opposed fragments. Ann and Patrick Poirier have captured this logic of dreams in their fragmented constructions which combine archetypes, half-remembered myths and miniature landscapes (20). We search these ruins for possible relations between such things as an arrow, bronze leaves and black lips; not fully comprehending the ancient story of which they may be fragments, but nevertheless invited to make a guess as to their significance. The enigmatic allegory makes use of dissociated and partial memories and, at best, creates a simulacrum of meaning where the overtones combine and harmonise. It is this harmonious aura which becomes the subject matter of this paradoxical genre – a narrative without a plot. Anamnesis is one of the oldest rhetorical tropes and today has become a goal in itself.

6) The well publicised 'return to painting' of Post-Modernism has also been accompanied by a 'return to content', and this content is as diverse and divergent as a pluralist society. The Hirschorn Museum exhibition, *Content*, 1974-84, showed some of this variety – the subject matter extended from autobiography to high and popular culture, from social commentary to metaphysical speculation, from paintings of nature to portrayals of psychological nature.[14] In addition there was the extension of the traditional genres, such as narrative painting, still-life and landscape painting, summarised in exhibitions on realism.[15] There is clearly no underlying thread, coherence, mythology or emergent rule in this heterogeneity beyond the general 'will to meaning' as it was termed by the Hirschorn. Yet, through pluralism, the overall movement has a *divergent signification* and allows multiple readings through the convention of enigmatic allegory. Many Post-Modern critics have emphasised intertextuality (the way several discontinuous texts com-

11.20 Ann and Patrick Poirier, *Untitled*, 1984, bronze and marble, 14x19½x39½in (Courtesy Sonnabend Gallery, NYC)

11.21 Thomas Cornell, *The Nurture of Dionysus II*, 1981, oil on canvas, 48x66in (Courtesy G.W. Einstein, NYC)

bine to form their own meaning) as both a strategy and contemporary reality. This has led to two precepts, *radical eclecticism* in architecture and *suggestive narrative* in art.

Where there is a commitment to a particular set of values, as with the Arcadian painters, the narrative is almost traditional. We see this in Thomas Cornell's pastoral work. His *The Nurture of Dionysus II*, 1981 (21), depicts the young god of wine being tended by nymphs on Mount Nysa, but this reading is crossed by several other texts: references to middle America (the contemporary pose and actors' faces); conventions adopted from Puvis de Chavannes, and repeated references to the ecological movement. Since most of us are unfamiliar with the particulars of Dionysus' early years, we may not realise that he was transformed into a ram, tended in a cave and disguised as a girl – events which are all alluded to in the painting. Only when we cross these mythological texts with those of the 1960s and 1970s – stressing the wholeness of rural life – does this divergent signification become clearer so that we read the work as both a nostalgic pastoral and political polemic.

7) This brings us to the most prevalent aspect of Post-Modernism, its *double-coding*, use of irony, ambiguity and contradiction. Irony and ambiguity were key concepts in Modern literature and Post-Modernists have continued using these tropes and methods while extending them to painting and architecture. The idea of double meaning and the *coincidentia oppositorum* ultimately goes back to Heraclitus and Nicholas of Cusa. Well before Robert Venturi and Matthias Ungers were formulating their poetics of dualism, a character in a Strindberg play exhorts 'Don't say "either . . . or" but instead "both . . . and"!'[16]

This Hegelian injunction has become *the* method for urban infill and is practised as a delicate art by Charles Vandenhove who stitches several parts of Belgian cities together with fragments of opposite languages. He has renovated the Hors-Chateau quarter of Liege with a variable order which has the dualism new/old consciously built in as a sign of reconciliation. His renovation of the Hotel Torrentius, a sixteenth-century mansion in the same city, is an exquisite compilation of opposites susceptible to several simultaneous readings: as real archaeological fragment, secessionist ornament and as the superimposition of abstract geometries (22). The ironies and juxtapositions are underplayed in favour of a 'both . . . and' harmony. This attitude to the past, more like Renaissance mixing than Modernist collage, implies the historical continuum which is so essential to the Post-Modern vision. Present style and technology are accepted as valid realities, but not required to overassert themselves; it is a case of peaceful, not antagonistic, coexistence.

When Vandenhove adds a new facade to a museum of decorative arts, he invents a new stylised Ionic Order, with oversize volutes made from concentric circles, but reconciles this with the previous geometry in a way that implies both continuity with the past and the separate identity of the present (23). This form of double-coding allows us to read the present in the past as much as the past in the present, as if history proceeded by a gradual

11.22 Charles Vandenhove, *Hotel Torrentius Renovation*, ground floor, Liege, 1981-2, decoration by Olivie Debré (Photograph courtesy the architect)

11.23 Charles Vandenhove, *Facade of the Museum of Decorative Arts*, renovation, Gent, 1986 (Photograph courtesy the architect)

evolution of permanent forms rather than a succession of revolutionary styles each one of which obliterates its predecessor. Double-coding can, of course, be used in an opposite way to emphasise the disjunctions, as for instance Stirling and Salle employ it; but however the method is articulated it acknowledges the simultaneous validity of opposite approaches and different tastes.

8) When several codes are used coherently to some purpose they produce another quality sought by Post-Modernists, *multivalence*. A univalent building or Minimalist work of art can have integrity but only of an exclusive and generally self-referential type. By contrast, a multivalent work reaches out to the rest of the environment, to many adjacent references, and to many different associations. It is inclusive by intent and, when successful, resonant as a symbol. The resonance consists in linking forms, colours and themes. This idea – an old one stemming from the notion of 'organic unity' – is relatively rare in our culture where art and architecture tend to have gone their separate ways: art to the gallery and architecture to a limited institutional practice. Recently there have been many calls for collaboration, mutual commissions have been promoted, joint organisations formed; but most of these efforts have produced a juxtaposition of the two disciplines, rarely an integration of the art work and its setting.[17] Nevertheless, artists such a Eduardo Paolozzi and Robert Graham, and architects such as Michael Graves and Cesar Pelli have sought a deeper collaboration that starts near the beginning of design, so that their work can be modified as it progresses. For mutual modification is the key to multivalence: only where the diverse meanings have been worked through will the art, architecture and daily activity begin to interact and form a greater unity.

Frank Lloyd Wright sought this organic unity in his work as did the Art Nouveau designers committed to the *gesamtkunstwerk*. An example I am well acquainted with, because it was painted for our dining room, is Allen Jones' *Dance to the Music of Time*, 1984 (24). Relating to the themes of summer which order this space, it pulls together in its frame, colour and iconography meanings both internal and external to its subject. A voluptuous young girl with a sheaf of corn in one hand, symbol of summer, dances to the music of Father Time, while a Janus figure, sign of the new and old year, exits to one side. Based loosely on Nicholas Poussin's work of the same subject, it lends this perennial theme a contemporary sense of anxiety as youth and age, male and female, hold each other in their gaze, frozen in a moment of suspense. The orange and yellow glow of the painting relates directly to the same tones of the room, just as the lighting fixture (an eclipsed sun) and ornament of the frame are transformations of immediately adjacent themes. In this way the room is brought into the painting and the painting's theme heightens those of the room. Even the furniture takes part in the overall plot.

Such integration is more common in churches where there is often incorporated a deliberate symbolic and aesthetic programme, but it is relatively rare in other building types. The great advantage and delight of

11.24 Allen Jones, *Dance to the Music of Time*, in the Summer Room, Thematic House, London, 1984 (Photograph C. Jencks)

multivalence is the continual reinterpretation it prompts, a result of the multiple links between the work and its setting. This unlimited semiosis (the continual discovery of new meaning in works that are rich in external and internal associations) is characteristic of both Post-Modernism and inclusive art in general. With Jones' painting, for instance, one sees traditional representations of time (the Egyptian corn god, the Four Seasons, Father Time, youth etc.) alongside more up-to-date ways of depicting the theme (such as the abyss of time dividing the aged musician from the exhibitionist dancer etc.). If a work is resonant enough it continues to inspire unlimited readings.

9) A precondition for this resonance is a complex relation to the past: without memories and associations a building is diminished in meaning, while if it is purely revivalist its scope will be equally restricted. Hence the Post-Modern emphasis on anamnesis, or the historical continuum, and another of its defining rules – the displacement of conventions, or *tradition reinterpreted*. Most discussions of Post-Modernism focus on one or other of the many 'returns': the 'return to painting', figuration, ornament, monument, comfort, the human body and so on. The list is virtually endless, but all these returns must to some degree be inventive in order to transcend replication. Terry Farrell, for instance, will reinterpret the syntax and colour of the traditional temple form and use it on a boathouse in Henley (25). The festive polychromy of the Henley Regatta obviously forms the pretext for the strong blues and reds which also relate to the colours of the site and, incidentally, to nineteenth-century investigations into Greek polychromy. The temple columns become paired pilasters, the broken pediment is extended down into the brick base to become a water gate for the boats, and the acroteria become spot lights. The Henley blue is also an obvious sign of both water and sky, as is the waving ornament etched in the stucco frieze. Thus in many ways old forms are given new meanings to justify their existence. The proportions and flatness of detail, not to mention the saturated polychromy, appear strange at first glance (as do all such displacements of tradition) and it is only after we understand their new validity and they become familiar that the aura of pastiche disappears. The reinterpretation of tradition must always carry some overtones of this kind, since conventions are simultaneously affirmed and distorted.

10) Another way of renewing past conventions is by consciously elaborating *new rhetorical figures*. Post-Modernists, like the Modernists before them, or for that matter any historical movement, are definable by stylistic formulae which they invent or adapt. Fashion and function both play a role in establishing these new figures and the most prevalent are the ones we have touched on here and in previous chapters: paradox, oxymoron, ambiguity, double-coding, disharmonious harmony, amplification, complexity and contradiction, irony, eclectic quotation, anamnesis, anastrophe, chiasmus, ellipsis, elision and erosion. Charles Moore has used the last three rhetorical

11.25 Terry Farrell Partnership, *Henley Boathouse*, Henley-on-Thames, England, 1984-6 (Photograph Richard Bryant)

11.26 Moore Grover Harper, *Sammis Hall*, central light well, Cold Spring Harbour, 1980-1 (Photograph courtesy the architect)

devices recently to create something of a personal style. Characteristically he will erode a classical arch, or set of them, to create an ambiguous, layered space equivalent to the Baroque. But whereas these traditional forms were built in substantial masonry, Moore constructs them in plywood and stucco because it is both cheaper and lighter. Inevitably this is censored by some critics as scenographic architecture which deteriorates quickly, but the postive aspects of this innovation must not be overlooked. 'Cardboard architecture' allows new spatial experiences, new ways of joining thin surfaces which elide different shapes to create the effect of a run-on sentence, or a homogeneous and continuous structure. In the Sammis Hall (26), for instance, cut out arches are held above by keystones, and on the sides by eroded Venetian windows, to form a magical, diaphanous space through which light pours and bounces. The complex ambiguity and layering are reminiscent of Vittone's Baroque domes, but the airy insubstantiality is very much of our time. Aside from economic motives, there is a psychological reason for the prevalence of such erosions – they are symptomatic of the taste for unfinished figures, incomplete classical shapes, and formality that is also informal. Marking a return to humanism, but without the full and confident metaphysics which supported it in the Renaissance, these erosions relate also to that feeling of loss which is a recurring theme within Post-Modernism: the 'presence of the absence', such as the void in the centre of the Tsukuba Civic Centre (page 294).

11) This *return to the absent centre* is one of the most recurring figures of Post-Modernism. It is portrayed both consciously by Arata Isozaki as a comment on the decentred nature of Japanese life (as we have seen in Chapter X), and unselfconsciously by James Stirling at Stuttgart, Michael Graves at the Humana Building, Ricardo Bofill at Montpellier and just about every Post-Modern architect who makes a central plan and then doesn't know what to put in the honorific place. This paradox is both startling and revealing: a desire for a communal space, a perfectly valid celebration of what we have in common, and then the admission that there is nothing quite adequate to fill it.

Perhaps this reflects the sense of loss which underlies so many of the departures which can be characterised with the prefix 'post'. For, if we return to the first usage of the term by Arnold Toynbee and others in the 1940s and 1950s, we detect a similar melancholic connotation. Post-Modern then meant a culture that was Post-western and Post-Christian; a culture that had a strong sense of its departure point, but no clear sense of destination. This ambivalence is worth stressing because, of course, the term also meant Still-Modern and Still-Christian – suggesting a very clear appreciation of the cultural roots and values embedded in everyday behaviour, law and language, which cannot disappear in one, two, or even five generations. The same is true of other global uses of the term – Post-Industrial and Post-Marxist – they point as much to the very real survivals of preexisting patterns as they do to the transcendence of them. A Post-Industrial society, for

11.27 Richard Shaffer, *Room with Figure*, 1982-3, oil on canvas, 126x108in (Courtesy LA Louver Gallery, Venice, California)

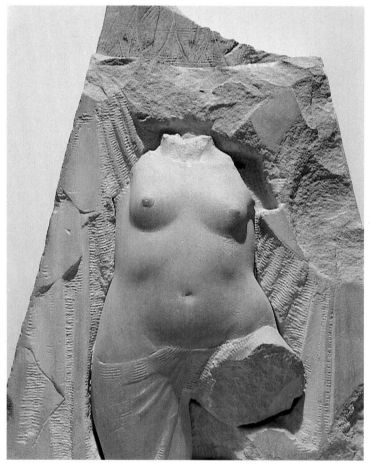

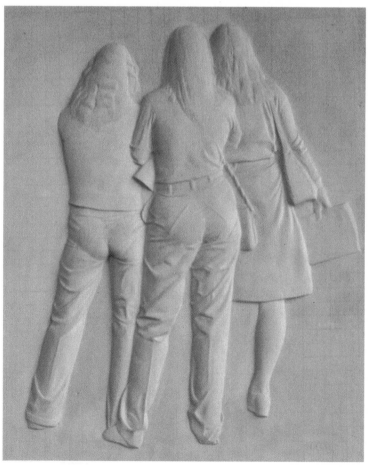

instance, still depends fundamentally on industry no matter how much its power structure and economy have moved on to the next level of organisation – computers, information exchange and a service economy. The ambivalence accurately reflects this double state of transition, where activity moves away from a well known point, acknowledges the move and yet keeps a view, or trace, or love of that past location. Sometimes it idealizes the security of this point of departure, with nostalgia and melancholy, but at the same time it may exult in a new found freedom and sense of adventure. Post-Modernism is in this sense schizophrenic about the past; equally as determined to retain and preserve aspects of the past as it is to go forward; excited about revival, yet wanting to escape the dead formulae of the past. Fundamentally it mixes the optimism of Renaissance revival with that of the Futurists, but is pessimistic about finding any certain salvation point, be it technology, a classless society, a meritocracy or rational organisation of a world economy (i.e. any of the answers which have momentarily been offered in the last hundred years). The 'grand narratives', as Jean-François Lyotard insists, have lost their certainty even if they remain locally desirable. The mood on board the ship of Post-Modernism is that of an Italian and Spanish crew looking for India, which may, if it's lucky, accidentally discover America; a crew which necessarily transports its cultural baggage and occasionally gets homesick, but one that is quite excited by the sense of liberation and the promise of discoveries.

Post-Modern artists directly mirror this ambivalence. Richard Shaffer, for instance, returns to a self-portraiture that owes much to Rembrandt's noble and saturnine disclosures *and* to modern phenomenology.[18] His *Room with Figure*, 1982-3 (27), like much of his other work, is almost totally black with a sad, enigmatic air, but its small areas of light invite the eye and mind to search the canvas for latent possibilities. One discovers on further investigation the reference to Velasquez's *Las Meninas* – that portrait of the absent royal family which inspired Isozaki's Tsukuba Civic Centre – there is a similar gesture of the artist in both paintings and the same kind of mysterious events set against a partially veiled background. As our eyes become adjusted to the dim light, we discern a male dancer who seems to enter the room from the left; it turns out he is a figure from another canvas, a representation of a representation, a 'sign of a sign', that typical Post-Modern emphasis on the reality of secondary reality. Then one notices other things – a man standing by a door, a tiny photograph of a nude occupying the space near the viewer, and the artist himself pointing out at you, bearer of significance to this suggested narrative. We can obviously read the plot several ways, epitomising, as it does, the idea of the artist's studio as a place where everything comes for comment but nothing ever happens. If anything occupies the centre of this story it is the act of interpretation itself.

Another artist's studio, that of sculptor Robin Shores, becomes a ruined labyrinth through which one searches to find the significance of the beautiful fragments adapted from different cultures and periods: Egypt, Rome, India

11.28 Robin Shores, *Installation*, overview, Boston, 1986 (Courtesy the artist)

11.29 Robin Shores, *Untitled*, 1986, limestone, 27x24x7in (Courtesy the artist)

11.30 Robin Shores, *Three Graces – Park Square*, 1986, plaster relief (Courtesy the artist)

and contemporary Boston (28). It's all related in Shores' maze of the past and fragmented present, so that the historical continuum unites the frozen dance of a voluptuous Greek courtesan with the 'Three Graces' waiting for a bus in Boston's Park Square (29,30). Each gesture, or fragment of a body, is depicted with skill and sensual neutrality. There is no single meaning to the maze, no thread we can follow through: it might be the ruined basement of any good museum, or an archaeological site of Post-Nuclear Civilisation (if that is not a contradiction in terms) or just the artist's studio with work in progress. Again it is the viewer who supplies the possible interpretations which lead back to himself, or herself: the presence at the absent centre.

*　　*　　*

There are more generative values in Post-Modern art and architecture than these eleven formulae and they are, inevitably, in a state of evolution. Furthermore, like the values and motives of any large movement, they are partly inconsistent. Nevertheless, these emerging canons are, in the third, classical phase of Post-Modernism, beginning to develop a discernible shape and direction, and we can say that this year's version of the ornamental building is likely to be more sophisticated than last year's. Urban building codes are evolving in a more enlightened direction as client and architect become more aware of the importance of context, while the many 'returns' in art have, in limited ways, made it richer and more accessible. Rules, however, do not necessarily a masterpiece make, and tend to generate new sets of dead-ends, imbalances and urban problems. Hence the ambivalence of our age to orthodoxy and the romantic impulse to challenge all canons of art and architecture while, at the same time, retaining them as a necessary precondition for creation: simultaneously promoting rules and breaking them. We are still near the beginning of the classical phase, which started in the late 1970s, and although one cannot predict its future, it is likely to deepen as it synthesizes the distant and more recent past, as it sustains more profoundly the western tradition of humanism. The modern world, which started with the Renaissance as an economic, social and political reality, has itself integrated as a twenty-four hour market-place on a much more complex level. Modern communications, scholarship and fabrication methods make any and every style equally possible, if not equally plausible. Even more than in the nineteenth century, the age of eclecticism, we have the freedom to choose and perfect our conventions and this choice forces us to look both inwards and outwards to culture as a whole. For the Modernist predicament, often epitomised in Yeats' words – 'Things fall apart; the centre cannot hold' – we have the dialectical answer – 'Things fall together, and there is no centre, but connections'. Or in E.M. Forster's words – 'connect, only connect'.

Notes

CHAPTER I
The Values of Post-Modernism

1) For some of these terms see Douglas Davis, 'Post-Everything', *Art in America*, Feb. 1980, pp.12-14. 'Post-Positivism' was used by Mary Hesse and other philosophers at a conference on Post-Modernism at Northwestern University in Oct. 1985: it refers to Thomas Kuhn's notion of a plurality of paradigms in science and the way they are non-commensurable and proceed by revolutionary jumps. The best short history of the term postmodern up to 1977 is Michael Köhler's 'Postmodernismus: Ein begrriffsgeschichtlicher Überblick,' *Amerikastudien 22* (1977), pp. 8-18, an issue which also carries other discussions of the term. Recent key references to Post-Modernism will be found below in notes 2, 7, 13, 15, 17, 20, 27, 28.

2) Jean-François Lyotard, 'What is Postmodernism?' included as an appendix in *The Postmodern Condition: A Report on Knowledge*, Manchester University Press, 1984, p.79. The essay was first published in French in 1982, the book in 1979. My own response to this, *What is Post-Modernism?*, Academy Editions, London, St. Martin's Press, New York, 1986, shows how the confusions of Postmodern with ultra- or Late-modern stem from Ihab Hassan's writings of the early 1970s.

3) For a discussion of many of these terms see E.H. Gombrich, 'Norm and Form, The Stylistic Categories of Art History and their Origins in Renaissance Ideals', *Norm and Form*, Phaidon, London, 1966, pp. 81-98 and the following essay in this collection 'Mannerism: The Historiographic Background', pp.99-106.

4) Ihab Hassan, 'The Question of Postmodernism', *Romanticism, Modernism, Postmodernism*, (ed.) Henry R. Garvin, Bucknell University Press, Lewisberg, 1980, p.117.

5) Harvey Cox, *Religion in the Secular City: Toward a Postmodern Theology*, Simon and Schuster, New York, 1970.

6) Irving Howe, 'Mass Society and Postmodern Fiction' (1963) reprinted in *The Decline of the New*, Horizon, New York, 1970.

7) Andreas Huyssen was the first to periodise postmodernism in this way and I am indebted to his arguments here with which I mostly agree; he does not however mention the third or 'classical' phase nor dichotomise Late- from Post-Modern. See his 'Mapping the Postmodern', *New German Critique*, No. 33, autumn 1984, pp.5-52.

8) Quoted from Lucy Lippard, *Pop Art*, Thames and Hudson, London, 1966, p.32.

9) This review in the *New York Times* is quoted from Judith Goldman, *James Rosenquist*, Penguin Books, New York, 1985, p.44.

10) In fact the *F 111* was shown in a small exhibit along with a Poussin and David in *History Painting – Various Aspects* at the Metropolitan Museum, 1968. This exhibit provoked Kramer's response. See note 9 for the source.

11) Lewis Mumford, 'The Case Against "Modern Architecture"' (1960) reprinted in *The Highway and the City*, Secker & Warburg, London, 1964, p.156.

12) Leslie Fiedler, 'The New Mutants' (1965) published in *The Collected Essays of Leslie Fiedler*, Vol.II, Stein and Day, New York, 1970.

13) Ihab Hassan, 'POSTmodernISM: A Paracritical Bibliography', *New Literary History* 3, No.1 (autumn 1971): 5-30 reprinted in *Paracriticisms: Seven Speculations of the Times*, University of Illinois Press, Urbana, Illinois, 1975, Chapter 2.

14) *Op.Cit.*, note 4, p. 123.

15) John Barth, 'The Literature of Replenishment, Postmodernist Fiction', *The Atlantic*, Jan. 1980, pp. 65-71.

16) *Ibid.*, p.70.

17) Umberto Eco, *Postscript to the Name of the Rose*, Harcourt Brace Jovanovich, New York and London, 1984, p.67 (first published in Italian in 1983).

18) *Ibid.*, pp.67-8.

19) The women's movement in art is summarised by Corinne Robins in *The Pluralist Era, American Art 1968-1981*, Harper and Row, New York, pp.49-75.

20) Craig Owens, 'The Discourse of Others: Feminists and Postmodernism' in *The Anti-Aesthetic, Essays on Postmodern Culture*, (ed.) Hal Foster, Bay Press, Port Townsend, Washington, 1983. Most of these essays are really concerned with Late-Modernism or the Schismatic Postmodernism that Hassan proffers. See note 2 for my critique.

21) Frank H. Goodyear Jr., *Contemporary American Realism Since 1960*, New York Graphic Society, Boston, 1981. This book, and catalogue, remains the standard text on the wide field of recent realisms.

22) Andreas Huyssen, 'Mapping the Postmodern', *op.cit.*, note 7, pp.13-16.

23) E.M. Farrelly, 'The New Spirit', *Architectural Review*, Aug. 1986 announces, as if for the first time, the 'death of Post-Modernism'; these obituaries started appearing in American magazines circa 1979.

24) See Anthony Vidler, 'Vidler on Jencks' or 'Cooking Up the Classics', *Skyline*, New York, Oct. 1981, pp. 18-21 and my reply the following month. Vidler later apologised to me for the tone and drawings in this piece. From about this time a new vicious tone starts appearing in architectural polemics as adversaries start treating each other with contempt, and the warfare moves to Britain with the so-called 'Great Debate – Modernism versus the Rest' at the RIBA in Nov. 1982. See my 'Post-Modern Architecture: the True Inheritor of Modernism' in *Transactions 3*, RIBA Publications, London, 1983, pp.26-41, which summarises some of the diatribe, more of which appears in the same journal. Much of this polemic results from the pluralism, or 'loss of authority', which characterises the Postmodern age and is obviously one of the costs paid for this variety.

25) The attacks on Graves' Portland Building resulted in the top pavilions and side garlands being stripped and simplified. For this controversy see my *Kings of Infinite Space*, Academy Editions, London, and St. Martin's Press, New York, 1983, pp.86-97, and the relevant issues of *Progressive Architecture* which carried the controversy for several months from 1982-3.

26) *Content, A Contemporary Focus 1974-1984* ran at the Hirshorn Museum in Washington DC from 4 Oct. 1984-6 Jan. 1985 and has a catalogue written by Howard Fox, Miranda McClintic and Phyllis Rosenzweig. Two small exhibits on the new classicism in art were 'The Classic Tradition in Recent Painting and Sculpture', The Aldrich Museum, Ridgefield Conn., 19 May-Sep. 1985, and 'Beyond Antiquity: Classical References in Contemporary Art' at the DeCordova and Dana Museum and Park, Lincoln, Mass., 15 June-8 Sep. 1985 (catalogues for both). Graham Beal organised 'Second Sight' at the San Francisco Museum of Modern Art, 21 Sep.-16 Nov. 1986 and, as the title suggests, the exhibit had a historicist bias.

27) The Inter-Design Conference on 'Modern Culture, Post-Modern Culture and What Will Come Next' was held in Sapporo, Japan, 17-20 Oct. 1984 and had over 10,000 participants; two other recent conferences I attended which also had wide agendas were at Northwestern University in Oct. 1985 and Hannover, Germany, later that month. Three conferences with published papers are: *The Idea of the Post-Modern – Who is Teaching It?*, Henry Art Gallery, University of Washington, 1981, with contributions by Lawrence Alloway and Donald Kuspit among others; *Postmodernism in Philosophy and the Arts* held in Cerisy-la-Salle, Sep. 1983, published later as *Postmodernism: Search for Criteria*, International Circle for Research in Philosophy, Houston, Texas, 1985, with contributions by writers and philosophers; *Postmodernism*, ICA Documents 4, London, 1985; a conference in May of that year which had contributions by Kenneth Frampton and Jean-François Lyotard among others; the conceptual confusion of Post-Modernism in the arts is well shown by two anthologies which discuss it from time to time and

elide it with Late-Modernism, *Theories of Contemporary Art*, (ed.) Richard Hertz, Prentice Hall, Englewood Cliffs, New Jersey, 1985, and *Art After Modernism; Rethinking Representation,* edited with an introduction by Brian Wallis, foreword by Marcia Tucker, The New Museum of Contemporary Art, New York, n.d (1985). In literary theory the clarity of postmodernism still remains blurred with Late-Modernism. See for instance Charles Newman, *The Post-Modern Aura, The Act of Fiction in an Age of Inflation*, Northwestern University Press, Evanston, 1985. The works of John Barth (note 15) and Umberto Eco (note 17) are exceptions to this lack of definition.

28) Charles Jencks, 'Post-Modern Classicism – The New Synthesis', *Architectural Design 5/6*, London 1980, also published as an *AD Profile*; quote from page 5.

29) Charles Jencks, 'Free-Style Classicism', *Architectural Design 1/2*, Jan. 1982, especially pp. 5-21 and 117-20.

30) See Nicholas Penny, 'Post-Modern Classicism', *Times Literary Supplement*, 3 Apr. 1981 and my response, *TLS*, 24 Apr. 1981.

31) John Summerson in conversation and letters to me between 1981 and 1982 concerning the two monographs mentioned in notes 28 and 29. For the positive view of Stirling see his 'Vitruvius Ludens', *Architectural Review,* Mar. 1983, pp. 19-21.

32) Gavin Stamp views Post-Modernism as 'Illiterate Vernacular'; see his essay of that title in *The Spectator,* 2 Aug. 1986, pp. 15-17.

33) C.P. Snow's notion of 'two cultures', the literary and scientific communities, has also been articulated in a different way as cultures which are 'highbrow, middle brow and low brow' and again into the seven taste-cultures that Herbert Gans defines in *Popular Culture and High Culture,* Basic Books, New York, 1974, pp. 69-103. Market researchers and advertisers group the market place differently again. Depending on what is being measured each one of these fragmented subcultures has relevance. It may well be that the most unifying force today in a pluralist society is mass-culture: TV, films, newspapers and processed food which most of society consumes. This would explain the fact that the British Royal Family enjoys watching *Dallas* and *Dynasty* and vice-versa.

34) For the definition of classical art see the first chapter of Michael Greenhalgh's, *The Classical Tradition in Art*, Harper & Row, London and New York, 1978, pp. 11-18. He mentions more than these definers, but these are the essential ones.

35) The definers that make an artist Free-Style Classicist fall into three general categories: implicit values, formal goals, and explicit goals that are non-formal. Needless to say some of these definers are shared with Canonic Classicists, most particularly the first set – implicit values. A Free-Style Classicist will often portray an idealistic view of the human condition which is fragmented or incomplete ('Ideal Realism, the Forced Contradiction', see Chapter V). He will convey serenity and classical *gravitas*, but with a certain pathos and tension as does Ron Kitaj. The epic grandeur and tragic quality of Canonic Classicism is rarely attempted except through parody – Komar and Melamid – or 'implicit allegory' – Stephen McKenna, the Poiriers and Gérard Garouste. All those Neoclassical qualities of restraint – 'noble simplicity', under-

statement, aristocratic taste – are used by artists such as Mariani and Robert Graham, but with irony and in quotation marks.

The formal goals are much more apparent and most Free-Style Classicists use syncopated proportions, a geometrical composition, a frontal layering to the picture plane or architectural space, an emphasis on clear outline and silhouette, and a sharp depiction of form seen in strong light so that it is 'rational' or intelligible. They may emphasise craft, *techné* and the mastery of the medium to which Pop Art adds a two-dimensional flatness. Integration, *concinnatus*, balance and unity in variety are also shared with Canonic Classicism, but harmonies are broken and dissonant. Thus the recurrent figure of 'dissonant beauty', the constant presence of the oxymoron 'disharmonious harmony' in the work of Salle, Morley, Fischl, Cox, Nava and most Post-Modernists. 'Distorted mimesis' is another oxymoron which current artists share as a formal goal, sometimes the result of using slides and photographs which are taken with telephoto and wide-angle lens; sometimes an indication of the distorted way we can see things; sometimes a mannerism and sometimes a way of adding interest to a predictable figure.

Among the non-formal goals are a new interest in the genres – still life, landscape, portraiture, nudes, narrative painting – and a renewed interest in political and social subject matter. These interests were summarised in two large American exhibits, *Contemporary American Realism Since 1960* (Philadelphia, 1981), and *Content* (Washington DC, 1984). Again contradiction and oxymoron are recurrent ways of dealing with these concerns so we find the mixtures: 'private/public', 'divergent symbolic', 'subversive classical', and 'enigmatic allegory'. Canonic Classicism emphasises the public realm and spirit, and often portrays grand historical themes didactically. Most Post-Modernists have eschewed this goal, but there are a few – Hans Haacke, Ron Kitaj, Ian Hamilton Finlay, Robert Longo – who are 'implicitly didactic' or 'cryptically moral'. Leon Golub and many feminist artists are explicitly moral.

36) Robert Rosenblum shows the wide stylistic range and variety of oppositions which underlie Neoclassicism. Among his categories there is the 'Neoclassic Horrific' (the Romantic Sturm and Drang), 'Neoclassic Erotic', 'Neoclassic Archaeologic' and 'Neoclassic Stoic' (the death bed scenes or theme of the virtuous widow). Historicism and the *Exemplum Virtutis* provide further variety to this complex period. See his important *Transformations in Late Eighteenth-Century Art*, Princeton University Press, Princeton, 1967, pp.11, 20, 24, 28, 34, 56.

37) O.J. Brendel, 'The Classical Style in Modern Art', in W.J. Oates (ed.), *From Sophocles to Picasso: the Present-Day Vitality of the Classical Tradition*, Bloomington, 1962, pp. 71-118.

38) See Donald Kuspit, 'Odd Nerdrum: The Human Constant', catalogue from the Martina Hamilton Gallery and Gallery Germans van Eyk, New York, 1986; partly reprinted in *Second Sight, Biennale IV*, organised by Graham W.J. Beal, San Francisco Museum of Art, 1986, pp. 42-5.

CHAPTER II
Metaphysical Classicism

1) *The Memoirs of Giorgio de Chirico*, 1962, translated from the Italian by Margaret Crosland, Peter Owen, London, 1971, p.15.

2) The Museum of Modern Art's 1982 exhibition organised by William Rubin places the artist's acceptable 'modern' work between 1911 and 1918. See also Claude Gintz, 'The Good, The Bad, The Ugly: Late de Chirico', *Art in America*, summer 1983, pp. 105-8. Also Robert Hughes, 'The Enigmas of de Chirico', *Time Magazine*, 12 Apr. 1982, pp. 70-1.

3) *Late de Chirico 1940-1976*, exhibition and catalogue, (ed.) Rupert Martin, Arnolofini Gallery, Bristol, 1985.

4) Rene Magritte, *Perspective of Madame Recamier*, 1951, Galerie Iolas, Paris.

5) For the influence of Piero della Francesca see Jean Leymarie, *Balthus*, Skiá/Rizzoli, New York, 1982, pp.10-11. For a negative assessment of Balthus as 'Pierrot della Francesca' see Robert Hughes, 'Poisoned Innocence, Surface Calm', a review of the New York retrospective at the Metropolitan Museum, *Time Magazine*, 16 Apr. 1984, pp. 75-6.

6) Mario Praz, 'Canova, or the Erotic Frigidaire', *Art News*, LVI, Nov. 1957, pp. 24-7.

7) For the variations of the Ganymedes myth see Robert Graves, *Greek Myths I*, Penguin Books, Harmondsworth (revised edition) 1960, pp. 115-18.

8) This notion of recalling many versions of a painting parallels the Post-Modern architects' use of anamnesis and, for instance, Claude Levi-Strauss' structural analysis of myth which shows the many versions, layers and transformations which occur in any living myth. The architects Hans Hollein and Robert Stern are particularly adept at layering these references to produce the Post-Modern trope of a 'sign of a sign of a sign'. See the discussion of their work in Chapter X.

9) See for instance Komar and Melamid's version of this allegory in Chapter IV, 'The Origin of Socialist Realism', photo 4.17.

10) See Achille Bonito Oliva, *The Italian Trans-avantgarde*, Giancarlo Politi Editore, Milano, 1980, and *Trans Avant Garde International*, Giancarlo Politi Editore, Milano, 1982.

11) Malcolm Morley statement, *Art in America*, Dec. 1982, p. 60.

12) *Ibid.*

13) For Peter Sari's broken reliefs see Chapter V, photo 5.20.

14) For this critical interpretation of Chia's work see Craig Owens, 'Honor, Power, and the Love of Women', *Art in America*, Jan. 1983, reprinted in *Theories of Contemporary Art*, (ed.) Richard Hertz, Prentice-Hall, Englewood, New Jersey, 1985, pp. 131-42. '*The Idleness of Sisyphus* testifies to the painter's ambivalence about his own activity, to a lack of conviction in painting . . .' Quote page 134.

15) Robert Hughes, 'Three from the Image Machine', *Time Magazine*, 14 Mar. 1983, pp. 83-4; quote page 84.

16) For the various myths of Orion which Garouste may have drawn on see Robert Graves, *op.cit.*, note 7, pp. 151-4.

17) For an early view of symbolist writing, its

obscurity and removal from the public realm see Edmund Wilson, *Axel's Castle*, 1931. For Symbolist Art see Edward Lucie-Smith, *Symbolist Art*, Thames and Hudson, London, 1972, and Robert Delevoy, *Symbolists and Symbolism*, Rizzoli, New York, 1978.

18) For the way the art market has distorted our appreciation of art and changed the way it is produced and seen by artists today see Robert Hughes, 'On Art and Money', *The New York Review of Books*, 6 Dec. 1984, pp. 20-7 and Suzi Gablik, *Has Modernism Failed?*, Thames and Hudson, London, 1984, especially 'Secularism, The Disenchantment of Art (Julian Schnabel Paints a Portrait of God)'.

CHAPTER III
Narrative Classicism

1) For these themes and the *exemplum virtutis* see Robert Rosenblum, *Transformations in Late Eighteenth Century Art*, Princeton University Press, Princeton, New Jersey, 1967, pp. 50-106.
2) Gérard, in 1793, claimed the arts should make 'one hate vice, love virtue, and they should charm the eye'. Quoted from Rosenblum, *op.cit.*, p. 85.
3) *Ibid.*, pp. 55-6. 'Les actions vertueuses et héroiques des grands hommes, les exemples d'humanité, de générosité, de courage, de mépris des dangers et même de la vie, d'un zele passioné pour l'honneur et le salut de sa Patrie, et surtout de défense de sa religion'.
4) Claudio Bravo has painted Danae in a bedroom being showered by gold coins, while Bruno Civitico has painted her more convincingly in a New England living room, see photo 4.6. I have appropriated the Danae theme in the design of a light produced by Aram Designs, London, 1985 (edition of five).
5) See catalogue devoted to his exhibiton, 'New Paintings and Drawings, James Valerio', Allan Frumkin Gallery, New York, (n.d) 1983, p. 7. For another interview see John Arthur, *Realists at Work*, Watson-Guptill Publications, New York, 1983, pp. 130-43.
6) For a good discussion of Ron Kitaj's work see *Kitaj, Paintings, Drawings, Pastels*, with articles by John Ashbery, Joe Shannon, Jane Livingston, Timothy Hyman; Thames and Hudson, London, 1983. The quote is, I believe, from an article by Timothy Hyman.
7) See Chapters X and XI where anthropomorphism is discussed in the work of Dixon, Graves, Robert Krier and others.
8) Thomas Lawson, 'Last Exit: Painting', *Artforum*, Oct. 1981 and reprinted in *Theories of Contemporary Art*, (ed.) Richard Hertz, Prentice-Hall, Englewood, New Jersey, 1985, pp. 143-57; quote page 150.
9) *Ibid.*, p.149.
10) Craig Owens, 'Honor, Power and the Love of Women', also reprinted in *Theories of Contemporary Art*, *op.cit.*, note 8, pp.131-41. 'What we are witnessing, then, is the emergence of a new – or renewed – authoritarianism masquerading as anti-authoritarianism. Today, acquiescence to authority is proclaimed as a radical act' (Donald Kuspit on David Salle), quote p. 136.

11) Eric Fischl, press release of Edward Thorp Gallery, New York, Feb. 1982, quoted in *Eric Fischl Paintings*, curator Bruce W. Ferguson, Mendel Art Gallery, Saskatoon, Canada, 1985, p.16.
12) Robert Hughes, 'Three from the Image Machine', *Time Magazine*, 14 Mar. 1983, pp. 83-4. See also the conclusion to this book, photo 11.6.
13) Maurice Berger, 'The Dynamics of Power: An Interview with Robert Longo', *Arts Magazine*, Jan. 1985, pp. 88-9.
14) Ian Hamilton Finlay, 'Liberty, Terror and Virtue, The Little Spartan War and the Third Reich Revisited', *New Arcadians Journal*, No.15, autumn 1984, p. 20.
15) *Ibid.*, p. 22.
16) See *Ian Hamilton Finlay, A Visual Primer* by Yves Abrioux, with introductory notes and commentaries by Stephen Bann, Reaktion Books, Edinburgh, 1985, pp.15-21. Also note 14 and articles in the *Observer, Sunday Times Magazine, TLS, Guardian*, etc.
17) *Op.cit.*, note 14; quote also from *Studio International*, Apr. 1984.

CHAPTER IV
Allegorical Classicism

1) Eunice Agar, 'Bruno Civitico, A New Spirit of Classicism', *American Artist*, Mar. 1982, pp. 42-7, 73, 78, 79.
2) *Ibid*, p. 78.
3) Eunice Agar, 'Lincoln Perry', *American Artist*, June 1984, p. 98.
4) The two shows on classicism in 1985 which included mostly American artists were 'The Classic Tradition In Recent Painting and Sculpture', 19 May-1 Sep., at The Aldrich Museum of Contemporary Art, Ridge-field, Conn.; and 'Beyond Antiquity: Classical References in Contemporary Art', DeCordova & Dana Park Museum, Lincoln, Mass., 15 June-8 Sep. Catalogues available for both. An earlier show 'Modern Masters of Classical Realism' was put on at the Univ. of Wisconsin, Oshkosh, 8 Nov.-14 Dec. 1984. These three small shows signal the emergent interest in contemporary classicism in art five years after the movement had started in architecture.
5) Peter Wollen, 'Komar & Melamid, Painting History', from *Komar & Melamid*, catalogue published in conjunction with exhibitions in Edinburgh & Oxford, 1985. Published by the Fruitmarket Gallery, Edinburgh, 1985, pp. 38-57.
6) *Ibid.*, pp. 55-6.
7) David Ligare, 'A Letter to Stephen Doherty', *American Artist*, Sep. 1984, p. 35.
8) Jon Thomson, 'The Warning Hand' in *Stephen McKenna* catalogue, Raab Galerie, Berlin, 1985, pp. 23-31.
9) *Ibid.*, p. 23.
10) *Ibid.*, p. 29. For another view see Ian Jeffrey, 'In Touch with History: Painting by Stephen McKenna', in *Stephen McKenna* catalogue to the Museum of Modern Art show of his work in Oxford, 1983, p. 22.

CHAPTER V
Realist Classicism

1) C. M. Bowra, *The Greek Experience*, Weidenfeld & Nicolson, London, 1957, pp. 148-9. The common word for statue, *eikon*, meant literally 'likeness or image' as Bowra points out, and sculptors were defined as those who 'make an imitation of the body'.
2) E. H. Gombrich, *Art and Illusion*, Phaidon, London, 1960, and *Meditations on a Hobby Horse and Other Essays In the Theory of Art*, Phaidon, London, 1963.
3) See Frank H. Goodyear Jr., *Contemporary American Realism Since 1960*, New York Graphic Society, Boston, 1981. The introduction and first chapter discuss pluralism as an essential quality of current realism, agreeing in this with other experts such as Linda Nochlin.
4) See Linda Nochlin, 'The Realist Criminal and the Abstract Law', *Art in America*, Sep.-Nov. 1973, reprinted in Richard Hertz, *Theories of Contemporary Art*, Prentice Hall, New Jersey, 1985, pp. 25-48.
5) Craig Owens, 'The Allegorical Impulse: Towards a Theory of Postmodernism', in *Art After Modernism*, (ed.) Brian Wallis, Godine & The New Museum of Contemporary Art, New York, 1984, p. 211. The article was reprinted from *October*, No. 12 (spring 1980), pp. 67-86 and No. 13, pp. 59-80.
6) See George W. Nuebert, 'Working Method' in *Robert Graham, Statues*, catalogue of Walker Art Centre show, 1981, pp. 39-42.
7) *Ibid.*, p. 17.
8) See William Bailey in discussion, Mark Strand, *The Art of the Real*, Clarkson Potter, New York, 1984, p. 37.
9) See Edward Lucie-Smith's critical essay,'Ben Johnson', London, 1984, n.p.
10) Edward Lucie-Smith, *Steve Hawley*, catalogue of the Alexander F. Milliken Gallery Exhibition, New York, 1984.
11) *Ibid.*, p. 8.

CHAPTER VI
The Classical Sensibility

1) Fairfield Porter quoted from Joe Shannon, 'Wintry Visions', *Art News*, Oct. 1982, pp. 98-100.
2) Rodrigo Moynihan in interview with David Sylvester, in *Rodrigo Moynihan*, catalogue, Galerie Claude Bernard, Paris, 1984, n.p.
3) See Michael Peppiatt, 'Avigdor Arikha: A Hunger in the Eye', *Art International*, Sep.-Oct. 1982, pp. 18-28.
4) Gerrit Henry,'Avigdor Arikha at Marlborough', *Art in America*, Mar. 1981, p. 129-30.
5) The rationalist myth of man starting society in a state of nature with a primitive camp fire and primitive hut is given architectural form by Vitruvius and many subsequent architectural writers after the first century B.C. See his *Ten Books of Architecture*, Book 2.1.2. For a general discussion see Joseph Rykwert, *On Adam's House in Paradise*, New York, 1972, pp. 29-113.
6) See *Resika, A Twenty-Five Year Survey*, 9 Apr.-19

May 1985, catalogue published by the Artist's Choice Museum, NYC, 1985, p. 8. Paul Resika also stressed this influence to me when we talked about the current classicism.

7) See 'The American Cemetery' in Albert Fein, 'The American City: The Ideal and the Real' published in *The Rise of an American Architecture*, (ed.) Edgar Kaufmann Jr., Pall Mall Press, London, 1970, pp. 81-3.

8) 'Contemporary Arcadian Painting' was an exhibition put on at the Robert Schoelkopf Gallery, Nov.-Dec. 1982. For an interesting discussion see George M. Tapley Jr., 'The Arcadian Ethos in Contemporary Painting', *Arts Magazine*, pp. 124-5. Besides those mentioned in my text, Bruno Civitico, Martha Erlebacher and Richard Chiriani also took part. The New Arcadians, a Yorkshire group led by the writer Patrick Eyres and the painters Ian Gardner and Grahame Jones, include in their *New Arcadians Journal* the work of this group and Ian Hamilton Finlay. Address – 40 North View, Wilsden, Bradford, West Yorkshire.

9) Lennart Anderson painted an abstract Bacchanale in the late 1950s as a parody and in the late 1970s saw the point of taking the idea seriously; see the interview in Mark Strand, *The Art of the Real*, Clarkson Potter, New York, 1984, pp. 140-9.

10) See below pp. 166-8, and the book *Ian Hamilton Finlay – A Visual Primer* by Yves Abrioux, Reaktion Books, Edinburgh, 1985, especially Chapter 10, 'Et in Arcadia Ego', pp. 205-13, which shows the subject transformed from various past versions, using tanks, machine guns etc. as emblems of death.

11) Post-Modernism is defined by Umberto Eco as recapturing traditional values and forms through irony etc. in an 'age of lost innocence'. See his *Postscript to the Name of the Rose*, Harcourt Brace Jovanovich, New York, London, 1983, pp. 65-72.

12) For these influences on Anderson and others such as Degas, Raphael, Titian, Tintoretto, Poussin and Ingres see reference above note 9.

13) See note 8 above for the New Arcadians.

14) As he told me in conversation 1985; see also the book on his work referred to in note 10.

15) This substitution of history as content for process as content is a quite logical development from Modernism to Post-Modernism. The idea was first suggested by my friend Judge Stephen Breyer in conversation.

16) For a brief discussion see Jill Wechsler, 'Alan Feltus: The Mystery in Painting', *American Artist Magazine*, Apr. 1980, pp.58-63.

CHAPTER VII
The Fundamentalists of Architecture

1) For Le Corbusier's irony see my 'Irony in Form and Content in Charles Jeanneret – Le Corbusier', reprinted from *Arena* in *Modern Movements in Architecture*, Penguin Books, Harmondsworth (second edition) 1985, pp. 153-65. For James Stirling's use of irony as double-coding see Chapter IX and my 'The Casual, The Shocking and the Well-Ordered Acropolis', *Architectural Design*, 54, 3/4, 1982, pp. 49-55.

Colin Rowe has also pointed out the dialectical nature of Le Corbusier's work in much of his writing and this leads to a form of irony. See also Vincent Scully, 'The Age of Irony' in his *Modern Architecture*, George Braziller, New York (revised edition) 1974, pp. 49-62.

2) Colin Rowe and Reyner Banham have continuously pointed out the classical strain within Modernism. See Rowe's 'Neo-Classicism and Modern Architecture I' (1956-7) and 'Neo-Classicism and Modern Architecture II' (1956-7) reprinted in *The Mathematics of the Ideal Villa and Other Essays*, MIT Press, Cambridge, Mass., 1976, pp. 119-58. For Banham's analysis of the classical strain see his entry 'Neoclassicism' in *Encyclopaedia of Modern Architecture*, Thames and Hudson, 1963, pp. 202-5, and the first three chapters and index entry 'classicism' of his *Theory and Design in the First Machine Age*, The Architectural Press, London, 1960.

3) For primitivism in Modern art see the catalogue and book to the MOMA show '*Primitivism' in 20th Century Art: Affinity of the Tribal and the Modern*, (ed.) William Rubin, and especially his chapter on Picasso, New York, 1984, pp. 252-4. For tragedy in Le Corbusier see my *Le Corbusier and the Tragic View of Architecture*, Penguin Books, Harmondsworth (second edition) 1987, especially the introduction. Vincent Scully mentions the concept of tragedy in his *Modern Architecture, op. cit.*, note 1, pp. 41, 49-51.

4) Vincent Scully, 'Introduction: The End of the Century Finds a Poet', in *Aldo Rossi, Buildings and Projects*, Rizzoli, New York, 1985, p. 12.

5) Aldo Rossi, *The Architecture of the City*, Opposition Books, MIT Press, Cambridge, Mass., 1982.

6) O.M. Ungers, *Architecture as Theme*, Electa, Milano, 1982; Colin Rowe, 'Collage City', *The Architectural Review*, Aug. 1975 and later *Collage City*, MIT Press, Cambridge, Mass., 1978; Kevin Lynch, *The Image of the City*, MIT Press, Cambridge, Mass., 1960 and *Good City Form*, MIT Press, Cambridge, Mass., 1981; Robert Venturi, *Complexity and Contradiction in Architecture*, MOMA, New York, 1966; Robert Krier, *Urban Space*, Academy Editions, London, Rizzoli, New York, 1979 (German 1975); Charles Jencks and Nathan Silver, *Adhocism*, Secker and Warburg, London, Doubleday, New York, 1972.

7) 'For Aldo Rossi the European city has become the house of the dead. Its history, its function, has ended . . .' Peter Eisenman, 'Houses of Memory' printed as part of an introduction to Rossi's American text *The Architecture of the City, op. cit.*, note 5.

8) For this idea see my 'The Irrational Rationalists – The Rats Since 1960' reprinted in *Late-Modern Architecture*, Academy Editions, London, and Rizzoli, New York, 1980, pp. 133-4.

9) *Ibid.*, p. 133-4. Also my *Current Architecture* (*Architecture Today*), Academy Editions, London, Abrams, New York, 1982, pp. 170-4. *The Language of Post-Modern Architecture, op.cit.*, pp. 91-2.

10) *Op.Cit.*, note 6, and for O.M. Ungers 'The New Abstraction' see my 'Abstract Representation', *Architectural Design*, 7/8, 1983, pp. 23-58.

11) *Ibid.*, pp. 36-7.

12) *Op.cit.*, note 6.

13) *Albert Speer, Architecture 1932-1942*, foreword by Albert Speer, (ed.) Leon Krier, introduction by Lars Olof Larsen, *AAM*, Brussels, 1985. The book contains an article by Leon Krier 'An Architecture of

Desire', which starts with the contentious remark 'Albert Speer is without a doubt the most famous architect of the 20th Century . . .', pp. 217-32. Krier is of course right that we should look again at Speer's work, and as James Stirling remarked to me 'Speer didn't ruin classicism for all time' (see the discussion in the last chapter), but there are two points to be made. Speer's architecture is intimidating and an oversimplified version of the classical language. As Speer himself remarks in the foreword – 'Karl Arndt is right to detect Hitler's desire for power and the submission of others in my buildings' (p. 213). Secondly, a point that is usually overlooked or denied, meaning in architecture is *always* partly associational and as long as the Nazi associations are still fresh in many people's minds they have a perfect right to object every time they see them revived. Post-Modern Classicism must acknowledge these associations and articulate the language to avoid it, which means the genre – 'intimidating/sublime' – must either be avoided in Germany or used in an unambiguous way to make some other point.

14) Colin Rowe, 'The Revolt of the Senses' in 'Leon Krier, Houses, Palaces, Cities', *Architectural Design*, 7/8, 1984, p. 8. This issue of *AD* is the most comprehensive survey of his work to date.

15) Jaquelin Robertson, 'The Empire Strikes Back', *ibid.*, p. 11.

16) For the semantic drawbacks see my discussion in *The Language of Post-Modern Architecture*, pp. 108-9. Subsequently Krier has started to elaborate a semantics of form. See his 'Names and Nicknames' in the monograph cited in note 14, pp. 108-9. This has a predictable Platonic bias as if 'the cathedral', 'the town hall', 'the palace' – the three types her names – were both eternal and comprehensive for our society.

17) Frank Gehry was attacked quite strongly by Leon Krier in a symposium on architecture in Florida, circa 1977. Subsequently he has adapted 'small block planning' in his excellent university buildings for Loyola University in Los Angeles (finished in 1984) and recommended Krier for his position as the Director of the new institute of Skidmore, Owings and Merrill; a nice and felicitous illustration of the way opposite polemicists, or designers of different persuasions, can influence each other and sometimes agree.

18) See the Museum of Modern Art Catalogue to the exhibition 'Ricardo Bofill and Leon Krier, Architecture, Urbanism and History', MOMA, New York, July 1985, p. 23.

19) Andres Duany and Elizabeth Plater-Zyberk, 'The Town of Seaside', designed 1978-83, *Design*, p. 3.

20) Cesar Pelli, like many architects, is not keen to be classified in any school, but more than most others, his work does cut across categories. His approach is pragmatic and Late-Modern in its emphasis on technology and construction, but realist and Post-Modern with respect to veiled imagery, especially anthropomorphism and classicism. Like Thomas Beeby, whose work his resembles in some respects, he likes to start from a constructional basis.

21) See my 'Mario Botta and the New Tuscanism', *Architectural Design*, 9/10, 1983, pp. 82-5. For a general discussion of the Tuscan style see James S. Ackerman, 'The Tuscan/Rustic Order: A Study in the Metaphorical Language of Order', *Journal of the*

Society of Architectural Historians, Mar. 1983, pp. 15-34.

22) Demetri Porphyrios, 'Classicism Is Not A Style', *Architectural Design*, 5/6, 1982.

23) Demetri Porphyrios and I have discussed our differences over the years and in print; for his argument against me see the previous note and for my answer see 'Abstract Representation', *Architectural Design*, 7/8, 1983, p. 15. The controversy continued in later issues of *AD*.

CHAPTER VIII
Revivalist Classicism

1) For the best critical discussion of the controversy on the Getty Museum see Ruth Wilford Caccavale, 'The J. Paul Getty Museum', *The Critical Edge*, (ed.) Tod A. Mareder, MIT Press, Cambridge, Mass., 1985, pp. 113-24. This article gives most of the basic sources and arguments surrounding a controversy that lasted from 1974-80. William Wilson's remarks are in 'A Preview of Pompeii-on-the-Pacific', *Los Angeles Times*, 6 Jan. 1974, CAL 44.

2) Reyner Banham, 'Lair of the Looter', *New Society*, 5 May 1977, p. 238; my counter opinion was expressed in *The Language of Post-Modern Architecture, op. cit.*, p. 95.

3) Norman Neuerburg, 'The New J. Paul Getty Museum', *Archaeology 23*, July 1974, pp. 175-81 and references in note 1.

4) My guide in these views is William L. MacDonald, the expert on Roman architecture and urbanism, with whom I had the good fortune to visit the Getty Museum in the spring of 1986.

5) J.Didion, 'Getty's Little House of the Highway', *Esquire*, Mar. 1977, p. 30.

6) Robert Stern was taught by Vincent Scully at Yale University, is a friend of Scully, and thus is fully aware of the arguments about the relevance of the Shingle Style to America's East Coast. See especially Vincent Scully, *The Shingle Style Today or The Historian's Revenge*, George Braziller, New York, 1974. For an imaginative analysis of Stern's Bozzi House see Gavin Macrae-Gibson, *The Secret Life of Buildings, An American Mythology for Modern Architecture*, MIT Press, Cambridge Mass., 1985, pp. 98-117.

7) See *Philip Johnson/John Burgee Architecture 1979-1985*, introduction by Carleton Knight III, Rizzoli, New York, p. 9.

8) *Ibid.*, p. 10.

9) See Ada Louise Huxtable, 'Rebuilding Architecture', *New York Review of Books*, Dec. 1983, pp. 55-61. Also *Progressive Architecture*, Feb. 1984, p. 68 (a special issue devoted to Johnson and Burgee).

10) *Progressive Architecture*, Feb. 1984, p. 69.

11) *Op. cit.*, note 7, pp. 6-11.

12) Leon Krier, Christopher Alexander and I have been emphasising the difficulties of producing good architecture under the present production system which requires high-speed volume building which tends to divorce the product from both its historical context and ultimate users. Johnson realises the problem more than other architects because of his enormous success and has said to reporters and at the symposium at the University of Virginia, 1983, such

things as: 'how to design two million square feet that should not be in this part of Boston . . . I am a whore and I am paid very well for high-rise buildings', an attitude which was recently censored by Anthony Lewis in 'The Golden Goose', *New York Times*, 17 July 1986.

13) For the comparison of the AT&T to a Chippendale Highboy see Paul Goldberger, 'A Major Monument of Post-Modernism', *New York Times*, 31 Mar. 1978, B4; Arthur Drexler apparently made this comparison first. For the Lincoln Continental and Rolls Royce comparisons see my 'Late-Modernism and Post-Modernism', *Architectural Design 48*, Nov.-Dec. 1978, reprinted in *Late-Modern Architecture*, Academy Editions, 1980, p. 20. The best compilation of critical reviews on the AT&T is in Gregory Gilbert, *The Critical Edge*, (ed.) Tod Marder, MIT Press, Cambridge, Mass., 1985, pp. 47-62.

14) *Op. cit.*, note 7, p. 7.

15) Assistant Dean Peter Wood, quoted in *The Daily Cougar*, University of Houston, Vol. 50, No. 43, 11 Nov. 1983.

16) *Houston Chronicle*, 12 Nov. 1983, p. 14, section 1.

17) John Burgee, *ibid.*, p. 14, section 1.

18) John Zemanek, associate professor of architecture quoted in *The Daily Cougar*, 9 Nov. 1983, pp. 1,9.

19) Robert Venturi, 'Diversity, Relevance and Representation in Historicism, or *plus ça change . . .* plus a Plea for Pattern all over Architecture with a Postscript on my Mother's House', *Architectural Record,* June 1982, pp. 114-19.

20) See *Progressive Architecture* devoted to their early work, Oct. 1983, pp. 69-91, p. 70 for the quote.

21) *Ibid.*, and in a lecture they gave at the RIBA, June 1985, coinciding with an exhibition of their work, 'The Architecture of Kohn Pedersen Fox', New York, 1985.

22) 'Cincinnati Centerpiece', *Progressive Architecture*, Oct. 1985, p. 71.

CHAPTER IX
Urbanist Classicism

1) Jane Jacobs, *The Death and Life of Great American Cities,* Random House, New York; quote from the Penguin edition, Harmondsworth, London, 1964, pp. 162-3.

2) Alice Coleman, *Utopia on Trial: Vision and Reality in Planned Housing,* Hilary Shipman, London, 1985.

3) Daniel Solomon, 'San Francisco, the Continuity of Urban Life', *Architecture California,* Sep.-Oct. 1982, pp. 10-13.

4) Douglas Davis, 'Raiders of the Lost Arch', *Newsweek,* 20 Jan. 1986, pp. 66-8.

5) Frank Israel, 'The Westside Pavilion', *LA Architect,* Feb. 1986, pp. 6-7.

6) Francis Tibbalds & Urban Design Group, 'Towards a U.D.G. Manifesto', Apr. 1986, p.4.

7) Terry Farrell Partnership, 'Charing Cross Development – an Urban Proposal', *Architectural Design Series,* Mar. 1986, pp. 14-15.

8) Jane Jacobs 'Urban Supertoy Subdues Renewal Bulldozer', *Progressive Architecture,* Sep. 1969, pp. 144-53.

9) Barton Myers and George Baird, 'Vacant Lottery',

Design Quarterly 108.

10) Barton Myers' presentation to the jury of eight (of which I was a member) was the most persuasive because of its understanding of democracy and the way it could be accommodated architecturally. Although I voted in favour of Graves' scheme because of its handling of architectural elements, Myers' project was superior in terms of the social use of the central square.

11) For Stirling's Düsseldorf project see Chapter VII. Bofill's Les Arcades du Lac was conceived in 1971, completed in 1983, but the major design work was done between 1973-5.

12) See the issue of *Architectural Review* which features the classical work of Bofill; Vol. CLXXI, No. 1024, June 1982, p. 30. This has an interview with Peter Hodgkinson and an interesting critique of the Taller.

13) Gavin Stamp, 'The Master Builder', *The Spectator,* 7 Feb. 1981, p. 24.

14) Conversation with Ricardo Bofill, Nov. 1980, before his exhibition at the Architectural Association. See my 'Ricardo Bofill and the Taller – Six Characters in Search of a Script', *AA Publications,* Jan. 1981, pp. 38-47.

15) For a discussion of Colin Rowe's *Collage City* see Chapter VII. Rowe has influenced Stirling since his university days as he recounts in the introduction to the monograph, *James Stirling*, Rizzoli, New York, Architectural Press, London, 1985.

16) The epithet 'punk clip-ons' was used at a Symposium held by *Architecural Design* in the summer of 1984 at which Demetri Porphyrios and Leon Krier spoke against the scheme; William Curtis in his attack on Post-Modern Classicism in general uses the epithet 'High-Tech Costume Jewellery': see William Curtis, 'Principle vs. Pastiche, Perspective on Some Recent Classicisms', *Architectural Review,* Aug. 1984, pp. 11-21, quote p. 20.

17) Jean-François Lyotard, *The Postmodern Condition: A Report on Knowledge,* Manchester University Press, Manchester, 1984, pp. 25, 82.

18) Stirling mentioned this to me when we visited the building in the summer of 1984. For a more extended discussion see my 'The Casual, the Shocking and the Well-Ordered Acropolis', *Architectural Design 54,* 3/4, 1984, pp. 48-55.

19) The opinion that the Neue Staatsgalerie is the most mature work of Post-Modernism for its time was also put by Paul Goldberger in his review in *The New York Times,* 10 Apr. 1985, p. 22.

20) 'James Stirling, Michael Wilford & Associates', *Architectural Design 56,* 1/2, 1985-6, pp. 70-95.

CHAPTER X
Eclectic Classicism

1) Robert Venturi, *Complexity and Contradiction in Architecture*, MOMA Publication, New York, 1966, p.23.

2) Robert Venturi, 'Diversity, Relevance and Representation in Historicism, or *plus ça change . . .* plus a Plea for Pattern all over Architecture with a Postscript on my Mother's House', Architectural

Record, June 1982, pp.114-19. Also reprinted in Robert Venturi and Denise Scott-Brown's *A View from the Campidoglio, Selected Essays 1958-1984*, Harper & Row, New York, 1984, pp.108-19.

3) Italian Architects and teachers at the design school in Ulm were the first to articulate the ideas on semiotics and architecture in the late 1950s. Christian Norberg-Schulz's book *Intentions in Architecture*, MIT Press, 1963, emphasised the symbolic component of the building task, while George Baird and I introduced the concepts of different kinds of architectural sign and multivalence into the discussion. 'Meaning in Architecture', *Arena*, June 1967, was an issue of the Architectural Association Journal devoted to the subject. Some of these articles with new ones were collected in *Meaning in Architecture*, Barrie & Rockliffe, London, George Braziller, New York, 1969.

4) The idea of the different kinds of architectural sign was developed in my 'Rhetoric and Architecture' a paper given at the semiotics and architecture conference in Barcelona in Mar. 1972; published later in *Architectural Association Quarterly*, Vol.4, No.3, pp. 4-17.

5) 'Symbolic or Signolic Architecture?', *Art and Design,* London, Oct. 1985, pp.14-17,48.

6) Robert Stern, 'Chicago Tribune Tower', *Post-Modern Classicism, Architectural Design*, 5/6, 1980, p. 35.

7) The Gable Building by Kazuhiro Ishii, Tokyo, 1978-80, uses Palladian, Venturian and Japanese motifs to give presence to the office; see my *The Language of Post-Modern Architecture*, Academy Editions, London, 1984, p. 157.

8) See Stanislaus von Moos, *Le Corbusier: Elements of a Synthesis*, MIT Press, Cambridge, Mass., 1979, pp.280-92, and my own new introduction to *Le Corbusier and the Tragic View of Architecture*, Penguin Books, Harmondsworth, London, 1987.

9) Arata Isozaki, 'Fujimi Country Club', *Post-Modern Classicism, Architectural Design, 5/6, 1980*, p. 83.

10) Arata Isozaki, 'Notes', in the special issue of *Space Design* devoted to his work, Jan. 1984, pp. 97-9.

11) *ibid.*, p. 99.

12) Hajime Yatsuka, 'Textual Strategy and Post-Modernism', *ibid.*, pp. 182-6; and Hiroyuki Suzuki, 'A Tale without a Message: Arata Isozaki's Tsukuba Centre Building', pp. 187-9.

13) 'Isozaki and Radical Eclecticism', *Architectural Design*, Jan. 1977, pp. 42-8.

14) *Op.cit.*, note 10, p. 98.

15) *Ibid.*, p. 153.

16) For some of this Japanese work see Chapter VII and my *The Language of Post-Modern Architecture*, Academy Editions, London, 1984, p. 138 ff.

17) Charles Jencks, *Towards a Symbolic Architecture*, Academy Editions, London, Rizzoli, New York, 1984, first and last chapters.

18) Hal Foster, '(Post) Modern Polemics', *New German Critique*, No. 33, autumn 1984, pp. 67-78, and Roland Barthes, 'The Death of the Author', *Image/Music/Text* (trans. Stephen Heath), Hill and Wang, New York, 1977.

19) See 'Plocek House', *Post-Modern Classicism, Architectural Design* 5/6, 1980, pp. 129-30; there are referential sketches here and in addition to the influences mentioned one can see those of Raphael's Villa Madama, Ledoux's Salt Work, and Le Corbusier.

20) Three aspects of Post-Modernism are mentioned in the Humana public relations brochure to justify the building – historicism, contextualism and anthropomorphism – an indication that by 1985 these values had become widespread enough to be used by a corporation; see *The Humana Building*, Louisville, Kentucky, 1986, especially the section prefaced by Paul Goldberger, 'The Building's Place In Architecture', p.19.

CHAPTER XI
The Emergent Rules

1) *Antonio Filarete Traktat über die Bankunst*, (ed.) W. Von Oettingen, Vienna, 1890, IX, p.291. Quoted and translated by Erwin Panofsky, *Renaissance and Renascences in Western Art*, 1960; taken from the Paladin Edition, Granada, London, 1970, pp. 19-20.

2) L.B. Alberti, *Della Pittura*, Florence, 1435, preface. Quoted from Michael Greenhalgh, *The Classical Tradition in Art*, Harper and Row, London and New York, 1978, p.80.

3) T.S. Eliot, 'Tradition and the Individual Talent', *Sacred Wood*, Methuen & Co., London, 1920, pp. 49-50.

4) E.H. Gombrich, 'The Tradition of General Knowledge', *Ideas and Idols*, Phaidon, Oxford, 1979, pp. 21-2.

5) For the idea that Raphael's *School of Athens* epitomizes the classical tradition and for a discussion see Michael Greenhalgh, *op. cit.*, pp.15-17.

6) For a discussion of this space and mural see David van Zanten. 'Felix Duban and the Buildings of the Ecole des Beaux-Arts, 1832-1840', *Journal of the Society of Architectural Historians*, Vol. XXXVIII, No. 3, Oct. 1978, pp. 161-74, especially pp. 170-1.

7) See Bruno Zevi, *The Modern Language of Architecture*, University of Washington Press, Seattle and London, 1978, pp.15, 17 (translated from the 1973 Italian edition).

8) *Ibid.*, p.17.

9) Sigfried Giedion, 'The Demand for Morality in Architecture', *Space, Time and Architecture*, Harvard University Press, Cambridge, Mass., (fifth edition), 1967, Part IV, especially pages 292-5 where morality is equated with forms that are not eclectic or historical and where they have a 'fitness for purpose'.

10) For the attacks on Charles Moore and the Piazza d'Italia, see the letters to the editor, *Progressive Architecture*, following its publication in Nov. 1978, especially Jan. 1979.

11) Wolf von Eckhardt, 'A Pied Piper in Hobbit Land', *Time*, 23 Aug. 1982, pp. 62-3.

12) The quote from Vitruvius' Seventh Book on Architecture VII, V, 3-4, is discussed by E.H. Gombrich, *The Sense of Order, A Study in the Psychology of Decorative Art*, Phaidon Press, Oxford (second edition) 1984, p. 20.

13) See E.H. Gombrich, 'The Origins of Stylistic Terminology', *Norm and Form, Studies in the Art of the Renaissance*, Phaidon, London and New York (fourth edition) 1985, pp. 83-6.

14) *Content, A Contemporary Focus*, 1974-84, Hirshorn Museum, Washington DC, 4-6 Jan. 1985;

curated by Howard N. Fox; essays by Fox, Miranda McClintic and Phyllis Rosenzweig.

15) For these categories and the best discussion of realist painting today see Frank H. Goodyear Jr. *Contemporary American Realism Since 1960*, exhibition catalogue and book, New York Graphic Society, Boston, 1981.

16) Strindberg's dualism is discussed in James McFarlane's, 'The Mind of Modernism', *Modernism 1890-1930*, (eds.) Malcolm Bradbury and James McFarlane, Penguin Books, Harmondsworth, London, 1976; quote from p. 88.

17) For the recent conferences, exhibitions and commissions involving the collaboration between artists and architects see *Collaboration*, (ed.) Barbara Lee Diamonstein, Architectural Press.

18) 'Richard Shaffer Interview' with Susan Freudenheim, 1983, in *Richard Shaffer, Selected Work*, 1979-1983, LA Louver Gallery catalogue, Venice, California, 1984.

Bibliography

GENERAL

Books

ALDEGHERI,CLAUDIO E SABINI, MAURIGIO, *Immagini del Post-Moderno*, Edizione Clura, Venezia, 1983.

COX, HARVEY, *Religion in the Secular City: Toward a Postmodern Theology*, Simon and Schuster, New York, 1984.

ECO, UMBERTO, *Postscript to the Name of the Rose*, Harcourt Brace Jovanovich, New York and London, 1984 (first published in Italian in 1983).

JENCKS, CHARLES, *What Is Post-Modernism?*, Academy Editions, London, St. Martin's Press, New York, 1986.

HASSAN, IHAB, *Paracriticisms: Seven Speculations on the Times*, University of Illinois Press, Urbana, 1975.

LYOTARD, JEAN-FRANÇOIS, *The Postmodern Condition: A Report on Knowledge*, Manchester University Press, 1984.

NEWMAN, CHARLES, *The Post-Modern Aura: The Age of Fiction in the Age of Inflation*, Northwestern University Press, Evanston, Illinois, 1985.

POGGIOLI, RENATO, *The Theory of the Avant-Garde*, Harvard University Press, Cambridge, Mass., 1968.

TAYLOR, MARK C., *E ЯRING, A Postmodern A/Theology*, The University of Chicago Press, Chicago and London, 1984.

Articles

BARTH, JOHN, 'The Literature of Replenishment, Postmodernist Fiction', *The Atlantic*, Jan. 1980.

BRADBURY, MALCOLM AND MCFARLANE, JAMES,'The Name and Nature of Modernism', in *Modernism 1890-1930*, Penguin Books, Harmondsworth, London, 1976.

FIEDLER, LESLIE, 'The New Mutants', 1965, *The Collected Essays of Leslie Fiedler*, Vol. II, Stein and Day, New York, 1970, and *A Fiedler Reader*, Stein and Day, New York, 1977.

GRAFF, GERALD, 'The Myth of the Postmodern Breakthrough', reprinted in *Literature Against Itself*, University of Chicago Press, Chicago and London, 1979.

HASSAN, IHAB, 'Joyce, Becket and the Postmodern Imagination', *The Quarterly*, XXXIV, autumn 1975.

——. 'POSTmodernISM: A Paracritical Bibliography', *New Literary History 3*, No. 1, autumn 1971, reprinted in *Paracriticisms*.

——. 'The Question of Postmodernism', in *Romanticism, Modernism, Postmodernism*, (ed.) Harry R. Garvin, Bucknell University Press, Lewisberg, Toronto and London, 1980.

HOWE, IRVING, 'Mass Society and Postmodern Fiction', 1963, reprinted in *The Decline of the New*, Harcourt Brace and World, New York, 1970.

HUYSSEN, ANDREAS, 'Mapping the Postmodern', *New German Critique*, No.33, autumn 1984.

INTERNATIONAL CIRCLE FOR RESEARCH IN PHILOSOPHY, *Postmodernism: Search for Criteria*, Houston, Texas, 1985.

KERMODE, FRANK, 'Modernisms', in *Modern Essays*, London, 1971.

KOHLER, MICHAEL, 'Postmodernismus: Ein begrriffsgeschictlicher Uberblick', *Americastudien 22*, (1977) 8-18.

STERN, ROBERT, 'The Doubles of Post-Modern', *Harvard Architectural Review*, Vol. I, spring 1980.

ART

Books

GOODYEAR, JR., FRANK H., *Contemporary American Realism Since 1960*, New York Graphic Society, Boston, 1981.

HERTZ, RICHARD, (ed.), *Theories Of Contemporary Art*, Prentice Hall, Englewood Cliffs, New Jersey, 1985.

WALLIS, BRIAN, *Art After Modernism: Rethinking Representation*, The New Museum of Contemporary Art, New York, 1985.

Articles

ALDRICH MUSEUM, catalogue for *The Classic Tradition in Recent Painting and Sculpture*, Ridgefield, Conn., 19 May-1 Sep. 1985.

DAVIS, DOUGLAS, 'Post-Everything', *Art in America*, Feb. 1980.

DECORDOVA AND DANA MUSEUM, catalogue for *Beyond Antiquity: Classical References in Contemporary Art*, Lincoln, Mass., 15 June-8 Sep. 1985.

FOX, HOWARD, catalogue for *Content: A Contemporary Focus 1974-1984*, Hirschorn Museum, Washington DC, 1984-5.

HENRY ART GALLERY, *The Idea of the Post-Modern – Who is Teaching it?*, University of Washington, 1981.

ICA, *Postmodernism*, Documents 4, London, 1985.

MUSEUM OF MODERN ART, catalogue for *Second Sight*, San Francisco, 21 Sep.-16 Nov. 1986.

OWENS, CRAIG, 'The Discourse of Others: Feminists and Postmodernism', in *The Anti-Aesthetic, Essays on Postmodern Culture*, (ed.) Hal Foster, Bay Press, Port Townsend, Washington, 1983.

ARCHITECTURE

Books

JENCKS, C., *Current Architecture*, Abrams, New York, 1982, Academy Editions, London, 1982.

——. *The Language of Post-Modern Architecture*, Academy Editions, London, 1977, 1978, 1981, 1984 (fourth edition).

——. *Modern Movements in Architecture*, Penguin Books, Harmondsworth, London, 1985 (second edition).

——. *Post-Modern Classicism*, Academy Editions, London, 1980.

——. *What is Post-Modernism?*, Academy Editions, London/St. Martin's Press, New York, 1986.

KLOTZ, HEINRICH, (ed.), *Die Revision der Moderne: Postmoderne Architektur, 1960-1980*, Prestel-Verlag, Munich, 1984, translated as *Postmodern Visions: Drawings, Paintings and Models by Contemporary Architects*, Abbeville Press, New York, 1985.

——. *Moderne und Postmoderne Architektur der Gegenwart 1960-1980*, Friedr. Vieweg & Sohn, Braunschweig/Wiesbaden, 1984.

PORTOGHESI, PAOLO, *After Modern Architecture*, Rizzoli, New York, 1982.

——. *La Biennale*, Venice, 1980.

——. *Postmodern, The Architecture of the Post Industrial Society*, Rizzoli, New York, 1983 (first published in Italian, 1982).

Articles

JENCKS, C., 'La Bataille des Étiquetes', *Nouveau plaisirs d'architecture*, Centre Georges Pompidou, Paris, 1985.

——. 'Post-Modern Classicism – The New Synthesis', *Architectural Design 5/6*, London, 1980 (also published as an *AD* Profile).

——. 'Post-Modernism: The True Inheritor of Modernism', *Transactions III*, RIBA Publications, London, 1983.

——. 'Revision of the Modern', *Architectural Design 7/8*, 1984.

——. 'The Rise of Post-Modern Architecture', *AA Quarterly 4*, London, 1975.

STERN, ROBERT, 'The Doubles of Post Modern' in 'Beyond the Modern Movement', *The Harvard Architectural Review*, Vol. 1, spring, 1980.

Index

Numbers in italics refer to pages containing illustrations